Business in Society

Business in Society
People, Work and Organizations

MARK ERICKSON, HARRIET BRADLEY,
CAROL STEPHENSON and STEVE WILLIAMS

polity

First published in 2009 by Polity Press

Polity Press
65 Bridge Street
Cambridge CB2 1UR, UK

Polity Press
350 Main Street
Malden, MA 02148, USA

ISBN-13: 978-0-7456-4232-1
ISBN-13: 978-0-7456-4233-8 (paperback)

A catalogue record for this book is available from the British Library.

Typeset in 9.5pt on 12pt Utopia
by Servis Filmsetting Ltd, Stockport, Cheshire
Printed in China by 1010 Printing Ltd.

The publisher has used its best endeavours to ensure that the
URLs for external websites referred to in this book are correct
and active at the time of going to press. However, the publisher
has no responsibility for the websites and can make no guarantee
that a site will remain live or that the content is or will remain
appropriate.

Every effort has been made to trace all copyright holders, but if any
have been inadvertently overlooked the publishers will be pleased
to include any necessary credits in any subsequent reprint or
edition.

For further information on Polity, visit our website:
www.polity.co.uk.

Contents

Acknowledgements viii
Illustration credits ix

1 Introduction 1
2 Understanding societies: from capitalism to
post-industrialism 30
3 Societies and change: globalization and the
knowledge-based economy 50
4 The nature of work 78
5 The meaning of work 113
6 Changing organizations? 144
7 Managers, workers and behaviour in organizations 173
8 Social divisions and inequalities 199
9 Work, community and action 233
10 Conclusion – looking to the future 260

Glossary and abbreviations 272
References 284
Index 296

Acknowledgements

We would like to thank Sara Bragg, Ljubica Erickson and Ben Fincham for commenting on drafts of chapters. At Polity, our thanks go to Jonathan Skerrett and Emma Longstaff for commissioning and supporting this book, and to Leigh Mueller for her copy-editing. We would also like to thank the four anonymous reviewers for their helpful and insightful comments on the draft manuscript.

Illustration credits

The publisher and the authors would like to thank the following for permission to reproduce copyright material:

Chapter 1:
Sean Locke/iStock
Paha_1/Dreamstime
Sean Locke/iStock
Kk5hy/Dreamstime

Chapter 2:
Ramona d'Viola/iStock
Art Renewal Center
helloyiying/iStock
Rich Legg/iStock

Chapter 3:
Ingsoc/Wikimedia Commons
Ronstock/iStock
Glenn Frank/iStock
Guenter Guni/iStock

Chapter 4:
James Steidl/iStock
Gautier075/iStock
Sedam35/Dreamstime
Brad killer/iStock

Chapter 5:
Andy Medina/iStock

Annett Vauteck/iStock
Mikeuk/iStock
Flashpoint/iStock

Chapter 6:
Helene Vallee/iStock
Nationwide
Chris Schmidt/iStock
Quavondo Nguyen/iStock

Chapter 7
Jacob Wackerhousen/iStock
Simonmcconico/iStock
Jim Jurica/iStock
Chris Schmidt/iStock

Chapter 8:
Margaret Cooper/iStock
Chris Schmidt/iStock
Roman Milert/iStock
iofoto/iStock

Chapter 9:
Chris Schmidt/iStock
Cornelia Schaible/iStock
Vakiliki Varvaki/iStock

Every effort has been made to trace copyright holders and to obtain their permission for the use of copyright material. The publisher apologizes for any errors or omissions in the above list and would be grateful if notified of any corrections that should be incorporated in future reprints or editions of this book.

1 Introduction

This chapter will:

- discuss the idea that to understand business we need to understand society
- introduce sociological analysis and briefly sketch the main theories that are used to make sense of the social world
- describe the main methods that social scientists use to examine society and business in society
- provide a short guide to using this book.

We are all a part of the society that surrounds us. We always have been and always will be. Everything in our world – from i-Pods to cemeteries, coal mines to call centres – is part of society too. We are all involved in constructing, through our actions, the society that surrounds us. In turn the society that surrounds us, through what sociologists term **social structure**, has significant effects upon us as individuals: how we think about the world, how we imagine ourselves, how we understand our role within it, how we make ourselves understood by others. This is the human social condition. Yet we rarely notice that this is the case and that it is affecting what we are doing, or if we do we may tell ourselves that this is just 'natural', as if there were no other way that the world could be. Often it is only when we are confronted by the difference of other societies that we may begin to question the 'naturalness' of our own. We don't regularly question how society works and how we are a part of society for two major reasons: because society is so deeply embedded within us it is hard to confront this reality, and because confronting this reality challenges our sense of security.

This is nowhere more so than in the world of work, **employment** and business. In our society the inevitability of work, the naturalness of business and the realities of employment are rarely discussed, let alone challenged. We tell ourselves that this is 'just the way that things are'; we look at the world of work and business as if it was something that emerges purely from economic activities alone and has its own internal logic and rationality. Yet if we begin to scratch the surface of this part of the social world we will see that, rather than being a separate sphere with its own internal mechanisms generating its features, the world of work and business is structured by social forces external to it, and is in turn responsible for structuring much of the society that surrounds it.

Think about the working day. In UK society the norm is for people in paid employment to work an eight-hour day, often starting at 9 a.m. and finishing at 5 p.m. Why is this the case? It certainly isn't a 'natural' thing to do. Nor is it 'traditional': this pattern of work became a norm only in the mid twentieth century. Nor is there any specific internal logic to this: that businesses choose to employ people on this work pattern is often a case of simply replicating a norm shared with other businesses. And if we begin to press a bit further here we will begin to see the importance of the social in structuring our lives. Why 'only' eight hours of work? Why not ten, or fifteen, or five for that matter? The reason we have an eight-hour day is largely the result of concerted actions on the part of trade unions in the late nineteenth and early twentieth centuries who campaigned for regulation of employment and restriction of the working day to protect the health and safety of their members. Before this happened the working day for many people was far longer: factory shifts of twelve hours were common, shop opening hours were erratic and unregulated, holidays were irregular and locally determined.

The point here is that to understand this aspect and, we argue here, all aspects of work, employment and business, we must take a wider, social view. To do this we need to employ a systematic and coherent set of methods, theories and **concepts** that we call 'sociology'. Sociology allows us to frame and then answer the crucial 'why' questions about society.

As we begin to challenge our ingrained and entrenched ideas about the social world, as we begin to look in a critical way at society, how it is made up, how it works and what its effects are, we will start to imagine society in a different, sociological way. The term 'the sociological imagination' was coined by American sociologist Charles Wright Mills in the 1950s (Wright Mills 1959), and his description of how sociology works still accurately sums up what sociologists do: they ask critical questions of society, and they challenge common sense assumptions about the world. In this book we will use this approach – taking a critical look at society, particularly those parts that relate closely to work, employment and business – to construct better and deeper understandings of why the world of work is the way that it is. To do this we will need some basic tools for analysis – sociological analysis.

Sociological analysis

The first thing that we need to do when we start to apply our sociological imaginations is to reflect upon what it is we are doing. We need to understand what our process of analysis is so that we can recognize the strengths and limitations of what we are doing. If we don't do this, we may confuse our analysis for the real world we are trying to describe, or fail to notice that our analyses can often be carried from one location to another, allowing us to make important connections between seemingly different parts of the social world.

Sociological analysis works by formalizing the way we think about the world. When we, in our everyday lives, try to explain why things are the way that they are, or why a particular event has happened, we may look for underlying causes, and we may try to group events that are similar together. For example, we may think that wars (which we might define as being outbreaks of organized aggression resulting in major loss of life between competing nation states) are caused by religious differences. In this example we have constructed a concept (war) and articulated a theory (wars are caused by religious differences). The problem here is that we may not have a particularly robust, well-defined concept – have we really described what war is? – nor a particularly sound theory – are all wars *really* caused by religious differences?

Sociology proceeds in a similar way, through constructing concepts and articulating theories. However, unlike our example above, it does this much more systematically so that concepts are very tightly and meticulously defined, and theories have a great deal of validity. Such theories need to be supported both by rigorous argument and by carefully collected evidence or 'data'. Theories and concepts are tested through sociologists carrying out research in the real world to 'test' and thus strengthen them. We can clearly see a parallel to the natural sciences where, for example, physicists may have a particular theory of what atoms are made of, will design experiments to test that theory and, after interpreting the results, will then either reject or confirm the theory. The social sciences operate on a similar model, constructing a theory, finding evidence that can support the theory, adjusting or rejecting the theory as a consequence.

Sociological concepts and theories together provide explanations of the social world, how it works and what it means. They do this by allowing us to re-imagine society, construct new and more revealing pictures of what society is, how it works and what effect it has on us as individuals. Each sociological theory provides a new picture, and each concept a new angle on something that may already be quite familiar to us. This account seems to imply that a myriad of different and competing pictures of the social world emerge from sociology: this is not the case. Sociology is sometimes described as an argumentative discipline, with competing theories attacking and denouncing one another. Although sociologists may like to argue with one another – most academics do – at root most are in broad agreement about what society is like, how it works and what its key features are. The obvious reason for this is that sociologists – just like physicists – are all looking at a shared object of inquiry: the social world. In the next few sections we will introduce you to some key sociological theories that will be of use in making sense of the world of work, business and employment. As you'll see, they each take a different focus on what is the most significant feature of our society, but they all describe a social world where our actions and forces external to us come into contact to generate the most complex thing in the known universe: human society.

Sociological theory

There are lots of different ways of characterizing and classifying socio-logical theory. Often a two-fold classification, based on the history of the discipline, is used to talk about 'classical theories' (those that emerged in the late nineteenth and early twentieth centuries) and 'contemporary theory'. A more theoretical classification would be to describe theories that focus on social structure and those that focus on **human agency** when providing descriptions and explanations of the social world. A third classificatory scheme uses the basic reply to a central, classic, question for sociologists – how is social order main-tained? – and finds three main groups of theories that describe conflict, constraint or consensus at the heart of society. In this section we will combine features of each of these approaches when presenting five key types of sociological theory that are central to understanding work, employment and business. These are Marxism, Durkheimian sociology (also known as functionalism), interpretive sociology, **feminism**, and postmodern social constructionism. You will see that they share some features, complement each other in some ways, and contradict each other at some points. Through the rest of this book we will refer back to these core theories and will suggest ways that you can apply aspects of them in your own sociological analysis of work, employment and business.

Marx and Marxism

Marxist sociological theory is based on the work of Karl Marx (see box 1.1). The starting point for Marx's analysis was an economic critique of his society: **capitalism** was the dominant mode of production, the prin-cipal way of providing goods and services, and all social phenomena became a reflection of this. Marx was one of the first writers to investi-gate the social, rather than just the economic, consequences of capitalism. He used a method of analysis that he called historical mate-rialism, the idea that the material conditions of human life structure and give character to human experience. Historical materialism is a theory of history and it compares previous epochs with the present day to investigate similarities and differences. In previous forms of society, such as feudal society, social relations and human experience were different because the underlying material conditions of society were different. Capitalist society was, for Marx, a new and very complex social formation that needed systematic analysis to understand it. Capitalism proceeds through the accumulation of capital (profit in the form of money) by those who own the means of production (e.g. facto-ries, shops, offices). The ultimate source of profit is the surplus value generated in the labour process by workers who themselves have no other means of subsistence than to sell their labour power in the capi-talist labour process. Hence the capitalist society is seen by Marx as

Box 1.1 Karl Marx

Born in 1818 in Trier, a province of Prussia and now in Germany, Karl Marx studied philosophy and history at university, but was unable to pursue an academic career due to his radicalism. He turned to journalism, writing for radical publications in Prussia until censorship closed these. Moving to Paris in 1843 he met his lifelong friend and collaborator Friedrich Engels. In 1847 they were involved in founding the Communist League, a pan-European political movement that sought to replace capitalist society with a socialist and subsequently communist alternative. Marx and Engels wrote their seminal text, *The Communist Manifesto*, in 1848, a year of massive political and social upheavals throughout Europe. These revolutions were largely unsuccessful, but the traditional order of many nations came under increasing pressure from radical agitators and political groups intent on bringing about a fairer and more just social order.

   Following the 1848 revolutions, Marx was expelled from France and he moved to London where he and his family lived in poverty. Marx occasionally earned money from his journalism, but largely relied on financial assistance from Engels. Marx remained politically active throughout his life, despite devoting himself to writing his magnum opus *Capital*, a systematic evaluation of the operation, character and course of capitalism. One volume was published before Marx's death in 1883 and two further volumes were published posthumously.

dividing into two great classes: those who own the **means of production** (the **bourgeoisie**) and those who do not (the **proletariat**).

   For Marx, and many subsequent theorists, modern society is characterized by conflict between these two competing social classes. In our society we can identify many different groups, some of which we might call classes – the upper **class**, middle class, **working class**, professionals, the self-employed and so on – but these are really just descriptive categories, not theoretically derived. According to Marxist theory, all members of society can be seen to fall ultimately into one or other of the two major social classes – the bourgeoisie or the proletariat. This is because in a capitalist society all action, culture and social institutions are determined by which of these two class positions people occupy. This leads to individuals having specific ways of living in, understanding and seeing the society that surrounds them: these characteristics are shared with other members of their social class, and we can describe people as having a specific class consciousness. Contemporary theorist Pierre Bourdieu has used the concept of **habitus** to describe this shared set of behaviours, values and attitudes, a term you may encounter in your reading. Bourdieu believes we are born into a particular habitus derived from our class position.

The extraction of surplus value, the core of the operation of capitalism, means that someone is losing out, primarily the worker who is selling her labour power. She is not being paid the full value of her work: the capitalist is keeping some of this for himself as profit. Yet it is not only the worker who is losing out in this arrangement: everybody is. Although it looks as if the bourgeoisie are getting a good deal and the proletariat a bad deal this is only partly the case, and only in the short term. According to Marx all people in capitalism experience **alienation**. This means that they are alienated from themselves, from each other, from nature and from their species-being (what their essence really is). As far as Marx is concerned, the irrationality of capitalism, the production of goods for profit not for use, the futility of constantly competing and not co-operating is what is wrong with the world. Only if we start working together and for each other will the world become a better place. Yet although Marx identifies irrationalities in the capitalist way of organizing production, he does point out that it is the most rational way of ordering production in history. It's just that things could be much better for everyone if we were to move to a different way of organizing production, one that didn't rely upon exploitation of one group by another group. For Marx this meant a social revolution leading to socialism and, ultimately, communism.

How does this affect society? The social world and the history of society can be described in terms of groups, classes, struggling and competing with each other for power and status – this is the underlying picture of reality that Marxism shows us:

> The history of all hitherto existing society is the history of class struggles. Freeman and slave, patrician and plebeian, lord and serf, guildmaster and journeyman, in a word, oppressor and oppressed, stood in constant opposition to one another, carried on an uninterrupted, now hidden, now open fight, a fight that each time ended, either in a revolutionary reconstitution of society at large, or in the common ruin of the contending classes. (Marx and Engels [1848] 1967: 1)

As a social and economic system capitalism thus contains the seeds of its own destruction, and in two significant ways. The first is that the class antagonism between the bourgeoisie and the proletariat will result in a conflict that the bourgeoisie will lose:

> What the bourgeoisie therefore produces, above all, are its own gravediggers. Its fall and the victory of the proletariat are equally inevitable. (Marx and Engels [1848] 1967: 12)

Second, the competition between capitalists and the expansion of the capitalist market will result in a falling rate of profit that will, eventually, make capitalist production unsustainable. From a standard Marxist perspective, capitalist society is structured around postponing these inevitable outcomes.

For Marxists, whatever social order appears around us is an imposed order, sustained by the rulers of society in order to preserve their interests. The mass of the population in society have to go along with this – without power and control of the means of acquiring power, they have no alternative but to bow to the pressure of the state and ruling-class interests. How do those in power retain their position and maintain the social order? Marx agrees with Machiavelli that a state is maintained by force and fraud. There is a vast state legal system that exists mainly to protect private property and the interests of the ruling class. We are educated by the state to learn the role that we need to fulfil in society – be it as bourgeois or as proletarian. But, crucially, in capitalism there is a pervasive and powerful ideological system that prevents us from seeing what the true state of affairs is. Our society can be characterized through an examination of collectively held norms and values. For Marxists, these norms and values are not freely chosen expressions of the interests of all people, they are forced upon the majority of the population and reflect the ruling ideas, those of the ruling class, in our society. Beneath the seemingly calm surface of social order, society is riven with conflict that must be suppressed in a number of ways. For Marxists, this is through the operation of the institutions of the state, and the production of an ideological framework to hide the true nature of society. Yet we are not simply pawns or robots being pushed about by external forces. People, communities, classes can, and do, resist at times, when opportunities arise. Marx describes a complex interplay of history, economics and individual biography. We can choose, but only from a restricted range of options:

> Men make their own history, but not of their own free will; not under circumstances they themselves have chosen but under the given and inherited circumstances with which they are directly confronted. (Marx 1973: 143)

Marxists are particularly interested in work, employment and business because, for them, the ultimate explanations of all social processes are rooted in how we organize work and employment, and how the economic base of our society patterns the social world that rests upon it. For Marxists, workplaces can be seen as microcosms of the social conflict that characterizes society, and we can see class struggles and interests being played out across all places where work and employment are taking place. As we will see, many of the most significant theories for making sense of work and employment have their roots in Marxist social analysis.

Durkheim and functionalism

Émile Durkheim's sociology, like that of Karl Marx, considers that the organization of work and employment is fundamental to the operation and understanding of society as a whole (see box 1.2 for a brief biography of Durkheim). His key sociological text, *The Division of Labour in Society* ([1893] 1964), describes how simple agrarian societies transform into complex industrial societies. But where Marx identified this process as being based on conflict and revolution, Durkheim identified consensus as being at the heart of any society. For Durkheim, and for subsequent functionalist sociologists, society is more than the sum of its parts. It is an achievement that is based on a shared moral order that patterns social action, institutions and culture. And at the centre of this shared moral order is the **division of labour**, the way that society assigns and distributes tasks to members of society.

Box 1.2 Émile Durkheim

Born in 1858 into a devout Jewish family, Émile Durkheim went against the family tradition and chose a non-religious career, becoming the founder of social science education in France. Ironically, given his religious background, much of Durkheim's work explains how religion emerges from social factors. He is best remembered for his classic study of suicide, in which he introduced the idea of 'social facts' – material and non-material things that are external to individuals and which exert an influence on individuals. Examples include money (a material thing) or values (non-material things); being poor changes how we act, particularly in a society which attaches a social value to being wealthy.

Durkheim was profoundly concerned with inequality and prejudice in his society, and his sociological work was an attempt to achieve a better and more just future. Battles with the French establishment and right-wing nationalists during the First World War led to his early death in 1917.

All societies can be characterized by the way that labour is divided between individual members of that society. Agrarian pre-industrial societies – societies where the majority of the population subsist through exploiting the land – exhibit a simple division of labour: most people are carrying out similar tasks and are largely replaceable by one another. As the majority of the population is carrying out similar tasks and simply subsisting through using the land, there is very little stratification: individuals will likely be either peasants or landowners. In such societies people are bound together by a form of **solidarity** that Durkheim calls mechanical, a solidarity based on likeness or resemblance. This form of solidarity is reinforced through shared experiences, shared rituals and shared symbols. Durkheim also referred to this as the '**conscience collective**', that part of our consciousness that we have in common with the rest of society.

Industrial societies, in contrast, have a complex division of labour. Rather than individuals carrying out broadly similar tasks, they are likely to perform different tasks. The forms of production that are taking place in such societies require specialization of one form or another, and tasks become increasingly specialized as production processes become more sophisticated. In such societies people are bound to one another by a different form of solidarity – organic. This form of solidarity is based on difference, and relies upon individuals recognizing the value of others through their different roles in society. Although there is still a conscience collective, we can develop our individual consciousnesses more fully, as we are freer to develop distinct and differentiated personalities.

Organic solidarity can also be reinforced by ritual and shared symbols (think about how events like Christmas or going to a football match can give one a sense of belonging with complete strangers), but relies more on society showing the need for diversity and difference. Stratification in such societies becomes complex, and based on more than just one's ownership of property or resources. Status in modern societies is ascribed through a complex social process where value is attached to, amongst other things, skill, income, gender and functional necessity.

Sport is part of the school curriculum ostensibly to encourage healthy living. However, it can also be an important socialization process to teach children competitiveness and how to work as a team.

In this picture of society, all parts of the social whole can be seen to be performing a function – meeting a need – that, ultimately, serves society as a whole. Sometimes functions are obvious, what we can call manifest. For example the education system in our society fulfils the manifest function of socializing and educating (mainly) young people so that they become full and productive members of society. However, we can also identify less obvious – latent – functions for many things in society. A good example is playing a sport: the manifest function is to keep participants fit and healthy, but a latent function is integration of individuals into society through **team work** and **solidarity**. Similarly the rituals we undertake in society have clear manifest functions – marriage confirms a legal status on couples, but has a latent function of promoting family values.

Indeed it is the family that becomes, for many functionalists, the fundamental unit of social analysis. It is inside the family that primary socialization takes place – in this process a child learns how to act, behave and understand in wider society. This process is followed by secondary socialization, a much longer and more complex process, which takes place outside of the family unit, most obviously in schools. In this process the child learns the **norms** and values of society, the 'social glue' that binds society together, and internalizes these. These two processes of socialization produce individuals who have very good knowledge of how to be a member of society. But socialization doesn't stop at this point, it continues throughout our lives. We may get more and more resistant to altering our existing patterns of behaviour, but each new social situation we enter, particularly those that will take up much of our time such as a new job, require us to be re-socialized so that we will know and conform to new specific norms and values. You may have experienced this quite recently if you left home and went to university or college in a different place. Making new acquaintances, learning how to be a student and how to behave in seminars and lectures, forming friendships on the basis of shared values are all aspects of this socialization process.

If we were to leave investigation of functionalism at this point, we would probably reject it out of hand for the simple reason that, so far, there has been no mention of conflict, dissatisfaction or unhappiness, and for some sociologists this remains a major criticism of this approach: that it ignores strife, sadness and inequality. Yet functionalism has a range of explanations for why things do go wrong in society, why conflict arises and why not everyone experiences society as a good thing. Central to these explanations is the key concept of **anomie**. Functionalism pictures society as a moral order, where collectively held norms and values bind individuals together such that the society they make is much bigger than the sum of its parts. We know society is a moral order because we feel constrained by this – and if you don't recognise this constraint, try departing from our moral order by insulting an elderly relative or stealing a charity collecting tin from a local shop:

see how you feel. We internalize the moral order of society to such an extent that we don't need to be constantly reminded of the norms and values of society – the moral order is a force we find very hard to resist. Yet resist some people do, and this, for functionalists, is best explained by examining the connection such individuals have between the core norms and values of society and themselves. Where such connections are stretched, stressed or even non-existent, we describe people as experiencing anomie – the sense of normlessness where individuals are unsure of their role and place within society. Anomie can be countered by reintegration; bringing people back into the heart of society 'cures' anomie.

Functionalists use anomie as an explanation for a range of social problems, particularly in relation to crime. Whilst some crime is normal and inevitable in society, and serves a goal of integrating the rest of society in opposition to it, excessive crime is seen as pathological, harmful to social cohesion. The impetus towards committing crime can be explained by the lack of connection to the core values of society and a lack of faith in the benefit of social norms. Criminals, by this account, are rational actors who are using other structural means, ones that are illegal and unacceptable to wider society, to achieve their goals. However, some problems, even if they are anomic in cause, cannot be solved by reintegration, and the social structure itself can be a cause of anomie. For example, many people in our society believe in the goal of hard work and upward mobility. Society establishes norms for how these goals should be achieved: doing well at school, getting a degree, etc. However, the social structure distributes the means to achieve these goals unevenly, so hard work and striving at school earn the typical working-class citizen less than the typical middle-class citizen. When opportunities are far from equally distributed, people begin to feel that they are deprived and they abandon their commitment to striving only by legitimate means. They feel cheated and lose faith in the rules and norms: they experience anomie.

Functionalism places a particularly heavy emphasis on the role of the **economy** as a subsystem of society: the functional imperative of the economy is adaptation (Parsons 1951). It is the economy that functions to make society adapt to the environment. It does this through constructing and organizing a market where necessary goods are acquired through trade or barter, and production is organized to provide such necessary goods. But it also does this through adaptation; as the environment changes (for example, as some raw materials become scarcer), the economy adapts to these changes by finding alternatives and shifting production to new goods, services or regions. Work and business are thus central to how society is organized and adapts to a changing world.

Overall, functionalism presents us with a cluster of theories and concepts that place heavy emphasis on the core structures of society: the division of labour, the collectively held norms and values of society, and the social institutions that represent and symbolize these norms and values. These core structures are replicated throughout society and at every level, down to the workplace and even the family and the individual. Functionalism may have difficulties in explaining individual acts and motivations, and may struggle to explain the range of conflict and inequality in society, but it remains a powerful way of analysing group formation and the connection between assigned social role and individual status in society.

Weber and interpretive sociology

> Sociology (in the sense in which this highly ambiguous word is used here) is a science concerning itself with the interpretive understanding of social action and thereby with a causal explanation of its course and consequences.
>
> (Max Weber [1921] 1978)

For Weber, behind the phenomena that we see in the social world are human social actions (see box 1.3 for a biography of Weber). Where Marx saw the economy and Durkheim saw the conscience collective and organic solidarity, Weber just sees people doing what they do. And people do what they do in different ways.

Box 1.3 Max Weber

Max Weber, like Durkheim, achieved fame and distinction as a social scientist in his lifetime. Born in 1864 he studied law at the University of Berlin and became Professor of Economics at the University of Heidelberg in 1896. However, his career was interrupted for over seven years due to him suffering a form of mental breakdown following the death of his father.

His subsequent work was largely academic but he also wrote for newpapers and periodicals, often on political issues of his day. Weber's interest in nationalism shifted from being purely academic to an active support of the German war effort during the First World War. The devastation of an entire generation of young people affected Weber (and many other Germans) and his later work is characterized by pessimism. He died in 1920.

Weberian sociology is characterized by the effort to explain and understand the social institutions produced by people and to explain and understand the values people have believed in. We need to have an empathetic understanding of what people do to make sense of others and their actions: Weberian sociology is about determining 'meaning'. Yet from this starting point Weber constructs the most comprehensive sociological framework, that not only is still one of the most commonly adopted modes of sociological analysis but is also the basis for the sub-discipline of organizational theory. How does this focus on understanding and interpreting the meaning of human social action translate into a systematic sociology?

The actor attaches meaning to his or her actions and this meaning is at the very least a contributory determinant to the action. Thus any scientific attempt to analyse human action requires the inclusion of meaning in an explanation of social phenomena. When Weber looks at human social action – and here he means anything that takes place in a social context – he will look at the meaning that is attached to it. When he does this he finds that we can break down human social action into four **ideal types**: rational action in relation to a goal, rational action in relation to a value, affective or emotional action, and traditional action (see box 1.4 for details of these types of action). It is important to note that Weber does *not* mean that these types of action are 'good' or 'ideal' in any way (although sometimes they might be). By 'ideal type', Weber means a 'pure' type that we can imagine existing, but that will probably never be achieved (a good analogy is that of a 'total vacuum' – it can never exist, but we can imagine what it is). So, these ideal types of action are categories that we can see real forms of action conforming to: some actions may come very close to matching up to the ideal type, others will deviate quite strongly from it. For Weber, and for many sociologists, using ideal types allows us to measure and make comparisons between different forms of the same thing in the social world. Sociological concepts are often ideal types.

Box 1.4 Types of action

Weber identifies four types of social action. For him, all human social action would broadly conform to one of these types:

1 Rational action in relation to a goal (*Zweck* – hence *zweckrational* action): an example could be the way that you choose to travel to work by picking the quickest and most expedient route. You have a goal and choose a rational means to achieve that goal.
2 Rational action in relation to a value (*Wert* – hence *wertrational* action). This form of action is characterized by an actor choosing their means by reference to their value system. For example, in some societies it is important to consult a horoscope before travelling. Such action may not be the best choice, particularly if horoscopes frequently say that travel is not a good idea at that time. But the action is rational according to the value system of which the actor is a part.
3 Affective or emotional action: actions that arise solely from one's emotional state such as smacking a child or being overcome by grief. This is non-rational action.

4 Traditional actions are actions that are carried out by actors because they have always done things that way. Habits and customs are good examples of such traditional actions. Traditional actions are also non-rational according to Weber.

Weber was particularly interested in the first two types of action. Whilst we might want to say that many of our actions are traditional, in that they are habits or customs, for Weber the prime characteristic of the world we live in is rationalization, and this is expressed by a widening of the sphere of *zweckrational* actions, actions rational in relation to goals. Economic enterprise is an example of such rational action, as is control of the state by bureaucracy, participating in a labour market and working for money for a living. Society as a whole tends towards *zweckrational* organization, and this is best characterized by the increasing power of organizations in modern societies. We'll discuss this in much more detail in chapter 2, but for the moment it is important to note that Weber's classic description of the emergence, consolidation and continuance of bureaucracy is, for him, a good example of the contradictions of **modernity**. Whilst it is plain that our society has become much more rationally organized, and this has provided huge benefits for many people, Weber also noted that rationalization led to a form of **disenchantment** and dehumanization. Bureaucracies are good examples: they (should) treat people fairly, equally and efficiently – a positive thing – but they do this in an impersonal and soulless way – a negative thing. Thus we complain about red tape and endless form-filling.

Bureaucracy is based around efficiency and should treat everyone equally. However, it can be very impersonal as a result and ignore individuality.

For Weber our modern society was characterized by this opposition, of efficiency penetrating all aspects of our lives making things easier and more predictable, but also making our lives less rich and meaningful. This was visible even in how sociology was becoming consolidated as a discipline. The construction of fundamental social laws, something that both Durkheim and Marx sought to achieve, and a fixed sociological framework was something that Weber was strongly opposed to. For Weber, incompleteness was a fundamental character of modern science, and sociology, no matter how scientific it tried to be, would always be changing and evolving, endlessly renewing the questions it asks about the social world as that world itself changes (Aron 1991).

Action, social action, is the thing that makes the social world – if you think about your university or college, you can see that this part of the social world is formed through the social action of teachers, lecturers and tutors performing their roles and doing their work, but also bureaucrats enacting their vocation, running the systems, managing the offices and maintaining the records that construct the structure around you. But to focus just on the obvious elements of the social structure is to miss out on one of the most profound insights of interpretive sociology: the construction of order from the everyday interactions of individuals in social settings. Society is emerging from all of us, all of the time. And to really understand what is happening we need Weber's method of **verstehen** – an empathetic understanding – so that we'll know what meanings are being attached to actions (and things in the social world) by actors and how to interpret them (hence interpretive sociology).

Interpretive sociology is exemplified by the work of Erving Goffman, a Canadian sociologist who described the way that all everyday social interaction, from the most mundane encounter to the most contrived piece of exhibitionism, is a performance. We act, we are actors, and we act as if we are on a stage all of the time – sometimes more consciously, sometimes less consciously. Goffman called this way of picturing the social world 'the **dramaturgical** perspective'. It is a useful perspective, not least for understanding how people act in workplaces and organizational settings, and a number of the case studies later in this book use this perspective to interpret the world of work. Goffman's research shows us that the veneer of social order is actually very thin in many social encounters, and we as societal members face constant risks of embarrassment, loss of status, stigma or anomie.

Overall the Weberian perspective and interpretive sociology show us that society is made up of human action, and that human social interaction is patterned by struggles for power and status. Underlying this are fundamental structures that make us think and act in particular ways – the most obvious and significant of which are **rationality** and **rationalization**. These things come together to make social structures and institutions like **labour markets**, legal systems, governments and social classes.

According to Goffman, in all social circumstances we are playing a role. There is a set way to act and behave, and deviating from it causes great embarrassment.

Feminism

Feminism is a sociological and political theory that you will almost certainly already have heard about. Feminism is frequently stereotyped: many people, for example, think that feminism is about lesbianism, man-hating, humourlessness and political correctness, and that feminists wear dungarees and unfashionable footwear. It will be useful to leave any prejudices about feminism to one side for the moment, but we also need our sociological imaginations to ask, first of all, why many people hold such negative opinions of feminism, and why society reinforces such opinions with negative cultural representations of feminism. You will be hard pressed to think of any positive cultural representations of feminism and feminists, at least in UK society. And yet the only reason that women are currently able to study at colleges and universities, be entitled to equal pay with men, vote, get divorced if they want to, have reproductive rights and the right to have control over their own bodies, make choices about the relationships they have, even have choice in the clothes they wear and where they go, is because of the actions of feminists. No other political movement in the UK in the twentieth century has been so successful in achieving its goals – and perhaps this is one reason why so many representations of feminism are negative: to depoliticize and marginalize it (Skeggs 1997). Feminism is not just a political movement, or a way of doing sociology, it is also a literary, cultural and artistic achievement that looks differently at all aspects of life. In the following section we will focus on feminist sociology rather than feminism as a whole, but bear in mind that feminist sociology is connected to feminist political struggles and these wider feminist movements. But to start with we will need an overview that maps out the emergence and development of feminist thought.

Feminism is often described as comprising two fairly distinct phases or waves. Much of contemporary feminist thought has moved on in some key respects, so we can talk of a third wave. Bear in mind that there are large continuities between these different 'waves'.

First-wave feminism, in the nineteenth and early twentieth centuries, focused on women's individual and collective social and political interests and self-determination – hence campaigns for equal democratic rights (women's suffrage), equal rights in the workplace, equal rights in marriage, reproductive rights over their own bodies. We can see parallels in the form of theory articulated by this wave of feminism with Marxism and other universal theories. This feminism sought to provide a universal good for all people, men and women.

Second-wave feminism, from the 1960s onwards, builds on these concerns for equality between the sexes, but goes beyond them to develop a woman-centred perspective on the social world. Women's lives – the moral standpoints and identities based on the shared characteristics that differentiate women from men and which include women's material, mental and emotional strengths – become the focus for feminism. Here the challenges women face are not just about the material conditions they live in, but are also challenges to knowledge, and what counts as legitimate knowledge, in society: central here is the belief that knowledge constructed from women's own experiences has a validity of its own, and certainly no lesser validity than androcentric (male-centred) knowledge. We can still describe this as a universal project, but here it is all women, primarily, who are to be liberated from **patriarchy** and oppression.

The third wave – postmodern feminism – is characterized by fragmentation and difference, with the feminist movement moving away from a shared central focus and towards specific sites of struggles and debates. The impetus for this differentiation was debates about whether second-wave feminism, with its universalist understanding of women's lives, could speak for all women. More diverse feminisms sprang up: black feminism, lesbian feminism, developing-world feminism, etc. The universal character of feminism became replaced by action on behalf of specific, particular groups. Indeed, many third-wave feminists argue that universal projects that attempt to encompass all women are doomed to failure and could in some ways be oppressive in their own right.

In sociology, feminist theory is a wide-ranging system of ideas that starts from a woman-centred perspective to understand social life and human social experience:

- the starting point is the experiences and situations of women in society;
- it recognizes that women have a distinct vantage point and perspective on society;
- it seeks to produce a better world for women and thus for everybody.

Feminism is different from other sociological theories in that it is inter-disciplinary – produced by sociologists but also others in other communities and disciplines. This range means that feminism takes on many forms. However, there are some key questions that most feminists address. Feminist sociology reminds us to ask:

- And what about women?

Women are present in most social situations, yet often play quite different roles from men, experience these differently, contribute to them differently and take different meanings from them. Given this, we have to recognize that most social theory simply ignores this. This isn't just a case of not seeing, it is a case of systematic exclusion and replication of the inequality of society. Women experience differently, but also often occupy subordinate positions to men. This brings us to the second crucial question:

- Why is this the case?

Feminism starts by describing the world of gender inequality, then goes on to explain why it has arisen. At this point we can note a divergence of opinions in feminist thought. Liberal feminists see social and cultural attitudes as being the cause of gender inequalities in society. For liberal feminists change can be brought about through legislation, such as the Sex Discrimination Act, and through education. In contrast, radical feminism places the concept of patriarchy at the heart of its analysis and finds patriarchy to be a fundamental cause of gender inequality and the oppression of women. Patriarchy is the *systematic* domination of women by men, and note here the emphasis on systematic: this means that patriarchy is a system that has interlinked branches.

Feminists see that the gendered division of labour in workplaces, where women get subordinate jobs to men, is reproduced and supported by the gendered division of labour in the home, where women carry out housework and caring tasks, things that are often not even seen as being 'work'. Men systematically deny women access to positions of power and influence in society, exploit women by taking their domestic labour for free, and oppress women through formal institutions of subjugation such as marriage. Under patriarchy, men commit acts of violence against women but often manage to evade prosecution for their actions due to our gendered legal system failing to adequately enforce laws. Patriarchy reproduces itself economically and culturally (through, for example, the media) and imposes itself on all aspects of social life. Patriarchy is perhaps the key concept of second-wave feminism, and Marxist feminists gave this analysis another twist by exploring how patriarchy was combined with capitalism; Marxist feminists are particularly concerned with the material and economic aspects of gender inequality.

Identifying the causes of gender difference, discrimination and **social exclusion** leads us to another fundamental question for feminists:

• How can we change this and improve the world?

Feminism requires a commitment to social transformation. It is a critical social theory. Radical feminism's roots lie in the activism of women coming together to challenge male power, male violence and male language: organizations such as Women's Aid and Rape Crisis Centres emerge from this (Bradley 2007: 41). Liberal feminism's roots are also embedded in campaigns for social transformation. They lie in the struggles of the suffragette movement of the early twentieth century – a campaign for legal reform to allow women to vote in elections. And a significant strand of feminism was informed by Marxism, where gender was seen as a relationship of oppression that rested on the fundamental social relationship of class (2007: 40). However, feminism as a whole has moved on, assimilating and re-articulating a range of different theories and ideas. Feminism has, across time, become increasingly diverse and, some would say, fragmented.

Feminist sociology forces us to consider gender as an issue, and women in particular, when we look at all and any aspects of the social world. It is particularly useful in understanding how workplaces are structured by forces external to the workplace, and particularly good at identifying power dynamics inside organizations. Feminism makes us alert to the reproduction of power structures that systematically disadvantage particular groups in society, and reminds us that gendered power and gender inequality is reproduced throughout society at all levels and in all social institutions. It makes us confront definitions of work and how it is valued and distributed in our society. For example, the subdiscipline of the sociology of work used to focus exclusively on paid employment, ignoring other forms of unpaid work which are,

however, vital to the well-being of our society. It was feminist sociologists, such as Ann Oakley (1974) and Hannah Gavron (1966), who
brought housework and caring work onto the sociological agenda.

Postmodern sociology – social constructionism

The types of theory we have discussed so far, such as Marxism, interpretive sociology and functionalism, can be understood as a tradition
that focuses on social structures and social actions. Sometimes these
are brought together, but more often a theory will focus on or emphasize one or the other. Even the challenge to traditional sociology from
feminism can be seen in this light, with Marxist and radical feminists
emphasizing the role of the underlying structure of patriarchy and
liberal feminists stressing the need to change social action through
education, legislation and culture. Postmodern sociology is different. It
starts from considering how western industrial societies have changed
in recent years, becoming societies that are characterized by fragmentation and difference, not unity and similarity. Postmodernists argue
that the universal frameworks that are applied by modern social theory
to all societies and all people in society are now inappropriate. They
challenge the possibility that a single account of society can ever be
achieved. They also question the universal frameworks for understanding society that modern sociology proposes, particularly the concern
with production and the underlying theme of structure and action
as two opposing factors. Instead, postmodernists focus on a range of
things, and deny the possibility of fixed and unitary frameworks for
analysis. So, their concern with language manifests itself in seeing language as something that shifts and changes; their focus on **identity** and
its relationship to consumption focuses on how identities shift according to what is being experienced or consumed.

Modernity is the epoch when sociology emerged. Although hard to
define, we can make some suggestions as to what modernity is. It is the
time when reason and rationality come to the fore in making sense of
society and human beings. It is the time when progress and science are
major forces in shaping society. It is a time where the world becomes
more rational, ordered, sensible, and less mysterious, religious and
superstitious. It was an ideal time for sociology because modernity
suggests that social problems can find technical cures, and that all
problems are potentially soluble. Sociology, with its systematic analysis of social issues and problems, sometimes saw its role in modernity
as helping to solve social problems. Many sociologists still think this is
their role.

Modern sociology has an aim of describing the totality of social reality, the social world, social action. Think back to Marx (we can best
make sense of society by looking at the operation of the economic
base), Durkheim (society can best be understood as a complex division of labour that reflects collectively held norms and values) or

Weber (social action is largely rational action and contemporary society expresses a process of rationalization). They present monolithic, universal frameworks. This is fine if everyone is the same – if we all have the same mechanisms inside our heads that make us act, or if we understand society in pretty much the same way. But according to postmodernists we don't. They suggest that we need to understand the social world from a relativist perspective (see box 1.5), to make sense of small parts in relation to the whole. They claim that a framework that describes everything in the world will tell you much more about the person doing the describing than about the social world.

Sociology, following a postmodern route, takes a linguistic turn. The linguistic turn requires us to understand language in a different way. Formerly, language was seen as a tool box in our heads where words had fixed meanings that we could take out of the box and use to describe objects we saw in the world. Postmodernists, rather than seeing language as being a set of fixed tools that we can understand in the same way in all places and times, see words as having shifting and changing meanings according to where, when and by whom they are used. Underlying human social life is our shared language, but this shared language is not a fixed foundation. According to postmodernists, our language constructs the world around us as we deploy it in our everyday lives, and this happens all of the time.

Box 1.5 Relativism

Relativism is something of a catch-all term that is used in many social sciences. In general, relativism is the theoretical stance adopted which says that things such as knowledge and culture cannot be understood as absolutes but must be understood in relation to one another. Thus a relativist position with respect to knowledge (knowledge relativism) sees that no form of knowledge is 'naturally' superior to any other form and all claims to knowledge must be qualified by statements showing where they arise from. This gives rise to the current usage of the term 'knowledges' to explain a multiplicity of knowledge claims in the world. Similarly 'cultural relativism' states that it is not possible to describe one specific culture as superior or inferior to another, as such a statement would rely on the selection of an arbitrary vantage point for analysis.

(Note: the relativism of the social sciences is not connected to Einstein's theory of relativity.)

One significant aspect of how language does this is through the formation and articulation of **discourse**. Discourse is language that is constructed in a specific context so that it combines power and knowledge; we can have political discourse, medical discourse, management discourse and so on. Discourses make people up and construct the

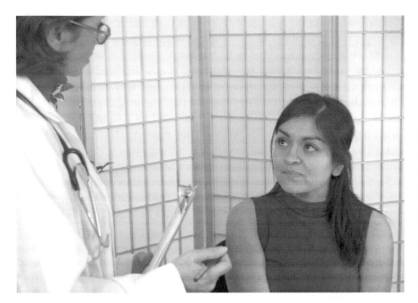

Some sociologists would say the medical discourse of practitioners such as doctors constructs people as 'patients', and this in itself can affect how they feel about themselves and their symptoms.

world around them. An example may be useful here. You may feel ill, have some symptoms and go and talk to your friends about having a sore stomach. You are using social discourse, and you are constructing yourself and your friends as just that – acquaintances who have no formal power differential between them and no specialized knowledge to deploy. But when your sore stomach doesn't get any better, you go and see your doctor who tells you that you have gastro-enteritis, must drink lots of liquids, rest and take a prescription for antibiotics. She is using a discourse that is making you up, constructing you, as a patient and constructing herself as a health care professional. She is using knowledge that you don't have and is exerting a form of power over you (just think about how differently you act when seeing your doctor to socializing with your friends). This conception of discourse is associated with the work of the French sociologist Michel Foucault.

Foucault's work is useful in making sense of the social world as it allows us to see how power and knowledge become widely distributed and have major effects through the articulation of discourses. Through history, Foucault says, we can identify the way that different discourses have arisen and led to society taking on particular forms. In the modern world, much more formalized and powerful discourses emerged: medical discourse, scientific discourse, governmental discourse, economic discourse, management discourse. All of these discourses served to articulate modes of power that subjugated and oppressed people, often in quite insidious ways through people internalizing subjugated positions by adopting these discourses. Foucault's examples often focus on marginalized and oppressed groups: the mentally ill, homosexuals, criminals. These groups became more oppressed in modernity as discourses constructed them as members of formal categories that were 'deviant' or 'damaged' in some way. For Foucault a crucial task for sociology is to identify these discourses and to find ways of articulating counter-discourses that challenge the operation of the complex of power and knowledge. There are clear parallels with third-wave feminism here, and Foucault's work has been a major resource for many third-wave feminists.

Postmodern sociology focuses on individuals, language and discourse, and consumption. Unlike the other theoretical paradigms we have looked at so far, work, employment and business are not key focal points for postmodern social constructionism, and for this reason we make less use of this group of theories in this book. However, we can clearly see how postmodern social constructionism can make a useful contribution to understanding work, employment and business in society. The construction of subject selves through the articulation of discourses is something that takes place every day in contemporary workplaces: management rhetoric and 'management speak' attempts to improve productivity through remaking, reconstructing workers as more efficient people, more quality-oriented people, more loyal people. For example, sociologists have discussed the emergence of an 'entrepreneurial self' formed by the discourses of the 'enterprise culture' of the 1980s (du Gay 1996). The emergence of mission statements, team work and total quality are all phenomena in contemporary business that show the significance of language and discourse in making workplaces. In addition, as will be discussed more fully in chapter 2, postmodern approaches look at the increased importance of consumption in everyday lives, and the rise of a consumer society.

Sociological methods – how do sociologists work?

We said earlier that sociology needs to find proof for its theories, and evidence to back up the way it has formed its concepts. There is a wide range of methods by which sociologists do this, and we will discuss some below. To start with, it is important to note that, without social research, sociology would be just a collection of theories of the world; with social research, sociology becomes a strong and significant way of making sense of society, with theories that have been tested and have attained validity. This is because social research methods are systematic, extend knowledge of the social world and allow strong inferences about the social world to be drawn. This means that social research is different from, say, market research: it combines collecting data with theoretical analysis so that it constructs pictures of parts of the social world that help us to explain *why* the world is the way that it is. Market research, in contrast, is solely concerned with description, not explanation.

There are two main groups of sociological methods: those that collect quantitative data and those that collect qualitative data. They do quite different things and are associated with different theoretical approaches. Quantitative social research relies on identifying and quantifying social facts: things in the social world that are considered to be fixed, static factual objects. For example, functionalists are often concerned with families in society, and knowing how many families there are and how they are composed is of great use. Collecting data of this sort often involves designing and administering questionnaires to large samples of the population, then using statistical analysis to identify trends and tendencies, and to validate theoretical hypotheses about the world. In quantitative social research, theory is often the starting point as it suggests objects of inquiry to look at, and it suggests causes for events in the world.

To take our functionalist example again, theory proposes that the cause of rises in crime and anti-social behaviour may be the decline of the traditional nuclear family. Researching this could involve collecting data on crime rates, divorce rates, attitudes towards crime and disorder, socio-economic factors and general demographics. Researchers may then use a range of multivariate statistical routines to try and find correlations – connections between these different variables. Strong associations between variables can help to validate, or disconfirm, our starting-point theory.

Quantitative studies of work and employment require the collection of large amounts of data, and this can be time-consuming and expensive. However, when such studies are carried out they are often influential, as they are seen as having a high degree of validity. The 'Affluent Worker' study (Goldthorpe et al. 1969) of the 1960s is one such classic study, as is the Social Change and Economic Life Initiative (SCELI) survey which was analysed in the 1990s (Gallie et al. 1994). SCELI was an entirely quantitative project, deploying complex questionnaires to over 6,000 respondents from 6 different locations in the UK in the late 1980s; the robustness and reliability of the research method is hard to fault. The survey investigated many aspects of work and employment, particularly career trajectories, attitudes towards work, management and workplaces, trade union membership and attitudes towards unions, and the researchers also collected extensive details on individuals, their families, financial situation and family relations. The resulting data set provided an immense resource for researchers to investigate how work is perceived and located in an individual's life course and how it connects to wider social processes.

Quantitative social research has many strengths: it is robust, objective, unlikely to be biased – in that researchers are distant from their subjects – produces results that help to construct theories that explain all of society, and produces hard and reliable data. However, some social researchers see many of these points as being disadvantages, not advantages.

Qualitative social researchers see the construction of numerical summaries of social phenomena as inappropriate, not least because it obscures the range of different human responses to specific things. Simply identifying someone's family status is not sufficient to explain how they feel about their family, why they act in a certain way in their family, or what their family means to them. Qualitative social research attempts to investigate the meanings, motivations and understandings that individuals and groups hold in society, in line with the principles of interpretive sociology which we discussed earlier. To do this it needs to get close to its research subjects, to use data collection methods that are sophisticated enough to reflect adequately this range of human responses, and to be flexible enough to change strategy in the course of research. Data collection techniques include interviews and focus groups, where respondents are asked specific questions which can be followed up, but also documentary methods where texts are analysed in detail, and observation techniques where social researchers simply observe how social actions and interactions are taking place. There are a great many qualitative sociological studies of work, taking a range of approaches. All, however, attempt to understand what is happening in a workplace in terms of action, interaction and how individuals understand their social situation. For example, Donald Roy's classic study of repetitive work in a machine shop used participant observation and symbolic interactionist theory (see box 1.6) to understand how workers coped with repetitive and boring work (Roy 1960). Roy took a job in a machine shop operating a die stamping machine, and simply observed and listened to his fellow workers. His aim was to find out how people managed the mind-numbing repetitiveness of their work. What he discovered was a rich, and highly structured, set of social interactions that individuals used to cope with their work. The men in the machine shop punctuated their repetitive work with childish games and ritualized interactions; every day there would be banana time, peach time, coca cola time and so on. Disrupting these ritualized interactions affected productivity as boredom became more acutely felt, and Roy's work served to show how workers construct meaning and significance in many different ways.

Box 1.6 Symbolic interactionism and participant observation

Symbolic interactionism is a powerful, micro-sociological theory that is of great use in explaining small-scale interactions between individuals and groups. Associated most closely with the work of Erving Goffman, symbolic interactionist studies look at how individuals relate to one another not only through gestures and language but also through symbols. Symbolic interactionist studies often rely on the method of participant observation, where the researcher immerses themselves in the environment they are interested in and actively takes part. Underpinning symbolic interactionism is an understanding of the self as composed of different components: the *I* which is the spontaneous self and the *me* which is the self as constrained by social rules and norms. In many situations there is a tension between these two parts of us, and we often feel restricted between what we want to do and what is expected of us. In society we cope with this tension by performing set social roles that we learn and internalize.

Qualitative research is closely connected to the interpretive socio-logical tradition, and is also the main data collection method used by feminist sociologists and social constructionists. The strengths of using qualitative social research come mainly from the richness and depth of the data collected. Unlike quantitative research, where complex social phenomena are reduced to simple categories, qualitative research pro-duces results with a lot of depth, reflecting the complexity of the social world. However, the disadvantage to this form of research is that it is very time-consuming, can only be carried out with quite small sample sizes, and is often not replicable as it relies on researchers forming close bonds with those they are researching.

Although these two approaches use substantially different methods, and produce different sorts of results, they are closely linked. They both rely on theory: theory provides a steer as to what researchers should be looking for, and subsequently both forms of research will confirm or reappraise theory. In addition, in qualitative research new theories can emerge from discoveries made in the research process. Both forms of research have a common goal of extending and deepening our knowledge of the social world, how it is formed and how it works. And both forms require the researcher to consider their role in the research process, how close or distant they are to their research subject, how objective or subjective they are and how their research fits in with other social research. Using social research and sociological theory we can pose and address important 'why' questions, articulate and extend theory, deepen our knowledge of society, challenge our assumptions about society and construct sophisticated pictures of the social world.

How to use this book

So far we have introduced you to the key principles of a sociological approach to understanding work and business. The following eight substantive chapters of this book provide overviews, analysis and case studies of four broad topics that are central to locating and understand-ing business in society:

society, what it is, how we can make sense of it and why it takes the form that it does;
work as a lived experience and as a social structure;

organizations, how they are structured, how they control and how they are resisted;

people, how they are united and divided, experience inequalities and are members of wider structures, institutions and communities.

Each chapter provides an overview of the main topic then looks at how the main issues can be examined sociologically. You can read the chapters in numerical order, which fits in with how we designed this book. However, you may want to dip in and out of the book and for that reason we have tried to make each chapter able to stand alone, at least to some extent.

We want this book to be user friendly, and we want this book to be read! To try and facilitate this we have included the following aids:

A glossary of key concepts and terms, each of which is presented in **bold** when they first appear.

Key concepts boxes, which supplement the main text. These will appear throughout the text.

Case studies, again in boxes. These also supplement the text and provide examples of the topics under discussion. Most of these case studies are recent examples from UK business practices, but we have also included some international examples and some older, classic studies.

Biographical vignette boxes that introduce key theorists with short summaries of their life and work.

At the end of each chapter you will find a short chapter summary that presents its key points. You might want to use these as a way of organizing revision notes or notes for an essay. Alternatively you can use the summary as a check list for learning and remembering the key points of the chapter.

Also at the end of each chapter we have included a short annotated bibliography suggesting further reading and websites that will be helpful in providing a more in-depth understanding of the topics discussed in the chapter. In addition you will find a number of questions for discussion. You may want to address these on your own or in discussions with friends, or use them in formal seminars. Please bear in mind that there are no 'right' answers to these questions; they are designed to help you identify your own position with respect to the question topic, and to illustrate the contested nature of business in society.

Discussion questions

1. What are the main sociological theories that are used to explain society?
2. How is our society 'modern'?
3. Is there a problem with common sense? Is common sense different from other ways of thinking?

4. How are social rules generated?
5. How can sociology help to explain why most businesses have similar organizational structures?
6. Why do these structures change with time?

Further reading

There are a vast number of 'introduction to sociology' books available, but these vary in terms of quality, level and accessibility. If you want a good, general overview of the main parameters of sociology, a university-level introduction to sociology textbook is the best starting place. Of these, Anthony Giddens' book is interesting, not least because Giddens is a major theorist of globalization:

Anthony Giddens, *Sociology*, 6th edition. Cambridge: Polity, 2009.

This book includes a chapter on work and organizations, and chapters on sociological theories and methods.

However, those sorts of textbooks may not be very good at getting across the idea of *thinking* sociologically. The following texts, both classic and contemporary, will give you an idea of what sociological thinking is like.

Charles Wright Mills, *The Sociological Imagination*. Harmondsworth: Penguin, [1959] 1970.
Nicholas Abercrombie, *Sociology*. Cambridge: Polity, 2004.
Zygmunt Bauman and Tim May, *Thinking Sociologically*. Oxford: Blackwell, 2001.

As well as a multitude of general sociology texts there are also hundreds of sociological theory textbooks. This book by George Ritzer, who invented the theory of **McDonaldization**, is a good one:

George Ritzer, *Contemporary Sociological Theory and its Classical Roots: the Basics*, 2nd edition. New York: McGraw-Hill, 2007.

For a more advanced introduction to social theory:

Austin Harrington, *Modern Social Theory: an Introduction*. Oxford: Oxford University Press, 2005.

Social research methods is an expanding area for publishers; a huge number of general and specialist texts are available. However, a good, well-written and illustrated social research methods book will cover most main topics and give you a good idea of how social research is carried out. Alan Bryman's book is a good example:

Alan Bryman, *Social Research Methods*. Oxford: Oxford University Press, 2008.

Websites

A useful (and free!) resource that will provide an excellent overview of the parameters of UK society is *Social Trends,* available from the UK government national statistics website. Download a copy from:

www.statistics.gov.uk/socialtrends/

This is an annual publication: the 2008 edition is issue 38. You can download both the main text and all the data that support the book; this comes in the form of Excel sheets. Put it on a memory stick and keep it handy as a resource for essay-writing, revision or even writing pub quiz questions (e.g. What percentage of internet users use it for banking? – the answer is on page 180 of *Social Trends* 38 (it's 45 per cent if you can't wait to find out – 2007 figures)).

2 Understanding societies: from capitalism to post-industrialism

This chapter will:

- introduce the idea of social typologies, particularly pre-industrial, industrial and post-industrial
- examine how societies change across time and how to understand this
- discuss a range of explanatory frameworks that help us to understand why contemporary society takes the shape that it does.

Introduction

Most of us, as we go about our daily life, do not think very much about the type of society we live in, tend to take our own society for granted and see the way things are in it as 'natural'. Indeed, if we start to gripe or grumble about things that we see as going wrong within it, such as a lack of well-paid jobs for young people, the trains running late, increased levels of vandalism and rubbish in the streets of our cities or the trend to obesity in young people, we tend to think of somebody or other to blame for it: the government, lazy workers, the local council, the younger generation, irresponsible parents are the sorts of groups that tend to be mentioned in the popular press or in debates in the pub. But for sociologists these kinds of phenomena are often explained as properties of *specific types of societies.*

Indeed, a core characteristic of what C. Wright Mills (1959) called 'the sociological imagination', the distinctively sociological way of looking at our world and trying to explain how and why things happen within it, is the creation of *social typologies*, that is of ways to categorize different sorts of society. Karl Marx, for example, described the western societies that preceded the advent of industrial production as 'feudal' and contrasted them with 'capitalist' societies, as he labelled the European societies of the mid nineteenth century, his own time. He predicted that tensions within them would finally lead to a new type of society, which he named 'communism', in which all social goods would not be privately owned but held 'in common'. Émile Durkheim, as we saw in chapter 1, constructed a different typology, contrasting tribal societies characterized by 'mechanical solidarity' (in which everybody did basically the same activities and shared the same values) with contemporary societies characterized by 'organic solidarity' (in which people carried out different activities from one another, had specialized jobs and were at liberty to hold their own different values).

In this chapter, and the one that follows it, we shall be exploring the different kinds of typologies that social scientists have developed and the different views they offer of the societies in which we live and work in the twenty-first century. In effect, typologies are different ways in which we can picture societies *as a whole*. This is a second core characteristic of a sociological approach. When studying social activities and phenomena, such as workplace relations or the functioning of businesses, sociologists normally wish to place them within a broader *context*. That context will help us to understand better the meaning of activities and phenomena, why they happen and how they may be changed.

As the examples given above show, there are many ways in which we can picture societies and thus many different social typologies can be developed (see table 2.1). In building typologies, sociologists seek to identify what they see as the central features of societies and how they differ. Thus Marx categorized societies in terms of the way their production systems were organized, while Durkheim categorized them on the basis of the mechanisms of social cohesion (that is, what holds societies together and makes them function). These are different, but equally valid, ways of picturing societies.

As we shall see in this chapter, many of the ways in which societies have been typologized relate to work or to economic activities more generally. That is because work arrangements are so vital to societies. In this chapter, we shall start by considering very briefly the contributions made within 'classical sociology' and then consider the variety of terms used to describe contemporary societies; the chapter will introduce you to the following key ideas: **industrialism, capitalism, modernity, post-industrialism, post-Fordism, postmodernity, reflexive modernity** and **consumer society**. Each of these influential concepts is very relevant to the study of businesses, organizations and workplaces. What does it mean to be a worker in these types of societies? What kind of jobs are prevalent? What problems do they create? How are businesses and organizations changing?

Table 2.1 Example of a social typology

Type of society	Nature of the economy	Core workers	When?
Traditional	Agriculture	Farmers and peasants	Pre nineteenth century
Industrial	Manufacturing	Male factory workers	Early nineteenth century
Post-industrial	Service-based	Female service-sector workers	Mid twentieth century onwards

The classical contribution: capitalism, bureaucracy and industrialism

We start by discussing some contributions made by early social think-ers, not just because they are of historical interest, but because they have had a major impact on how others have subsequently con-ceptualized societies. For example, the highly influential account of 'postindustrialism' by Daniel Bell (1973) is in many respects a direct critique of Karl Marx and his followers. Moreover, many concepts devised by these early contributors are still in use today, as we will note in subsequent chapters.

We start with Marx, who offered a powerful account of societies he described as 'capitalist' which still holds much relevance today. As we stated earlier, Marx's social typology was based on the way in which societies organized their resources to produce the necessities of life, what he called the **mode of production**. **Feudalism** was, according to Marx, the mode of production before capitalism. It was a system based upon a specific kind of landholding. The feudal lords held their lands or *fiefdoms* from the king (who might confiscate them if the lord, who had sworn loyalty to him, displeased him). In turn the lords leased land out to peasant farmers who grew crops and raised animals upon them. A certain amount of what they produced was handed over to the lord (sometimes along with money for rent). The lord accumulated his wealth from this 'surplus production' generated by the peasants, and in turn had to pay taxes to the king. Thus the core **relations of produc-tion** in feudal societies were those between the lords and the peasants, or 'serfs' as they were called in medieval times (the word itself deriving from the Latin word *servus* meaning 'slave'). It was a characteristic of Marx's thought that he distinguished in each type of society a corre-sponding form of **social division** which would sooner or later lead to conflict. The lords squeezed the serfs to extract as much surplus from them as they could, pushing them towards starvation and poverty. This would lead, said Marx, to social conflict, with peasants protesting, rebelling and rioting as a response to the lords' oppression. One exam-ple of such conflict was the famous Peasants' Revolt in Britain during the reign of Richard II.

Conflicts and other tensions within the mode of production would eventually lead to the breakdown of one mode of production and the development of another. Marx called these tensions *contradictions*. For example, a key contradiction within feudalism was that peasants were not free to utilize their labour as they pleased: they were tied to the land and working for one specific master. This blocked the develop-ment of new forms of mechanized production which needed supplies of untied free labour to work in mills and factories. So, slowly, a new dominant class emerged, of factory owners, capitalist investors and entrepreneurs, the bourgeoisie as Marx termed them. The labourers who worked in their enterprises were the working class or proletariat who, unlike the peasants before them, owned no land or anything but their labour which they had to sell to the capitalists to survive.

As we saw in chapter 1, this new mode of production, capitalism, then had its own form of central social division between capitalist employers and working people whose labour produced the products which the capitalists took from them (appropriation of surplus) and sold for a profit. These are the key two classes within capitalist societies; one result of the conflictual relations between them was the development of trade unions to act as the collective voice of the working people. Just as under feudalism, the people who performed all the necessary labour were not those who profited from it. Marx believed the working people's growing realization of the injustice of this system would eventually lead the working classes to rise up against the capitalists, and the resulting revolution would lead to a new classless mode of production, which Marx called 'communism' or 'socialism'. In such a society, there would be an end to the capitalist institutions of private property and private profits. Lands and capital assets would be held 'in common' and the surplus of production would no longer be monopolized by an elite class, but shared out among all the people: 'from each according to his means to each according to his needs' as Marx put it.

Marx's ideas have been and continue to be hugely influential, even if people do not accept his theory in its totality (for example the notion of an inevitable socialist revolution). Most theories of industrial conflict either draw on Marx's thinking or attempt to refute it. The popular 'labour process theory', discussed in chapter 4, rose from the work of Harry Braverman (1974) who developed some of Marx's ideas about how the arrangement of production would change over time. Another key concept is that of **alienation**, Marx's proposition that, under conditions of *unfree* labour, such as capitalist production, human beings are distanced – alienated – from the products that they make and the process of producing them. Human labour, which should be creative and joyful, became monotonous drudgery. While a craftworker (say a skilled silversmith or potter) can take delight in the beautiful things she or he has produced, the typical factory worker has no involvement with the end product. In Miriam Glucksmann's fine study of an electrical components factory *Women on the Line* (Cavendish 1982), some workers did not even know what the plastic pieces they made were for! Alienation also means that workers may see their fellow workers as competitors not collaborators. Marx believed people were also alienated from their true nature, which he stated was to be co-operative, looking at the way people in simple tribal societies worked together to produce food, clothing and shelter for all the tribe's members. Young people who go off to live in tepee villages in Wales or share goods within a squat are living out some of Marx's ideals about sharing, creativity and **community**.

Marx's ideas have been much criticized. Max Weber was one of his most powerful critics and provided an alternative account of

capitalism. Weber shared some of Marx's ideas about how capitalist societies worked, although he totally rejected the notion of a socialist revolution. However, he saw the key features of capitalism not as production relations and class conflict but as **bureaucracy** and rationalization.

You will remember from chapter 1 that Weber explored motivation and meaning: what makes us behave in certain ways, what influences our decisions. What are the intentions that lie behind the behaviour we observe? As we saw, Weber developed his own typology of action (box 1.4), distinguishing between *traditional* action, based on habit and custom, and *rational* action, in which we calculate the steps we need towards a given end. In capitalist societies Weber believed that *zweckrational* action targeted on goals had come to dominate, so that increasingly all decisions were made on the basis of means–ends judgements.

The broader process of *rationalization* refers to the way all facets of society were increasingly designed to promote rational behaviour: rather than thinking 'we'll do this because we've always done things this way', people tend to think 'this is the best way to get what I want' (you may like to think about this in relation to how you plan your own lives). For Weber, this process was allied to secularization and what he termed the 'disenchantment of the world'; increasingly, human beings were turning their back on religion and other forms of mystical and superstitious thinking. All phenomena and all human behaviour were

Skilled, traditional artisans are closely involved with the work they do and with selling the goods they produce. Marxists would argue that capitalist production destroys this relationship and alienates workers from their work.

increasingly explained in scientific, not religious, terms. However, as we shall see in later chapters, events have rather disproved this part of Weber's vision of modern societies, given the resurgence of some forms of religious fundamentalism (within Christianity and Islam, for example) along with new forms of spirituality, ranging from Druidism to Wicca (paganism) and other forms of 'New Age' thinking.

Another important part of Weber's theory of capitalist development was the idea of the **Protestant ethic**, which is explored fully in chapter 4. This was an idea of work as a calling or vocation which was the key motivation for developing capitalist enterprise, rather than squandering one's wealth on conspicuous consumption.

However, Weber's main contribution to the understanding of work was probably the concept of bureaucracy, which is covered fully in chapter 6. Weber believed that work organizations would inevitably become more bureaucratized, as this was the organizational form which was most suitable for the pursuit of rational objectives. Bureaucracies were impersonal, so that they ensured more equal treatment than the patriarchal or paternalist systems which predated them, in which judgements and decisions might rest on the arbitrary whims of kings and other leaders (we can see the dangers of this if we think of the careers of Saddam Hussein or Idi Amin). An example of the bureaucratic principle is the way large organizations set up procedures to ensure equal opportunities in selection and promotion; these forms of bureaucracy have been initiated to ensure that certain groups, such as women, people with disabilities or members of minority ethnic groups, do not suffer from discrimination in the decisions made by managers and recruiters. Before these procedures were devised, there were many accusations of unfairness, arbitrary judgements on the basis of personal preference, as managers, supervisors and foremen sought to promote their 'blue-eyed boys'!

However, although fairer and more efficient, bureaucracies also led to the entanglement of individuals in rules and red tape and the stifling of creativity and individuality. In that sense, there are similarities between Marx's concept of alienation and the Weberian view of bureaucracy. In both cases, individuals are seen as powerless and lacking in control within workplaces, slaves to systems originally devised for human benefit but which end by reducing individuals to cogs in a machine or numbers within a system of rules. 'I am not a number, I am a free man' cried Patrick McGoohan's hero in the cult TV series *The Prisoner*. Franz Kafka's *The Castle* and *The Trial*, Fritz Lang's film *Metropolis* and Charlie Chaplin's *Modern Times* are literary and cultural expressions of this kind of bleak view which Marx and Weber formulated. They portray workers under capitalism as, literally, wage slaves! However, Weber's visions were much bleaker than Marx's as Marx believed that socialism would free people from exploitation and alienation, while Weber, who lived to see the dawn of the Soviet system, thought that socialism would only lead to a more centralized and oppressive form of state bureaucracy. In fact, the societies of Eastern Europe during the Soviet era resembled Weber's predictions rather than Marx's.

A more optimistic version of work relations in the modern world was provided by Émile Durkheim, who can be taken as representative of a different framework for modern societies, the notion of industrialism. As we noted earlier, this approach focuses on what holds societies together, rather than what divides them. Proponents of the industrial perspective tend to see technology as a beneficent and driving power, capable of generating so much wealth and prosperity that it will 'trickle down' to everyone. Such was the perspective of Clark Kerr, author of a well-known book, *Industrialism and Industrial Man* (Kerr et al. 1962). Kerr believed that the 'inner logic of industrialism' would lead all societies to converge towards a dominant model, exemplified by the USA: a wealthy democracy, with high levels of education and skills. This was for Kerr a very positive trend.

Durkheim, however, put less emphasis on technology and more on morality. He was interested in what holds people together in collectivities. In his famous work *The Division of Labour in Society*, discussed in chapter 1, he explored the link between work arrangements and social solidarity. While Marx saw the division of labour in society as stifling and alienating, Durkheim saw it as liberating. He believed that industrial societies freed people from the conformity forced on them in pre-industrial societies. In tribal societies, for example, everybody does much the same range of tasks, with little specialization. People are strictly bound by the customs of the tribe, as is demonstrated in Bruce Parry's excellent television programmes in which he lives with various tribes in remote quarters of the world (see case study 2.1). In feudal societies people tended to follow in their parents' footsteps: the son of a lord became a lord, the son of a carpenter became a carpenter. Only with the advent of a much greater range of specialized occupations did choice open up: Durkheim believed that in industrial societies people could find jobs which would fit their personal aptitudes and interests. The other great advantage of specialization is that it unites people through their awareness of their dependence on others. We need the work of all sorts of people (from doctors, to plumbers, to train drivers, to waste collectors) to enable us to lead our comfortable and liberated lives. Of course, as the people of the planet of Golgafrincham found, not all specialist activities are necessarily that useful! Fans of Douglas Adams' *Hitchhikers' Guide to the Galaxy* will recall that the Golgafrinchans decided to get rid of the 'useless third' of their population, including hairstylists, TV producers, insurance salesmen, telephone sanitizers, security guards, along with management consultants and personnel officers! Those deemed useless were told of imminent planetary disaster, packed into the giant 'B' Ark and sent into space, having been told that the other two Arks would follow: one solution to overpopulation!

Durkheim's might seem a very rosy view of society, compared to the visions of Marx and Weber, but he did see some problems associated with modern industrial societies. He believed that sometimes people's desires and aspirations got out of control when they were not subject to the common values typical of pre-industrial societies. This was the problem of anomie (see chapter 1). Durkheim suggested it was particularly common in times of rapid change (such as the times we are living through now). Durkheim felt that some kind of new institutions were needed to set new standards and values for people to live by and suggested this function might be carried out by what he called 'corporations', a type of professional association which would set rules and values for each occupational group. People belonging to these associations would follow the rules, as had been the case, for example, in the medieval craftsmen's guilds.

Durkheim's work has had a general influence on some approaches to understanding work relations, particularly through the idea of **meritocracy**. This states that in current societies people acquire jobs and positions on the basis not of their birth, but of their merits (talents, capabilities, skills, hard work). This is a widespread if disputable view of societies such as Britain and America (Saunders 1990). The other area in which Durkheim's ideas are influential is in the currently fashionable idea of social inclusion, which is a major element of public policy in the European Union (Levitas 2005). In this approach, work is seen as the major mechanism for ensuring that people are included as citizens. This lies behind the policy on unemployment known as 'workfare' (as opposed to welfare), which makes unemployment benefits dependent on demonstrable attempts to find a job or become 'employable'. For example, New Labour governments have encouraged single parents to find jobs rather than stay at home in dependence on social security payments, through schemes such as the New Deal which helps with training, job placements and childcare needs.

Finally, we should note that, alongside the ideas of capitalism and industrialism, another concept evolved which is also used to signify the nature of contemporary societies; that is the notion of modernity. This term derived originally from the idea of modernism, a movement in art, architecture and literature at the beginning of the twentieth century, which challenged the values of tradition and valued the new. Often striking new materials (the concrete and glass of office blocks) or approaches (the poetry of T. S. Eliot or the novels of James Joyce) were used. The term then expanded to describe society itself, again with the accent placed on newness and rejection of the past. The term has been used particularly by the influential British sociologist Anthony Giddens, who refers to the era we live in now as late modernity (1990, 1991). This is a way of thinking about society which makes great play of cultural notions of change, dynamism, mobility. Krishan Kumar (1978) discusses J. M. W. Turner's dramatic picture *Rain, Steam and Speed*, an impressionistic vision of a railway train crossing a bridge built by

Isambard Kingdom Brunel, as an iconic emblem of 'the modern'. John Lienhard, a professor of engineering, describes the impact of this picture, painted in 1844:

> The artists of the mid-19th century saw it. They knew what those incredible engines were doing to their world. Turner's engine roars out of the mists of a twilight zone. It leaves the 18th century behind and hurtles straight into the world of my childhood. (Lienhard 1998)

Modernity remains associated with evolving technology, with air travel, computers and mobile phones (the term 'mobile' is itself a signifier of

J. M. W. Turner's *Rain, Steam and Speed* represented the arrival of all things 'modern' for its nineteenth-century viewers.

Cities around the world increasingly resemble one another. The Shanghai skyline, although distinctive, is similar to that of New York, London or Sydney.

modernity). Developing nations, such as India, China or Malaysia, portray themselves as being in the throes of a process of modernization which will allow them to catch up with the western societies. Being 'modern' is also a very important value within contemporary business. We talk a lot about the need to 'modernize' firms and organizations, and condemn institutions which are old-fashioned and out of date. 'New ideas' and 'new blood' are highly valued in contemporary organizations; after all, we have been governed recently by a party which presented itself specifically as 'New' Labour.

Box 2.1 *Grandad's Back in Business*: the cult of 'modernity' in contemporary organizations

This BBC2 TV series from 2007 featured an episode set in a fashionable London restaurant, *Pied à Terre*, where chef Shane Osborn has gained two Michelin stars. A young man and an older man competed to be taken on as a trainee chef. James was tall, slim and well-groomed and had just finished a course at catering college. Malcolm, in his fifties, had had a distinguished career in the past as a chef in the Royal Navy, where he had cooked banquets for members of the royal family. A member of James' family speculated that the older man would be short, bearded with a beer belly, and that his taste in food would be 'prawn cocktails and pâté with toast' (seen as old-fashioned in the world of Michelin stars). In the highly pressurized restaurant kitchen, overseen by the authoritative and charismatic Osborn, Malcolm was calm, efficient, fitted in with the young staff with great ease and tried to hone his old skills. James was badly organized, kept losing focus and forgot to taste all the food he sent to table (Osborn's number one rule). He was told off, and on one occasion sent home, for forgetting his timing instructions. However, the recipes he devised were seen as imaginative, stylish and contemporary by Osborn and a team of fellow chefs, while Malcolm's ideas were criticized as old-fashioned, traditional and uninteresting in appearance. On one occasion, when he suggested a dish of roast lamb with raspberry sauce, Osborn threw a tantrum! He told Malcolm he felt totally let down as it was unthinkable in contemporary cooking to serve a fruit-based sauce with lamb: a salad of endive and broad beans was the kind of accompaniment he proposed. The team of chefs commented that Malcolm's dishes would not match up to people's expectations of what would be served in a two-starred restaurant.

No prizes for guessing who was offered the job! Despite his lack of concentration and organization, James was seen as having the potential to make it in the world of modern *haute cuisine*, while Malcolm, notwithstanding his efforts to learn about new values in cooking, appeared to the chef Osborn (in his thirties) as hopelessly traditional.

Many areas of contemporary business are based on youth, glamour and style; being 'modern' is a key selling point and discrimination at work on the grounds of age has increasingly been recognized as a problem. The young, aggressively self-confident women and men who compete

to become Sir Alan Sugar's apprentice typify the modern business world. Older people such as Malcolm are seen to lack **flexibility** and adaptability. Will they be able to take orders from young ambitious managers? Will they understand the needs of a new generation of customers and clients? Will they fit with the image of a successful modern enterprise?
What do you think?

Notions of modernity are used in some of the best-known writings about the contemporary world of work. For example, Ulrich Beck uses the term 'the second modernity' (2000) to refer to the contemporary global economy. The notion of reflexive modernity has been used by Beck (1992; 2000; Beck et al. 1994), Giddens (1991) and Paul du Gay (1996), whose work will be discussed elsewhere in this book, to describe the way that we perpetually reflect upon and monitor our own actions and lifestyles and change them if they are not working for us. Contemporary selves are seen as constantly changing and adapting in response to our rapidly moving environment. Business organizations, too, can be seen to be 'reflexive' in that they use all sorts of mechanisms to review their progress, instead of carrying on because 'that's the way we've always done it'. It is argued that, to stay competitive in the 'modern world', it is necessary to be self-critical. Consultants, away-days , team-building exercises and staff development programmes are all part of this reflexive modern business culture: though fans of Ricky Gervais in *The Office* will know that these do not always work quite as intended!

Case study 2.1 Life in a pre-industrial economy

'There is no such thing as an earthly paradise, but I think Anuta comes close to it.' Anuta, a small island in the Pacific visited by Bruce Parry as part of his *Tribe* BBC 2 TV series, has many of the features of pre-industrial societies as described by Marx, Weber and Durkheim. There is a limited division of labour: apart from those of the Chief and the Assistant Chief, there are no specialist occupations. Each of the twenty-four families on the island carries out the same range of activities to fulfil subsistence needs. They build houses and canoes; they hunt for fish and seabirds, and grow crops such as manioc, taro, banana and coconut. What division of labour exists is based, as in most tribal societies, on gender and age. Only men go out in canoes to fish. However, women and men combine to drive fish into walled trap areas; once trapped, the men spear the big fish and the boys the little ones. Bruce Parry was allowed by the women to join in one of their tasks, the washing of turmeric roots: turmeric is used in cooking, but also to decorate their bodies in the various tribal rituals and feasts that take place, for example to welcome visitors, to celebrate a boy's first fishing trip or to mark a funeral.

Weber reported that, when German pre-industrial peasants were offered the choice of extra hours' work for more money, they rejected it, saying their needs were all met and they preferred to retain their spare time (Weber 1958: 59–60). Weber saw this as a limiting factor in pre-industrial societies since it inhibited the drive to accumulate a surplus of capital for investment. The Anuta are like other tribes in working mainly to fulfil their needs; as they are almost totally dependent on their environment, they respect and preserve it by not over-utilizing particular resources, so that at certain times they will not catch particular animals or fish. Spare time is spent in leisure – dancing, singing and swimming.

What struck Parry above all, however, was their central concept of aropa which ensured the well-being of the whole community. Aropa is a concept for giving and sharing, which roughly equates to compassion, love and affection. The catch of a fishing trip would be divided up equally between the twenty-four families, as were the gifts Parry brought to the island. Since the island is susceptible to tropical storms and crop failure, the islanders dig what they call maa pits, lined with banana leaves, in which they store food for emergencies. In times of need this is shared between the whole community.

Part of the Solomon Islands, Anuta is remote, with limited contact with the outside world. Even so, such contacts are beginning to threaten the continuation of aropa, the 'primitive communism' that Marx attributed to tribal societies. The Anuta catch sharks and preserve their fins to sell to the Japanese, where they are a rare and expensive delicacy. The Anuta do not have a very developed money economy, but money gained from the sale of the fins is not shared out, but is kept by the family who caught the fish. This could be the start of commerce and surplus accumulation. Some men go on trips and work for money which is used to buy western goods like clothes or fuel.

In the modern world, with its tempting luxuries and global communication capacities, it is difficult for such societies to retain their traditions. The tribe's culture and customs are already under threat: they were converted to Christianity in 1916, although this religion fits well with their communitarian and egalitarian values. But the community is divided over the setting up of a clinic providing modern western medicine. The Chief refused to have a clinic, believing it would threaten the culture; however, without modern medicine, members of the tribe may suffer or die unnecessarily and some of the Anuta saw his decision as an abuse of his power.

How long the Anuta lifestyle can survive is unknown, but it provides a good example of the 'simple life' of harmony within the community and with nature which some of us crave for. However, this has to be traded for the choice, variety and cornucopia of consumer goods which was brought to us by capitalism and industrialism.

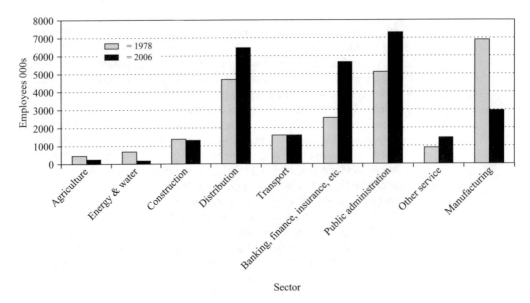

Sector

Afterwards? The post-industrial society?

What about today? As we shall see in subsequent chapters, many people still use the terms 'capitalism' and 'industrialism' to describe contemporary Britain, and draw on the ideas of Marx, Weber and Durkheim to explain work relationships. However, many others believe that changes occurring, especially since the mid twentieth century, mean that we need new terms to describe societies and work relations. In particular, in current western societies traditional manufacturing jobs have been in decline for some time, while service jobs, including a whole range of new types of occupations, have increased rapidly. A 'new international division of labour' emerged, as we shall explore in the next chapter. This means that production of many goods which were made in Britain and other western countries (including cars, electrical goods, clothing and shoes) has been moved to other parts of the world where labour and raw materials are cheaper, developing new chains of supply and demand. The graph in figure 2.1 shows the resulting pattern of change in jobs in the UK. The distribution of employment between industrial sectors has changed considerably over time, and we can see the decline of the manufacturing sector and the rise of the service sector in terms of numbers employed within these industries. The decline of manufacturing jobs is quite marked when seen against the rise of service sector jobs. However, we should note that two other significant sectors – agriculture and energy – have also declined significantly in this period.

As conditions of service work are rather different from those of factory jobs, many commentators have seen this as bringing a radical change in the nature of work and a need for new theories and typologies of society. One very influential notion is that of post-industrialism, which was initially developed by Daniel Bell (1973) and Alain Touraine (1971).

Fig. 2.1 Change in employment patterns; employees per industrial sector 1978/2006 Source: Labour Force Survey time series data, 1978–2006

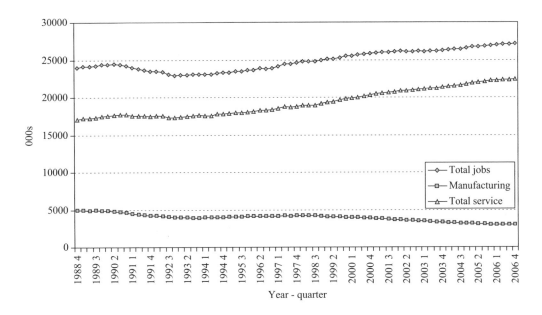

Fig. 2.2 Service, manufacturing and total jobs, 1978 to 2006

Source: ONS data, 2008

Bell's ideas were developed specifically as a critique of Marx's theory of capitalism, which he thought was no longer relevant. According to Bell, the main dynamic of modern society, what he called its 'axial principle', was no longer profit accumulation but knowledge. This was bringing a less exploitative type of production, in which people's skills were being upgraded. Higher education would be increasingly important and widespread so that occupational levels would be raised. As a result there would be an end of class conflict between workers and management. Bell also believed that the greater technological capacity of the new economy, with computerized techniques and processes, would free up labour, bringing a shorter working week and what others have termed the '**leisure society**'. Thus in the 1970s politicians worried about educating schoolchildren into making creative and positive use of all the leisure time they would be experiencing.

Table 2.2 Work in industrial and post-industrial society

	Industrial society	Post-industrial society
Axial principle	Profit	Knowledge
Dominant sector	Manufacturing	Service
Dominant occupations	Manual workers	Scientists, technicians, professionals
Nature of work	Jobs	Careers
Skill levels	Degrading of skills	Upskilling
Industrial relations	Conflictual	Co-operative
Key institutions	Companies	Universities, R&D

The notion of post-industrialism was part of a wider family of 'post' concepts which were elaborated in the 1980s and 1990s. The classic typologies of capitalism, industrialism and modernity were challenged by ideas such as post-capitalism, post-Fordism and post-modernity, as well as post-industrialism. All these ideas implied that the classic theories were no longer relevant because of major changes since they were written. They related to what were seen as new structures of society, and social relations which had evolved in the second half of the twentieth century.

'Post' and present

American industrial sociologist George Ritzer (2007) has recently provided a useful update on Bell's ideas. He lists some major characteristics of the contemporary **post-industrial** society.

- There is a transition from goods production to the provision of services. Although services predominate in a wide range of sectors, health, education, research and government services are particularly important areas.
- Manual work declines and professional and technical work increases.
- Practical know-how (such as engineering and machine operation) become less important than theoretical knowledge, with scientists and researchers being particularly important.
- There are attempts to harness and control new types of technologies, such as bio-technologies and nano-technologies.
- New intellectual technologies and frameworks, such as complexity theory or chaos theory, are needed to understand the potential of the new technologies.
- Universities and higher-level education are crucial to post-industrialism as they produce all the necessary scientists and technical experts.

You can see that this version of post-industrialism incorporates very recent forms of technology, and we shall consider in the next chapter how these developments will affect our lives; technology is changing the nature of business and employment in ways which we still have not perhaps fully grasped.

The post-industrial thesis has come in for considerable criticism, particularly in relation to the assumptions about the nature of jobs and the predicted harmony of industrial relations. As we shall see throughout this book, deskilling of jobs is still a major feature of employment change, while very many 'new' service jobs (for example in catering, in retail and in customer service) are as repetitive and monotonous as manufacturing jobs and less well-paid. Rather than a leisure society, Britain and America have become 'long-hours' societies with workers experiencing stress and work overload. Also, although there have

The growth of science and technology is symptomatic of post-industrial society's pursuit of knowledge rather than production.

been flows and variations in the nature of industrial relations since Bell wrote *The Coming of Post-Industrial Society*, there is no end in sight to conflict. While the defeat of the National Union of Mineworkers (NUM) in the great mining industrial dispute of 1984 was seen by some as the last great burst of industrial militancy in Britain, it resulted from a bitterly fought battle, not from consensus; and **strikes** have not been ended. While we were writing this book in 2007, there was talk of a new 'winter of discontent' (borrowing the term used to describe the wave of strikes in 1979 which led to the election of the Conservative government of Margaret Thatcher). Public-sector workers were disgruntled with their pay, teachers and local government employees held short strikes, and there was unrest among postal workers, railway workers and the staff of the London Underground, whose one-day strikes were causing considerable disruption to Britain's capital city.

However, there is clearly some validity in the idea of post-industrialism, as it is true that in the advanced economies manufacturing jobs continue to decline, with industrial production becoming relocated to newly industrializing countries. The decisions of the successful vacuum manufacturer Sir James Dyson in 2002, to move his production from Wiltshire to Malaysia, and of the Burberry clothing company in 2007, to close its factory in Rhondda, South Wales, and produce its polo shirts overseas (see box 3.1), were well-publicized recent examples. The growing importance of education and science is also verifiable. Students reading this book will probably not need to be told of the importance of higher education in securing career opportunities. The problem with the post-industrial thesis rested more with the interpretation of its social and political consequences than with the economic changes discerned by its advocates.

The notion of post-industrialism was part of a broader tendency to focus on how things have changed since Marx, Weber and Durkheim set out their typologies of society. Many of these ideas involved the idea of being 'post', i.e. 'after', these influential theories: post-Fordism, postmodernity, post-feminism, post-materialism or post-bureaucracy. For example, the idea of post-Fordism, which is discussed in full in chapter 4, refers to changes in the nature of manufacturing production techniques. The classic assembly line arrangement, particularly associated with the production of identical Ford motor-cars, has been replaced by more 'flexible' production systems which could cater for more sophisticated and differentiated consumer tastes. Like Bell, post-Fordists suggested that jobs would be upgraded and industrial relations become more democratic.

The other 'post' concepts listed above refer more generally to social trends beyond the economic realm and are less relevant to our study of work and business organizations. However, it is worth saying something more about the ideas of postmodernity and postmodernism which we discussed in chapter 1. This way of thinking has been very influential and pervasive in past decades across the social sciences, including management theory. To recap, these sometimes rather confusing terms refer to the idea that a new way of living, postmodernity, has replaced the older forms of culture and society, which evolved with industrialism and capitalism; and associated with this a new way of thinking and understanding, postmodernism, has replaced modernist thought, the body of theories developed in the nineteenth and early twentieth centuries, including the work of Marx, Durkheim and Weber. These earlier approaches, often also described as 'Enlightenment' thought, believed that societies were systematically ordered and could be systematically analysed. The application of science and rationality could then be used to cure social problems and move towards a better, fairer way of living. Postmodernists, however, see the world more pessimistically, as chaotic and disordered. They are sceptical of science and its claims and highlight the irrational nature of much human behaviour.

The ideas of postmodernism and postmodernity are particularly associated with Zygmunt Bauman (1998; 2000) and Richard Sennett (1998), who have applied them to the world of work. Bauman views the postmodern world and its organizations as shifting and fluid; work and business are ever-changing, requiring individuals to adapt themselves ceaselessly to fit in with their demands. According to Bauman, we lead 'liquid lives' (2006), geographically and socially mobile as we try to develop ourselves to cope with change. We shall return to these ideas of flexibility and liquidity in subsequent chapters. But it may occur to you that these ideas of postmodernity are really not very different from the notions of reflexive or late modernity we explored earlier. Perhaps the key differences are that the advocates of postmodernity are more inclined to highlight unpredictability and uncertainty, and are less optimistic about the promises of technology and economic development.

Bauman is also associated with the widespread and popular notion of the consumer society. In his version, consumption has taken over from production as the force that drives our lives (1998). People used to think of their identities in terms of occupations, careers or jobs, and shape their lives around work (as in Weber's idea of the work ethic, discussed fully in chapter 4). Now their identities are more determined by their consumer needs and choices. According to Bauman, divisions in society are now more shaped by how you consume than what job you do. An elite of high-paid managers and professionals lead jet-setting lives, marked by extravagant lifestyles, expensive leisure pursuits (yachting, jet-skiing, dining at restaurants like *Pied à Terre*) and fashion goods (Chloe and Mulberry bags, Jimmy Choo and Manolo Blahnik shoes). Bauman also points to an under layer of 'failed consumers' who are too poor to buy into the world of luxury and leisure goods. Such people are often unemployed and dependent on state benefits. They are, in Bauman's view, victims of a new phase of capitalism in which capital relates to people as consumers not producers. If you cannot buy things, you are socially redundant. We gain our place in society by what we consume and this is displayed in our lifestyles.

Whatever the truth of this contention about the place of work in people's lives, there can be little doubt that consumption is an important driver of the modern service-based economy. Throughout the second half of the twentieth century, there was substantial growth in the retail and leisure sectors. Shopping is big business and there is no sign of this changing. It is likely that wherever you are living and studying you will see new retail developments, shopping malls and out-of-town retail and leisure parks being constructed in your vicinity.

Summary and conclusions

In this chapter we have introduced some of the key concepts and typologies that sociologists employ to explain and to make sense of the world we live in, especially the world of work and enterprise, which has always been central to sociological thinking. We started by exploring the work of three theorists who are taken to be among the key founders of modern social science: Marx, Weber and Durkheim.

Students often question the relevance to the modern world of work written by people who are long dead. However, in this chapter we have taken the view that to understand the present we need to know something about the past and the ideas used to understand it. But we have also shown in this chapter that many of the ideas produced by these classic social science figures are still relevant and in familiar use today: ideas such as capitalism, alienation, class conflict, bureaucracy, rationalization, the work ethic, the division of labour and anomie are still used today, not only in academic life but in many cases in everyday thinking. In subsequent chapters we shall find many instances of these ideas being reused and adapted.

We also introduced some of the most influential ideas used by contemporary theorists, which often developed by building on the work of the classic theorists or in critical response to them. These may help us to gain a better understanding of changing contemporary societies. Two extremely important ideas were those of post-industrialism and reflexive modernity. The notion of post-industrialism refers to the way the objective realities of working life have changed, with the growth of service jobs, the importance of new technologies and the increased stress on educational qualifications and high levels of skill. These are the working arrangements which will shape your own careers. Reflexive modernity refers more to the subjective dimensions of work – that is, the way we approach it, the stress put in the modern world on self-assessment and self-development. Thus it is already likely that your way of thinking about your working futures will be different from that of your parents' generation. Young people are encouraged to plan ahead much more than in the past.

Another change is the growth of a rampant form of consumerism, which has affected the market and the range of jobs available, as well as the way work links to the other aspects of our lives. You are likely to be familiar with the display of expensive fashionwear, 'bling' and luxury goods from your own observations, and from their display in the media, whichever part of the world you come from. Indeed China and Russia are seen to be taking over as world leaders in the consumption of luxury, with an avid thirst for gold and diamonds, designer clothes and accessories and high-performance cars. Is Bauman correct in his statement that our identities are shaped more by consumption than by our occupations and jobs?

In the next chapter we shall be considering some even more recent accounts of how the world of work is changing, with our focus on the notions of globalization and the changes it is bringing.

Discussion questions

1. Are contemporary workers rightly characterized as 'wage slaves'?
2. Look at the account of the ideas of Marx, Weber and Durkheim. Discuss how their ideas might still be relevant to contemporary working life.
3. Would it be possible to reproduce some of the positive features of tribal life in contemporary societies? What would be the barriers preventing the persistence of the ethics of aropa in modern social life?
4. With reference to the lives of yourselves, your friends and your families, consider how consumption and work affect your lives. Which is more important in defining who you are?

Further reading

If you are interested in reading more about Marx, Durkheim or Weber, there are a number of introductory books available. These include:

Pip Jones, *Introducing Social Theory*. Cambridge: Polity, 2003.
John Hughes, Wes Sharrock and Peter Martin, *Understanding Classical Sociology: Marx, Weber, Durkheim*. London: Sage Publications, 2003.
George Ritzer, *Contemporary Sociological Theory and its Classical Roots: The Basics*, 2nd edition. New York: McGraw-Hill, 2007.

You might enjoy the cartoon guide, *Marx for Beginners* (by Rius – first published in 1975), published by Pantheon, 2003.

A lively and simple guide to postmodernism and post-industrialism is:

David Lyon, *Postmodernity*. Milton Keynes: Open University Press, 2000.

Two short books by Zygmunt Bauman, *Work, Consumerism and the New Poor* (Milton Keynes: Open University Press, 1998), and *Consuming Life* (Cambridge: Polity, 2007) will introduce you to many of Bauman's influential ideas in a very readable way.

3 Societies and change: globalization and the knowledge-based economy

This chapter will:

- introduce two important concepts that help us picture society and businesses in it: globalization and neoliberalism
- discuss how these concepts are related to the emergence and operation of a knowledge-based economy
- examine how work and labour markets have changed in recent years as a result of globalization and neoliberalism, highlighting the trends of feminization and increased migration
- present a number of critiques of neoliberalism
- introduce the concept of corporate social responsibility and link it to environmental issues.

This chapter focuses on the key concepts which are currently being used to explain changes in work and employment relations in contemporary western societies as the twenty-first century develops. These kinds of conceptualizations present the world in which we live as highly dynamic, and indeed unstable. Moreover, the pace of change is hotting up, to the extent that people find it quite difficult to foresee beyond the immediate future. Technological developments, from robots to i-Pods, from mobile phones to memory-sticks, are changing the way we live, communicate and work, with effects not yet fully comprehended. All societies change, but in the pre-industrial era changes were slow and imperceptible and might take generations to work through. Now the world you live in is quite noticeably different from the one in which your parents grew up.

In the last chapter we explored various social typologies and noted how they all identified certain structures as organizing principles of society. This type of analysis sometimes can give a false impression that societies are static, as it emphasizes features that persist over time. Recently, however, social analysis has tended to focus on the driving forces which promote change. As opposed to social structures, we talk more of social processes or social dynamics. A number of important concepts are currently used to explain major processes of change in work relationships. Of these the most important is **globalization**, the idea that social relationships are moving from a national to international basis. This concept is often linked to two other concepts, that of **neoliberalism** as the prevailing form of economic policy, and the **knowledge-based economy** as an accompaniment of globalization in the West. We shall also consider the related ideas of **feminization** and **migration** and their impact on the workforce. Change brings new problems and challenges and we will end by looking at two issues which increasingly preoccupy social scientists: the threat to the **environment** and the growing influence and importance of information and communication technologies (**ICT**).

What's going on? Picturing current societies

The range of 'post' concepts discussed in the last chapter were extremely popular in the 1980s and 1990s. Do they help us understand what is going on today? Well, 'yes and no' must be the answer. You will still come across the ideas of post-industrialism and postmodernity (although equally you will still encounter discussions of industrialism, capitalism and modernity). However, in terms of understanding the current phase of social and economic development, some new terms have become increasingly popular. In the next section of this chapter we will focus briefly on three of these current terms: globalization, neo-liberalism and the knowledge-based economy.

Globalization

The notion of globalization has become a popular buzzword among politicians, journalists and business leaders, by whom it is often used in a rhetorical way. It has also been increasingly employed in academic debate since the 1980s. It is in truth a rather imprecise term that is used to convey large-scale economic and social changes without exactly specifying what they are. The *Collins Dictionary* provides a rather narrow definition focusing specifically on the economy: globalization is 'the process enabling financial and investment markets to operate internationally, largely as a result of deregulation and improved communications'. A more typically broad definition is provided by Abercrombie et al. – globalization consists of:

> Processes operating on an emergent global level which over time are compressing the distances between people and places within different societies and which increase the sense that we live in a single world. (2000: 13)

This definition indicates that there can be economic, social, political and cultural accounts of globalization, depending on which particular aspects of the relations between 'people and places' we focus on. Here we shall be primarily concerned with the economic aspects, only touching briefly on culture.

If we concentrate on economic globalization we can distinguish a number of interrelated processes:

1. internationalization of the processes of production, distribution and exchange, so that national economies are less distinct and markets become global;
2. dominance of large multinational corporations (MNCs) which operate across national boundaries;
3. decreased ability of nation-states to control fully their own economic systems;
4. increase in number and power of supra-national bodies and institutions (such as the European Union or the G8);
5. improved methods of transport and communication which allow rapid movement of people, goods and, in particular, information flows between countries;
6. the increasing integration of newly industrializing countries (such as India, China and Indonesia) into these global networks;
7. the development of a 'new international division of labour', in which unskilled manufacturing work shifts to poorer, less developed countries, while research and development are centred in the richer, advanced industrial societies;
8. a movement in which goods and services become much more culturally homogenized around the globe (symbolized by the spread of McDonald's restaurants, Starbucks coffee shops, pizza and Nike shoes to virtually every country).

At the core of globalization is the increased movement of labour and capital, of finance, goods and services between countries, which is often described by sociologists and cultural theorists as the shrinking of space and time. Although nations and localities retain their own traditional cultures, they are increasingly weakened by the spread of mass western culture (often Americanized), around the world, for example via the internet, TV and cinema.

Just one example of economic globalization.

Globalization has had effects on all our lives, as we are more likely to travel (think of the rise of the 'Gap Year', hardly heard of when the authors of this book were students), to encounter people and products from other cultures and to communicate with people across vast distances with the latest ICT devices. Some of us may take jobs abroad or be sent abroad by our companies, since businesses increasingly think and operate in global terms. Obviously these are beneficial trends, which enrich our lives. But perhaps the most remarked-on aspect of globalization is less benevolent: the heightened nature of international competition leading to pressure to cut costs and maximize quality and efficiency. In particular this has led to job losses in European countries and to firms resorting to 'offshore' activity, such as locating their customer service departments and **call centres** in India. The story of Burberry (box 3.1) is a good example of the impact of such pressures. Globalization is thus associated with increased insecurity in the labour market.

Box 3.1 Burberry and the global economy

This is how the famous Burberry clothing company defines itself on its website:

> Burberry is a luxury brand with a distinctive British sensibility, strong international recognition and differentiating brand values that resonate across a multi-generational and dual-gender audience. The Company designs and sources apparel and accessories distributing through a diversified network of retail, wholesale and licensing channels worldwide. Since its founding in England in 1856, Burberry has been synonymous with quality, innovation and style.
>
> (www.burberry.com)

Its story illustrates well the process of globalization. Burberry was founded in 1856 as a small shop in Basingstoke by Thomas Burberry, a draper's apprentice aged twenty-one. The business expanded and became an 'emporium', pioneering the weatherproof material, gabardine, which became synonymous with rainwear. In 1891 a shop was opened in the Haymarket in London. The Burberry trenchcoat was introduced in 1914 and the trademark check pattern, both a signal of upper-class status and now of 'chav' culture, was developed in the 1920s and became part of a repertoire of products that signalled 'Englishness'. The products became popular in the overseas market. The Norwegian explorer Amundsen used Burberry products in his expedition to the South Pole.

Recently the company has developed a worldwide distribution network and has also moved from its traditional outerwear range into *haute couture* women's clothing under its Prorsum trademark. It owns stores in some countries, while in other places where it does not wish to invest directly it operates through enfranchised partners. Thus it has become a distinctly global player. In 2005–6 only 35 per cent of its sales were in

Europe, with 46 per cent in Japan and Asia. Some of its ranges are now targeted at specific market groups internationally, especially young adults (Black Label and Blue Label in Japan and Thomas Burberry in Spain). In the USA it markets a limited range of its products electronically.

As its markets became international, Burberry started to produce some of its garments overseas through what it terms an 'external sourcing network'. Most of the goods are made in Europe but some in Asia and South and Central America. This policy became a source of public controversy when the company announced it was closing its plant in Treorchy in the depressed valleys region of South Wales, with the loss of 300 jobs. It argued that it could not produce goods of sufficient quality competitively in Wales and was moving production to China.

This resulted in a major campaign led by the GMB union, and supported by a number of celebrity figures, as reported by BBC Wales:

> Protests have taken place in six cities across the world as part of a campaign to stop the closure. Co-ordinated protests against closure were held in London, Paris, New York, Chicago, Strasbourg and Las Vegas earlier in February. A number of celebrities have added their support to the workers' campaign including singer Sir Tom Jones, Manchester United manager Sir Alex Ferguson, actors Michael Sheen, Ioan Gruffudd, Rhys Ifans and Emma Thompson, opera star Bryn Terfel, singer/presenter Charlotte Church and comedian and author Ben Elton.

The strategy of global resourcing operated by Burberry is put down by them to the need to remain profitable in an increasingly competitive international market for luxury clothing. Consequences of such global competition are frequent losses of manufacturing jobs in the richer societies as a result of the search for cheap labour. Unions and others who seek to resist these processes of global change often find it more effective to organize protests on a global base, as shown in this case.

Commenting on the Burberry case, *Personnel Today* pointed to the loss of nearly 8,000 manufacturing jobs in Britain in January 2007: these included jobs at well-known and established firms, such as Birds Eye, Tate and Lyle and Young's Seafood.

When the concept of globalization was first developed, there was considerable critique of it, especially as to whether the autonomy of the nation-state was really being undermined (Hirst and Thompson 2000; Bradley et al. 2000). Ackroyd (2002) is doubtful whether hard data can be found to prove that Britain's economy is increasingly global. Commentators also pointed out the extraordinarily long history of international trade and wondered if this was really a new phenomenon. Generally it is agreed, however, that the volume and intensity of inter-national exchanges are much greater, indicating that there has been a real qualitative shift. However, as Abercrombie et al. (2000) argue, we are very far from an end-state in which nations are fused into a single economy. Languages, cultures and nationalist values stand in the way; for example, many countries in Europe, including Britain, remain resistant to the integrative structures of the European Union (EU), such as the single currency (the Euro) or the relaxation of border controls. Anthony Giddens, one of globalization's foremost proponents, admits that, paradoxically, global pushes can actually strengthen nationalist fervour and attachment to locality and local customs. However, there can be little doubt that economic globalization is impacting on our working lives.

So far, as the analysis may have indicated, the push for globalization has come primarily from the societies of the advanced capitalist economies, as their businesses seek new markets and new ways to increase their profits. In particular the United States has been seen as the key player and promoter of globalization, and its huge corporations as the major beneficiaries. In the critical approach to globalization the countries of the developing world are usually portrayed as becoming losers, whose natural resources are squandered, while their citizens provide cheap labour in factories and call centres. Box 3.2 offers some examples of how profits accrue to businesses in the western societies, although there may be stings in the tail: loss of working-class jobs in the UK and USA, displaced to cheaper offshore locations, has led to unemployment and the rise of ghettoes or areas of deprivation, where criminal activity and drug-taking may appeal to disillusioned young people.

Box 3.2 Global supply chains: bananas and cocaine

Bananas: from Costa Rica to Tesco via the Channel Islands

Bananas are big business: they are the largest single product by volume sold in British supermarkets. The industry is controlled by big US companies such as Dole and Chiquita, along with Irish-based Fyffes. Between 2002 and 2007 Dole, Chiquita and Del Monte had combined sales of $50 billion and profits of $1.4 billion. For every pound spent by a consumer on bananas in the UK, only 1.5 pence goes on labour costs. As well as manufacturing costs and profit for producers and retailers, many other middle men profit along the way, taking money for shipping, insurance, branding and marketing, and for business services, many of which are purchased by the companies in tax havens such as Bermuda or Jersey to enable them to reduce their tax bills.

Back in the Caribbean and Latin America, women workers toil on the plantations in unpleasant conditions, standing up beside large tanks of water to wash, grade and pack the bananas. A worker described her long working day, with only two fifteen-minute breaks and half an hour for lunch, to a *Guardian* reporter:

> I get up at 4 am, get the children ready for school, and then walk 20 minutes to the roadside where a company bus picks me up.

It's an hour's ride to the plantation. We get there by 6 am, just when the sun is rising and start work right away. I'm a selector inside a big warehouse with 42 other workers sorting through the bananas. They arrive on a conveyor belt and you have to be quick. . . . we work through to 6 or 7 pm. By then it's dark and your feet are killing you after all that time standing . . . I earn 7,000 colones a day (£6.60). It's not much but what really upsets me is that we have to work longer hours than we're supposed to. Eleven hours is the maximum but often we're there for more than 13 hours. We work six days a week, Monday to Saturday. Sometimes it doesn't feel like a life.

Cocaine: from Colombia via Jamaica to London

Drugs are big business, too, dominating the 'black' or illegal economy. A study published in 2007 by the Home Office, *The Illicit Drug Trade in the United Kingdom*, estimated that there are in Britain 300 major importers, 3,000 wholesalers and 70,000 street dealers in the drugs business, with a turnover of £7–8 billion per year.

Drugs are grown by poor farmers in third world countries: opium poppies in Afghanistan, coca plants in Peru and Colombia. Cocaine has production costs of £325 per kilo, but is sold to the first set of South American dealers in the chain for over £2,000, and is then passed to others in the Caribbean for £7,800. When it finally reaches Britain, often carried by 'mules' desperate for money to pay for mortgages or other debts, it has a street value of £51,650. Successful traffickers and dealers can become very rich, although landing up in prison is seen as an occupational hazard.

It is estimated that there are around 332,000 problem drug users in the UK. Although many users of heroin or crack cocaine are unemployed people from poor backgrounds, they have fixed on an expensive habit. Their supplies may cost them around £100 per day, often procured by stealing, mugging or prostitution. An ex-user of heroin, now working, as many do, on community projects with vulnerable people, describes her past lifestyle:

Some people commit horrendous crimes to get money for drugs. I didn't. I worked at a lap-dancing club practically every night and earned up to £500 a week. I didn't think about what I was doing. When you're an addict you spend all day running around to get your drugs. Some days you haven't got enough money to buy any. Sometimes you can't find a dealer to supply you. When you come off drugs, one of the most difficult things to deal with is boredom. What else do you do with your time?

While drugs make a lot of money for many individuals and for the drug trafficking cartels, the economic and social costs are monumental: maintaining prisons and looking after prisoners, costs of policing and the justice system, costs of rehabilitation and counselling, community schemes designed to prevent addiction in the first place, benefits paid to unemployed addicts, plus all the losses and distress caused to the victims of crime (often family and acquaintances of the addicts). The lives of the addicts themselves are miserable, frequently ending in prison, illness and early death.

Both examples show how global chains of production and selling act to bind nations and individuals together. A whole multitude of people hold occupations or earn their livings from activities either directly or indirectly related to the production of bananas and cocaine.

Interestingly, shortages on the world market of morphine are making British farmers turn to growing opium poppies – a lucrative crop.

(References: *Guardian* newspaper 2007; Travis 2007; Murray 2007)

However, given the dynamism we have emphasized here, the fortunes of various nations may change as global economic development proceeds. The booming economy of the Republic of Ireland has led to it being nicknamed the 'Celtic tiger'. The countries of the Pacific Rim, such as Japan, Hong Kong and Singapore, have been seen by America as potential economic rivals. In recent years, attention has focused on 'the sleeping giant' of mainland China as its economic growth proceeds at an extraordinary rate. As a result Chinese citizens have come out of their former isolation and are taking advantage of openings in the West. Many Chinese students come to the UK and Europe to further their studies, and many may read this book!

Recently, the *Guardian* newspaper asked a question about another country experiencing rapid growth: 'Is this the Indian century?' With the advantage of familiarity with the English language and western cultures which was gained during India's time as a British colony, its companies are now beginning to invest substantially in the West. India is famed for its output of high-quality IT graduates. Its companies are putting these skilled assets, along with managerial and entrepreneurial expertise, to notable global use. For example India's richest family, the Tatas, own many global hotel chains. Along with another giant Indian firm, the software company Infosys, Tata is buying up call centres around the world, including in Britain. In 2007 Infosys took over the call centres in Poland belonging to the well-known Philips electronics group. It hired 32,000 new employees in that year. According to its CEO, Kris Gopalakrishnan:

> The company is building up a network of offices stretching from Mexico to eastern Europe to China to provide an 'anytime, anywhere' solution to its clients. 'Our customers are global so we have to become so.' (Ramesh 2007)

In recent years the Indian economy has been growing at around 9 per cent of GDP (Gross Domestic Product) per annum. In 2008 the World

Bank forecast it to grow again at 8.4 per cent of GDP, with China predicted to be the world's fastest growing economy at 10.8 per cent. By contrast, forecasts for the USA and UK, both economies whose credit systems were running into dire trouble, were for growth of 1.9 per cent and 2.25 per cent respectively. Of course, the developing countries have a long way to go to catch up with the West, and their societies are marked by huge gaps of wealth between rich and poor and conditions of poverty which would be unacceptable in Europe. However, the coming decades could witness some interesting shifts in global power if these trends continue.

Neoliberalism

Those interested in the critique of globalization often combine it with discussion of neoliberalism. This term denotes a political doctrine, associated particularly with Margaret Thatcher and Ronald Reagan, and a set of economic policies to realize that doctrine. Harvey (2005) explores neoliberalism as the belief that market exchange is in itself a beneficial ethical process which should be allowed to drive all economic action, free from interference or external regulation. Radical activists Elizabeth Martinez and Arnoldo García argue that it evolved as a response to shrinking profits and difficulties within capitalism which led institutions such as the International Monetary Fund (IMF) and the World Bank to return to the economic liberalism of the early capitalist era.

Martinez and García list the essential features of neoliberal economic policy:

1. The rule of the market. 'Free' or private enterprise must be liberated from any bonds imposed by the government (the state), no matter how much social damage this causes. The aim is to secure total freedom of movement for capital, goods and services.
2. Cutting public expenditure. Spending on health, education and social infrastructure must not be allowed to become a burden on free enterprise.
3. Deregulation. Reducing any kind of government regulation (such as wage and price controls) which might hamper the search for profit.
4. **Privatization**. Selling off state-owned enterprises, goods and services to private investment, including utilities, public transport, schools and hospitals, in the name of greater efficiency.
5. **Individualization**. Eliminating notions of 'the public good' and 'collectivities' and replacing them with 'individual responsibility'. The poor are urged to make their own efforts to become independent and blamed if they fail. (Martinez and García 2000)

In line with the latter point, Pierre Bourdieu (1998) describes neoliberalism as a programme for destroying collective structures which may impede the pure market logic. This would include trade unions, which are seen as enemies of free choice and individual rights.

Neoliberalism can produce huge wealth but it often goes hand-in-hand with increasing gaps between rich and poor.

Thus at the core of neoliberal policy is the deregulation of markets and dismantling of the welfare state, a process started in Britain by Margaret Thatcher in the 1980s but to some extent carried on by New Labour, with its fondness for shared private/public ownership. However, New Labour also introduced some regulation of the market, such as the minimum wage. The neoliberal argument is that the unimpeded market will help businesses become more effective in accumulating profit, thus the society will become more wealthy and the wealth will 'trickle down' to the rest of the citizens and benefit everybody. That is the 'ethic' of neoliberalism referred to by Harvey (2005).

In reality the trickling down of wealth can be limited and most countries which have adopted neoliberal policies, such as Britain, have seen the gap between the rich and the poor increase, as Susan George points out:

> Another structural feature of neo-liberalism consists in remunerating capital to the detriment of labour and thus moving wealth from the bottom of society to the top. If you are, roughly, in the top 20 percent of the income scale, you are likely to gain something from neo-liberalism and the higher you are up the ladder, the more you gain.

Conversely, the bottom 80 percent all lose and the lower they are to begin with, the more they lose proportionally. (George 1999)

The notion of neoliberalism is also often used by contemporary theorists such as Harvey in combination with an analysis of capitalism. There is an acknowledgement that capitalist societies may differ from each other. Thus the Scandinavian countries such as Sweden and Denmark have to a certain extent resisted neoliberalism, retaining a commitment to the welfare state and believing in the 'common good' and collective social provision. This is an important point as it contradicts the common tendency to believe that economic development must inevitably take a specific direction. We have in fact, as citizens, real choices to make, between, for example *neoliberal capitalism* and **welfare capitalism**. Also, as we shall see later in the chapter, many people are beginning to take seriously the notion of an environmentally friendly 'green capitalism', as set out in box 3.3.

Box 3.3 The green critique of neoliberalism

Once in every generation a political revolution takes place in which thinking and behaviour shifts not just by degrees but qualitatively . . . Today, every pressing issue we face demands a collective response – climate change and flooding, terrorism, the housing crisis, insecurity at work, immigration and the ageing population. Neoliberalism promised a utopia but has failed to deliver. Britain has become a hideously unequal society. The poor are not treading water but sinking under the rising tide of the rich. . . . Working harder to keep up on the treadmill of the learn-to-earn consumer society is deepening our social recession. We are at a tipping point.

People want reassurance once more but this time it's that globalization can be tamed, climate change averted and social cohesion created.

(Neal Lawson of Compass, writing in the *Guardian* 8 August 2007)

Is Lawson right? Have we reached a 'tipping point'? What changes might happen? Will collective actions replace individualism?

The knowledge-based economy

Next we discuss another concept which has become very popular with politicians, and has been much explored by management theorists and industrial sociologists. This is the idea of the knowledge-based economy. According to Sylvia Walby, 'the knowledge economy is the future of the world of work' (2007: 3).

This term was officially endorsed by the Special Council of Europe in Lisbon in 2000 as the part to be played by the EU in the evolving 'new world order'. It can be seen as essentially a newer version of post-industrialism and bears many similarities to George Ritzer's model discussed in chapter 2. It sees the future role of the more advanced economies as developing a highly educated, highly skilled workforce who can act as 'knowledge workers'. At the Lisbon Council, the EU took as its goal to become:

> the most competitive and dynamic knowledge-based economy in the world capable of sustainable economic growth with more and better jobs and greater social cohesion. (quoted in Walby 2007: 9)

As with so many of the ideas discussed in this chapter the term is often employed rather loosely, but Walby usefully distinguishes three ways it can be used:

1. as a name for specific sectors of the economy, particularly the ITC occupations, but also the 'knowledge-intensive occupations' (such as finance, health and education);
2. as a way to understand the development of the whole economy, with knowledge seen as a key driver of overall development;
3. to explore the processes of knowledge development within the economy.

Here we are concerned with the second meaning, though the importance of ICT should not be overlooked. The knowledge-based economy can be seen as a distinct new phase of capitalism or industrialism in which high technology and high-level services replace manufacturing as key activities. Manuel Castells, whose work has been very influential here, talks of a 'new technological paradigm centred round microelectronics-based information/communication technologies & genetic engineering' (2000: 9). Knowledge becomes a key asset for societies, businesses and individuals. Thus Danny Quah (2003) defines the knowledge-based economy as characterized by 'knowledge goods' and suggests that the ability of things to be digitized lies at the core of this.

We can see the knowledge-based economy as having the following characteristics:

1. a changed occupational structure with new service jobs at both higher and lower skill levels;
2. a new elite of 'knowledge workers' in areas such as computing, electronics, consultancy, design, bioscience, pharmaceuticals, creative industries, media;
3. the continued importance of Research and Development (R&D) in western economies with manufacturing moving to less developed countries;
4. increased outsourcing of lower-level service jobs to developing societies, such as call-centre-based customer services;
5. an infrastructure allowing for the training and retraining of workers to allow them to acquire high-level and rapidly changing skills

– for instance, the rapid growth of the international student market shows how the developing societies appreciate the crucial role of knowledge acquisition.

Reading this list you can see how this builds on many of the theories discussed earlier in this chapter and the previous one. It has important consequences for governments, in terms of training and education provision, and for businesses, in terms of how they construct jobs and utilize the skills and qualifications of their workers. We can see that the EU vision also includes the idea that jobs will be upgraded and society become more harmonious, as in Bell's vision of the post-industrial society. But in reality we can distinguish between jobs which them-selves are based on the possession of expert knowledge (for example computer programming, medicine or accountancy) and large numbers of jobs which are embedded in the knowledge industries but which require only basic skills (data entry clerks, hospital auxiliaries and call centre workers, for example). As we shall see in later chapters, the knowledge-based economy remains a segregated and divided one.

The changing nature of the workforce: migration and feminization

The discussion so far has highlighted the changing nature of jobs within the global, neoliberal and knowledge-based economy, but has not given any attention to the nature of the people who fill these jobs. There have been some very significant changes here, too, as globaliza-tion has occurred simultaneously with the increasing participation of women in the workforce in many parts (though not all) of the globe, a process known as feminization, and increased levels of movement around the world in new patterns of international migration. Neither feminization nor international migration are new phenomena but it can be argued that they have taken new forms in combination with globalization.

In fact, increased-density migration was seen to be one of the defin-ing features of globalization, as listed earlier in the chapter. Of course, from the earliest known civilization onward, migration has been a fea-ture of human societies. People move around the globe for reasons of warfare and conquest (such as the great empires from Rome onwards); to find new homes or land to cultivate (for example the American pioneers moving the frontier westwards); to find new jobs and better opportunities (Irish and Scandinavian emigrants to America in the nineteenth century); or to escape persecution (the Jews throughout much of history).

Such migrations may be small-scale, as individuals or families move to 'seek their fortunes', or wide-scale as a result of disasters or conflicts, when they may be known as 'diasporas'. The latter term was used in relation to the Jews when they had no homeland and were scattered round the globe. Now it is also used to refer to other situations: we talk of the Indian diaspora, in relation to those from the sub-continent who reside in Britain, America and elsewhere. Some migrations may be forced, as in the case of the wholesale export of African slaves to the Caribbean and the United States; some may be invited, such as the movement of citizens from the British colonies to fill labour shortages in public transport, hospitals and factories during the period of post-war reconstruction; and some may be purely the voluntary decision of individuals. The study of migration has focused on push and pull factors. Wars, poverty, natural disasters and political persecution can be among the push factors; better wages, plentiful jobs, reuniting with family members or a more attractive lifestyle are some of the pull factors.

Our focus here is particularly on economic migration, the movement of people who are seeking better living standards and job opportunities. Several features of globalization have encouraged people to look outside their home countries for work: high-level staff of multinational companies are often required to move country for career reasons; the quick pace of change in markets, products and services means that some types of skills may be in short supply, encouraging skilled workers and professionals to take opportunities abroad; better and cheaper modes of transport make movement easier; the expanding international student market opens young people's eyes to possibilities of working abroad; international processes of trade and marketing create a need for people with language skills and cultural knowledge to help businesses succeed in other countries.

Castles and Miller state that the end of the twentieth century and start of the twenty-first can be seen as 'the Age of Migration' (1998). They list a number of key trends:

1. migration has become globalized so that more countries are involved;
2. more people are migrating and they are able to do so more quickly;
3. migrants are more diverse, and there are many differing types of migration;
4. migration is increasingly the focus of political concern and political conflict;
5. migration has been feminized, with many more women coming as migrants in their own right, rather than accompanying or joining fathers and husbands.

Britain, as the first industrial nation and one of the world's leading economies, has long been a target for economic migrants. As we noted above, in the post-war period most immigrants came from the former British colonies, in particular from the Caribbean and the Indian sub-continent. There has also been a long tradition of migrants filling 'niche' markets in British cities, for example Chinese and Turkish families providing cheap and popular takeaway food. Persistent nursing shortages over the years have led to the employment of women trained as nurses in many other countries, including the Caribbean, the Philippines, India, Sweden and Australia. When it has been difficult to fill jobs with native British people, employers and organizations have persistently turned to the use of migrant labour.

However, this process has been attended by periodic anxieties and panics about the consequences of immigration, such as Enoch Powell's infamous speech in 1968 about commonwealth immigrants 'swamping' the British culture. As a result, from the 1960s, when the first Commonwealth Immigration Act was passed, Britain has exercised tight control over immigration and turned back many applicants, including numerous refugees and asylum-seekers from war-torn countries such as Iraq, Somalia and Rwanda.

However, recently, the picture on migration has changed considerably as citizens of the EU exercise their right to take up jobs anywhere within the community. This has led to large numbers of economic migrants seeking work in Britain and the Republic of Ireland (which has minimal restrictions on immigration), especially from Portugal, Poland and the newer countries of EU enlargement such as Romania and Bulgaria.

There is now a heated debate about the consequences of the arrival of these 'new migrants'. Particularly in depressed or rural areas, the influx of migrant workers may be seen as a threat to the employment of the locals or a way to undercut wage levels. Indeed, less skilled migrant workers are dangerously exposed to exploitation, for example by gangmasters who use them as cheap agricultural labour for picking fruit or vegetables. There is particular concern over the role of manpower agencies in pushing down labour costs and undermining job security. However, in many cases such workers are filling jobs which British people are not prepared to take because of low pay and poor conditions. Also, many of the 'new migrants' are expert and committed workers who are contributing substantially to the growth and health of our economy. Notoriously, Britain in past decades experienced shortages of skilled craftsmen, such as plumbers and carpenters, gaps in our skills base which were filled by Polish migrants. We also need doctors and software experts from overseas, and many academic lecturing posts in science, medicine and economics can only be filled by recruiting candidates from abroad. It is also important to point out that there has always been a correspondingly high 'out-migration' from the UK, particularly to the Anglophone areas of the world such as the United States and Australasia, but also to Britain's former colonies and, increasingly, round the EU countries. However, social panic over competition for jobs has led the government to consider further curbs on migration, including that of skilled workers.

James Wickham (2007) argues that such moves are mistaken, as policy-makers have failed to understand the changed nature of migration. Indeed, he argues we should talk of mobility rather than migration.

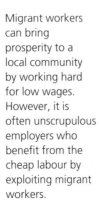

Migrant workers can bring prosperity to a local community by working hard for low wages. However, it is often unscrupulous employers who benefit from the cheap labour by exploiting migrant workers.

Based on his research in the Republic of Ireland, he challenges the old model of migrant labour, involving individuals moving from country A to country B for work; although the migrants might have believed initially that this was a temporary move, in fact most stayed and became settled. This is how Britain's settled ethnic minority communities were formed. However, according to Wickham, this no longer applies. Instead, workers may make repeated moves between their home country and others for work and study. In his research among Ireland's very large numbers of Polish workers, Wickham found that they had no intention of settling, but expected to return home when they had accumulated savings and when conditions back home improved. In other words, globalization has changed the old pattern of migration, generating much more fluid, complex and rapid movements of labour between countries.

We have focused here on people who move because they cannot satisfy their economic needs in their home countries. But among the 'new migrants' we must also include those who move for social or lifestyle reasons as well as economic ones. Many students enjoy the challenge and adventure of taking degrees and courses in other countries, while also improving their language skills. People move because they fall in love with a country after going there for a holiday, or because they are in a relationship with one of its natives. Young people in particular may experience this lifestyle mobility, having grown up in an epoch where capital cities are highly multicultural. Many regard the world as 'their oyster'. This is another important consequence of globalization. Playwright Neil Biswas described his cousin from Bombay, who had completed a master's in International Business Management in England and was about to take up a consultancy job in Dubai:

> Tuntai is only 23 and seems to me a shining example of the new
> generation transforming India into a 21st century super-economy.
> As such he has three defining qualities – he is streetwise, technologi-
> cally literate and hungry for it. Tuntai's generation of Indians view the
> world as their marketplace. They think nothing of abandoning their
> homes and hometowns and setting up on their own in a foreign land.
> (Biswas 2008)

The increasing volume of such flows of mobile workers obviously has
important effects on the composition of the workforce in the receiving country. There are many non-white and foreign-born employees
in most large organizations in the UK. Thus, organizations have had
to address the handling of this diversity, as will be discussed in later
chapters. As well as being more ethnically diverse, most organizations
continue to experience the impacts of feminization.

   Elsewhere we pointed out that feminization had three aspects
(Bradley et al. 2000):

1. The feminization of the *workforce* as the proportion of women rose
   and that of men declined. This has been a long-term trend in Britain
   since the 1960s, although it may now be approaching its limit (see
   figures 3.1 and 3.2).
2. The feminization of *occupations* as women advanced in former
   male strongholds such as medicine and accountancy. The feminization of occupations, however, may be accompanied by declining
   status and reduced pay levels. Such has arguably been the case with
   academic work. Men have continued, however, to maintain some
   strongholds such as engineering, construction, craft production
   and transport, where women have made little headway. Neither

Fig. 3.1 Women's economic activity rate 1984–2003 Source: Labour Force Survey 1984 to 2003

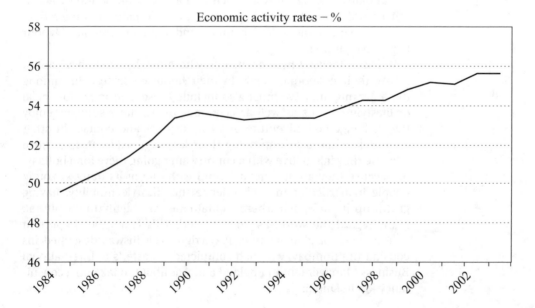

Economic activity rates – %

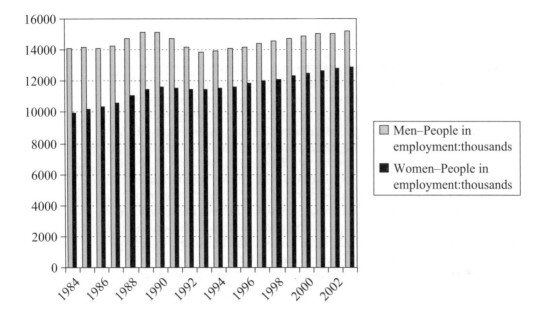

Fig. 3.2 Gender and employment Source: Labour Force Survey 1984 to 2003

has there been much evidence of the 'masculinization' of 'women's jobs', such as secretarial jobs, cleaning or hairdressing. Entry of men into such jobs is seen as a kind of emasculation by many men.

3. The feminization of *work* as jobs in the service sector increased and were seen to demand qualities associated with 'women's work', such as caring for customers and good communication skills. Women are seen as specialists in '**emotion work**', such as the air hostesses studied by Arlie Hochschild (1983), whose key function was to make the passengers feel happy and cared for during the flight. Increasingly, service jobs in areas such as catering and leisure also demand glamour and charm as characteristics of their employees. Lisa Adkins studied hotel employees (1995) who were supposed to act as objects of sexual fantasy for customers. However, while these kinds of changes are ongoing, the characteristics which are still associated with the top jobs are those linked with masculinity, such as toughness, ambition and decisiveness. One of the authors was told at a management job interview, where her pitch was her desire to promote both aspirations and compassion, that compassion was an unsuitable value for an organization where 'tough decisions' had to be made.

Feminization of one type or other is a continued trend in many countries. This means that in many occupations the workforce is more mixed. This has led managers to take more notice of forms of prejudice and discrimination, backed by national and EU equality legislation which makes discrimination illegal (Bradley and Healy 2008). The complex issues surrounding 'managing diversity' will be fully explored in chapter 8.

The 'elephant in the room': environmental catastrophe and business

Earlier on in the chapter, we noted the 'green critique' of neoliberal capitalism. We are now beginning to see the malign impacts on the planet of the unchecked operation of globalization. As global capitalism continually seeks new products and markets, it greedily consumes more of the world's increasingly scarce natural resources, especially oil. The demands on energy have been compounded by the long consumer boom enjoyed in the West since the mid 1990s (discussed in chapter 2) and the engagement of the populations of the newly industrialized nations with western-style consumption. The growth of consumption means new or enlarged businesses; new businesses mean more factories consuming energy to produce goods, more vehicles on the road as employees travel to work, more international business travellers clocking up air miles. Our houses hum with the latest electronic gadgets (think of all those MP3 players and mobile phones continually demanding to be charged) and wealthier people take more and more long-distance holidays. These are the results of 'economic growth' so valorized by governments and corporate interests. But events of 2007 and 2008 (spiralling oil prices with knock-on effects on gas and electricity charges, food shortages leading to sharp rises in basic foodstuff costs) are bringing home the fact that the world's resources are not limitless and that there may be an end to persistent economic growth.

So it is not only the critics of capitalism who have become worried about the consequences of unchecked economic development. Journalists, politicians of all parties, young people, academics and directors and managers of companies, including the multinationals, have all become focused on the threats and challenges posed to the world by environmental pollution, global warming and the over-utilization of the world's resources. Many people, including large companies such as suppliers of gas and electricity, are telling us to use less energy in our houses, consume locally produced goods to save air miles, recycle our waste materials, change from cars and planes to bicycles and trains, and live more modestly, consuming less blatantly. At the end of the first decade of the twenty-first century, the environment has become possibly the key social concern. What will we do when the oil runs out? Will global warming lead to large areas of the world becoming deserts, while others are flooded as the polar ice caps melt? How disastrous will be the release of methane gases currently trapped by the polar permafrosts? How can we best conserve the oceans' dwindling fish stocks? Can we outlaw plastic bags from shopping and save the sea turtles who mistake them for jellyfish from extinction? How do we cope with the massive volumes of waste produced by our consumption habits? Are wind-farms, bio-fuels or nuclear power stations the best way to generate energy in the future? These and a whole host of other truly worrying questions are preoccupying politicians, consumers and business traders alike.

Such environmental issues have had a considerable impact on the way businesses present themselves and market their goods and services to us. Supermarkets vie with each other as to which is the greenest, offering organic food, locally grown fruit and vegetables and environmentally safe cleaning materials. Sainsbury's swapped its old white plastic bags for orange ones which it claims are recyclable. Energy providers give us tips on how to make more efficient use of the power they are selling us.

Box 3.4 Firms promote sustainability: an example from energy provider EDF

Save today, save tomorrow

We're constantly being told about how climate change is one of the biggest risks facing our planet today. There's no doubt we all have to start cutting down the amount of energy we use to reduce our carbon emissions. However, it's not easy being green which is why we'd like to help you.

We've created the EDF Energy 2012 Carbon Challenge

You can join in by making a pledge to try to reduce the annual carbon footprint of your household by 15% by 2012. We'll help you with useful, free ideas and advice to achieve your target. You'll also get to hear about incentives and grants that might be available to you, such as money off insulating your walls and loft which could save you up to £200 on your energy bills.

(EDFenergy.com)

EDF sets out the Challenge in its impressive website with graphics and animations. In the 'magic book' you can read a number of tips about everything from low-energy bulbs, to efficient use of kettles, to insulation. It offers energy-saving products like a thermal kettle, eco-balls for your washing machine and a solar MP3 charger. You can sign up to Climate Change or Green tariffs by which you pay more but some of your money is donated to sustainability projects at home and overseas, including reforestation schemes. EDF also sets out a programme of social commitments, with an endorsement from Will Hutton of the Work Foundation, who is chair of their stakeholder board.

The record looks impressive, but is this a case of passing on costs to customers as a way to comply with government targets? You decide. . .

We may treat some of these claims with a degree of scepticism; nonetheless, there is a growing degree of panic and urgency which is bound have long-term impacts on your future lives as workers and consumers. We may be pressured to reduce our carbon footprints by working closer to home and by taking fewer holidays involving long-haul flights. The glamorous world of international jet-setting celebrities, businessmen – and even academics and exchange students – may have to change if air travel is restricted or rationed. Providers of cheap flights such as EasyJet and Ryanair have changed the way we make our travel plans, as well as bringing wealth and public prominence to their CEOs. The ease and comparative cheapness of travel has encouraged the younger generation to consider studying or working abroad, when they can easily return home. Will there be an end to cheap flights? Might that put some of the dynamics of globalization, as discussed earlier in the chapter, into reverse? There are hard choices that face us all and will confront all organizations and businesses as the century progresses.

Box 3.5 The Greening of Ambridge?

The long-running Radio 4 soap, *The Archers*, has featured a number of environmental issues in its storylines. Young Pip Archer campaigned against local farmers who were destroying the habitats of skylarks, persuading them to leave unploughed islands in their fields. Other young characters have opposed the spread of GM (genetically modified) crop varieties. Controversy surrounds the plans of a consortium led by David and Brian Archer to invest in an anaerobic extractor which converts crops into fuel and fertilizer. The plan is hotly opposed by Pat Archer, long-term advocate of organic farming methods and seller of organic yoghurts, on the grounds that we should be saving energy rather than taking land from food crops to produce biofuels. Nigel Pargetter has given up his car for a bicycle, though Kenton Archer continues to drive a 'gas-guzzler'. Meanwhile Pat is campaigning for Ambridge to become a 'transition village', leading the way as a model for an environmentally friendly future.

The series, with its claim to be about the 'everyday life' of 'everyday country folk', reflects the kind of dilemmas and choices that we, like its characters, will increasingly face, as producers and consumers. Farming communities like the fictional Ambridge are at the sharp end of environmental pressures as they have to supply us with wholesome food while still making a profit to ensure the livelihood of themselves and their families. However, increasingly these dilemmas will face the rest of us too. Do we shop at farmers' markets and organic shops which embrace sustainability but are more expensive? If we buy only locally produced fruit and vegetables, how will that impact on cash crop farmers and their workforces who grow strawberries, pineapples and carrots for us in the developing world? How will we travel into work? Will women with families stop buying the fast foods and convenience products which enable them to participate in the long-hours working culture? If we all become ethical consumers and change our habits, how will that impact on individual businesses and on the wealth of the society as a whole? George W. Bush and the American government have been particularly resistant to signing national agreements on reducing carbon emissions, which they see as a threat to the American way of life (large cars, air-conditioned buildings and high levels of consumerism). Will people – and that means you! – be prepared to 'downsize' their lifestyles?

Buying locally grown produce can help the environment. However, it could have a devastating effect on developing countries whose economies are based on exporting produce to developed nations.

Green businesses and corporate social responsibility

This has important consequences for how businesses are organized beyond the choices of individual consumers. Some idealistic businesses display green credentials and even big capitalist organizations are starting to change their practices, as mentioned above. This ties in with the influential and important notion of **corporate social responsibility (CSR)**. Since large firms and organizations hold a lot of power in our society, it is argued that they should also act responsibly in their business practices and be aware of their need to give something back to the community. Thus, many businesses sponsor sports teams or events (though they get something back in free advertisements when events are televised) or support specific charities. You may have buildings on your campus named after organizations that have given sums towards their construction. Contributions to the environment are a new way in which companies can demonstrate their commitment to CSR.

As a result, many companies are thinking of ways to change their own practices to be more sustainable, while others are actually making money by selling 'green' products to people, from recycling bins to rechargeable batteries, from electric cars to holidays categorized as ecotourism. There are websites to help businesses become more sustainable and reduce their carbon footprints (BusinessGreen.com) and networks for green businesses such as the Green Tourism Business Scheme which gives out awards for initiatives devised by its over 1,400 members. Politicians and leading businessmen have combined to form BASE (Business and a Sustainable Environment) which holds a yearly forum and conference:

> Business leaders need to realise that we do not inherit the earth, but merely borrow it from our children. (Sir David Arculus, BASE board member)

External political pressures towards sustainability are also increasing. For example in his 2008 budget, the UK Chancellor, Alastair Darling, ruled that supermarkets must either abolish plastic carrier bags or charge customers for them.

BASE claims that sustainability is an imperative and that change can bring opportunities and profits to companies who embrace it. But is this activity merely rhetoric for public relations purposes, sometimes nicknamed 'greenwashing', or does it indicate a sincere espousal of green principles? Ramus and Montiel (2005) studied companies with written environmental policies, finding that these were widespread and were a response to ethical and legal pressures from outside the organization; but they concluded that companies only actually implemented them when they gained some economic advantage from doing so. Similarly, Sachs (1993) has highlighted the danger of the green movement being hijacked by 'eco-crats', who do not really feel concerned about the long-term threat to the planet but wish to protect it as a source of commerce and profits. Some of our most crucial problems surround the production of energy. Will the oil barons and the oil-rich nations (from the Gulf States to Norway) be prepared to put limits on extraction? Should companies have the freedom to dispose of such scarce resources just for the sake of shareholder profits? And what *will* we do when and if the oil runs out?

Can technology save the world?

When things get tough, we often turn to technology to help us solve our problems. Many suggested solutions to environmental pressures are technical, involving new sources of low-level energy, such as solar panels, and new products that require less energy, such as the electric car. However, sociologists have pointed out consistently that technology is not a power in itself; it is what use we make of it that matters:

> In the dominant paradigm, technology is seen as being above society both in its structure and evolution, in its offering technological fixes. Its course is seen as self-determining . . . It is assumed that society and people must adjust to change, instead of technological change adjusting to the social values of equity, sustainability and participation. (Shiva 1995, quoted in Irwin 2001: 136)

It is in our power to control the use of technology, rather than allowing technology to control us, particularly as our working lives are being so radically altered by it. The introduction of new forms of information and communication technology (ICT) has repeatedly brought new jobs and altered the way we do older ones. Within the knowledge-based economy, the new occupations constitute an elite of knowledge workers: computer programmers, software engineers, graphic designers, web designers, data analysts and so forth. But all our jobs are being affected by the dominance of the internet and the computer: how we buy and sell things (Amazon, e-Bay, online supermarket orders), what goods we want and need (MP3 players, Blackberrys, digital cameras, an array of electrical chargers). Despite the wider variety of occupations now on offer, ironically, in many ways our modes of working are increasingly similar, as Ursula Huws points out:

> Across the workforce an extraordinary and unprecedented convergence has been taking place. From tele-sales staff to typesetters, from indexers to insurance underwriters, from librarians to ledger clerks, from planning inspectors to pattern-cutters, a large and increasing proportion of daily work time is spent identically: sitting with one hand poised over the keyboard and the other dancing back and forth from keys to mouse. (Huws 2003: 65)

Huws suggests that this is linked to processes of deskilling, which will be discussed in chapter 4, and posits that a new 'cybertariat' (an IT-based proletariat) may be emerging among the lower-level service workers who sit at these PCs in call centres and offices.

The internet and PCs raise other interesting questions. They make it much more possible for service work to be done from home, and businesses to be set up without highly expensive initial investment. Thus we have seen the steady growth of **teleworking** and of self-employment. Teleworking simply refers to people working outside the core site of an organization, frequently from home (we discuss this in more detail in chapter 4). Because computer technology is cheap and portable, work-stations can be set up virtually anywhere. Increasing numbers of people are spending some of their time working from home (see chapter 4, 'Homework and telework' section for recent figures). This reduces travel costs for employees, and will help cut carbon emissions, while for the organizations it may decrease overheads and help build employee loyalty.

Teleworking is but one example of how working practices are changing as a result of ICT. Mobile phones allow us to keep in touch with employers and offices as we travel around; more and more buying, selling and organizing are done online or through call centres. Moynagh and Worsley discuss the increasing levels of what they call 'mobile working'. Between 1981 and 2002 the proportion of people working mainly in different places, using home as a base, had risen from 3 to 8 per cent:

> It is possible to work in a hotel, an airport lounge or motorway service station, in a train, plane or car, in a cottage in Wales, at a wedding reception in Australia or on a beach in the Caribbean. You can work morning, noon and night, during the week or at weekends. You can be visiting suppliers, wooing customers or interviewing a job applicant in a hotel lounge. This mobile fluid work will continue to spread. (Moynagh and Worsley 2005: 105)

Many production processes have become more automated; robots supplement the use of human beings on assembly lines. Email has changed the way we communicate at work and there has been much talk of the 'paperless office'. Face-to-face relations are diminishing as we interface more with machines and screens. Wi-fi conferencing systems raise new options. New gadgets utilizing ICT are coming into use daily, with the intention of making our lives more efficient – although, as anyone who has used a lengthy computerized answer system or waited in a queue to talk to a customer service operative will know, computer technology can also be frustrating.

Case study 3.1 Hackers: knowledge, power and resistance

'Savoir est pouvoir', which translates as 'knowledge is power': French philosopher and historian Michel Foucault developed this idea, arguing that expert systems of knowledge, such as those of medicine or law, are the basis of particular 'regimes of power' which operate in our daily lives. This idea of knowledge as power is also at the heart of the notions of post-industrialism and the knowledge-based economy, which we have discussed. The new well-paid elite of knowledge workers includes those with technical expertise around computing. It is no coincidence that Bill Gates of Microsoft is one of the world's richest men.

Foucault also stated that wherever there is power there is **resistance**, and that leads us to consider the contemporary phenomemon of hacking, which forms the base of an interesting and very readable study by Paul Taylor, simply entitled *Hackers* (1999). Hackers are people who use their understanding of computers to create new techniques and procedures, including breaking into ('hacking') other people's computer systems, such as those of large corporations or government and military departments. They also may use their skills to access telephone systems and make free calls, or to purchase goods illegally using credit card numbers. Some hackers are also responsible for viruses and worms, although these are generally frowned upon by many in the hacking community, or 'computer underground' as they call themselves. Although a lot of hacking activities are technically illegal and their skills may be used to make money, Taylor emphasizes that the core motivation of hackers is not making money but curiosity and the desire for knowledge. Many of those he interviewed saw themselves as revolutionaries in a struggle against corporate power.

Taylor's point is affirmed by American ex-hacker Neal Patrick who states:

> Hackers are intelligent people. They've worked with computers for years, examined them inside and out. Some have created new additions to their home computers; some have even designed their own machines. Put simply, the workings of a computer hold as much interest for hackers as the workings of a '57 Chevy do for the car fanatic.
>
> This interest is due to curiosity. There is nothing sinister or destructive about it. Hackers are eager to learn as much as possible

in computer classes at school or in user groups and computer clubs, where other hobbyists share their insatiable curiosity. Always driven to working with larger and more powerful machines, all hackers aspire to mastering a mainframe.

('Hacker ethics' by Neal Patrick (n.d.) www.atariarchives.org/deli/hacker_ethics.php)

Taylor's study also emphasizes the close links between computer professionals, hackers and computer security systems. Many hackers work for computer companies (although others are schoolchildren or students). As Taylor points out, they are members of a generation who have grown up from infancy in a computerized environment. While older people often feel anxious or incompetent when faced with computer technology, young people take it for granted and feel at home with it – witness the incredible popularity of internet networking sites.

There is therefore a continual flow of knowledge between professionals and hackers. Skills and ideas which they develop as a way of challenging the power structures of capitalist organizations and bureaucracies may subsequently be made use of to enhance the security and profits of the same organizations.

To answer the question posed at the start of this section, it is not at all clear whether technology can help us to preserve the environment or save the world; but it certainly can transform our working lives and will continue to do.

Summary and conclusions

We have covered a lot of ground in this chapter. We explored the way globalization is changing our lives: while it enriches lives of many individuals by enhancing flexibility and mobility, its critics show how increased international competition heightens social divisions between rich and poor, at national and international levels. Paradoxically, it binds winners and losers closer together through global chains, and may challenge the existing hierarchy of nations with the rise of new super-economies such as India and China. Globalization has been accompanied by the spread of neoliberal policies which privilege the market above all else, as can be seen in the way our UK universities are changing. Universities and students are also bound up with the posited development of a 'knowledge-based economy' with its elite of skilled workers. However, this idea may conceal continuing realities of power which lie in the control of wealth.

Globalization has been accompanied by social changes in gender and ethnic relations, involving continued feminization of work and changing patterns of migration. This has affected the composition of the UK workforce, producing a more multicultural and diverse society.

While these changes can be seen as bringing greater equality and cultural richness, other changes linked to globalization are much less beneficial. Increased levels of travel, consumerism and use of energy are posing serious threats to the future of our planet. While there are rapidly increasing levels of environmental awareness, are individuals and companies doing enough to secure the earth's future?

There are questions, too, about ICT and its widespread effects on the way we work. While it brings many benefits to individuals and organizations, it can also increase waste and inefficiency. We are still exploring the ways work is likely to change in future; for example the spread in teleworking may help people, especially those with children, to achieve a better '**work–life balance**'. But it also offers us all the chance of self-exploitation by buying into the long-hours culture that is replacing the old factory and office rhythms of the 'nine to five'. Societies have choices to use these technologies in diverse ways. We should all be concerned to see that those choices are made responsibly.

Discussion questions

1. Choose any *two* of the following terms and construct an argument to explain why you think this is a good way to characterize contemporary societies
   a. Capitalism
   b. Post-industrialism
   c. Modernity
   d. Consumer society
   e. Globalization
   f. Neoliberalism
   g. Knowledge-based economy
2. 'The knowledge economy is the future of the world of work.' Do you agree? What will this mean for the future of you, your friends and your families?
3. Discuss in a group if and how your own habits have changed recently as a result of environmental concerns. What examples of organizations displaying eco-friendly values have you recently observed?
4. Will ICT create a new 'cybertariat'? Explain why or why not.

Further reading

Two easy-to-read books which give a good overview of changes in working practices are:

Ulrich Beck, *The Brave New World of Work*. Cambridge: Polity, 2000.
Michael Moynagh and Richard Worsley, *Working in the Twenty-First Century*. Leeds: Leeds University / ESRC, 2005.

Useful introductory texts to these topic areas are:

Manfred B. Steger, *Globalization: A Very Short Introduction.* Oxford: Oxford University Press, 2003.

Malcolm Waters, *Globalization*, 2nd edition. London: Routledge, 2000.

David Harvey, *A Brief History of Neoliberalism.* Oxford: Oxford University Press, 2005.

Khalid Koser, *International Migration: A Very Short Introduction.* Oxford: Oxford University Press, 2007.

Ursula Huws, *The Making of a Cybertariat: Virtual Work in a Real World.* London: Merlin, 2003.

Susan Buckingham and Mike Turner, *Understanding Environmental Issues.* London: Sage, 2008.

4 The nature of work

This chapter will:

- introduce the concept of labour markets and investigate how labour markets are regulated
- examine the relationship between labour markets and society
- look at the structure of the UK labour market
- examine unemployment from a historic and contemporary perspective
- examine how work has changed in recent years and investigate new, significant forms of work and employment including team work, flexible specialization, telework, home work and call centre work.

Work is central to advanced industrial societies, in a way most of us take for granted. We organize our societies around work and employment, organize values and norms around social understandings of work and employment, and see work as something that is intrinsic to the individual and the human condition. Although we sometimes hear people talking about a leisure society (a society where people have much free time and are primarily oriented towards enjoying their leisure time), an **information society** (a society which focuses on the production and circulation of knowledge and information) or a consumer society (where identities derived from our **consumption** patterns are more significant than our work identity), we would argue that the UK is fundamentally a work society. In such a work society, the division of labour and how it is carried out is a central feature.

In this chapter we will look at the main mechanism that organizes the division of labour – the labour market – and see how labour markets have changed and transformed in the last two decades with the decline, in the UK economy, of manufacturing, the rise of the service sector and the changes brought about by privatization. As well as considering the local context of the UK labour market, we will also consider the change and transformation that have taken place in the global organization of labour, changes brought about by geopolitical shifts in power relations, and the emergence of the phenomenon we now call globalization, as discussed in chapter 3.

Labour markets

As we noted in discussing the work of Marx and Durkheim, all societies can be characterized by the way that labour is divided between individual members of that society. Agrarian preindustrial societies – societies where the majority of the population subsist through producing from the land – exhibit a simple division of labour, since most people are carrying out similar tasks. Consequently there is very little stratification: individuals are likely to be either peasants or landowners. Industrial societies, in contrast, have a complex division of labour. Rather than individuals carrying out broadly similar tasks, they are likely to found in different jobs and occupations. The forms of production that are taking place in such societies require specialization of one form or another; indeed, the more sophisticated production processes become, the more specialized jobs will become. For example, the steady development of bureaucratic organizations we have discussed in previous chapters has generated a whole host of new jobs: communications and public relations officers, press liaison officers, marketers, trainers, staff development officers, equality and diversity officers, counsellors, recruiters, health and safety officers, company lawyers, researchers, planners, accountants, tax advisers, risk managers, customer service staff, etc. (a bit reminiscent again of the Planet Golgafrincham!). In the early days of capitalism, business owners with a few managers and supervisors would have carried out all these functions themselves. Stratification in such societies becomes complex, and based on more than just one's ownership of property or resources. Status in modern societies is ascribed through a complex social process where value is attached to, amongst other things, skill, income, functional necessity and gender. We can see the division of labour taking place in modern industrial societies through the operation of labour markets. The labour market in any society is both a concept – an idea that organizes our thoughts about parts of the world that we can see – and a real thing that people can interact within. We define a labour market as being a place where employers and employees interact to make arrangements with each other. These arrangements are usually governed by some form of contractual obligation: employers agree to pay employees a certain amount of money and employees agree to carry out a certain amount of work.

However, 'labour market' is, like much of the language that surrounds the world of business, a quite misleading term. In contemporary society we often talk about markets as if they were free and open spaces where individuals come together freely to choose goods and services, and agree to pay for them. We imagine individuals coming together with a series of needs or desires and meeting those needs through interaction in an unforced way in a neutral space. It is unlikely that such free markets exist anywhere (just think about how you are manipulated into buying goods or services that you don't really want or need), and labour markets are particularly subject to control, regulation, distortion and power differentials. As Richard Brown notes:

> Markets are rarely if ever neutral allocative mechanisms which efficiently secure the best possible outcome for all participants.

> The buyers and sellers in any market typically possess differential resources, and the more powerful can to a greater or lesser extent dictate the terms of the exchange to those with fewer resources. This is especially true in the labour market. (Brown 1997: 81)

Indeed, this is true, because employers have greater resources than employees, are fewer in number, and have a vested interest in driving down costs to maximize profits. Also their potential employees may be desperate to get a job in order to survive, under, as Weber put it, 'the whip of the compulsion of hunger': that is, their freedom is only formal.

There are, however, ways in which this imbalance can be redressed: through employees joining together in trade unions or other forms of association to ensure that labour is hired at an agreed and 'fair' rate; or through external agencies – normally a nation's government – intervening and imposing rules and regulations, such as minimum wage legislation and **equal opportunities** legislation, upon a labour market.

We can take an abstract view of labour markets when we think about the sum total of all employee–employer relations in a given region, nation or even the globe. Here we would look at large-scale trends in terms of the forms of contracts being used (short-term, long-term, full-time, part-time), the rates of pay, and forms of remuneration being offered (low, high, piece rates, commission-based); the kinds of state intervention into the labour market (equality laws, minimum wage legislation); and, most crucially, **gender**, class, age and **ethnicity**, in considering who gets which sorts of jobs. When we do this, particularly if we take a longitudinal perspective, we can see how labour markets change and transform as societies change and transform.

However, we can also see the reality of labour markets as being embodied in interpersonal relations between employees and employers, and in the actual human actions and transactions that take place in formalizing contracts of employment and employment itself. At its most stark, we can see labour market operations in the hiring of informal and casual labour by employers who are avoiding as much regulation as possible: the anonymous white van stopping at a particular street corner to pick up willing workers for a day's cash-in-hand work on a building site or vegetable picking is still a common occurrence in the UK labour market. Migrant workers, as we saw in chapter 3, are particularly vulnerable to exploitation by such unscrupulous employers. The UK media reported cases of migrant vegetable pickers, employed on a casual and ad hoc basis, being paid less than subsistence wages and being forced to scavenge for food (Morris and Lawrence 2007). More familiar labour market operations are job adverts and recruitment centres where employers and employees are placed in contact with one another.

Labour markets often fail to provide either the right sort of labour for employers (resulting in a skills shortage) or the right amount of work for employees (resulting in **unemployment**), and are thus flawed mechanisms of allocation. However, the consequences of these flaws are very different for employers (a fall in the rate of profit) and employees (the personal and community tragedy of unemployment). The labour market, as a site where power struggles between individuals and groups take place, remains a major source of social problems, primarily through being unable to meet the needs of all those individuals who want to work.

> Nothing stands still. We are aware that the labour market is in constant flux, expanding and contracting with the economic cycle. But like other institutions it is also in a continuous process of change and renewal, adapting to new technology and other social and economic innovations, so that the composition and character of workers do not stand still. (Hakim 1998: 1)

The labour market reflects society in a number of ways. Social divisions are reflected in the labour market in terms of who gets which jobs. Most notable is the way that working-class people get working-class jobs, and middle-class people get middle-class jobs. In a classic study, *Learning to Labour*, Paul Willis (1981) explored how school channelled working-class boys into manual labour, as they failed to identify with its goals and developed an 'anti-school' culture of 'having a laff'. This rejection of school and its values condemned them to a lack of qualifications. But other forms of division and inequality are also reflected in the labour market. Historically, women were confined to a small range of tasks in the labour market, and were less well paid and valued for the work that they did, even when it was exactly the same as male workers'. As social pressure for change in terms of women's rights increased, the labour market became a battleground. Women workers fought for recognition of their equal worth, and demanded, through collective action, legislation that would protect their employment rights.

In many employment sectors, people from middle-class backgrounds hold positions of responsibility, whilst less-skilled and lower-paid jobs go to those from working-class households.

The Equal Pay Act (EPA) was passed by the UK government in 1970, and was enforced from 1975. The EPA was designed to eliminate the **discrimination** in pay between women and men in the same employment: prior to the Act it was perfectly legal for employers to offer jobs with a male and a female rate of pay. At the time that the Act was passed, the pay gap between men and women was 37 per cent, and by 1975 this had closed to 30 per cent (Women and Equality Unit, www.womenandequalityunit.gov.uk/legislation/equal_pay_act.htm). The EPA did not address the way that employers chose their employees, and until the passing in 1975 of the Sex Discrimination Act it was still wholly legal for an employer to choose to employ a man rather than a woman, purely on the grounds of preference. Despite over thirty years of equality legislation, women still receive lower pay than men: in 2006 the full-time gender pay gap stood at 12.6 per cent using the median, and 17.2 per cent using the mean, which means that women who work full-time are paid on average just 87.4 per cent of men's hourly earnings using the median, and 82.8 per cent using the mean (Women and Equality Unit, www.womenandequalityunit.gov.uk/legislation/equal_pay_act.htm).

This legislative intervention into the UK labour market is a reflection of a number of things. First, we can see that the labour market is being made to reflect the values of society, in this case a desire for fairness and equality of opportunity. Secondly, the continuing discrimination that women face in the labour market reflects wider discrimination in a society that is sexist and patriarchal. But, overall, we must bear in mind that the labour market is still a 'buyers'' market, where employers' interests are reflected to a much greater extent than employees'. The introduction of equal opportunities legislation is a small measure of control on a system that still operates to maximize profit for employers through controlling and, if possible, holding down wages. We can view the current labour market parameters as the outcome of a range of social forces, such as interest groups seeking to achieve their aims (employers' organizations, trade unions and political parties), and a reflection of societal attitudes, such as a general concern for fairness and equality. This is reflected, in part, in the way that labour markets are regulated – and the way they change as the balance of power shifts.

Mapping the UK labour market

What does the labour market in the UK look like today, and what conclusions can we draw from this? The UK government collects a huge amount of data about the economy, and much of this data concerns the labour market. Most of the following data are taken from either the Labour Force Survey, a rolling survey of about 59,000 households that has been carried out in the UK since 1973; the Annual Survey of Hours and Earnings (which replaced the New

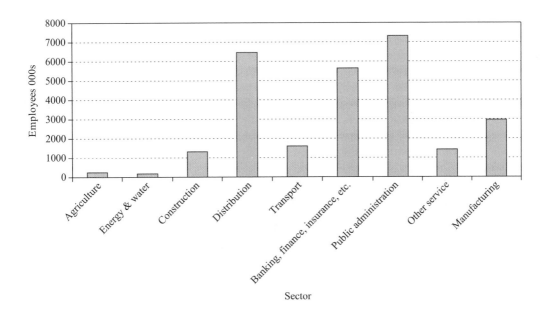

Sector

Earnings Survey from 2004), which uses a combination of question-naire survey data and data from the Inland Revenue PAYE returns to construct a picture of employment and pay in the UK; or a few compendium sources of UK government statistics (such as *Social Trends* and *Regional Trends*). Readers are advised to go to the UK government statistical service's website at www.statistics.gov.uk for access to many of these sources (see 'Further reading' section at the end of this chapter).

However, we need to be wary of government statistics. Although they are usually extremely robust – it is unfeasible for academic researchers to carry out a continuous survey of 59,000 households that are largely representative of the whole of the UK population – and readily avail-able, we have to bear in mind that these figures are not collected for the benefit of academic social scientists. This is particularly pertinent when we think about how definitions are constructed: the ONS collects data for the government to make decisions about society and the economy, and will use the categories and definitions that it thinks are best. We will return to this point when we discuss definitions of unemployment. For the time being, bear in mind that the statistics we are using here are a description of our society and economy and also a reflection of the con-cerns of those in power.

The UK labour market is segmental, providing labour for a number of different industrial sectors. A 'snapshot' picture of these sectors shows us the relative sizes, by employment, of different parts of the economy (figure 4.1).

When we look at wages associated with each sector, the picture in figure 4.2 emerges.

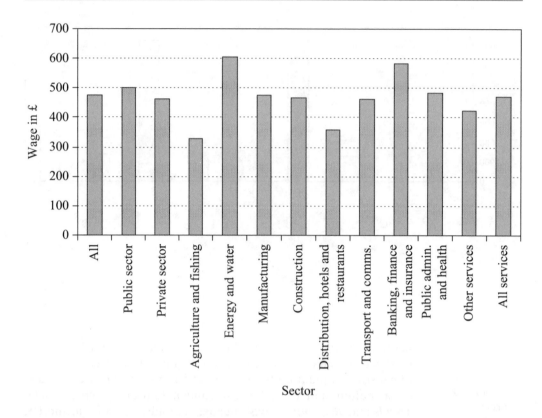

Fig. 4.2 Average weekly earnings by industrial sector, Winter 2005–6 Source: LFS Historical Quarterly Supplement, Table 37

There is a large variation in wages across the sectors. Jobs requiring more skills and qualifications provide better returns than the service and manufacturing sectors, and public sector jobs continue to provide higher wages than the private sector.

In chapter 2, we saw how jobs in manufacturing had declined and service-sector employment expanded. Across a similar period, as we saw in chapter 3, there was a dramatic increase in the number of women in employment (see figure 3.1). This rise in female economic activity is reflected in the gender distribution of employment (see figure 3.2).

Pay distribution

Pay distribution is uneven through the labour market, and pay differentials between the best and worst paid are increasing. In 2006 the median weekly pay was £364.10, whilst the mean was £440.19. This discrepancy, between the 'average' (mean) wage and the median (midpoint) wage is created by a small number of very wealthy people distorting the average by pulling it upwards. The gap between median and mean pay is thus one indicator of income inequality, and it has been steadily increasing (see figure 4.3).

Most people in the UK labour market receive modest or low pay as table 4.1 shows.

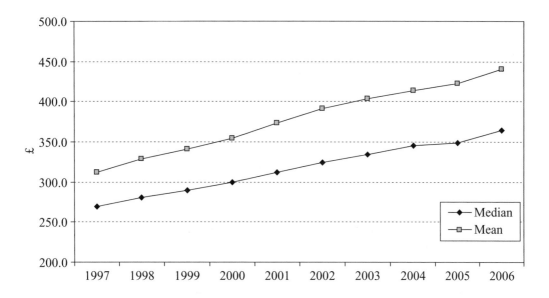

Fig. 4.3 Gross weekly pay – median and mean comparisons (£s) Source: Annual Survey of Hours and Earnings (ASHE) and New Earnings Survey (NES) 1997 to 2006

Table 4.1 Distribution of gross weekly earnings (employees on adult rates, whose pay was unaffected by absence)

	Full-time (£)	Part-time (£)	All (£)
10 per cent earned less than	244.1	45.4	110.0
25 per cent earned less than	316.3	83.3	222.4
50 per cent earned less than	447.1	136.6	364.1
25 per cent earned more than	632.9	207.4	563.3
10 per cent earned more than	886.1	324.5	799.6

Source: ASHE 2006

The table shows that 25 per cent of the population earned less than £222 a week before deductions such as tax and national insurance. It is very difficult to pay for a mortgage at current rates at this level of pay. Since the early 1990s, it has been extremely difficult for first-time buyers to enter the housing market. In 2008, as we write this book, the rising cost of petrol and the price of basic foods like bread and meat is pushing many people towards poverty. Despite the high pay of the top 10 per cent, Britain is becoming a low-wage economy.

The labour market, discrimination and division

There is widespread consensus across academia, government and campaigning organizations that paid employment – access to the labour market – is central to social inclusion. A labour market that excludes or discriminates against some people or sections of society is one that contributes to social divisions and social exclusion – as well as, of course, reflecting pre-existing prejudices in society. The UK labour market is a reflection of, and a cause of, social structures of inequality and social divisions. This is particularly visible in terms of key social divisions: women, members of ethnic minorities, people with disabilities, and older people are much more likely to be disadvantaged in the labour market in terms of participation and remuneration. We'll look at each of these significant social divisions in the labour market in turn, and consider how the labour market reflects and reinforces social divisions, and contributes to social exclusion.

Gender

Figure 4.4 shows that the pay gap between men and women has gradually diminished over time. Nonetheless, 'women are still substantially lower paid than men in Britain. On average the pay difference between men and women is around 23 per cent' (Dickens and Manning 2003: 211). The ONS figures for 2001/2 are even starker: the average male income was £415 and average female income was £235 (though we should note that this includes all people, both economically active and inactive) (ONS 2006).

Ethnicity

People from the UK's visible minority groups are less likely to be in employment than the white majority, as table 4.2 shows.

Fig. 4.4 Hourly earnings sex differential 1970 to 2003
Source: NES 2003

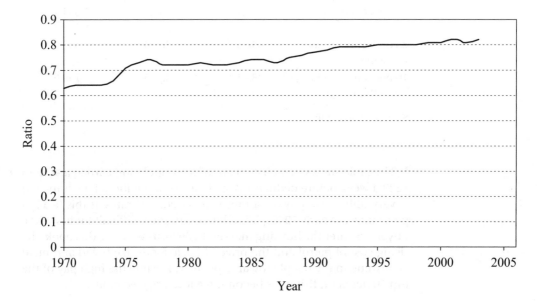

Year

Table 4.2   Working-age employment rates by ethnicity, United Kingdom, 2002–3 (percentages)

All	White	Non-White
74.0	75.5	57.3

Source: annual Labour Force Survey (Brook 2004: 409)

Table 4.3 Working-age employment rates for individual non-white ethnic groups, United Kingdom, 2002–3 (percentages)

Mixed heritage	Indian	Pakistani/ Bangladeshi	Black	Other
59.8	68.4	42.9	60.2	55.2

Source: annual local area Labour Force Survey (Brook 2004: 410)

However, there is considerable variation between ethnic groups. People of Indian and Chinese origin have employment rates closer to the white group rate. As table 4.3 shows, Muslim groups are the least likely to be employed. This is true for both men and women.

Both these tables show a much higher rate of exclusion from the labour market for people from ethnic minority backgrounds, which reflects the difficulty they have in finding suitable jobs and their greater vulnerability to unemployment.

Disability

Finding work is hard if you are a Bangladeshi or a Pakistani, but it is even harder if you are disabled, as table 4.4 shows. People with disabilities clearly face exclusion from participation in the labour market – over three times the number of economically inactive disabled want a job but can't get one, compared to non-disabled people.

> Despite the emergence of disability politics, social scientists generally demonstrated little interest in critically examining the living conditions of disabled people, and concentrated instead on chronic illness and disability as a health issue. This silence is not new. There has been a notable absence of discussion of disability across classical sociological theories, but the general thrust is inescapable: the absence of people with impairments from the industrial labour market dictates their wider social exclusion. (Barnes and Mercer 2005: 532)

Sociologists of **disability**, and disability rights campaigners, have shown that the societal view of disability as a personal and medical tragedy for individuals is a misrepresentation of the cause and experience of disability for most disabled people. Instead of this personal

Table 4.4 Economic activity status of working-age people by whether disabled, 2003 (percentages)

	Disabled	Not disabled
Economically active		
In employment	49	81
Unemployed	4	4
All economically active	53	85
Economically inactive		
Wants a job	15	4
Does not want a job	32	12
All economically inactive	47	15

Source: LFS – reproduced in *Social Trends*, 34

Table 4.5 Employment rates by age, United Kingdom, seasonally adjusted: December 2006 to February 2007 (percentages)

	16 and over	16–59/64	16–17	18–24	25–34	35–49	50–59/64	60/65 and over
All persons	59.9	74.3	34.4	64.9	79.8	82.1	70.8	10.9
Men	66.7	78.6	31.7	68	87.8	88.8	72.3	9.9
Women	53.5	69.6	37.3	61.8	72	75.6	68.8	11.6

Source: LFS

and medical model they propose the adoption of a social model, where disability is seen as a consequence of a society that systematically excludes and disables individuals who are different. Much of the social model focuses on the systematic exclusion of disabled people from labour markets, and the disability rights movement has campaigned for decades for legislation outlawing discrimination to be introduced. This has been successful in some parts of society, but the labour market still shows signs of continued discrimination. We discuss this further in chapter 8.

Age

The labour market is also shaped by **ageism**: some employers show a preference for younger workers, believing that older employees may lack current skills and are less adaptable (as discussed in chapter 2). Table 4.5 shows the decline of employment among older age groups. Note that the table incorporates the differential retirement rates for women and men at sixty and sixty-five, respectively (although this has subsequently been equalized). Therefore the last column represents people over retirement age. You will see, however, that there is also a decline in employment among people over fifty. This can be partly explained as a result of older people experiencing health problems that prevent them from continuing in employment, or voluntarily opting for early retirement if they can afford it. But it also results from age discrimination. People who are made redundant over the age of fifty find it particularly difficult to find new jobs.

Labour market policy

The degree to which the labour market reflects social divisions or causes social divisions is difficult to ascertain, but the connection between the persistence of social divisions and the structure of the labour market is quite clear. The question of how to change this, or whether this should be changed, presents both a political and a moral problem that centres on the role of labour market regulation. Since 1979 there has been a general trend towards deregulating labour markets, and removing from them any 'barriers' that may prevent the free hiring and firing of labour. This trend has been checked to some degree by both UK and EU legislation, notably the introduction of the national minimum wage (NMW) and some anti-discrimination legislation, which has often used the EU Charter for Human Rights as its basis.

However, these forms of regulation must be placed alongside the continuous lobbying by employers' groups and political parties of the right for a decrease in labour market regulation, often with, initially, the two-fold rationale of aiming to reduce unemployment and improve efficiency and productivity. The argument that labour market regulation was a cause of unemployment emerged in the late 1970s and was often the reason provided by the Conservative government of the 1980s and 1990s for reducing regulation, although as the figures below will show this had little or no effect on unemployment. Indeed, the idea that labour market regulation needs to be removed to reduce unemployment has largely disappeared from the political landscape of the UK, being replaced by the argument that flexibility of capital, i.e. freedom for capital, will promote an economic structure that encourages growth and wealth creation. Gordon Brown, then UK Chancellor of the Exchequer, in a speech in 2006 presented just such an argument:

> So we know that we, Britain, will have to become a more flexible economy – more ready to change, with more local and regional pay flexibility, better equipped for the long term, with more focus on the jobs and skills of the future. In some economies energies are devoted to sheltering the last job, when the job is redundant. In the successful economies of the future like Britain, energies will be focused on helping people move into the next job. (Gordon Brown, Mansion House speech, 22 June 2006)

The current UK government economic policy with respect to employ-ment can be summed up as the support of free trade, open markets, flexible labour forces and 'investing heavily in education and skills so that people became the masters and beneficiaries of change' (Gordon Brown at the World Economic Forum, Davos, February 2007).

Unemployment

We can find other instances where the labour market is controlled or constrained by external forces. In the 1970s, as we saw earlier in the chapter, the labour market in the UK became characterized as being inflexible, a cause of inflation and a contributor to the UK's alleged lack of competitiveness. The incoming Conservative government of 1979 set to change that through a process of **deregulation**. Freeing up the labour market would ensure that employers would not be 'burdened' by regulation that made them less willing to offer new jobs (Department of Employment 1985: 13–14), thus alleviating the rising unemployment of the time. Although the labour market was deregulated to a large extent, and the trade unions, which had managed to control the supply of labour, had their power curtailed to a huge extent (see chapter 7), unemployment did not fall. The 1980s and 1990s were characterized by a labour market that provided for the needs of employers through ensur-ing a supply of cheap and skilled labour, but failed to provide for many employees as unemployment stubbornly stayed at the 2 million mark.

Box 4.1 Defining unemployment

Unemployment, the condition of individuals wanting paid employment but being unable to find it, is endemic in industrial societies. However, defining unemployment is difficult, provokes controversy, and is politically charged. Behind these arguments lies the fact of continuing mass unemployment in the UK and many other western industrial societies. The 2008 UK unemployment rate of 5.3 per cent, or 1.64 million people, reflects a particular definition – those who are actively seeking work – but excludes people who have given up looking for work, are excluded from the labour market due to sickness or disability, are unable to take up work because they are caring for others (e.g. children, older relatives) or who have become 'hidden' by being in training or education of one form or another. In the UK there were, at the same time, 7.86 million people who were classed as economically inactive.

Writing in the 1930s during the Great Depression the economist John Maynard Keynes analysed unemployment in terms of specific causes. He found three reasons for unemployment, two of which (frictional and voluntary unemployment) are inevitable, but not as serious as the third form, what he called 'involuntary unemployment' (Keynes and Royal Economic Society [1936] 1974: 6–7, 15).

Frictional unemployment is a consequence of the operation of labour markets, where there is a lag between a job becoming vacant and an employee taking up a post, and a consequence of the operation of a capitalist economy, where competition between capitalist enterprises will inevitably lead to some companies closing with a resultant loss of jobs. This type of unemployment was inevitable given that there was competition and a certain amount of freedom in the economy and labour market. However, unemployment of this kind should be of short duration. Similarly, voluntary unemployment, caused by workers refusing to take jobs due to the wage being too low, not liking a particular type of job, or as a result of collective bargaining, was an inevitable consequence of capitalism (as, indeed, 'classical' economists had noted).

In contrast, involuntary unemployment occurs when there are simply no jobs available for individuals, either due to individuals having the wrong skills for vacant positions, or there being too few vacant positions for the number of unemployed individuals. Keynes' involuntary unemployment has been re-named a number of times and is called, variously, 'demand-deficient unemployment', 'core unemployment' and 'structural unemployment'. Here we will use the term 'core unemployment' to identify unemployment that is not caused by voluntary or frictional mechanisms, and is resistant to reduction in overall numbers regardless of fluctuations in supply and demand (Philpott 1997: 5).

In the UK, unemployment in the period 1945 to the mid 1970s was seen as being largely frictional, and government policy was oriented towards maintaining the level of unemployment at around the 3 per cent mark – the level that Keynesian economists agreed would be equivalent to full

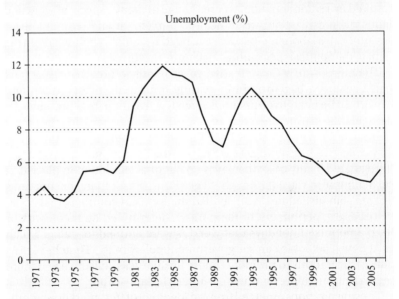

Fig. 4.5 Unemployment in the United Kingdom, 1971 to 2006
Source: LFS, various years

employment. Towards the end of the 1970s core unemployment took off, and large-scale redundancies from the closure of heavy industries, such as mining, ship building and steel making, and shrinkage in medium industries such as engineering and car making boosted the unemployment rate as redundant workers failed to find new jobs. This was particularly acute amongst unskilled workers.

Labour market regulation

Historically the UK labour market has been largely unregulated. If we consider that the capitalist system has two sides – employers and workers – then it is possible to look at the emergence of regulation in recent years as a struggle between two competing groups. But it is important to note that the immediate post-war years are best characterized as being subject to a doctrine of 'collective laissez-faire' (Davies and Freedland 1993; 2007). Under this doctrine the labour market was left largely unregulated by the state: employers and workers, through the trade unions that represented them, controlled the flow of labour into and out of many businesses and industries. Voluntary collective bargaining, where employers and trade unions would negotiate wage levels and working conditions, was encouraged by the government as a way of avoiding or defusing industrial disputes, and this setting of wages and conditions served to regulate flows of labour in the labour market. However, such a situation, while benefiting workers in terms of security of service and, arguably, good levels of pay, resulted in a static situation, where change in many aspects of work and industrial organization was difficult to implement and required negotiation. Such a labour regime was seen by some, notably politicians on the right of the political spectrum, as lacking in 'flexibility'.

The election of a Conservative government to power in 1979 took place against a backdrop of increasing industrial unrest, strikes and closures. The new government pledged to solve industrial problems by deregulating labour markets to promote flexibility, removing the power of trade unions and pushing back the collective agreements on voluntary collective bargaining. As we noted, the labour market was largely unregulated in any case: there was no national legislation in place that set a minimum wage (although Wages Councils for many occupations existed – abolished in 1993), defined the forms of contracts that could be used (e.g. permanent or temporary), determined hours of work or fixed amounts of holidays that workers were entitled to – all of which exist now (2008). We can see government policy in the Thatcher era as a set of aspirations to promote a more flexible, less collective and more individual, and more competitive industrial landscape.

These aspirations emerged from an **ideology** of free-market economics, where success is seen as dependent on removing all barriers to the operation of capitalism, whether it be government rules, trade union actions or legislation. This was the doctrine of neoliberalism, discussed in chapter 3. Its ideas were developed by conservative economists such as Milton Friedman and Patrick Minford, who had a major influence on the policies of Margaret Thatcher and her government. The degree to which this ideology mirrored the ideas of society as a whole is debatable, particularly in light of large-scale public unrest in the UK in the 1980s and into the 1990s. The result of the government adopting this free-market ideology was a raft of anti-trade-union legislation, the abolition of what little regulation of the labour market there was, and the promotion of privatization policies.

The Labour government, elected in 1997, came to power promising to introduce a range of labour market reforms and legislations to counter the most negative effects of the unregulated labour market, and to bring the UK into line with most other EU member states. However, despite the government introducing a wide range of legislation that has had an effect on labour markets, and also repealing anti-trade-union legislation, it would be wrong to see this simply as an attempt to shift power in favour of workers. Government legislation has been designed to maintain flexible options for employers and ensure that unions are relatively weak (Smith and Morton 2006). The goal of competitiveness in international markets, as discussed in chapter 3, remains primary.

The principal legislation that has been introduced addresses three areas of working life: working time, work–life balance and equality legislation. We will briefly discuss each of these in turn. The other major piece of regulation, in the form of the introduction of a national minimum wage (NMW), is discussed later in this chapter.

Working time

The EU, in the Maastricht Treaty, adopted a standard framework in 1991 that regulated the maximum amount of time employees could work. The UK negotiated a 'derogation' – an opt-out – from this legislation. However, the incoming 1997 Labour government immediately set about adopting the framework, although the initial 1998 legislation – the Working Time Regulation – still included a number of derogations and opt-outs. The legislation ordered that the maximum working week be fixed at forty-eight hours, and that there must also be a minimum period of paid annual leave. In practice, due to the derogations it was fairly simple for employers to get employees to opt-out of the regulations voluntarily. The legislation has been amended and tightened many times over the years, mainly to include more groups of workers, but individuals still have the 'right' to opt-out as long as they confirm this in writing with their employer.

Work–life balance

The term 'work–life balance' has emerged in popular and academic discourse in the past decade or so. It reflects, in the view of the authors, the changes in the structures and experiences of work that have been engendered by post-Fordist work regimes and the adoption of neo-liberal economic policies where the dominant characteristic of work is that we have to do more of it and with more of our own resources. People work harder for longer hours, have less security and thus more stress, and often have a number of jobs. Work–life balance legislation attempts to try and provide employees with some means of ensuring a quality of life outside the workplace, and respite at important times.

There are two broad forms of legislation that apply here. The first is what have come to be called '**family-friendly**' policies. Key legislative steps have been the consolidation and extension of maternity leave to twenty-six weeks, the provision for paid (two weeks) and unpaid (thirteen weeks) paternity leave, adoption leave and the right to (unpaid) time off to look after dependants. As of 2003 (Flexible Working Regulations) employees who have caring responsibilities for children have the right to request that they work part-time, or have some other flexible arrangement, and the employer is obligated to take this request seriously.

The second category of regulations and policies addresses issues of flexibility, job security and employment contracts. A key principle of this legislation is to ensure that employees on short-term, zero-hours or other forms of non-standard contract can build up an amount of service to qualify for the same rights as full-time workers. In addition, employers must now justify their use of temporary contracts and use permanent contracts where possible. Employees must be compensated at the end of a fixed-term contract by, for example, receiving statutory redundancy pay (SRP).

Anti-discrimination legislation

A wide range of anti-discrimination legislation has been introduced in recent years. The 2006 Employment Equality (Age) Regulations make it unlawful to discriminate against employees or potential employees on the grounds of age, although there are numerous exclusions to this legislation. Similarly the Employment Equality (Religion or Belief) Regulations (2003) and the Employment Equality (Sexual Orientation) Regulations (2003) make it unlawful to discriminate against employees or potential employees on the grounds of sexual orientation or religious belief. These pieces of legislation add to the already existing legislation outlawing discrimination on the grounds of sex, **race** or disability. The body of discrimination legislation which has accumulated in a piecemeal fashion over the years is now very complicated and disjointed, and the new watchdog body, the Equality and Human Rights

Commission (EHRC), is seeking to consolidate all these laws into a single anti-discrimination bill.

Skill and jobs in the new knowledge-based economy

It is not only through legislation that labour markets can be controlled or manipulated. Labour markets are places where skills will be valued and rewarded or rejected and ignored. Across time, different skills will come to be valued according to the needs of employers. Again, we need to be careful in conceptualizing the 'labour market': the language itself may make us think that there is a free market for skills taking place, with winners and losers occurring largely through the luck of the draw. This is not the case, due to the fact that acquisition of skills and knowledge is a social process that is structured by one's location in social institutions and hierarchies. Skills for use in the labour market are acquired in a variety of places: on-the-job training, college, university or apprenticeships. But most obviously, such skills are acquired through formal and compulsory school education, and here governments can, and do, have a great deal of input. This is clearly visible if we look at **knowledge work** and the emergence of a 'knowledge-based economy'. There has been, since the 1960s, a debate as to whether there is a general trend towards **upskilling** in employment, and a shift towards 'knowledge work' (Bradley et al. 2000: 114). However, this debate, and the desire of the UK government to construct an economy around knowledge (a knowledge-based economy), have intensified, something we discussed in more detail in chapter 3. UK industry has been presented with an unparalleled barrage of rhetoric exhorting it to embrace the new knowledge-based economy, to participate in the technological (ICT) revolution, and to promote skills and knowledge in the workforce. But what has resulted has been an intensification of **job polarization**: increase in the gap between the pay of the richest and the poorest, alongside a decline in 'middle-order' jobs.

Box 4.2 Skills and knowledge

All forms of work require skills and knowledge. Skills and knowledge are distinguishable, but connected. When we talk about skill we usually mean the technical competence to complete or contribute to a task in a productive process (be that physical or mental production). Skills may be simple and easily learned, or complex, requiring a lot of training. An influential perspective, **labour process** theory, has focused on the role of skill in the capitalist labour process and has described how, across time, large groups of workers have been deskilled through the introduction of machinery, scientific management and repetitive forms of production (Braverman 1974; P. Thompson 1983). Skills have been taken from them and invested in machinery or managerial control of the labour process.

The deskilling of work results in lower wages and more easily controlled workers as employers are less dependent on specialist groups and individuals.

However, it is possible to see that in some forms of work a process of upskilling takes place. New workers need to be inducted into patterns of work, and to do this they need to be trained. Some more recent forms of work, such as **telesales**, whilst often controlled in great detail by managers through the use of scripts and supervision, still require workers to innovate and use initiative, both of which are often consequences of experience gained through work.

In manufacturing production processes, the drive towards **flexible specialization** has resulted in forms of **multi-skilling** emerging, where workers will be responsible for a range of skilled (or semi-skilled) tasks, rather than being responsible for just one element of the production process.

Knowledge is part of all forms of work, in that individuals need knowledge about how and where to apply skill and effort. However, not all work is 'knowledge work', and we can define knowledge work as being work that draws on a body of theoretical (specialized and abstract) knowledge, and this is used under conditions of relative autonomy. Knowledge work is about innovating products and processes (Warhurst and Thompson 2006).

Skill and knowledge are gendered, both in terms of their acquisition and their perceived value in the labour market and the labour process. The skills and knowledge of women have been consistently undervalued, and this has, in the past, been institutionalized through occupational roles considered to be 'women's work' receiving lower rates of remuneration, and being marginalized in terms of organizational hierarchies and values (Bradley 1999).

How do we measure skill? There is no easy way of measuring skill, and picking an indicator that reflects skill will always be contentious. A straightforward approach is to choose formal qualifications as an indicator, and if this is chosen then the overall level of skill in the UK workforce has clearly risen. The number of people without a qualification has declined from 24.7 per cent in 1993 to 17.3 per cent in 2001 (McIntosh 2003: 255). However, this rise is largely due to the increase in numbers of young people staying in full-time education, getting A-levels and going to university. Skill levels as measured by vocational qualifications have risen slightly in the same period, but the take-up of such qualifications remains low. One reason for this may be that the returns on having a vocational qualification are relatively poor.

Another method is to look at skill as a reflection of output or forms of production. Thus it is possible to 'measure' skill through the uptake of ICTs by an employer, using the assumption that an ICT-heavy industry must be a 'knowledgeable' industry. Similarly, we could use spending on R&D in an industry as a way to locate skills and knowledge (Warhurst and Thompson 2006). However, none of these measures is without its flaws.

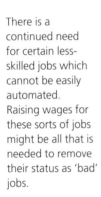

There is a continued need for certain less-skilled jobs which cannot be easily automated. Raising wages for these sorts of jobs might be all that is needed to remove their status as 'bad' jobs.

Polarization of jobs: MacJobs and McJobs

There has been a rise in the number of well-paid jobs in the UK (what Goos and Manning 2003 call 'MacJobs' – a reference to the use of Apple Macintosh computers by creative industries), but also a rise in poorly paid jobs such as those flipping burgers in a fast-food outlet (often called McJobs – although the McDonald's Corporation are now forcefully challenging the use of the term 'McJob' as a negative construction, insisting that McJobs can be rewarding, fulfilling and lead to good career opportunities; they have challenged the *Oxford English Dictionary*'s definition of 'McJob' as 'an unstimulating, low-paid job with few prospects'). Jobs in the middle are gradually disappearing. The most likely explanation for this is the introduction of new technology; the mechanization of jobs replaces middling jobs, but the lowest-paid jobs such as cleaning and portering cannot be replaced by machines, so employment in these occupations tends to rise (Goos and Manning 2003). Goos and Manning measure this job polarization by looking at wage levels: jobs with low wages are increasing at the same time as jobs with high wages. Their conclusion, that job polarization is likely to increase, presents a number of challenges for employers and for the government. Educating people is, of course, a good thing, but educating people for jobs that don't exist is likely to lead to frustration, dissatisfaction and a loss of confidence in the purpose of education. But there may not be the possibility to create more 'good' jobs while there is a continued need for people to do less-skilled work, such as cleaning, catering and assembly work, much of which cannot be automated. A solution to this could come in the form of raising wages – after all, a 'bad' job is largely seen as being a job that pays poor wages. Abolishing poor rates of pay could abolish 'bad' jobs of this type.

Job seekers in the labour market are often quite averse to taking badly paid, low-status McJobs (Lindsay and McQuaid 2004). In a recent survey of unemployed job seekers, researchers found that 36 per cent, 41 per cent and 51 per cent would 'never consider' working in retail, hospitality and call centres, respectively. A major factor in this was the level of pay: at the time of the research in 2004, the average service-sector gross wage in the relevant area was £174 per week, which was well below the level that most job seekers were looking for. Other factors included considerations of status and self-assessed lack of skills (Lindsay and McQuaid 2004).

Flexibility

> The UK's labour market is increasingly driven by choice. Employees are demanding flexibility from employers; about the hours they work, how they work and increasingly where they work.
>
> (Digby Jones, Director General of the CBI, 2003)

Discussions of flexibility in relation to work refer to two separate but linked things. The first is labour market flexibility: the ability of a labour market to respond to the demands of business and employers in providing appropriate workers at the right price. The second refers to the way that an organization operates, and this has four dimensions:

1. the ability of an employer to vary the number and composition of a workforce, according to demand (numerical flexibility);
2. the ability of employees to have a range of skills and knowledges for a production process (functional flexibility);
3. the degree to which an organization can restructure itself according to changing conditions (organizational flexibility);
4. the degree to which an organization can provide appropriate resources to support restructuring (financial flexibility).

Numerical and functional flexibility are most heavily dependent on the operation of the labour market. In turn, the labour market itself is dependent on a number of external factors for its own flexibility, two of which are particularly significant: regulation, and education and training.

The drive towards competitiveness in the global economy, and the focus on the UK economy as a 'knowledge-based economy' is reflected in these two external factors. The UK government has spent heavily on providing training and education which will, in theory, lead to a better-educated and better-trained workforce that can achieve better wages in knowledge-based industries. In addition, the identification of competitor economies' labour markets as being less regulated has prompted the UK government to promote labour market flexibility through a reduction of regulation and 'red tape'. The theory underlying this strategy is that employers will be more keen to employ workers if they have fewer commitments to fulfil, and less bureaucracy to contend with. This has been a

consistent strategy of UK governments since the rise of mass unemployment in the late 1970s; there is only one example of a UK government
increasing what some might consider to be regulation in this period: the
introduction of a national minimum wage (NMW) in April 1999.

The NMW – a national, legally binding, wage floor – was a reflection
of a widespread concern in UK society that deregulation of the labour
market had resulted in significant exploitation of vulnerable groups of
workers. The NMW was a cornerstone of the 1997 Labour government's
election manifesto but, although it had widespread popular support, it
was also seen by some as being a likely disaster for UK industry, and
a major threat to labour market flexibility. Right-wing political parties
and much of the UK print media offered vociferous opposition to its
introduction, and the CBI forecast a rise in unemployment, decline
in productivity and even possible closures of industries. Conservative
Party MP John Redwood (then (1999) shadow Secretary for Trade and
Industry and now chair of the Conservative Party's Policy Review Group
on Economic Competitiveness) predicted that the minimum wage
would destroy jobs and that the government would be forced to amend
its own legislation to introduce many exemptions: 'That is the way it
has gone in other countries . . . Then we'll be in broken promise territory' (*Guardian*, 28 November 1997). However, the CBI were involved
in extensive consultation on what the level of the NMW should be and,
when the original level of £3.60 was announced, they agreed that the
measures were 'sensible and fair' (*Guardian*, 29 March 1999).

The NMW, despite the dire predictions, has turned out to have had
almost no effect on employment levels (Dickens and Manning 2003:
201), but also has had only a modest impact on household incomes and
poverty. Further, despite the 'fact that three-quarters of the beneficiaries of the NMW are women the impact on the gender pay gap is small'
(2003: 201), with the differences between average wages of men and
women closing by 0.5 per cent.

Studies of labour market regulation have found contradictory effects.
Esping-Anderson and Regini's comparative study of European labour
market regulation (2000) concluded that, whilst regulation may offer
some explanation of who is unemployed, labour market regulation
itself was not a cause of unemployment (2000: 337), and deregulation
reforms would be unlikely to reduce levels of mass unemployment.
Overall, they found complex and contradictory effects between
flexibility and regulation. However, we should note that labour market
regulation in the UK in the form of working-time regulations and the
NMW has had positive effects in terms of quality of life for many of the
lowest-paid and most vulnerable workers in the labour market.

Emerging forms of work in a changing economy

In chapter 5 we will look in detail at the meanings that are attached
to work, and particularly how these arise out of people's experiences

of work. Before that, we need to consider some of the ways that work and work organization have changed in the last thirty years, as society and economic structures have changed. Most central is the shift from Fordist production regimes to post-Fordist production, with an emphasis on flexibility in the workplace.

Fordism and scientific management

Capitalist production has always been concerned with efficiency, but there was little systematic study and application of 'scientific' techniques to promote efficiency in the workplace until Frederick W. Taylor began to study work in the late nineteenth century. Taylor wanted to use the tools, methods and techniques of scientific investigation to produce more efficient workplaces and work practices. His work produced a change in production regimes, initially in the USA and subsequently throughout the world, and his theories became the underpinning of the scientific management movement. His work attracted controversy because it promoted the idea that human beings can be considered to be machines whose efforts, just like those of a machine, can be maximized by using technical analysis. In particular, Marxists saw scientific management as yet another means of subjugating workers in the labour process:

> Scientific management, so-called, is an attempt to apply the methods of science to the increasingly complex problems of the control of labor in rapidly growing capitalist enterprises. It lacks the characteristics of true science because its assumptions reflect nothing more than the outlook of the capitalist with regard to the conditions of production. (Braverman 1974: 86)

Taylor was the first management guru of the twentieth century, and **Taylorism** was adopted in many spheres of capitalist production. The

The creation of production lines was a 'scientific' innovation of capitalism intended to increase human efficiency in the same way one might increase a machine's output.

principle of Taylorism is to organize the labour process in such a way that production is maximized. To do this, Taylor advocated the strict splitting of mental and manual labour, and the close observation of what exactly was done in the labour process. It is because of Taylor that management became obsessed with timing activities with stop-watches. Quite simply, Taylorism meant that management could integrate and maximize production in a rational and efficient way. Basically, you could put together a production facility just like a machine, and then fine-tune this machine so it would run at peak performance.

But – note – Taylor is concerned with getting the machine to work well. He wasn't concerned with getting the humans to fit in with the machine. It was later management theorists, notably Elton Mayo, whose human relations approach tried to fit the people to the work processes (Mayo 1933). For Taylor, it was the execution of tasks that was the key, not the attitude or orientation of the worker; Taylor didn't seem to care what workers thought about their work. Essential to this is *control*. Control has always been important to management, but Taylor pushed it much further. Before Taylor, a worker was under management control when conforming to the rules laid down by management. Braverman lists these progressively: gathering together workers in a workshop, dictating the length of the working day, supervision to ensure diligent application, enforcement of rules against distraction, setting of production minimums.

For Taylor, that's just 'ordinary management'. Scientific management was different: it was an *absolute necessity* for adequate management to dictate to the worker the *precise* manner in which work is to be performed. Management has always had the 'right' to control labour. But now, Taylor advocated that management would always be a frustrated and limited undertaking so long as the worker had *any* decisions to make about his work (Braverman 1974: 90).

Taylor really was hugely influential. The USA, UK, France, Germany, all took to 'scientific management' or 'rationalization'. Even Lenin was an admirer! It fitted in with the social, political and economic climate – rapidly expanding capitalist production, rapidly increasing urbanization, rapidly escalating global competition. There was of course a significant backlash from trade unions and workers themselves. Taylor claimed he was merely trying to get people to do a 'fair day's work'. The problem here is with Taylor's version of what a fair day's work was: all the work a worker can do without injury to his health at a pace that can be sustained throughout a working lifetime.

Taylorism is at the heart of **Fordism**, the production regime that characterized much of manufacturing and services in the twentieth century. Fordism, named after Henry Ford whose River Rouge, Michigan, car plant instigated the first major assembly-line production, is a form of mass production where complex production processes are split into basic, individual tasks, and single workers are made responsible for single tasks. Consequently, work becomes repetitive and monotonous, and workers are bored and disengaged. This, indeed, exemplifies the meaning of Marx's concept of alienation, discussed in chapter 2. Whilst such production regimes are often very efficient, particularly in terms of the detailed labour process, they can lack flexibility, and are resistant to change – as well as being degrading for participants in such processes. Indeed critics of Fordism and scientific management point out that all workers, both production and knowledge, are 'degraded' in a capitalist labour process.

We can point to three aspects of the **degradation of work**.

1.   First, technology and labour under conditions of capitalist accumulation are directed *against* skill. In the past, workers' power was based upon their skills – as artisans. Artisanal workers were craftspeople whose skills made them autonomous and protected them from the diverse forces of the labour market. As capitalism developed, it launched a continuous assault on the knowledge of skilled workers by deskilling – separating them from the craft knowledge that gave them power. This is exemplified by Taylor's scientific management – this redefines the logic of capital from the formal subsumption of labour (control over the product of labour, that is the goods and services which the employer can offer in the market) to real subsumption of labour (control over all the activities of labourers as they contribute to the process of accumulation). Capitalism wanted to control the labour process as a whole. This was neatly summed up by Braverman as: the separation of conception from execution. Skilled workers who did both manual and mental aspects of work were to be split away from their specialized knowledge of the labour process and transformed into semi-skilled or unskilled workers, no longer involved in mental work. A fractured workplace results with a detailed division of labour as its organizational principle. The 'new worker' was a non-autonomous, detailed labourer.

However, this degradation of work required some new, specialized workers to be brought in: scientists and engineers were used to design the labour process, the machinery, the new products; managers were brought in to command and co-ordinate the whole process. In the name of science and productivity, the shopfloor worker was dominated by others.

2.   The **displacement** of labour. Deskilling results in the recomposition of the workforce: less-skilled workers replace more-skilled workers, low wage earners replace high wage earners. Workers lose their jobs. Displacement is a continuous process, and all levels of workers, from unskilled to engineers and managers, may be affected. The replacement of middle-aged middle managers with recent MBA graduates is an example of displacement. Machinery and new forms of workplace organization will replace skilled work, creating permanent tendencies of structural unemployment.

3.   With the destruction of skill, the labour movement is disempowered. Its only option is to resist new technologies that further degrade

the labour process. Withdrawal of labour becomes increasingly precarious as skill is eroded and power is removed from workers' hands.

Is the degradation of work inevitable? Braverman, one of the key theorists here, considered that it was, and argued that all craft-based forms of production needed to be defended, whilst all forms of technological innovation and new technologies that could challenge craft production must be opposed. Not all commentators agreed. Some Marxists considered that the degradation of work would result in the ultimate collapse of the capitalist mode of production and the emergence of better forms of production, based around co-operation and use of technology to remove the drudgery of work.

Fordism and scientific management are still mainstays of production regimes; indeed, these strategic approaches have moved from production processes to the service sector, where, notably, telesales and telemarketing operations are often based on Fordist principles of a detailed division of labour and very strict control of the labour process. However, the inflexibilities of Fordist production have resulted in the emergence of new ways of dividing labour and controlling the labour process, a raft of tools and techniques that is usually called 'post-Fordism'.

Post-Fordism, flexibility and skill

Because it has different needs, post-Fordism needs different sorts of workers from Fordist mass production. Rather than relying on producing lots of similar goods and services, post-Fordist production systems produce a range of goods and services for highly differentiated markets. Different sorts of workers are required, and a different system to produce these workers. This means a shift in power relations and social relations, particularly in terms of gender and class.

Post-Fordism is often regarded as a move away from degradation, involving greater levels of workplace democracy and a new demand for skilled workers. However, the degree to which it represents a true break with Fordism is debatable: we've already seen that new forms of work such as telesales and call centre work are subject to many Fordist principles. Nonetheless, we can identify some trends in the organization of work that have emerged in recent years (flexible specialization and **team work**), and some new forms of work that have now become significant sources of employment (**telework** and homework, and call centre work). We'll look at each of these in turn, and in the next chapter will consider in more depth how these have affected workers' experiences.

Team work and flexibility

Although team working can be identified throughout modernity (and earlier), in the context of contemporary work organizations, business and management team work is closely linked to a Japanese model of production and to a work system called Just In Time (JIT). Whereas

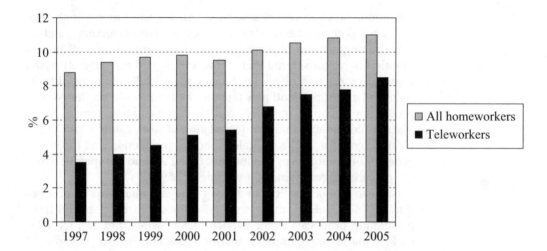

Fig. 4.6 Home-workers and teleworkers in the United Kingdom as a percentage of people in employment Source: *Social Trends*, 36: 58

a Taylorist/Fordist assembly line relies on individuals doing single tasks over and over again, and an assembly line that produces many copies of an identical product, JIT organizes itself around the production of a range of goods, with workers organized into teams which will carry out a number of different tasks and, usually, a company ethos that requires employees to develop and demonstrate commitment to the company and to their team. Where Fordist production relies on fragmenting tasks and standardization, a JIT production process introduces variation and relies on multi-tasking; the latter is sometimes referred to as multi-skilling, although this may be a misnomer where employees are just doing more tasks rather than applying a range of skills.

Teleworking and homeworking

Homeworking is a broad category of work which includes **telework** as its main subset. We can define homework as work mainly carried out in the home or with the home as a main base. Telework is a form of homework where workers use ICT to carry out their tasks. Both these forms of work have grown significantly in recent years (see figure 4.6). In Spring 2005 there were around 3.1 million people who were classified as homeworkers, of whom 2.4 million used a phone and a computer (i.e. were teleworkers). This equates to 8 per cent of the workforce, double the number in 1997. In some regions of the UK, notably the South East, 14 per cent of the workforce are homeworkers, and the vast majority of these are teleworkers.

Teleworking

> Modern information and communication technologies are changing the way UK business works. Telework, using technology to work away from the traditional office environment, has the potential to bring a wide range of benefits to both employers and . . . [b]y allowing more

flexible ways of working telework can increase employment opportunities, particularly for those with families or who have long journeys to work. In turn this can ease pressure on infrastructure, facilitate regional development and help employees improve the balance between work and home life. For business these new ways of working can offer new business opportunities, improve productivity and maintain competitiveness. (Gerry Sutcliffe, Parliamentary Under Secretary of State for Employment Relations, Competition and Consumers, quoted in DTI 2003)

Defining teleworkers is difficult – lots of different people may work at home using a phone and a computer (for example, the authors of this book and a telephone canvasser selling double glazing and earning the minimum wage plus bonus or commission could both be considered to be teleworkers, but have considerably different social relations of production). The International Labour Organization uses this definition of telework:

> A form of work in which (a) work is performed in a location remote from central office or production facilities, thus separating the worker from personal contact with co-workers there; and (b) new technology enables this separation by facilitating communication. (ILO, 1990)

Teleworkers may work exclusively from home, divide their time between an office and their home, or may be mobile workers who use their home as a base. They may voluntarily choose to telework, perhaps to alter their work–life balance or to alleviate childcare issues, or their job may require that they work in this way.

Despite the advantages noted above, teleworking presents some problems for both managers and workers. Given the distance between workers and managers, there are often issues of control and supervision. Similarly, workers can be prone to self-exploitation through working long hours, not taking breaks, and may experience stress associated with isolation and lack of support. There have been a variety of attempts to address these issues, most notably the tripartite guidelines to regulate telework drawn up by the employers, trade unions and government in 2003 (based on a set of EU guidelines). These voluntary guidelines specify that all telework agreements should be voluntary, should be reversible (i.e. employees can opt back out) and should not be to the detriment of the employee.

Although telework has been hailed as the future of work, indeed an almost universal panacea for both employers and employees, not all organizations have found it beneficial: Hewlett Packard recently announced that it was bringing back in-house most of its US teleworkers – homeworking was bad for team work (see box 4.3: 'HP and telework'). Managers state that it can promote tensions within the workforce, as office-bound workers regard those working outside with jealousy and suspicion. However, telework does mean that employers can recruit from a wider pool of applicants, reduce the cost of office

Teleworking increases opportunities for self-exploitation (working longer hours, not taking breaks, etc.). It may sometimes be used as an attempt to perpetuate unfair division of labour between the sexes, for example by supposing that a woman can undertake a paid job and childcare at the same time.

accommodation, reduce commuting times and achieve a better work–life balance for some employees. The emergence of **homeshoring** as an alternative to offshore call centres, where home-based workers respond to customers' queries, may increase the number of people in telework, particularly as offshore call centres can attract high levels of customer dissatisfaction. The Automobile Association (AA) has a proportion of its staff working in this way already, and a number of US organizations are taking this route to provide customer services.

Box 4.3 HP and telework

HP Downshifts Telecommuting

Computer maker Hewlett-Packard recently curtailed telecommuting options for hundreds of employees. HP calls the move a key to reshaping its information technology unit. But the decision marks a shift from the company's famed support of flexible work arrangements. What's more, some telecommuting advocates say work-at-home policies make more sense now than ever, and that by withdrawing the option, HP risks losing talented employees.

Workforce Management, 28 June 2006
www.workforce.com/section/00/article/24/42/47.html

Homeworking

Many types of homeworking also involve aspects of teleworking. The Chartered Institute of Personnel and Development report in 2006 was scathing of the apparent increase in teleworking, and argued that the inclusion of all who rely on a phone and a computer meant that 'white van man amongst others, was being included' (Philpott 2006). However, perhaps more significant is that the increase in teleworkers leads to us ignoring other forms of homeworking, which may be hidden, under-reported or unknown. Much homeworking is routine, manual work carrying out assembly of components, food preparation, garment manufacture or envelope addressing. Homeworkers are often disadvantaged in terms of pay and conditions, and they are the lowest-paid workers in the labour force (Felstead and Jewson 2000).

Alan Felstead and Nick Jewson attempt to redress this. Rather than starting from a subdivided field, they propose that we see all forms of homeworking as 'home production' (2000: 16), where the spatial location of home-located production is its defining feature. Doing this reveals that different social relations emerge because of this new way of organizing production. We shall return to their work in the next chapter when we consider the meaning of work. For the moment it is enough to note simply that many forms of home production are characterized by low pay, health hazards, absence of benefits and hidden costs, and what emerges is a profoundly depressing picture. All research on contemporary home production is agreed on this, and where there 'is debate it concerns how bad conditions are' (2000: 88).

Call centre work

Call centre work is a form of employment that has emerged and rapidly expanded in the 1990s and early twenty-first century. The term 'call centre work' covers a range of different forms, although all share a common form of labour process, where workers are under close supervision and use telephones and computers to contact clients and potential customers either to offer new goods and services (the quantitative market) or to support already-purchased goods and services (the qualitative market). The major growth in call centre work has been in the quantitative market.

Call centre work is distinct from homework as an employer provides specialized premises, and employees work fixed shift patterns. Call centre work has been characterized as a new manifestation of a Taylorized labour process (Taylor and Bain 1999), as it involves a detailed division of labour, tightly enforced targets to be met and very close supervision: call centre workplaces are often organized on panopticon patterns to allow supervisors to oversee employees at all times. They use technology to listen in to calls as they are being made. But call centre work has also been described as a new form of work that can be liberating for workers as it allows them more discretion and application of creativity and interpersonal skills (Frenkel et al. 1999). Overall, however, most commentators are agreed that call centre work can be stressful. Polly Toynbee, reflecting on her own experiences of call centre work, said:

Call centres and telesales sweatshops are the modern slave galleys of the labour market, with workers chained to their desks by their headsets. (Toynbee 2003: 151)

Case study 4.1 Call centre work

Research carried out by Taylor et al. (2003), who studied a privatized Scottish energy company (given the pseudonym Energyco), investigated in depth the causes of stress, and other causes of ill-health, associated with call centre work.

Energyco is a national utility provider that was privatized in the late 1980s. Its clerical functions are spread over seven sites, with Grampian House operating as an inbound and outbound call centre dealing with debt and pre-payment calls from across the UK. Working hours are from 8:00 to 20:00 Monday to Friday, and 8:00 to 18:00 on Saturdays, with a 'twilight' administrative support function from 14:00 to 22:00 on weekdays. The site comprises two large, open plan call centres (bureaux) where staff are organized into teams, each comprising 23 customer service advisors (CSAs), two senior CSAs and a customer manager. Customer managers sit with their teams, monitoring individual and collective performance using Call Scan. The performance of each bureau, measured as a 'Grade of Service', together with call queuing data, is displayed on electronic boards, which update in real time. CSAs are extensively monitored on call-handling times, with those handling debt calls required to achieve 'smart' and 'stretch' targets of 10 and 12 calls per hour respectively. Two factors exacerbate the pressure to meet quantitative performance levels. First, CSAs must complete essential clerical 'wrap up' lasting between 1 and 3 minutes for each call and, second, much customer contact is potentially conflictual, as it involves repayment of outstanding bills and possible service disconnection. CSAs are also obliged to promote services to inbound customers and failure to meet such quality standards can lead to CSAs being placed on a 'Poor Performers List'. In sum, this is a call centre where management prioritizes call volumes, numerical targets are strictly imposed and encounters with customers are routinized.

Of the 1100 staff, 70 per cent are directly employed and the remainder are agency workers on long-term assignments. Energyco recruits permanent workers from this agency pool if they meet established performance and attendance criteria. Women comprise 55 per cent of the workforce, a lower proportion than the Scottish call centre average (63%), while the proportion of full-time employees (75%) is higher than average (63%). The relative youth of the workforce – 65 percent aged 35 years or less – is similar to the industry average. Whereas before privatization employees often joined Energyco straight from school and 10 per cent had periods of service of 20 years or more, high levels of turnover have been evident since the establishment of the call centre in 1995.

(Taylor et al. 2003: 439–40)

Management at Energyco were determined to reduce levels of sickness and absence, whilst the unions were increasingly concerned about levels of stress and sickness. Sickness averaged 4.7 per cent, and the annual staff turnover rate was 37 per cent. Between them the unions and management agreed to an independent investigation of the causes of sickness levels and absence rates, and Taylor and his colleagues were approached to carry out a study. Using quantitative and qualitative methods comprising questionnaires, interviews and observations of work processes, the researchers collected evidence and categorized symptoms and absences.

Their main findings are quite disturbing in terms of health and safety at work implications: a quarter of employees reported feeling stress daily or several times a week, and this was largely due to the process of call handling. A quarter reported pain in shoulders, neck and back from work, 50 per cent reported eye strain and pain from excessive and continuous PC use, and many reported sore throats. In addition, many employees experienced the symptoms in clusters, and call handlers experienced most symptoms.

What was causing such high levels of stress and ill-health symptoms? The ergonomic design of workstations was a factor, although not as significant as the overall ambience of the call centre itself; many workers complained of overheating, underheating, poor air conditioning:

> The air conditioning does not work. It's not bad today but normally if it's hot outside it's either roasting or freezing. It's feast or famine. With the draught from air vents sometimes my hands get cold and sometimes I bring in my fleece and put it over my jacket. If you are working late you can hear the heating going off with a bang and it can be really cold.
>
> (CSA interview, 19 September 2000)

But neither of these factors was as significant a cause as the overall control and operation of the labour process itself. Employees felt little or no control over organizing their own work, setting their work pace, or setting targets. The call handlers found the work repetitive and stressful; 69 per cent of them found their work to be 'quite or very pressurized' (Taylor et al. 2003: 448). Targets were the number one cause of pressure in the workplace:

> I have yet to encounter any evidence that management at policy level regard their staff as anything other than telephone-answering automatons who must not be allowed any flexibility or latitude. We are constantly pressured to improve call-rates, even when these are already within expected target rates, for the sake of getting through an extra few calls every day. After a certain point this inevitably causes errors, which lead to repeat calls and problems. . . . The sickness rate has been an ongoing problem as long as I

> have worked here. I believe the major cause is stress due to targets and the repetitive nature of most of the work, compounded by [management's] apparent indifference.
>
> (Questionnaire comment, female CSA, aged thirty-six)
>
> Factors relating to job design, work organization and management – repetitiveness, targets, call volumes, lack of breaks – were the primary causes of sickness and absence from work. Yet the main outcome of the research was for management to change the environmental factors, i.e. those factors that had *least* adverse effect on the health and well-being of call centre workers.

Summary

The UK labour market has changed significantly in recent years, particularly in terms of the gender composition of the workforce. These changes have occurred as a result of economic change and social change, and we can see that the labour market is both a reflection of UK society and a factor in changes in social structure. However, despite social change, government action and legislation, we can still see deep divisions in terms of access to employment and systematic discrimination against particular social groups.

As production has shifted from running on Fordist to post-Fordist lines, work organizations, structures and specific jobs themselves have changed. In addition, new forms of work – notably telework, homeworking and call centre work – have emerged. Continuities, however, remain in terms of control and organization in workplaces. The degree to which such shifts represent 'deskilling' or 'upskilling' remains a debating point, but the range of skills required by workers in a new knowledge-based economy is certainly different.

Overall, work and the division of labour remain at the heart of society and social organization. This is underscored when we investigate in more depth the meanings that are attached to work – the subject of our next chapter.

Discussion questions

1. Who does labour market regulation benefit? Employees, employers, the state or society?
2. What are the main forms of labour market regulation?
3. In what ways does the structure of the UK labour market reflect UK society?
4. How do new forms of working differ from older ones?
5. Does team working promote or hinder flexibility?
6. What challenges to employers and trade unions respectively do homeworking and teleworking present?

Further reading

This chapter has shown that labour markets have been subject to considerable change in recent years. This book provides an excellent overview of the main trends in the UK:

R. Dickens, P. Gregg and J. Wadsworth (eds.), *The Labour Market under New Labour: The State of Working Britain 2003*. Basingstoke: Palgrave Macmillan, 2003.

A much more detailed account can be obtained from Catherine Hakim's book:

C. Hakim, *Social Change and Innovation in the Labour Market: Evidence From the Census SARs on Occupational Segregation and Labour Mobility, Part-time Work and Student Jobs, Homework and Self-employment*. Oxford and New York: Oxford University Press, 1998.

Lisa Adkins, in contrast, presents a specific case study of the hospitality industry to examine labour market changes:

L. Adkins, *Gendered Work: Sexuality, Family and the Labour Market*. Milton Keynes: Open University Press, 1995.

Ajit Ghose's book provides an overview of global labour market change in the context of globalization, international trade and migration:

A. K. Ghose and International Labour Office, *Jobs and Incomes in a Globalizing World*. Geneva: International Labour Office, 2003.

Accessing sources of online data

A lot of the material and analysis in this chapter relies on using official statistics. The following is a list of useful websites that will provide good-quality data on many aspects of work, employment and business. But it is worth remembering that these data have not been collected specifically for you: data collectors have a particular purpose in mind and it is rarely to help sociologists and business studies students. Keep an open and critical mind when using these data and ask who collected them, why did they collect them and, most importantly, how are they defining key concepts, variables and indicators.

Sources of official statistics

The main site for finding useful data is the Office for National Statistics website at www.ons.gov.uk whose front page may have a link to exactly what you are looking for. If not, use the search facility to locate data on the topic you are investigating. You can also access and download useful compilations of ready-analysed government data in the form of annual publications: *Social Trends* and *Regional Trends* are particularly useful and both contain a wealth of information on work, employment and labour markets.

As well as this central site, each UK government department will have its own listing of relevant statistics and links to the National Statistics website. The Department for Work and Pensions is probably the most useful in this general topic area, and includes clickable links to statistics on most government benefits at www.dwp.gov.uk/asd/statistics_a_to_z.asp.

As well as government statistics, many trade unions will provide useful data and other information about work, employment and unemployment. The UK Trades Union Congress provides a lot of information on its website at www.tuc.org.uk and also lists, with links, all the TUC-affiliated trade unions in the UK.

For international data concerning work, employment and unemployment, the ILO based in Geneva is the best starting point. The ILO seeks to promote better working conditions and poverty reduction around the world, and monitors international trends in work, employment, workers' rights and exploitation. The ILO collects data from many countries and compiles international labour market indicators, very useful for getting a comparative perspective. The website is at www.ilo.org.

Using statistical sources

Good social research methods books always contain information on how to use secondary sources of data like official statistics. However, if you are uncertain or unsure about your own skills in evaluating statistics, there are some useful texts that introduce the topic in an approachable and even fun way. Particularly good is:

M. Blastland and A. Dilnot, *The Tiger That Isn't: Seeing Through a World of Numbers*. London: Profile, 2007.

That may not be in your university or local library, but almost certainly there will be a copy of:

D. Huff, *How to Lie with Statistics*. Harmondsworth: Pelican, 1973.

Although slightly outdated, Huff's book will introduce you to all sorts of numerical trickery used to make statistics tell the story that someone wants. Very useful, particularly for recognizing how advertisers and others will use statistics to sell products or policies.

5 The meaning of work

This chapter will:

- examine motivations towards work
- look at the range of rewards people receive from working
- discuss how our identities are bound up with our work
- explore negative consequences of work
- use theory to explain why it is that we work.

Introduction

> The work of our hands, as distinguished from the labour of our bodies
> . . . fabricates the sheer unending variety of things whose sum total
> constitutes the human artifice.
>
> (Hannah Arendt 1959)

Is work still central to the lives of most people? It certainly used to be, and we can see this in cultural representations, shared social values of hard work and thrift that older generations espoused, and social theories that explain the structure and form of modern societies. The German sociologist Max Weber described the rise of a work ethic and how western industrial societies largely conformed to a type where work and personal effort were considered to be core values, and even core elements of human life. For Weber, industrial societies produced particular types of people who were oriented towards work as a goal, and built their lives around a career or a specific role (Weber 1958). Karl Marx and later similar-minded thinkers also placed work at the centre of a picture of what it is to be a human being (Marx 1975; Arendt 1959). Social theorists who saw society in more functional terms placed the division of labour – the way that tasks and roles are allocated – at the centre of their understanding of what a society is and, in turn, understood individuals largely through their work roles.

All of these ideas about the social and personal centrality of work presuppose that work is both available and largely continuous. And, in most cases, they also presuppose that work means employment: they are talking about paid work, not voluntary work, domestic labour, hobbies and pastimes or illegal occupations such as sex work or drug dealing. The idea that paid work is central to individuals makes sense where production is at the core of social arrangements, as it is in modern, industrial societies. Indeed, we could go so far as to define modernity as the time when social identities are closely linked to employment status and role, and where many social structures are organized to facilitate production.

But if the main 'mode' of work – paid employment in a single career for one's lifetime – becomes untenable, if that form of work begins to disappear, then the meaning of work for individuals and for society may change, and social identities may also begin to change. This is what German sociologist Ulrich Beck argues. Beck is famous for defining contemporary society as a '**risk society**' (Beck 1992), and he has extended this definition to a consideration of, as he puts it, the 'brave new world' of work (Beck 2000). Work, as with most things in contemporary society, is risky. Not risky in the sense of being potentially hazardous or dangerous to one's health (although many jobs are), but risky in the sense of being insecure, precarious and uncertain. Work is no longer a safe and secure future in a world of mass unemployment, short-term contracts and flexible working practices. In fact, work could never be safe and secure once capitalism passes a certain point of productivity. As Beck points out, the aim of productivity is to *remove* human labour to promote efficiency. There is a paradox here: work is both the centre of a work society, around which everything and everyone revolves, but it is also something that people strive to eliminate as much of as possible. This presents a challenge for a 'work-society': how does a society reorganize itself around the fact that work is diminishing? We'll return to Beck's, and some other contemporary social thinkers', ideas at the end of this chapter to consider some possible scenarios.

Box 5.1 Risk society

Are our lives becoming more risky? Is our society more risky than previous societies? German sociologist Ulrich Beck, in his 1986 *Risk Society: Towards a New Modernity*, presents a strong case that we live in much more risky and dangerous times, and that we all know this. While formerly risk mainly came from natural phenomena such as storms or floods, it is now increasingly man-made: risk is associated with technology and science – global warming, radiation threats, genetically modified foods, things we have ourselves created.

We know that the world is more risky because, according to Beck, as our societies have become more modern we have developed an increasing ability to reflect on our own conditions of existence. This reflexivity makes us more aware of the technical conditions that surround us – we know, for example, much more about possible threats to us and our lifestyles from, say, global warming than would have been possible for people of previous generations.

Beck's ideas of reflexive modernity and risk society create a picture of the human condition that suggests high levels of anxiety for individuals and decreasing faith in the competence of specialists and those in authority. However, we should note that Beck's account may be overstated:

technology and science may have increased risk in some areas of our lives but they have also removed other risks, especially to our health, and brought massive benefits to us. We are now more healthy and live longer than ever before, and much of this is the result of scientific development providing sanitation, medicine and improved food technology.

Many social analysts have taken up Beck's ideas, and risk and risk management are now major themes of research and investigation in the social sciences. Beck would consider this in itself to be an example of reflexive modernization.

We face problems of definition when we try and talk about work and its meaning, problems that arise from the ubiquity of the word, the pervasiveness of work, and the hidden nature of work; we rarely see or examine the work of others, or even ourselves, closely. A key aim of this chapter is to examine what work and employment mean to individuals, to society and to us as social scientists.

What is work?

In the previous chapter we looked at the nature of work by examining changes in patterns of employment, labour markets and work organization. In doing so we were making an assumption, a commonly held one, that work is the same thing as employment. Whilst much of this chapter, and indeed this book, is about work as employment, we also need to challenge this assumption in order to understand fully the meanings that we as individuals, as communities and as a society attach to work and working.

The idea that work is the same as employment is embedded firmly in social science studies of work from the nineteenth century onwards. Following the industrial revolution, a particular form of work emerged – wage labour, where individuals contract to sell their labour power to an employer in return for a wage – and came to dominate the economic operation of societies. The dramatic changes in the division of labour that the introduction of wage labour brought about completely changed the way that production was organized in society; we can very briefly summarize this as the shift from household production to factory production: the production of goods and the provision of services moved from the locus of the home with its mixed functions (living space, production premises, reproductive space) to specialized premises which only had one function – the production of goods and provision of services to generate profit for capitalists and wages for employees. These changes brought about a different understanding of work for participants and for commentators: much more of economic life and growth came to rest on the world of wage labour, and other forms of work began to recede in the importance placed upon them. Of course that did not mean that housework, caring, volunteering and other forms of unpaid and hidden work ceased to take place. But it meant that, for the past century, most study of work has focused on employment. This is an important task, but, as in other areas of study, we also need to consider what we are excluding. In this case, defining 'real work' as employment led to much of women's work being excluded from scrutiny and consideration. Thus academic study of work and organization largely left out women. In addition, the consequence of focusing on only the formal aspects of labour – contracts, labour process, work organization – was an omission of the most significant aspect of work, its social character:

> Why do we say that a woman 'works' when she takes care of children in a nursery school and 'does not work' when she stays at home to take care of her own children? Is it because the one is paid and the other is not? But the mother at home would still not 'work' if she received an allowance equal to the wages of a nursery school teacher. She would not 'work' even if she too had a teaching qualification. Why is this? Because 'work' is defined from the outset as a social activity, marked out as forming part of the flow of social exchanges on a society-wide basis. The remuneration of this 'work' confirms its insertion into that flow, but that is not essential either: the essential point is that 'work' performs a *socially identified and normalized function in the production and reproduction of the social whole.* And to perform a socially identifiable function, it has itself to be identifiable by the *socially defined skills* it deploys, according to *socially determined procedures.* In other words, it has to be a 'job', a 'profession': that is to say, *the deployment of institutionally certified skills according to approved procedures.* (Gorz 1999: 3)

Here Gorz is reminding us that work is a social construct, something that is created by and for society through the interaction of the members of a society. We make work up, define it and reproduce it through our own actions, although we often have very little choice about how these processes take place. It is society that decides what will and will not count as work, and in our society much of the work of women and carers is excluded from the definition of work – it remains hidden and undervalued, despite being vital for the reproduction of society. This process reflects the power structure of our society, and we can see similar processes taking place through history. Ancient Greek and Roman societies defined work (such as politics, military activity or artistic production) in distinction to labour, and largely ignored what they considered labour – the carrying out of tasks necessary for subsistence – as it was carried out by slaves, not by freemen and citizens. Indeed, as Hannah Arendt points out, most European languages have two words for productive activity, one associated with creative production (in English it is 'work') and the other associated with drudgery, subsistence and repetition ('labour').

But not all labour is drudgery, and not all work is creative; just splitting up productive tasks into these two categories is probably not sufficient to help us understand what work actually is. We might want to conceive work, as the sociologist Wilhelm Baldamus did, in terms of the application of effort and skill. Baldamus' work in the 1960s was groundbreaking; he started from the point of challenging the current orthodoxy of his day, that 'efficiency' was essential to all aspects of business. On examination, Baldamus found that efficiency was usually left undefined by those advocating it. Instead, what people were really talking about was the application of effort (an aspect of employment) and skill (an aspect of occupation) (Baldamus 1961: 9–10). The distinction is an important one: effort is a consequence of individual action, whereas skill is constructed through education and training – a set of social processes. But Baldamus' schema is too limited as well: it implies that we are quite passive as employees, and will either be slotted into an occupational hierarchy according to our skills, or employed according to how much effort can be extracted from us. Subsequent attempts to make sense of work have focused more closely on how individual workers will resist attempts to exploit them (labour process theory – see chapter 4) or use their discretion to regulate their application of effort according to their own criteria of what they feel is fair, or necessary, or enjoyable (Brown 1992).

We are beginning to move towards a definition of work that reflects the complexities of the concept. We can see that work is necessary, and can be divided into paid and unpaid forms. On top of that we can see that work has different components: skill, effort and discretion. Employment is where these components are brought together in a formal, paid situation. Each will be valued differently: this is the outcome of a bargaining process, albeit one in which many employees have very little power. Beyond this we know that work is central to the way that value and status are assigned in our society: it is important to the individual's identity, to how they make sense of themselves in the world around them.

In some professions, identity can be bolstered by a uniform and a clear role in society. How might other professions contribute to one's identity? Is identity dependent to a large degree on occupation nowadays?

Box 5.2 Identity

When we talk about identity, what do we mean? The sense of self that we have, and the way that we are perceived by others, come together in the concept of identity. We know who we are, but we construct this sense of self from our interactions in the social world: the perception others have of us is crucial to our understanding of self.

Identity is thus a complex amalgamation of personal feeling and social action, and we are likely to have a number of identities that are available to us at any one time (employee, mentor, lover, parent) as well as our own core (but perhaps shifting across time) sense of self (who I think I really am). However, as well as knowing what identity is, we also need to know where it comes from – what gives us our identities?

Janette Webb's recent analysis of the relationship between identity and organization points to some significant shifts in our society with respect to the self, from a situation where our identity was inscribed at birth, and life was mapped out by traditions and institutions designed to maintain a rigid social hierarchy, to a time where the normative idea of the self presents us as agents in control of our own destiny (Webb 2006: 18). If we focus on identities associated with production and consumption, particularly a consumer society such as ours, identity becomes something to be achieved in the market for labour and goods. Rather than being ascribed, identity must be achieved (2006: 19). However, this definition is restrictive, and doesn't reveal the ways that our identity shifts and changes according to both our context and how others see us. Although identities associated with production and consumption are significant, particularly in terms of relations among people in organizations, our social identities are also constructed in relation to wider social and political processes, for example through social norms surrounding gender and age.

Bradley's conception of identity addresses these problems:

> I suggest that it is helpful to identify three *levels* of social identity: passive, active and politicised. 'Passive identities' are potential identities in the sense that they derive from the sets of lived relationships (class, gender, ethnicity and so forth) in which the individuals are engaged, but they are not acted on. Individuals are not particularly conscious of passive identities and do not normally define themselves by them unless events occur which bring those particular relationships to the fore. Class in the late twentieth century is a passive identity for many people. The majority of the British population do not appear to think of themselves in class terms, although they recognise the existence of class inequalities.
>
> (Bradley 1996: 25)

Identities, however, become really significant when activated, that is when we become aware of them, and especially when they spur people on to political action.

Thus our identity is dependent on the social circumstances we inhabit, the material conditions we experience, our active imagination in assimilating experiences, and the attitudes of others towards us. The degree to which our identity is seen as fixed, formed by processes we have no choice over, or fluid and actively constructed through our own decisions (as two opposing poles on a continuum) will depend on which study of identity we look at. But regardless of these theoretical differences, given that identity has a large social (as opposed to purely personal) component, and that most people spend much time in a (social) workplace, the role of work and organizations in forming identity will be significant.

We will see all of these components coming together when we look at some examples of the world of work and how different people experience it, and, given the subject matter and audience of this book, we will be concentrating mainly on paid work and employment. Before that, however, we need to consider *why* it is that people work.

Why do we work?

The obvious answer is that people work for money by which to live. But this is not a very helpful answer in that, as we often simply define work as paid employment, all we are doing is reproducing the definitions: we haven't learnt anything about why people choose particular forms of work, how they feel about the work that they do, and whether or not these factors have an effect on how well or otherwise people work. However, it is the reason many people ascribe to others when they think about their work: we assume others carry out tasks because they are being paid to do so, and we tend to ignore: (a) the possibility that they have other motivations, and (b) that we ourselves don't necessarily have only economic reasons for working. Elsewhere we describe this idea of people primarily working for money as a 'myth' (Bradley et al. 2000); here it is sufficient to note that we need to investigate in some depth what motivates people in particular occupations. To do this properly we need to think about not only individuals' economic needs, but also their psychosocial needs, along with the social and economic contexts within which people and their work are located.

Motivations and orientations to work are often classified according to a simple schema of rewards: extrinsic, intrinsic and authority. We will briefly look at each of these.

Extrinsic rewards

Extrinsic rewards are those associated with the external conditions surrounding work that affect an individual's attitudes: things that come from outside – primarily money or other forms of payment, but also job security, hours worked and career prospects through, for example, promotion. The SCELI research project, a major academic investigation

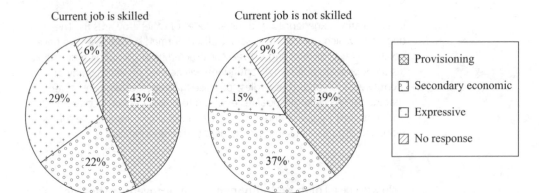

Current job is skilled   Current job is not skilled

Provisioning

Secondary economic

Expressive

No response

Fig. 5.1 Rationale for employment (percentages) Data source: Rose (1994: 298)

into a wide range of aspects of work and employment, looked in detail at orientations and motivations towards work. This survey-based research used a very large sample (the work histories study, from which some data are reproduced here, used a sample of some 6,000 adults). Although the data were collected in the late 1980s the conclusions are still worth examining, particularly as independent research of this magnitude is rare.

SCELI data show that a primary motivation, or rationale, for work is economic, but that other factors are also important to workers. Figure 5.1, abbreviated from Rose (1994: 298), shows some of the findings. Respondents were asked to identify why they worked and the researchers constructed three broad categories: provisioning, which provides the primary economic needs for a household; secondary economic, which provides an additional income for a household, to provide money for such things as holidays and an enhanced lifestyle; and expressive, where the work is not primarily motivated by economic need.

The diagram shows that provisioning was the most common reason for working. However, other motives were also mentioned, especially by the skilled workers. Moreover, the normative commitment to work, as expressed by agreeing that one would continue to work even if one did not need to, is perhaps the most telling evidence that work is still a central part of society and vital to our view of our selves. In the SCELI survey, 66 per cent of all respondents said they would continue to work even if they did not need to (Rose 1994: 291). However, the SCELI data also show clearly that the lower one is in terms of wages and skills, the less strong one's commitment is to work, and the more likely one is to be working for largely economic reasons.

Intrinsic rewards

Intrinsic rewards, satisfactions to the inner self that arise from working, such as the use of skill, the challenge of work, the sense of self-worth that arises from work, and the construction of identity, particularly occupational identity, come in a variety of forms that we can classify according

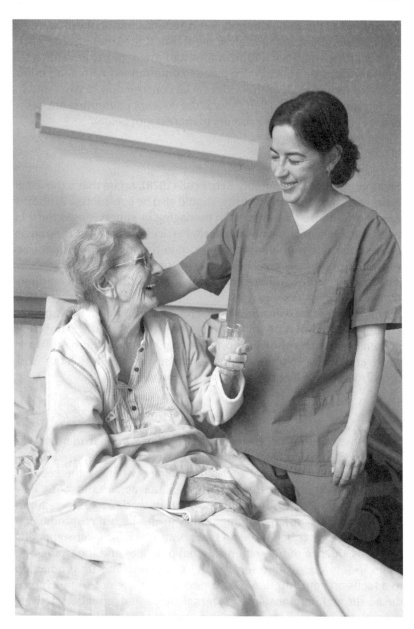

Intrinsic reward is particularly significant in health and social care professions, such as nursing, social work and occupational therapy.

to their importance to the self. At one end of the scale are motivations where an individual has a very strong urge to follow a particular career or vocation: you may have friends who are firmly committed to becoming a doctor or lawyer – or a professional footballer or rap artist. At the other end are looser rewards and motivations; feelings of pleasure and satisfaction in work, a sense of belonging to an organization or group, positive associations with knowing one is being productive or helping others, even in quite abstract ways. Young adults interviewed by one of the authors of this book about their aspirations often spoke of 'wanting to make something of themselves', or of 'wanting to make a difference' through their work. Such motivations and orientations towards work can vary through time, are frequently compounded with each other, and are often a result of the wider social construction of work and its importance. Central to all of these is the concept of identity, our sense of self in society, which we discuss in more depth below.

Authority rewards

Some commentators, notably Berg et al. (1978), argue that a third category of reward, that of authority, should also be considered. Authority rewards are those that arise from managing or supervising others, or being managed or supervised oneself. Particularly among the younger generation there is often a strong desire to rise to be a manager, thus controlling other people's efforts, or to set up one's own business, which, if successful, will involve having others work under your direction.

This threefold classification is a useful starting point in beginning to explain orientations and motivations towards work. But it is not comprehensive: there are diverse orientations and motivations to work, which still merit exploration. There are many ways in which our work contributes to our identity and sense of who we are.

Work as the site of identity construction

Two key studies in the 1990s challenged the way that identity was understood in workplaces. Catherine Casey (1995) proposed a new post-structural and critical social psychology, whereby the self was seen as something constructed through the active and conscious consumption of signs and symbols, often in workplaces. In examining 'Hephaestus', a large multinational in the high-tech production sector, Casey described the ways that new forms of self were emerging as a consequence of new organizational practices and the changes in wider society – basically a social shift from a concern with production to a focus on consumption. These new selves were not so much produced through circumstances external to the individual, as actively constructed by individuals through a process of consumption.

The new post-Fordist corporation that Casey describes is one where traditional occupations are in decline. Rather than having single task-oriented roles, employees were encouraged to be part of teams and families, and to identify very strongly with the company. The company, in a society where traditional social bonds such as those of occupation, family and community are in decline, takes over the role of being the main provider of social solidarity. Workers stop being workers and become employees – they cease forming their identity around their occupation (as engineer, designer or manager) and begin to form their identities around belonging to the corporation ('I'm not an engineer, I'm a Hephaestus employee'). The corporation is deliberately active in designing this new corporate culture as a way of promoting solidarity, team work and productivity.

> The corporation's new designer culture provides a solidarity locus that compensates for the demise of former industrial loci. It provides a simulated community that is manufactured for a vital function of production. (Casey 1995: 189)

The self, the individual within the corporation, is presented with stark choices in constructing their identity, and Casey's research revealed three main modes of doing this.

1. The 'defensive self' has internalized the disenchantment of bureaucratic life. They would rather be somewhere else, living under the conditions of their own self-narrative. But they are attracted and tied by the package of financial rewards and status offered by the corporation.
2. The 'colluded self' is characterized by compulsive optimism and espousal of the new values of the new culture. A strong supporter of the corporation and its new culture.
3. The 'capitulated self' has negotiated a weary surrender with the corporation. Although their identity has been produced by the corporation, they don't foreclose the possibility of some form of resistance. But the circumstances in which they find themselves make resistance difficult, and their pragmatic attitude is to stick with what they have as an alternative may be worse.

While employees keep working for reasons of pragmatic need (e.g. money), Casey found that some employees had a sense of almost religious duty:

> Promotion of secular religious character, and not just economic need, ensures that people come to work every day and perform their utmost in the service of the company's goals. ... Religiosity – belief and practice – is the sustaining principle of Hephaestus Corporation. Faith is most simply displayed in belief in the product, the values and wisdom of the company and in its work principles: teamwork, excellence and customer satisfaction. (Casey 1995: 191)

Compliance is thus achieved through creating a corporate culture that fulfils a need inside the human employee: it makes a place for the person to enter, and satisfies their needs of belonging. The team–family intimacy of work replaces the declining intimacy of the home, and ensures the compliance of the workers. The corporation becomes almost a second family. In addition Casey observes very little of what labour process theorists would call resistance, and she notes that such passive modes of resistance as not taking part, not being a team player, are virtually not possible in the new corporate climate. Even better, for the corporation at least, has been the disruption of previous sites of resistance (such as trade unions): with such intimacy at work, employees are reluctant to socialize with each other after hours.

Casey's account is ultimately fatalistic; the new corporate culture has 'won': sites of resistance are neutralized and the corporation is, in Foucault's terms, becoming a panopticon that sees all and predicts all, gaining a pervasive influence in all aspects of the employees' lives both within and outside the workplace.

Paul du Gay's study of the UK retail sector (1996) uses theory similar to Casey's, but he produces a more robust theoretical account, and a less fatalistic perspective. Du Gay describes the 'de-differentiation' of consumer culture and retailing organizations, where the way an organization is run and the way that people shop and consume become similar. We see a reduction of difference, a process of reducing everything to a similar level. Material, aspirational and entrepreneurial values operate in all spheres of life, cultural, social and economic. So we see the penetration of this form of organization (broadly post-Fordist) into areas of the world other than the retailing sector.

Du Gay sees the post-Fordist consumerist culture as being highly dangerous to society. There is a blurring of the separate spheres of society – all are becoming controlled by similar processes, namely that of enterprise and the entrepreneur. While their advocates tend also to use the rhetoric of increasing egalitarianism and diversity, these two concepts are 'remarkably thin'. We are entering a culture where everything becomes defined by a bottom line of enterprise and profitability (think of how schools and universities are currently managed). This may look good; it seems to suggest that all are, initially at least, equal in the market, but such a form of **pluralism** is incorrect. For du Gay, equality is the hallmark of unjust societies.

> Justice requires the defence of difference – different goods distributed for different reasons among different groups of people – and enterprise, as we have seen, flattens difference by naming distinct spheres commensurable through the medium of the market mechanism. (du Gay 1996: 191)

It looks like there is an equalizing process taking place – enterprise traversing previous boundaries of the social world, redefining individuals as entrepreneurs of their own lives; enterprise appears to offer the possibility of spreading satisfaction and well-being throughout the social fabric. But this is at the expense of difference: this means that we are redefining people, socially constructing them as being all the same. According to this doctrine, there should be no complex multiple ethical selves – just a single conception of human life as 'enterprise of self'.

The imposition of such corporate cultures, particularly 'enterprise' culture in du Gay's case study organizations, is resisted and resented by many employees, and at all levels, including senior management (1996: 151). Du Gay identifies overt and covert conflict and resentment when new corporate cultures are imposed, with employees reporting that they feel they are being deskilled, marginalized and even humiliated (1996: 153). Resistance, often through passivity, refusal to comply with new directives or offer false emotional support for new programmes is a widespread reaction to the imposition of enterprise culture. Instead of embracing the corporate culture with religious fervour, as Casey suggested, workers may become cynical and disillusioned. So the discourse of enterprise, with its emphasis on interpersonal skills, actually makes itself vulnerable to more enterprising workers who can disrupt or subvert the process (1996: 168).

Work as duty, calling and vocation

Many people feel compelled to work, and may experience this compulsion to be a combination of factors. They are compelled because they need to earn money, but also by the need to feel fulfilled and to be recognized and valued in society. For some, this compulsion is so strong as to be almost irresistible: they are 'called' and feel a strong sense of duty to take up a particular vocation. The paradigmatic example is those called to a religious vocation – as a priest, for example – but Weber noted that this sense of calling and duty is felt by many others, even, perhaps, all of us (Weber 1958: 54). Weber looked in detail at how politicians and scientists felt called to their vocation, and many subsequent studies have seen how individuals feel a sense of duty to accompany their work.

Case study 5.1 Scientific workers' motivations to work

Contract research staff (CRS) (also known as postdoctoral researchers or 'postdocs.') in UK universities are responsible for the vast majority of the research work that takes place, particularly in science, engineering and medical disciplines. These workers are amongst the most highly trained in the UK labour force: gaining a position as a science researcher on a CRS contract requires at least a very good first degree and usually a Ph.D. (and a master's-level course, taken between these other two degrees, is not uncommon): a minimum of six years' university-level study. Despite their very high level of skills, and the dedication needed to work in advanced scientific research, formal working conditions are often poor, with low wages, poor chances of career progression and high levels of job insecurity (most CRS are still employed on temporary contracts of between six months and three years). In addition, very many of these workers are women (despite the fact that the majority of senior research scientists and science academics in the UK are men), and many come from developing-world nations.

Given that this group of workers has such high levels of skill, and also have many transferable skills, why do they choose to work in conditions that would be unacceptable to others?

Erickson (2002) carried out a piece of qualitative research interviewing scientists about, amongst other things, their motivations to work. Twenty-six interviews were conducted with scientists working in UK universities, half from a team of biochemists, the other half from a team of physicists.

CRS recognize that they have job insecurity, and that their pay levels are lower than they could earn in industry. They also recognize that their career may face an abrupt change if the science research project they are working on runs out of funds. But they choose to continue in this form of employment for two main reasons. The first is that they are making a calculation concerning their future, as this biochemistry postdoc. explained:

> If I had a choice between a secure but boring post and an exciting but temporary position, I think I would go for the temporary position with the exciting work because usually there will be options further down the line and the most important thing is your c.v., the work that you have done and your publications. That will make you a stronger researcher and make you a more viable asset for obtaining a more permanent position in the future.
>
> (Female biochemistry postdoc., 27, Greek)

The second is that they feel compelled to follow their calling to a vocation – in this case to be scientists. This was reported by a majority of respondents in this research when asked why they chose this career:

> From junior school I wanted to be a mathematician or a physicist.
>
> (Female physics CRS, Yugoslavian)

> I like it. I was good at science in high school. I enjoy it and like physics and studied physics in University and I wanted to carry on with research.
>
> (Female physics postdoc., 36, Chinese)

> I still find it the most exciting thing in life, just finding out things. Really very straightforward Mark, I just genuinely find it interesting.
>
> (Male biochemistry postdoc., 48, British)

> It is a duty to use my talents. I enjoy it very much and am very very very happy when I come here to work. If I have too little work I become nervous, I like to be busy, but busy in science.
>
> (Male biochemistry postdoc., 29, Egyptian)

Many of these people would not have chosen an alternative career, and they were definitely not following this career path for economic reasons. Some even reported that they would work exactly the same long hours for less money, or even for no pay:

> I'm not doing this for going to work and having a job. I'm doing this because I want to do this, I want to work in science and getting paid is a bonus. OK, I could complain about not getting paid enough but I'm not in it for the money. If I was I wouldn't be doing this. (Male physics postdoc., 23, French)

Overall, the motivations to work reported by this group of scientists were:

- job satisfaction and money: 50 per cent
- job satisfaction alone: 25 per cent
- duty, a sense of achievement, need for intellectual challenge: 25 per cent.

Scientists are not different from other people, other than having a particular form of skills training, and the idea of a calling to a vocation should not be restricted to thinking about religious, political or scientific careers. However, these scientists are lucky in that they have managed to achieve their goal of getting the career and position that they want. In addition, they also get a great deal of job satisfaction from their work, with almost all those interviewed finding it fulfilling and stimulating. Not all other workers are so fortunate.

Work as fun

Intrinsic rewards that we have looked at so far have been prosaic: vocation, calling, sense of duty, identity. But some jobs are, at least for those doing them, fun and exciting. Ben Fincham's study of cycle couriers in London and Cardiff offers an insight into just such an occupation (Fincham 2007). Fincham argues that the orientations to work of bicycle couriers are based around membership of a specific subcultural group, a shared sense of danger and the enjoyment of cycling.

Case study 5.2 Bicycle courier work

Bicycle courier work is fairly simple, involving the collection and delivery of packages around a city. Cycles are used to navigate congested traffic, but given current levels of congestion the work is dangerous and strenuous. It is also low-paid and the labour market position of couriers is peripheral. Most messengers are paid on a commission basis, and most are sub-contracted to a business: they are effectively self-employed. In 2004 the average daily wage for messengering in Cardiff was £45, and in London £65 (Fincham 2007: 192).

Fincham's research revealed a rich and deep subculture shared amongst bicycle couriers. The couriers saw themselves as being apart from other members of society. This subculture emerged from shared experiences both at work and outside of work. At work, bicycle couriers all experienced a shared sense of fun associated with cycling, and this fun element was what attracted them to the work:

> I thought it would be good fun.
>
> (Pipstar, Cardiff)

> The first year I loved it, you know. Being outside all day. Because everything's new . . . and it was a real good laugh.
>
> (Edwardian, Cardiff)

> I just thought it would be sort of fun. Just like they said in the ad, seeing different parts of London and being fit and happy.
>
> (Catwoman, London)

The motivation for many becoming involved is that cycle messengering is enjoyable (2007: 200). In addition to the enjoyment and fun of cycling, messengering provides a strong shared subculture, based around a common sense of danger and superiority to other road users, shared entertainment activities (often revolving around recreational drugs and alcohol), and a reinforcement of 'outsider' values, notably those associated with 'normal' work. Many bicycle couriers reported that they liked a job that was connected to their social life and allowed them to express themselves; this was not a 'boring 9 to 5' job.

> When you've got a job like this where your work isn't too much of a hassle and it doesn't take away too much of your personality and your social life, you can have your own sub-culture which does express itself a lot more like skateboarding or surfing or something like that.
>
> (Cargo Chris, London)

Other forms of work are seen as oppressive, even alienating, and this group of workers have an identity, community and culture that are very important to them, and are maintained by a 'unifying process of shared experiences and shared world-views' (2007: 201).

Choice and work – temporary employment, flexibility and work–life balance

In recent years we have seen attitudes towards work change, in terms of employees, employers and the state all addressing issues of work–life balance, attempts to match the needs of individuals outside the workplace with the needs of an organization (see chapter 4 for details of recent legislation addressing work–life balance issues). This change in attitude has occurred at the same time as patterns of work have changed, particularly through the increase in part-time work and women entering the labour market.

Women now make up over 45 per cent of the workforce, although a large proportion of these are working part-time. The increase in part-time work can be taken as a marker of the increase in flexible employment practices and non-standard work. Part-time jobs are often seen as being as inferior to full-time jobs, and the uptake of these jobs by women has been used to explain their continuing low-status position in the labour market. Where the (male-set) norm is a forty-hour working week, those failing to fulfil this norm are seen as being deficient. However, some sociologists have challenged this picture. Some suggest that women are less strongly committed to work in any case, and hold 'weak' orientations to work (Hakim 1996), thus making them more likely to choose part-time jobs, and to be less career-focused. This validation of non-standard work as a positive choice was investigated in depth by Casey and Alach (2004). They interviewed forty-five temporary workers, all women, in New Zealand, and found that these workers were positively choosing non-standard work, and for a range of reasons. The three main categories of reasons they found were: being in a transitional period of life, wanting flexibility to prioritize other commitments such as family or community involvement, and dissatisfaction with conventional permanent and full-time positions (2004: 466). For these women, temping was a positive choice, and non-standard work, despite its associated insecurity and perceived lower status, was a positive thing for them:

> I don't like to stay in one place for too long . . . temping means that you can work for a week and then you can have a break, or you can do whatever you want to. . . . It's really flexible, and like, I'd say (to the agency) that I want Monday and Tuesday off, have you got any assignments starting on Wednesday? (2004: 468)

> There's a lot of freedom in temping to just up and go, you know. Because as a temp, to a degree you are your own boss. I mean you. . . can state when you want to work and when you don't want to work. Would I go back permanent? . . . No, I don't think so. Even if I were to go onto any sort of permanent role it would be on a contract type situation . . . (2004: 468)

They reported the value of not working, of being able to have 'a four or six week holiday whenever you want to, as well as being able to take days off here and there'; or of having more control over their day:

> I think times are changing and people are moving into the temping thing and they're realizing that a lot of their day goes into working . . . and I've met so many people that say, 'oh, I don't want to go to work today' and me, you know, I get up and think 'oh cool, another day of work, for a few hours.' (2004: 468)

Casey and Alach conclude:

> The assertion of non-commitment to conventional work, and work-based social expectations, and to traditional cultural expectations, in order to 'do what I'd rather be doing' exposes a rupture in the economistic and rationalization trajectories of modernity. . . . These women regard their participation in labour market work and their development of occupational competencies as one set of constituents among others in their complex projects of self-identity construction. . . . The ability to pick and choose when and how to work, long assumed a rare privilege of the rich and powerful, is ironically being demanded and practiced by otherwise ordinary (historically working-class or lower middle-class), lifestyle seeking women. (2004: 476–7)

As well as identifying a shift in the status of non-standard jobs, this research suggests that new subjectivities are emerging, ones where work is not the central facet of identity construction, where multi-active lives are lived. However, much evidence points in the other direction. For instance, Colin Bryson's 2004 survey of academic workers on fixed-term contracts (FTCs) found high levels of disadvantage and discrimination for non-standard workers in this sector. In marked contrast to Casey and Alach, Bryson found:

- more men than women viewed FTCs as advantageous in terms of flexibility
- more women than men cited disadvantages, particularly insecurity, and would prefer a permanent contract
- no evidence that women on FTCs are less likely to want a permanent job
- no evidence that FTCs provide 'desirable' flexibility for women
- no evidence that women exhibit 'weak' orientations to work.

Bryson concluded that the FTC workers experienced unfavourable conditions and felt marginalized. Bryson's work addresses a crucial question ignored by Casey: whose interests are best being served by flexibility and non-standard work? Hyman et al.'s 2005 study of call centre and software workers found that many employees reported significant spillover from work to home, and that spillover is a consistent outcome of work in the contemporary economy. The authors talk of work–life tensions rather than work–life balance. Call centre workers felt strong pressure to be flexible in the employer's favour:

> I hate getting up in the morning to come to work, I really do, because I just think 'you are coming in and you are going to get hit with something else that's changed. . . .' They leave you messages on the phones saying next week on Monday we are doing 8–5 shift, we are getting our lunch at 11 o'clock in the morning . . . Just leave a bit of paper on your desk . . . They want you to take half an hour for your lunch and stay and do a couple of hours overtime. That would be a 12 hour day . . . They want us to be 100% flexible but they are not flexible in return. (Hyman et al. 2005: 712–13)

Non-standard work employees felt a significant range of negative effects, particularly in terms of family life:

> I've been on secondment for two months to do this constant backshift . . . and they pay me quite a lot more money to do it but the money's not enough, because my son was saying to me the other day, a couple of weeks ago, Daddy, I don't like these shifts you are working because I never see you. (2005: 713)

Overall, the authors conclude that, in the new sectors of the economy, employers only grant flexibility on their own terms.

Negative consequences of work

As we have seen, work can be rewarding, stimulating, fun. It is something that provides us with resources in constructing our personal identity and our sense of self in the world. But for many people work is rarely stimulating, fun or rewarding. As the noted economist J. K. Galbraith pointed out:

> There is no greater modern illusion, even fraud, than the use of the single term 'work' to cover what for some is ... dreary, painful, socially demeaning and what for others is enjoyable, socially reputable and economically rewarding. (Galbraith: 1992)

Work can have significant negative consequences, particularly if it is dirty, dangerous, physically and mentally exhausting, or is work that we feel we are not suited to, are forced into doing, or that challenges our moral framework. Much research points to the fact that what we have now is *more* work: more to do, longer hours.

Box 5.3 How much do we work?

The average full-time worker in the UK works 42.4 hours against an EU average of 40.5 hours (Eurostat). That works out at about 8 hours a month more, a whole extra day's work. We work high levels of unpaid overtime: 39 per cent of people in IT, and 38 per cent of workers in education do at least 1 hour of unpaid overtime per week. Indeed, on average education workers are providing a massive 9 hours 47 minutes' additional work per week (*Guardian*, 19 February 2007). The TUC has responded by introducing an annual 'work your proper hours day' to highlight this issue.

Not only are organizations persuading us to work longer, we are also expected to give more – not just our labour power or brain power but our emotions as well.

Box 5.4 Emotional labour

The term 'emotional labour' was first coined by American sociologist Arlie Russell Hochschild in her book *The Managed Heart: The Commercialization of Human Feeling* (1983). Emotional labour is associated with an increasing number of occupations, and more and more people are now employed in positions that require them not only to deploy skill and effort, but also to present certain emotions. Increasingly, corporations require employees to show their commitment to customers or clients and to employers by overt displays of emotions.

Hochschild's research investigated this emotional work, and found that a complex process of controlling emotions took place. Workers had to manage their emotions in precise ways, particularly to ensure that their real feelings did not come to the surface: surface acting, in which employees pretend to feel an emotion and subsequently express it, is separated from deep acting through this process of managing emotions.

According to Hochschild, jobs that deploy emotional labour have three distinct characteristics:

> First, they require face-to-face or voice-to-voice contact with the public. Second, they require the worker to produce an emotional state in another person – gratitude or fear for example. Third, they allow the employer, through training and supervision, to exercise a degree of control over the emotional activities of employees.
>
> (Hochschild 1983: 147)

Hochschild's original case study is that of air stewardesses, who are trained to manipulate the emotions of the public through controlling their own emotions, and to express the company's public image through their actions. But we can see similar processes in many forms of service sector work: call centre operatives who are obliged to follow closely worded scripts, fast-food outlet staff who must greet customers in a specific way – indeed most front-line customer service workers. Emotional labour is about 'keeping the customer happy'. Such labour can be draining, since it involves the acting out of emotions that may be very different from those one is actively feeling. Emotional labour has been strongly associated with women because of its link with care and nurturing, the archetypal qualities of a mother, and, increasingly, much of it is highly sexualized (Bradley 2007).

The popularity of the term 'emotional labour' has led to a proliferation of studies and usages, so much so that Bolton (2005) argues that something of a bandwagon has formed. Nevertheless, emotional labour has been identified in many forms of work, particularly in the service sector, and is increasingly seen by employers as an important resource. Bolton points out that there are many complexities hidden by the term, but argues that 'it has never before been so important to a capitalist economy' (Bolton 2005: 157). Given this, the question of how emotion work should itself be managed must be addressed. Central to this is the degree to which workers are being exploited and abused by employers managing their emotions as well as their skill and effort. A number of studies have found that high levels of control over emotions will result in resistance from employees, and that, as these forms of resistance will often involve potential damage to the public face of the corporation, stakes are high. Emotional labour can rob workers of their dignity, and this has prompted calls for the restoration of autonomy to front-line workers.

We saw in previous chapters that the division of labour and the labour market in our society are not perfect, or even ideal for many people. The social construction of work and the social institutions that emerge from it are themselves imperfect and many social scientists think that these have negative consequences for the whole of society,

Table 5.1 The impacts of work

Work realities	Physical conditions	Repetitiveness	Routines
Deprivations	Impairment	Tedium	Weariness
Relative satisfactions	Inurement	Traction	Contentment

Source: Baldamus (1961: 76)

as well as for individuals. We will briefly explore some of these negative consequences of work. Whilst much of business studies is devoted to considering how and why it is that employees stop working – through strikes, absenteeism or illness – we should recognize that it is also difficult to explain why it is that people work in the first place, particularly when the work they are offered is sometimes terrible.

Wilhelm Baldamus offers us a useful set of classifications, based on research, that describes the realities of work for many, and begins to explain how employees will continue with work that many may consider unpalatable, tiring, degrading or boring (see table 5.1).

Impairment arises due to the physical discomfort of work, often strenuous work. But this can result in a relative satisfaction of inurement – getting used to the hard work and coping with it. Similarly, boring and routine work produces tedium, but as time proceeds the worker copes with the routine and boredom and actually begins to enjoy being taken up and propelled along by the task – traction. Finally, weariness arises from the work realities of routine, the daily grind of work activities, the coerciveness of having to keep a job. This engenders a relative satisfaction of, as Baldamus put it, 'contentment, a state of mind that is often expressed by saying that one is in the mood for work. This is usually a kind of dull contentment' (Baldamus 1961: 70). There is a strong connection and a mutual dependence between these pairs of deprivations and satisfactions: the worker cannot experience one without the other, cannot experience contentment without having first experienced weariness. We could compare it to the contentment that follows the weariness caused by some athletic activity, a vigorous workout in the gym, partaking in a half-marathon run.

Do Baldamus' categories describe all aspects of work processes? No. However, they do two useful things for us. They remind us that work is often unpleasant for many people, and they show us a route to beginning to understand the complexity of our engagement with work. In addition, they are rooted in the real experiences of individuals – both Baldamus and you will have experienced similar feelings, particularly with respect to traction: the feeling of being caught up in a task and carried along by it, regardless of whether or not you really want to do it.

Such feelings and experiences are not quantifiable, are not even comparable, for we all have different sensations of how we are expending our effort, but we can use them as a way of making better sense of how people work. These ideas will be useful when looking in more depth at forms of work that are considered dirty, degrading, hard or dangerous.

Dirty, degrading, hard and dangerous work

We mentioned above that the current situation of work tends to be one of more: more work, more insecurity, more exploitation of emotions normally associated with the personal sphere, more commitment to organizations, sometimes at the expense of personal relationships. In formal language we can describe this situation as intensification, and the negative consequences, at least for workers, have been widely noted. There is a tension between the drive towards a more flexible, committed and compliant workforce that can compete in global markets and the needs of individuals who have to cope with **work intensification**, job insecurity and the problems that low-wage lifestyles engender. The practicalities of living on a low wage, even following the introduction of the NMW in April 1999, are complex and often dispiriting. Public concerns about the continuance of poverty in the UK despite government attempts to raise living standards prompted a number of studies of life in low-wage Britain. Polly Toynbee and Fran Abrams, both *Guardian* journalists, produced separate and quite different accounts of life in low-wage Britain (at about the same time in the USA, Barbara Ehrenreich, a prominent journalist, produced *Nickel and Dimed* (2002) an account of her time in the low-wage economy, and followed it up with *Bait and Switch* (2006), an examination of unemployment and despair inside the white-collar corporate workforce).

Abrams' book focuses on the everyday difficulties of trying to live on the minimum wage, and on the sharp practices and dishonesties of unscrupulous employers who can take advantage of vulnerable and non-unionized workers. For example, companies would hire in temporary staff from agencies who specialize in providing such workers, thus releasing them from any burdens associated with employing people: no human resource management (HRM) problems, no need to provide sick or holiday pay, no need to provide uniforms or even safety equipment as this becomes the sub-contractor's responsibility (Abrams 2002). Abrams is at an advantage in comparison to many of her colleagues in low-wage work in that she has no dependants, few obligations and is mobile. For others, the low-wage economy is a hand-to-mouth existence of constant worry, insecurity, psychological pressure and humiliation. Toynbee is particularly acute in her observation of the petty meanness and humiliations that low-waged workers in the service sector have to suffer every day, and what people will do to avoid further humiliation; on being turned down for a minimum-wage job (£4.10 per hour) in a cake factory, she wrote:

> I had forgotten that it doesn't matter how low the job, rejection is always an affront which is another reason why people don't job-swap upwards as much as they should and could. It is not pleasant to subject yourself to scrutiny and risk failure. (Toynbee 2003: 170)

But it isn't just low-waged employees who are facing stress and insecurity at work. Burchell et al.'s (2002) study of twenty diverse workplaces around the UK (in the Job Insecurity and Work Intensification Survey (JIWIS)) found widespread job insecurity (which is not only the fear of losing one's job, but also worries about losing valued job features), alongside stress and work intensification: 64 per cent of respondents had experienced an increase in the speed of work in the past five years, and 61 per cent an increase in effort in a similar period. The outcomes of this intensification were demotivation, sickness and absenteeism in the workplace, and decreased levels of psychological well-being.

Perhaps surprisingly, job insecurity was felt more acutely in better-paid positions:

> Workers in higher-paid occupations, those employed in construction or financial services, those who had been in their current job for over ten years and the self-employed were significantly more insecure in 1997: those in the manufacturing industry and in sales occupations were more secure in 1997 than in 1986. But the biggest change was experienced by those in professional occupations, who went from being the most secure workers in 1986 to the most insecure in 1997. (Burchell et al. 2002: 66)

Similar conditions pertain in the USA, where the '**dot com**' collapse of the early twenty-first century, accompanied by massive outsourcing of IT jobs to Asia and the Pacific Rim, led to endemic job insecurity. Andrew Ross, in *No-Collar*, a 2003 study of US New Economy workplaces, notes that:

> For those who have retained their high-value jobs, the pressure to boost productivity has been all the more intense. . . . If you work for a large corporation, the threat of losing your job to a lower-priced Asian counterpart will have the desired effect. For those at smaller and medium-sized companies, the rapid opening and closing of market opportunities tends to shape short-term expectations about employment opportunities. Consequently, a layoff is no longer the opposite of employment, it is part and parcel of the job definition. (Ross 2003: ix)

Why is job insecurity and work intensification so stressful? One reason is that continued uncertainty makes planning for the future difficult, and a continued lack of control can be compounded by other factors, such as work overload. Employees experiencing both at the same time find themselves depleting their reserve capacities. This can result in chronic overload and ultimately even a complete breakdown of task performance. One of the most powerful findings of the JIWIS research is that we do not 'get used to' job insecurity and intensification (Burchell et al. 2002).

When considering causes of stress and insecurity at work, it can be easy to forget that many people are employed in jobs that regularly put their lives at risk.

Beyond these threats to our well-being, some forms of work can actually be fatal. In the UK in 2001–2 there were 251 fatal accidents at work, about a third of which were in the construction industries. There were over 130,000 workplace injuries that resulted in more than three days' absence from work. Moreover, these figures do not cover deaths and injuries in sea fishing and the armed forces.

As well as ill-health or even the danger of death, work can present us with psychological and personal problems that are difficult to cope with, and can have a detrimental effect on the quality of life of individuals. Examples include people involved in 'morally contested work' such as arms dealers, nuclear waste workers, vivisectionists, sex workers and defence industry workers (Bradley et al. 2000: 180). The psychological stresses that employees in these industries face are varied and may be mitigated by membership of a supportive **occupational community**. However, when we consider these forms of work as 'deviant' or morally contested we find, on further examination, that all forms of work may contain morally contested elements, in that the work that we do is surrounded by socially generated discourses that ascribe or deny value and importance to particular productive processes. Work is not neutral: many of us may have secret anxieties about things we are asked to do in the name of profit.

Alienation

Is work itself, then, a problem for us? We can, as we have seen, identify forms of work and work practices that have harmful effects on people, but is there something about work itself, particularly work in capitalism, that is in essence harmful?

The work that most of us are involved in could be viewed as

profoundly unnatural and strange, although to most of us it appears to be the most natural thing in the world. Karl Marx's theory of alienation – the concept that describes how we become estranged from ourselves, each other and the world around us – rests on identification of this unnaturalness and how it is heightened by the operation of capitalism. Marx's theory of alienation suggests that work in capitalism will inevitably have a negative effect on the worker, and that the only escape from this alienation is through abolition of capitalism itself.

As discussed in chapter 2, alienated work means being denied control over one's own activities within the labour process. This results in alienation, the sensation of being a 'disaffected stranger' (Edgell 2006: 29). It is worth noting the similarities here with Arendt's ideas about the work/labour distinction: alienated work is the 'dehumanized opposite of a satisfying experience which develops the human capacity for creativity' (Edgell 2006: 29). For Marx, everyone living under capitalism is alienated: workers, managers, owners, unpaid domestic workers, unemployed people. This is because the whole of a capitalist society is oriented and geared towards the production of profit.

Marx's theory of alienation underpins much twentieth-century study of work and workplaces, notably Robert Blauner's investigation of the relationship between workplace technology and alienation (Blauner 1964), and labour process theory's focus on the estrangement of the worker from the manufacturing process (Braverman 1974). The loss of craft skills through the introduction of machinery to the workplace was, for Blauner, a central factor in causing alienation. Craft workers who still had significant control over how they worked experienced lower levels of alienation than those who were machine tending or, worst of all, assembly line workers, the archetypes of alienated people. For Blauner the core of alienated labour was meaninglessness, and this was endemic through much of industry, particularly factory work. However, he presented an optimistic vision of the future. Writing in the early 1960s he reported that chemical process workers (those working in oil refinery and other continuous-process plants) had a much higher degree of autonomy than assembly line workers. He believed the introduction of automated processes could be significant in reducing alienation, even though the worker would, possibly, have no direct contact with the product being made (Blauner 1964). Yet despite his identification of widespread alienation throughout industry, Blauner still reports that:

> [T]he majority of industrial workers are satisfied with their work and with their jobs. (183)

Why do we work? Ethic, social role or dogma?

When we look in depth at all these negative aspects of paid work, we can see why for Baldamus the real question was not why people don't work, but why they work at all.

We have seen how there are many motivations for working and a range of rewards from work. But surrounding these individual factors are much wider, more entrenched and persistent societal attitudes towards work. Our society values work highly, considers laziness and idleness to be bad things, and exhorts us to work hard to be a full member of society. We can say that work is seen as being the norm (although lots of people don't have paid employment) and there is a normative commitment to paid work in our society. Where do these societal values concerning work come from?

This normative commitment is sometimes called the 'work ethic' or the 'Protestant work ethic', after its identification in Max Weber's *The Protestant Ethic and the Spirit of Capitalism* (Weber [1905] 1958). Weber's book had a number of aims, but the central goal was to explain why capitalism rose in Western Europe but nowhere else. For Weber the reason was that the Protestant religious revolution of the seventeenth century brought about a change in ideas of the self and one's relationship to God. Where previously individuals would seek salvation through confessing their sins, the new Protestant doctrines emphasized the need to appear to be chosen through working hard, living frugally and living an unadorned lifestyle. The desire to amass wealth in this culture was quite different from in other societies, where wealth accumulation was seen as a means to an end, making one free from want. The Protestant societies of this time saw wealth as something that indicated one's status as part of the chosen or elect. Therefore, wealth should not be used for luxury or pleasure, but should be reinvested in enterprise.

This spirit of capitalism – making profit, reinvesting and making more profit – emerged from the religious ideas of the time, and became firmly entrenched as the values were embedded in the culture and the economy. Success in work, success in having a vocation and working diligently, became a sign that one was one of the elect, chosen and called by God.

Weber thus provided an explanation for why people work so diligently and why society values work so highly. We internalize our normative commitment to work from a very early age and proceed through life without often questioning it. We are, according to Weber, different people when we internalize these ideas – we become, in his term, *Berufsmensch*, a spiritless 'person of vocation' who follows the work ethic.

Weber's description of the work ethic is a narrow one, and perhaps it is too fatalistic. There is more to proving one's worth than simply turning up for work, and Weber appears to be ignoring the pleasure that can be received from work, particularly craft and creative work. But most commentators agree that 'the work ethic is competitive, requires comparative judgments of worth; those who win may turn a blind eye to those who lose' (Sennett 2003: 58).

The degree of commitment to the work ethic has been questioned by commentators. In the 1980s, with mass unemployment, there were fears that the unemployed would lose their commitment to work and would refuse employment if offered jobs. These fears, although widely broadcast, were unfounded. Indeed, the commitment to work held by the unemployed was actually stronger than those in employment, according to the SCELI research:

> Among employees and the self-employed, 66 per cent would wish to continue working if there were no financial necessity. Among the unemployed, the proportion rises to 77 per cent. The evidence, then, provides no general support for the view that the unemployed have particularly low levels of work commitment. (Gallie et al. 1994: 124–6)

Michael Rose's analysis of these data shows that there is probably more commitment to the work ethic than in previous times, and that men and women at the same skill levels were just as committed. However, a crucial factor in this commitment is level of skill. Of those who considered their job to be skilled, 67 per cent would continue working if there were no financial necessity, compared to 56 per cent of those in unskilled jobs (Rose 1994: 298). Clearly, satisfaction in use and deployment of skill is a key factor in commitment to work.

In contrast, André Gorz argues that our commitment to work is waning, and that it is only an 'elite' of professional workers who carry the burden of the economy who are really focused on their jobs. Were work to be more equally shared out amongst those who want and need it, the level of commitment would drop much further:

> The passion for, devotion to, and identification with work would be diminishing if everyone were able to work less and less. . . . Technically, there is really nothing to prevent the firm from sharing out the work between a larger number of people who would work only 20 hours a week. But then those people would not have the 'correct' attitude to work which consists in regarding themselves as small entrepreneurs turning their knowledge capital to good effect. (Gorz 1999: 45)

Gorz suggests many people have realized that work is not the be-all and end-all of their lives, and he argues that we all need to move away from current harmful patterns of work distribution. Central to this project is the need to 'de-socialize' ourselves away from our commitment to a work ethic and thus to capitalism and consumerism. He advocates a move away from a wage-based society where individuals are set against one another and towards more collective forms of work and production, where value is invested in all, rather than just the paid elite. Individually, we know that we are all potentially unemployed, part-time, under-used, undervalued, insecure, but this individual awareness needs to be replaced with a collective awareness for change to occur: we need to recognize our shared insecurity. There is only one possible outcome, for Gorz, if we are to be a better, more secure, more environmentally aware and responsible society: 'Let us make no mistake about this: wage-labour has to disappear and, with it, capitalism' (Gorz 1999: 77).

The idea that we are committed to work largely through habituation is plausible, but could hide from us some important aspects of attachment to work that Gorz highlights: that our work ethic and commitment serves the purposes of those in power. Without our commitment to work, capitalism could not operate, or at least not in the form we see today. For this reason many commentators on the left describe the promulgation of a work ethic as an ideology – a codified set of ideas that represents the interest of one class and is used to subjugate people by inducing a sense of false consciousness, effectively hiding the reality of the world from people. Debates about ideology dominated social science for much of the last century, often rather unproductively. At the heart of these debates were arguments over *where* such ideologies come from and whether all people would be equally susceptible. Many neo-Marxists have moved away from using the concept of ideology, with its overtones of heavy determination, in favour of more subtle explanations for compliance and lack of resistance.

Stanley Aronowitz and William DiFazio (1994), in their examination of new forms of sci-tech work, use the term 'the dogma of work' to describe the persistence of work ethic and work commitment. Dogma is a good word here. It doesn't suggest singularity, a single set of values or ideas or class location. Their conception of dogma reminds us that work is socially constructed as a need, and internalized by workers as a part of their self-identity. It is not merely the comparative advantage that paid work has over the dole that motivates people to take jobs. Nor does the meaning of work derive entirely from its intrinsic interest: technology increasingly eliminates our skills. Instead, we are driven by the fact that the 'self' is constituted, at least for most of us, by membership in the labour force, as a member of either what they call the 'job bourgeoisie' – the professions – or the working class. Paid work is a socially and psychologically constructed 'need' shared by those who have been successfully habituated to think that the link between holding a job and having 'dignity' is a given.

Dogma suggests permanence, inescapableness, continuity, but also wrongness, and it is the identification of this wrongness of work that frees us up to look at how we might challenge the dogma to bring about better and more equitable ways of working, sharing out opportunities and rewards more fairly.

This theme is taken up by Beck (2000), who argues that the rapid changes in work which have been described in this chapter – particularly the decline of traditional work, the rise of non-standard work, increasing insecurity and risk, and the end of lifetime jobs – must be addressed, but in a way that looks to the future and not the past. Rather than trying to swallow the 'bitter neoliberal medicine' (91) and hope that everything will be fine, Beck argues we need to see work in a much wider social context and consider rethinking how we work. This is for a number of reasons, not least of which is the need for more ecologically sustainable patterns of production and consumption in a world that is rapidly undergoing environmental change.

Many people continue to work in paid employment in some capacity after they retire. Why might this be?

Summary

Work is central to society, organizations and the individual. It is central to the way that value and status are assigned in society, a major component of individual identity, and a necessary thing, be it unpaid or paid. Yet, as we have seen, defining work is difficult: merely saying that work is the same as employment excludes important forms of productive and caring activities and gives us a distorted picture. And even if we do equate work with employment, we need to recognize that employment is changing as society changes, particularly as capitalism becomes more entrenched and pervasive across the globe, and as states privatize enterprises and services. Work is constantly becoming more 'risky': insecure, uncertain and intense.

We keep on working in any case, and sociologists have provided a range of explanations for our motivations. We can see that some people experience a calling to a vocation, while most others feel compelled to work through a combination of financial need, self-fulfilment and habit or tradition. Recent sociological studies of workplaces have shown how some employers are playing on the psychosocial needs of employees to ensure greater commitment, and hopefully higher productivity, through providing a sense of belonging in organizations. Perhaps more common is the increasing requirement for individuals to give more of themselves in their employment; emotional labour, with its debilitating consequences for individuals who continually have to give their emotions as well as their effort, is expanding into more areas of work and organizational life.

Such new negative consequences of work are additional to those identified by sociologists and others through the twentieth century: alienation, boredom, danger and moral challenges are implicit in many forms of work in our society. As work becomes more intense and insecure, these negative consequences are likely to increase: lower pay to achieve greater competitiveness leads to higher stress levels and accident rates.

Work is important to us, and provides us with meaning and a sense of identity. Yet work also presents us with great challenges in terms of its riskiness, particularly when we think we may lose our work, and also in terms of its unfairness, particularly when individuals are badly treated and discriminated against in organizations: we discuss this topic in chapter 8.

Discussion questions

1. Is work a good thing?
2. Are work and employment the same thing?
3. Why do we work? What are your, your family's and your friends' motivations for working?
4. Is your work part of your identity? In what ways?
5. What has brought about the rise in temporary and part-time work?
6. Do recent trends in the organization of work indicate a shift towards individualization?

Further reading

Work has been a significant topic for sociologists since the discipline began, and for this reason there are a lot of books about work and research studies on work. In writing this book we have relied on a range of classic sociological texts to provide details of the main theoretical orientations to work, contemporary research studies and contemporary commentaries on work. A few examples from each may be useful.

Classic sociological texts on work

Baldamus, W. 1961: *Efficiency and Effort. An Analysis of Industrial Administration.* London: Tavistock Publications.

Braverman, H. 1974: *Labour and Monopoly Capital. The Degradation of Work in the Twentieth Century.* New York: Monthly Review Press.

Casey, C. 1995: *Work, Self and Society. After Industrialism.* London: Routledge.

Cockburn, C. 1985: *Machinery of Dominance. Women, Men and Technical Know-how.* London: Pluto Press.

du Gay, P. 1996: *Consumption and Identity at Work.* London: Sage.

Goffman, E. 1959: *The Presentation of Self in Everyday Life.* Harmondsworth: Penguin.

Goldthorpe, J., Lockwood, D., Bechhofer, F. and Platt, J. 1969: *The Affluent Worker in the Class Structure*. Cambridge: Cambridge University Press.

Gouldner, A. W. 1954: *Wildcat Strike. A Study in Worker–Management Relations*. New York: Harper Torchbooks.

Hochschild, A. R. 1983: *The Managed Heart: Commercialization of Human Feeling*. Berkeley: University of California Press.

Oakley, A. 1974: *The Sociology of Housework*. London: Robertson.

Pollert, A. 1981: *Girls, Wives, Factory Lives*. London: Macmillan.

Roy, D. 1960: '"Banana time". Job satisfaction and informal interaction'. *Human Organization*, 18, 4, 158–68.

Witz, A. 1992: *Professions and Patriarchy*. London: Routledge.

Contemporary research studies

The British Sociological Association (BSA) journal *Work, Employment and Society* publishes contemporary studies of work, usually from a sociological perspective. This is the best starting point for studies of emerging and recent forms of work, work organization and employment.

Contemporary commentaries

These books look at recent trends in work and employment and offer a range of analyses. All of the following could be described as 'critical', challenging the dominant ideas of management thinking.

Bauman, Z. 2004: *Wasted Lives: Modernity and its Outcasts*. Cambridge: Polity.

Beck, U. 2000: *The Brave New World of Work*. Cambridge: Polity.

Bradley, H., Erickson, M., Stephenson, C. and Williams, S. 2000: *Myths At Work*. Cambridge: Polity.

Gorz, A. 1999: *Reclaiming Work. Beyond the Wage-Based Society*. Cambridge: Polity.

6 Changing organizations?

This chapter will:

- explore the main features of the bureaucratic approaches to organizations
- introduce the notion of post-bureaucracy
- examine the extent to which there has been a shift from a bureaucratic to a post-bureaucratic paradigm among organizations in contemporary societies
- assess the durability, vitality and adaptability of the bureaucratic form of organization.

Introduction

In this chapter, the first of two that focus on organizations, we are largely concerned with the main ways in which organizations are designed and structured. Our starting point is the nature of the bureaucratic form of organization, rooted in Weber's pioneering sociological analysis which was introduced in the first two chapters. Therefore we start by outlining the main features of bureaucratic organization, consider the implications for the management of labour and present the main criticisms of the bureaucratic approach. Since the 1980s many writers and management gurus have claimed that bureaucracy is on the wane, usurped by the rise of more flexible, dynamic and decentralized organizational arrangements that are more appropriate to changing market and technological contexts. Thus a shift away from the dominance of the bureaucratic organization, towards an emerging **post-bureaucratic** paradigm, has been proposed.

We will examine the main features of post-bureaucratic organizational forms, consider why the post-bureaucracy concept has grown in significance and look at the implications for managing and working in organizations that function in a post-bureaucratic way. However, the extent to which a shift from bureaucracy to post-bureaucracy has occurred is a matter of some debate. We will consider the evidence for the continuing relevance of the bureaucratic form, based on studies that highlight its variability and adaptability under changing circumstances, something that leads us to question the extent of the trend towards post-bureaucracy.

Weber and the nature of bureaucratic organization

The work of the German sociologist Max Weber has exercised a pro-found influence over studies of organizations. Writing in the early years of the twentieth century, just as large-scale companies were beginning to dominate the advanced economies of Europe and North America, Weber pioneered the analysis of organizations as social entities. Perhaps Weber's main contribution was to emphasize the importance of bureaucracy in modern societies. He considered it 'the most impor-tant social invention of the modern period' (Ackroyd 2002: 17).

As we saw in chapter 1, Weber was particularly concerned with the nature of authority in societies. Bureaucratic organization is under-pinned by rational–legal authority. Weber was interested in how managers, administrators and other office-holders could legitimately issue commands, and expect compliance from their subordinates. Thus 'obedience is owed to the legally established impersonal order. It extends to the persons exercising the authority of office under it only by virtue of the formal legality of their commands and only within the scope of authority of the office' (Weber 1947: 328). In other words, we obey the commands of a policeman, a headmaster or a doctor because of the *role* which they embody, not because of their individuality.

Weber never advanced a specific definition of bureaucracy. However, he did articulate the features of an 'ideal-type' bureaucracy, distin-guishing it from the more general usage of the term to describe any organization that is administered by appointed specialist officials. (The formation and use of ideal types in social analysis is discussed in chap-ter 1.) What are the main features of Weber's ideal-type bureaucratic organization? Among other things, they include:

* the presence of a clear hierarchy 'of offices', that is of the positions in the organization
* the specialization of job roles among the managers and administra-tors who are the holders of those positions
* the importance of impersonal considerations in reaching decisions
* the widespread use of formal rules and procedures to govern the conduct of office holders
* formal processes to appoint people to offices.

Perhaps the main distinguishing feature of bureaucratic organization is the attempt to co-ordinate and control organizational activities through the use of hierarchies (such as lines of management) and rules. Weber was convinced of the superiority of the pure type of bureaucratic organization. It is, 'from a purely technical point of view, capable of attaining the highest degree of efficiency and is in this sense formally the most rational known means of carrying out imperative control over human beings' (Weber 1947: 337). We examined the concept of rationality in chapter 2. With regard to the ideal-type bureaucracy, rationality implies that organizations will choose the most logical

Even social institutions that have a traditional hierarchy and authority, such as the army, have become increasingly bureaucratic in recent years.

and efficient means for realizing their goals. This is exemplified by the important role played by formal rules and procedures in providing impersonal and objective criteria for determining organizational action and making decisions.

Formal rules proliferate in organizations. A considerable amount of management time is devoted to devising new rules, and amending existing ones, for dealing with matters such as sickness absence, equal opportunities, bullying and harassment, health and safety, confidentiality, data protection and so on. As Kersley et al. (2006) state, formal procedures for dealing with employee grievances and for disciplining and dismissing staff have become almost ubiquitous in large organizations. When you start a new job, you are likely to undergo an induction which will introduce these procedures to you. The proliferation of rules and procedures has also contributed to the growth of Human Resources departments, discussed elsewhere in this book.

The existence of formal rules and procedures serves managerial interests in a number of important ways. They prescribe acceptable standards of conduct and behaviour to be expected from staff. Moreover, by reducing the scope for arbitrary managerial action, they also provide for greater fairness, consistency and transparency in management decision-making, all of which can help to secure the co-operation of the workforce. Formal rules and procedures are a highly productive way of effecting managerial control over employees, not least because their presence can help to legitimate managerial decision-making. Opposition to controversial decisions, such as the dismissal of a popular member of staff for example, may be forestalled if they are seen to be the outcome of an apparently fair and transparent procedure.

Weber's interest in bureaucracy both inspired, and has to be seen in the context of, related efforts to highlight the rational character of organizations and the implications for how they are managed. Such 'classical' approaches to understanding organizations and management dominated the field of organization studies during the first half of the twentieth century. Among other things, they emphasized the importance of formal command and control structures and rigid hierarchies of authority. Organizations were thus seen mainly as 'machines' for realizing their objectives.

Weber's writings on the nature of bureaucratic organization were a major influence on, for example, Henri Fayol's administrative theory of management. Fayol elaborated five elements – planning, organizing, commanding, co-ordination and control – and fourteen principles of general management, which included an emphasis on the importance of specialized job roles (Fayol 1949). Other examples include the work of the American economist Alfred Chandler who stressed the importance of formal structures of command and control to the success of the large, vertically integrated and rigidly hierarchical corporations which dominated the economy of the United States during the middle part of the twentieth century (Chandler 1962).

While Weber's theory of bureaucracy was essentially concerned with the structure and administration of organizations, within his work there is also an implied recognition that in order to maximize efficiency managers need to exercise control over their workforce (Brown 1992). In chapter 4 we examined another perspective in the classical tradition, the concept of scientific management pioneered in the early years of the twentieth century by Frederick Taylor. The purpose of the scientific management approach was to rationalize work and how it is managed (Wilson 2004). Weber's theory of bureaucracy and Taylor's concept of scientific management therefore reinforce one another; the former's concern with the administration and design of organizations being complemented by the latter's emphasis on the desirability of exercising control over the workforce.

This emphasis on securing control over labour as a managerial priority, particularly through the use of scientific management techniques, shifts our attention away from the insights accorded by Weber to the relevance of a Marxist perspective on organizations and management. In chapter 4 we assessed the contribution of Braverman. Whereas Taylor advocated the rationalization of labour for reasons of efficiency, for Braverman its consequences were the degradation of work and the exploitation, deskilling and impoverishment of those charged with undertaking it (Braverman 1974). This resulted in the kinds of negative aspects of work we looked at in chapter 5 and confirms Marx's ideas about alienated labour.

Also writing from a Marxist perspective, Edwards (1979) maintains that the exercise of control over labour is the primary concern of managers in large enterprises. But he rejects the view that this is achieved through the simple application of scientific management techniques. Instead, control is effected by means of an array of bureaucratic rules and procedures. These are used to manage labour: selection procedures, promotion ladders, machinery for handling grievances and disciplinary matters, remuneration arrangements and so on. The importance of the bureaucratic organizational form cannot be properly appreciated without acknowledging the implications for management control over labour.

As an organizational form, bureaucracy, with its emphasis on rules, hierarchy, efficiency, order and control, is the institutional expression of rationalizing tendencies in modern societies. Given its rational character, Weber reckoned that bureaucracy would become an ever more important feature of modern societies. Since it made possible the efficient production of goods and services on a large scale, the spread of the ideal-type bureaucratic organization was inevitable. Yet Weber himself was decidedly ambivalent about the consequences of **bureaucratization**; he did not necessarily approve of it, voicing concerns about its potentially adverse effects, most notably the alienating and de-humanizing consequences of working within an impersonal and strictly regimented 'iron cage' of bureaucratic rationality (Grey 2005). In this he came close to Marx's ideas, though he emphasized strongly that office workers were just as deprived of control as their factory counterparts in the industrial sector.

The notion that rationalization is a pervasive trend in contemporary societies is central to Ritzer's concept of McDonaldization (Ritzer 2004). Writing from a Weberian perspective, he argues that the way in which the fast-food chain McDonald's operates exemplifies the process of rationalization that characterizes contemporary societies. This is based around four key principles: efficiency, predictability, calculability and control. With regard to efficiency, McDonald's and other organizations operate in a highly streamlined way with an emphasis on delivering their products as quickly, and with as little effort, as possible. A limited set of menu options helps. McDonald's and other service providers also offer a highly predictable experience. People 'want to know that when they order their Big Mac today it will be identical to the one they ate yesterday and the one they will eat tomorrow' (Ritzer 2004: 86). The principle of calculability refers to the emphasis on the quantity of a product, such as a quarter-pounder burger, rather than its quality. Finally, a lot of the success of McDonald's, and companies like it, rests upon the control which they exercise over their employees and customers. With the help of technology, the jobs of McDonald's workers have been deskilled, removing any scope for judgement or discretion. They are given a minute set of instructions for how to prepare, cook and serve their burgers or chicken nuggets.

Ritzer also maintains that the rationality evident in the way that McDonald's organizes its activities is, ironically, a source of irrationality. The emphasis on efficiency, for example, has seen at least one drive-in McDonald's customer in the UK incur a parking fine for spending too long consuming his meal in the establishment's car park, something that is hardly consistent with the supposed importance to contemporary businesses of generating consumer satisfaction.

Ritzer's concept of McDonaldization has been widely discussed, and extended to many other areas of contemporary social life, including

Call centres often afford no scope for variation to employees who must follow a script. This can be an irrational choice for the company, since it can create many angry customers!

Box 6.1 The McDonaldization of sex?

The McDonaldization concept has been extended to various aspects of contemporary social life, including the sex industry. There is an efficiency rationale underlying the consumption of 'fast-food sex'. In the United States, for example, brothels operate in a highly rationalized manner, governed by rules and rituals that enhance the profitability of the commercialized sexual encounter. In the phone sex sector, companies deploy scripts or guides 'that direct the phone sex worker to say certain things in particular ways in order to generate the highest fees from the customer' (Hausbeck and Brents 2006: 105).

The sex industry is also underpinned by a predictability rationale, with the standardization of the sexual encounter being a primary consideration. This is evident in the common layout of strip clubs and lap-dancing establishments for example. The aesthetics and language of pornography, moreover, are highly standardized. There is 'a language of pleasure and desire scripted into the plot line (however simplistic it may be), encoded in the camera angles, and reinforced by the soundtracks' (2006: 109).

The exercise of control is a notable feature of how the sex industry operates. Sophisticated information technology permits managers to monitor closely the activities of their sex workers. Medical technology enables greater control over the appearance of sex workers. Thus diversity 'in women's bodies can be reined in – fat cut off here, implants added there, scars removed, makeup permanently added' (2006: 112). Finally, the way in which the sex industry operates is marked by a considerable degree of calculability. See, for example, the importance ascribed to the quantification of sex – the size of a man's penis for example, or the dimensions of a woman's breasts – in the commercialized sex encounter. The McDonaldization of sex is important because it highlights the spread of rationalizing tendencies into the most personal and intimate aspects of human behaviour.

But the McDonaldization of the sex industry has important limits. The profitability of sex as a commodity is to a large degree predicated upon irrationality, the appearance of intimacy for example, something that by its nature is unpredictable, and not liable to control and quantification. This suggests that for commercial reasons rationalization is not entirely desirable.

agriculture and higher education, as well as the sex industry (see box 6.1). It has also been subjected to considerable critical scrutiny. One major problem with the McDonaldization concept concerns its inherent pessimism. It proposes the development of an ever-tightening straitjacket of rationality and ignores the way that social actors – whether as citizens, consumers or workers – resist and challenge it. They are treated as though they are dupes who are easily pliable and manipulated by coercive corporations. Another criticism of the McDonaldization concept is that it represents a form of cultural conservatism, harking back nostalgically to an earlier era before the arrival of giant corporations. Yet there is a valid argument which says that the activities of large multinational corporations like McDonalds have given many hundreds of millions of people access to goods and services that they would otherwise never have enjoyed. These criticisms notwithstanding, at the very least it is clear that the McDonaldization concept, and the debate which it has provoked, says a lot about the vitality of Weber's ideas about rational–legal authority, bureaucratic organization and rationalization, and their continuing relevance to interpreting developments in contemporary societies.

Critiques of bureaucratic organization

Perhaps the main criticism of Weber's ideal-type bureaucratic organization, despite its theoretical strength and prophetic power, is that it is just that, an 'ideal type', a model that does not exist in practice for the simple reason that its consequences are so unappealing, meaning that people tend to develop deviations from it. So the idea that rational bureaucracy, of the kind envisaged by Weber, is necessarily the most efficient way of designing organizations has been challenged by writers concerned with the 'dysfunctional' characteristics of bureaucratic organization, the negative features of delays, frustrations and 'red tape'.

One strand of this literature is concerned with the adverse effects of bureaucratic organization. Strictly following the provisions of the rulebook may actually compromise organizational effectiveness. This is because administrators and some managers may view the execution of rules and procedures as their main objective, rather than looking to see if they are consistent with enhancing organizational effectiveness. This 'goal displacement', as social scientists call it, is commonplace in organizations. The management of sickness absence in organizations illustrates goal displacement in action. There is an increasing concern with reducing sickness absence levels, using tools such as return-to-work interviews, where managers hold a meeting with the worker concerned after every instance of absence. Managers, however, have a tendency to perceive return-to-work interviews as an unavoidable chore, demonstrating that the interview has taken place as required by the procedure, and not as an effective means of identifying and tackling absence issues. This can also lead to tensions between people in different positions in the organization, in this case between HR staff and the line managers required to carry out the extra work.

Too narrow a concern with following the rules and procedures can have adverse organizational consequences for another reason. Trade unions often use 'work-to-rule' because it is a highly effective form of industrial action. Given the extent to which organizations rely on the co-operation of their staff, simply following the rules can be highly disruptive. The case of school-teaching is a good example of how a work-to-rule can disrupt organizational effectiveness. During the 1980s, as part of a dispute over pay and conditions, teachers in England and Wales operated a work-to-rule, working strictly to the provisions of their employment contracts. Such behaviour resulted in major disruption to school sports events and other extra-curricular activities, which had hitherto been supported by the goodwill of teachers going beyond what they were obliged to do by their contracts.

On its own, the enactment of bureaucratic rules and procedures does not necessarily maximize organizational effectiveness. This points us towards another problem. Decisions are often made in organizations in ways that depart from the principles of the ideal-type bureaucracy. Frequently, rules and procedures are not the outcome of rational processes of decision-making; rather they reflect imbalances of power between different sectional groups within organizations (as in the sickness interview example).

Gouldner (1954a) was concerned with the difference between the content of the formal rules and procedures and what actually happens in practice in organizations. He identified three types of rules. 'Punishment-centred' rules are ones devised and used by managers for the purposes of directing and controlling the behaviour of staff, who are liable to sanctions should they transgress. Rules governing misconduct at work are examples of this type. 'Representative' rules are those which are accepted, and regarded as legitimate, by managers and workers. While rules concerning health and safety matters often come into this category, managers may sometimes adopt a more punishment-centred approach in this area. 'Mock' rules are those that are not taken seriously by either managers or workers and are, as a result, largely ignored.

Perhaps the most significant aspect of Gouldner's contribution was his identification of the 'indulgency pattern' as a characteristic feature of organizational life. This term refers to situations where managers tolerate, or indulge, breaches of formal rules. A good example is the behaviour of the hotel and restaurant staff in a study undertaken by Harris and Ogbonna (2002). Their actions, which included deliberately compromising hygiene standards, by putting dirt in food for example, clearly contravened organizational rules. However, managers tolerated such behaviour, recognizing the likely adverse effects on motivation and co-operation if they were not to do so. This kind of indulgency is particularly likely to occur in areas such as hotel work, where pay is poor and staff turnover is high and it may be hard to recruit new employees.

Informal and tacit understandings that arise between workers, and between workers and managers, are therefore an important effect on behaviour at work. There can be important differences between the rhetoric of organizational policy and the reality of day-to-day life in organizations. See, for example, the use of policies for promoting equal opportunities (EO) in organizations. These are becoming increasingly commonplace; according to Kersley et al. (2006) nearly three-quarters of UK workplaces have an EO policy in place. Yet they are often of limited effectiveness in challenging inequality and disadvantage at work, generally because there are few interventions in place to support them.

We should mention two other important critiques of bureaucratic organization. First, during the twentieth century there arose a concern about the de-humanizing effects of large-scale bureaucracies. The emphasis on impersonal rules, procedures and structures, and the lack of recognition given to individuals, personal relationships and emotions, were thought to have adverse consequences, perhaps extreme ones. For example, Zygmunt Bauman (1989) argued that the Nazi holocaust was a logical expression of bureaucratic organization. It was implemented by means of a highly intricate set of formal arrangements that involved the recording and rounding-up of Jews and other groups, sophisticated transportation facilities and the organization of gas chambers, all of which enabled mass murder to be instigated on an unprecedented scale.

On a more mundane level, the de-humanizing effects of bureaucracy pose challenges for managers in organizations. Narrow job roles, highly specialized work tasks, hierarchical relationships, and detailed rules and procedures all conspire to reduce the motivation, morale and satisfaction of workers. Huw Beynon's study of Ford car workers, which was undertaken in the late 1960s, gives an insight into the alienating effects of working in a large-scale, mass-production-based industrial bureaucracy. One worker expressed a determination to quit his job for this reason:

> I *will* leave soon. It's getting me down. It's so monotonous, tedious, boring. I was just going to make a convenience of Ford's for a few months but I'm still here. Not for much longer though. Yes: I'm leaving soon. I'm not happy here. I'm definitely not going to stay for much longer. (Beynon 1973: 118)

Second, we must also recognize the important feminist critique of bureaucratic organization. There is no room for gender in Weber's rational–legal model of bureaucracy; organizations are assumed to be gender-neutral. Such an approach poses a problem, however. How does one explain the persistence of gender inequality in organizations, such as the failure of women to reach senior leadership positions to anything like the extent to which men have? For liberal feminists, such as Kanter (1977), ongoing gender disadvantage occurs because bureaucratic arrangements in organizations do not operate sufficiently and effectively and can be subverted or ignored. More rigorous procedures for handling equal opportunities in selection and promotion decisions would erode the privileged position of men. This position has been challenged by more radical feminist writers such as Pringle (1989) who believe that bureaucratic procedures are in practice biased towards the interests of men although they purport to be 'impersonal' and 'objective'. For example, banking promotion procedures used to require employees to move between different branches, often in different parts of the country, which posed difficulties for married women who were unable to move because of domestic ties.

Both liberal and radical feminist perspectives have their uses. On the one hand, the presence of bureaucratic arrangements, particularly formal equality and diversity policies, potentially challenges gender disadvantage at work. On the other hand, we have already seen that equal opportunities policies often lack teeth. As a result, their existence may legitimize the persistence of gender inequality by giving the misleading impression that it is being tackled when, in reality, as Linda Dickens' research has shown (2000) many managers only pay 'lip service' to it and continue to discriminate in favour of men.

Post-bureaucratic organization

There is nothing new about critiques of bureaucratic organization. In the last section we examined the concept of bureaucratic dysfunctionalism, questioning the existence of the 'ideal-type' bureaucracy and also its desirability. It has long been recognized, moreover, that the development of the bureaucratic form during the twentieth century was by no means a universal tendency. In their famous book *The Management of Innovation*, Burns and Stalker (1961) distinguished between 'mechanistic' and 'organic' firms. Whereas the former were organized and structured according to classic bureaucratic principles, the latter, mainly small firms operating in highly competitive markets, functioned with a much greater degree of flexibility, fluidity and informality, at odds with the ideal-type model of bureaucracy.

Moreover, bureaucratic organization itself is not monolithic. During the 1950s and 1960s, an influential group of writers and researchers, such as Woodward (1965) and Pugh and Hickson (1976) proposed, on the basis of extensive empirical research, that the structural characteristics of organizations varied according to the nature of their product market, their size and also the sophistication of the technology they employed. This 'contingency' approach to understanding organizational structure argued for the existence of alternative types of bureaucratic organization. Within the prevailing overall framework of bureaucracy, there were different ways of designing and structuring organizations. They might have relatively 'tall' or relatively 'flat' hierarchies, for example, but still be structured according to broadly bureaucratic principles. Contingency perspectives emphasize variations in bureaucratic organization, rather than the predominance of one particular approach.

However, since the 1980s many influential management writers and organizational theorists have suggested that conventional bureaucratic organizational forms are becoming, or will become, obsolete. Scholars such as Child and McGrath (2001) argue that new 'post-bureaucratic' organizations and ways of managing have been emerging in response to current business needs. They focus on the characteristics and implications of post-bureaucratic organization and management (2001), which, its proponents claim, is 'sweeping through the business world, leaving no organization untouched by its powerful force' (Williams 2007: 170). In this section we provide an overview of the post-bureaucracy concept. We will also explore three main forms of post-bureaucratic organization – inter-organizational networks, network enterprises and virtual organizations – before going on to consider the implications for businesses and for work.

Post-bureaucratic organization: an overview

What are the main features of post-bureaucratic organizations? To some extent, the concept of post-bureaucracy has been elaborated as an explicit reaction against the bureaucratic paradigm, and so is defined by its opposition to bureaucracy, rather than as a discrete phenomenon in its own right. Perhaps the most influential effort to specify the characteristics of the 'ideal-type' post-bureaucratic organization has come from the US management writer Charles Heckscher (1994). Among other things, he identified:

- an emphasis on sharing information
- an assumption that people's careers would not be restricted to one organization
- co-ordination is predicated upon broad principles, rather than specific rules
- the importance of trust relationships
- consensus is generated through dialogue between organizational actors, not obedience to impersonal authority embodied in formal rules.

Heckscher is careful to emphasize that his ideal-type post-bureaucratic model is a construct: something that, at the time he was writing, did not exist in its entirety. Yet certain trends, developments and practices that he identified, such as the rise of team-working arrangements, led him to believe that a shift towards post-bureaucracy was not only happening, but also inevitable.

What factors have prompted the development of post-bureaucratic organizational forms? One key influence has been the rise of an anti-bureaucratic ethos among the leaders of large corporations, originating in the United States. The existence of a 'broad bureaucracy busting movement in US corporations' (Adler 1999: 36) is exemplified by the determination of chief executives, such as General Electric's Jack Welch, to eradicate whole layers of organizational hierarchies, and the middle management jobs that once filled them. The 'excellence' literature associated with management 'gurus' Peters and Waterman (1982) encourages organizations to develop more entrepreneurial forms of governance in order to secure greater flexibility. This involves removing the constraints posed by rigid and inflexible bureaucratic decision-making structures. If managers are to improve the performance of their organizations, they need to abandon established way of doing things and 'throw away the organizational rule book' (Grey and Garsten 2001). The principles of bureaucracy are no longer considered as beneficial for organizations as they once were. Instead, success is determined by an organization's ability to respond quickly to business needs, its flexibility and its capacity for innovation.

A series of new models for managing organizations has emerged, all of which, it is claimed, provide a template for re-designing organizations in a way that dissolves bureaucratic structures. The **Business Process Re-engineering (BPR)** approach developed by Hammer and Champy (1993) is perhaps the most notable example. They suggest that organizational goals are best achieved by re-designing them so that the

Increasing numbers of organizations – especially those in creative industries – claim to be breaking down the rigid structures of bureaucracy.

focus is on operating processes that add value to the firm, by meeting the needs of customers, avoiding hierarchy and unwieldy decision-making procedures.

The 'war against bureaucracy' (Grey 2005) that has been waged in organizations also needs to be seen in the context of two sets of factors; first, economic change, notably the diminution of standardized, mass markets and the rise of more specialized, differentiated ones; and second, the influence of the sophisticated new forms of information technology, which we discussed in chapter 3. As we saw in chapter 4, the last decades of the twentieth century witnessed the decline of standardized mass markets associated with the Fordist period, and the rise of increasingly differentiated markets for more specialized products characteristic of post-Fordism. This was seen to imply the break-up of the huge vertically integrated corporations that had hitherto dominated economic life into more decentralized units, and a revival of small firms, which were better capable of adapting to, and thriving in, more uncertain, specialized markets (Piore and Sabel 1984). Managers were encouraged to adapt to the changing circumstances by re-designing organizations to render them more flexible.

The most well-known approach was Atkinson's (1984) model of the **flexible firm**. He suggested that firms would benefit from organizing their workers into 'core' and 'peripheral' categories. Functional flexibility would be achieved by employing a group of highly skilled, well-remunerated and secure 'core' employees who can move from task to task relatively smoothly. Around the core rests a peripheral group of workers whose flexibility comes from being more easily disposable, including part-time staff, employees on fixed-term contracts, agency workers and self-employed sub-contractors. Their numbers can be adjusted to meet variations in demand, thus insulating the core employees from losing their jobs.

There are numerous problems with the flexible firm model. For one thing, it is not clear whether it was advanced as a description of organizational practice, as a programme for organizational trans-formation, or as a prediction of how organizations would inevitably change, three conceptually different approaches (Pollert 1988). Did the flexible firm really exist? The distinction drawn between so-called 'core' and 'peripheral' workers is also very crude, with little evidence for it in practice. However, Bradley suggests there is evidence in recent research that businesses have come to see 'flexibility' as necessary and important, even if their attachment to it is sometimes more rhetorical than real, and many firms do adopt some aspects of flexibility, if not the whole package as set out in Atkinson's model (Bradley 1999; 2009).

New technology, particularly the implications of sophisticated information technology, has also contributed to the post-bureau-cratic trend. While, in bureaucratic organizations, the co-ordination of activities is achieved through hierarchies of managerial decision-making, this is a role increasingly undertaken by advanced forms of ICT. As we discussed in chapter 3, ICT is seen to be of central impor-tance to the development of a knowledge-based economy and the rise of knowledge-intensive firms, for whom information and knowledge are key sources of competitive advantage. There is a widely held view that rigid and restrictive bureaucratic structures are inappropriate for firms that look to derive economic success from knowledge-based assets.

The rise of post-bureaucratic organization has been linked to broader social change associated with the shift to postmodernity (see chapters 1 and 2). Whereas bureaucracy and rationalization were seen by Weber as fundamental to the project of modernity, some sociologists of organizations assert that the development of post-bureaucratic, or in their terms 'postmodern', organizations is a key feature of postmoder-nity. For Clegg (1990), a key distinction is that in the era of modernity organizational structure was rigid, while under conditions of postmo-dernity it becomes flexible. Postmodern organizations differ from their modern counterparts in other significant respects. There is a diminu-tion of rules, hierarchies and formal structures, paving the way for more democratic and participative relations. Reed presents the argument in the following way: if 'modern organizations are constructed around a culture of repression and control, then their postmodern counter-parts are thought to generate a culture of expression and involvement within which autonomy, participation and disagreement are openly encouraged' (Reed 1992: 229). This definition is striking and thought-provoking, but perhaps idealized. What we have seen of contemporary workplaces so far in this book does not suggest that disagreement and autonomy are welcomed. It may be that there is an element of wish-fulfilment in the writings of post-bureaucracy theorists!

Forms of post-bureaucratic organization

We have already discussed the tendency for the term 'post-bureaucracy' to be used as an umbrella label for a diverse range of developments. In this section we focus on three principal forms of post-bureaucratic organization: inter-organizational networks; the network enterprise; and the virtual organizational form.

Ashkenas et al. (1995) hold that one of the main features of post-bureaucracy is the 'boundaryless' character of organizations. Firms co-operate with one another in more sustained ways to produce goods or deliver services, making the conventional organization, as a discrete, self-contained entity, increasingly redundant. Key trends include the use of sophisticated supply, or value, chains of more than one organization in the production of goods and services; the consolidation of market share by means of strategic alliances between businesses; joint ventures, particularly when entering new markets or developing new products; and the outsourcing of activities that were once undertaken by organizations on an in-house basis. All this is a stark contrast with the self-contained nature of bureaucratic organizations whose boundaries were fixed and relatively impermeable.

Great importance is assigned to the 'network' metaphor as a means of understanding contemporary organizational forms. Co-ordination of economic activities is realized, not through the price mechanism as in a market, nor by means of hierarchy as under bureaucracy, but through co-operative networks of inter-organizational relationships. The network mode of organization is seen to possess a number of key advantages: it facilitates co-operation, encouraging knowledge transfer; it enables businesses to share the risks of innovation; and it also permits greater flexibility, generating efficiency savings. The way in which sports footwear company Nike operates exemplifies the network form. Research, design and marketing activities it does itself, but production is undertaken by means of a complex, multi-level network of suppliers.

The trend towards outsourcing in the UK is a good example of the development of inter-organizational networks as a way to co-ordinate economic activity. For many years, organizations have entered into arrangements with outside firms to deliver certain non-core services, particularly cleaning and building maintenance, catering and security functions. Companies such as Compass, for example, and Group 4, grew rapidly as specialist providers of catering and security services to firms that found it more efficient not to organize them on an in-house basis. Such outsourcing, though, has now become commonplace in the UK. A major survey of workplaces found that 93 per cent of them outsourced at least one type of service; half of them outsourced four or more services (White et al. 2004: 25). See box 6.2 for details of how some organizations have outsourced aspects of the HRM functions.

Box 6.2 Outsourcing the management of human resources

The process of outsourcing business activities has spread to aspects of how people are managed. Some organizations have relinquished elements of their human resource management (HRM) work, preferring to buy them in from specialist external providers. Perhaps the most notable example of this trend concerns the BBC. In 2006 it outsourced many of its human resource services, including recruitment activities, pay administration and occupational health facilities, to the business services group Capita. The BBC claimed that the resulting efficiency savings would enable more money to be invested in programme making. Some firms, including Brakes, the catering supply company, and Pickfords, the removals company, have outsourced aspects of their absence management arrangements to an external provider, the specialist healthcare company AHP. Instead of notifying their manager that they cannot attend work, sick workers are obliged to contact the qualified nurses used by AHP who are available 24 hours a day, 365 days a year. As a result, any medical issues relating to the absence can be more effectively recorded, perhaps making staff who are fit to attend work more reluctant to claim they are sick.

While the development of inter-organizational networks is one manifestation of post-bureaucracy in practice, firms themselves are also said to be increasingly restructuring themselves on network principles. In bureaucratic organizations, co-ordination is achieved through hierarchical decision-making structures. The rise of the *network enterprise*, however, is facilitated by the availability of sophisticated forms of information technology. This makes it possible for businesses to be leaner and flatter with boundaries between departments eroded; cross-functional teams come together to work on specific projects. Team working is a crucial component of the post-bureaucratic network organization, implying that job roles are less specialized. Ackroyd (2002) points out that the use of IT allows large companies to decentralize and disperse their activities to a greater degree, with the monitoring and control functions carried out by a relatively small number of staff in the corporate centre.

Firms, then, are increasingly re-organizing themselves as horizontal networks of decentralized economic activity, as opposed to the vertical, hierarchical model characteristics of traditional bureaucracy. Manuel Castells, who is the major theorist of what he calls 'the network society', points to the main advantages of the network enterprise, which contribute to its current dominance. These are its capacity to generate and process information efficiently, its adaptability, its flexibility, and also the ease with which it helps to promote innovation (Castells 2000). Successful firms such as Cisco Systems, Nokia and fashion retailer Zara re-arranged themselves on network principles and benefited as a result.

Finally, there has also been an increasing amount of interest in the development of 'virtual' corporations or organizations. Whereas sophisticated forms of information technology make a key contribution to the concept of the network enterprise, supporting and facilitating the co-ordination of activities, the virtual organization is, in effect, totally transformed by ICT. Thus 'a central idea is that computer coordination becomes so important to an organization that the organizational structure is actually changed from being a set of processes coordinated by human beings (which technology supports) to one coordinated by technology (which human beings support)' (Ackroyd 2002: 174). Examples of virtual organization in practice include firms whose business model is dominated by online activities, such as social networking sites Friends Reunited, Facebook and MySpace.

What are the principal characteristics of the virtual organization? Perhaps the main feature is its lack of physical assets. In contrast to the emphasis on tangible formal structures, hierarchies, rules and processes seen in the bureaucratic model of organization, the virtual organization relies more heavily on intangibles, like knowledge, that can be stored, processed and manipulated electronically. There is also an assumption that traditional physical locations of work, like offices, are rendered unnecessary by developments in IT. Work can be undertaken from a variety of locations, such as from home, or on the move. Nohria and Berkley (1994: 115) elaborate the main features of the 'ideal-type' virtual organization. They include:

- electronic arrangements for storing data, with no need for physical files
- dependence on electronic communications for co-ordinating activities
- blurring of inter-organizational boundaries such that it becomes difficult to determine where one organization ends and another begins
- disappearance of narrow, specialized job roles, since, with the help of ICT, they are made redundant by the spread of cross-functional team working.

Yet we need to be wary about claims for the existence of virtual organizations. Even firms whose business model seems to depend upon virtuality, such as the retailer Amazon, rely heavily upon tangible, physical assets, such as warehouses. Instead of focusing on whether or not the virtual organization exists in practice, perhaps it is better to examine the degree to which organizations in general have embraced virtuality in their operations. Warner and Witzel (2004) point out that most organizations mix physicality with virtuality, albeit to varying degrees. All 'conventional' organizations possess a 'virtual dimension' to their activities. A company like the giant retailer Tesco, for example, uses sophisticated IT systems for all sorts of purposes from stock replenishment to market research. Yet its business model depends upon the management of evidently physical assets, including its net-work of distribution centres, stores and their contents. While virtuality may be influencing business practice, the arrival of the virtual organi-zation is not imminent just yet.

Managing and working in the post-bureaucratic organization

What are the implications of post-bureaucracy for managing and working in organizations? Proponents of post-bureaucratic organiza-tional change contend that, in contrast to bureaucratic organizations, which were managed using hierarchical decision-making structures to ensure that workers complied with formal rules, managers in post-bureaucratic organizations prefer to concentrate on building trust relations. Thompson (2005) argues that, with the absence of hierarchies, and in the context of an increasingly knowledge-driven economy, trust is seen as a particularly effective way of co-ordinating activities between and within organizations. Trust is essential to the effective operation of co-operative inter-organizational networks, for example. Collaboration, knowledge-sharing and mutual learning can only be effectively realized if the parties in a network can rely on and co-operate with each other. See box 6.3, however, for a case study of the absence of trust in an inter-organizational network.

The post-bureaucracy thesis also states that relations between man-agers and their subordinates within organizations have become more trust-based. The reduction of hierarchies, the decreasing significance of formal rules and procedures and the trend towards broader job roles

Box 6.3 Missing trust in an inter-organizational network

One cannot assume that relations between firms in an inter-organizational network will necessarily be marked by high levels of trust and co-operation. See, for example, the case of the airport studied by Rubery et al. (2003). A number of different organizations – including airlines, handling agents and the airport operator itself – collaborated to deliver airport services. Yet relations between them were riddled by tensions and conflict, demonstrating a lack of trust, as each sought to reduce its own costs, while at the same time working towards a common goal.

Similarly, the supermarket Waitrose and its affiliated home-delivery service provider Ocado have clashed over Ocado's decision to undercut Waitrose on some goods, and Waitrose's decision to start its own home delivery service in competition with Ocado. 'They are a pain in the arse to deal with at the corporate level', said Ocado's head of finance and marketing, Jason Gissing; 'They don't speak with one voice' (J. Finch, 2008: 'Ocado plans expansion after delivering first £1bn of sales' *Guardian*, Monday 21 July 2008).

mean that work in post-bureaucratic organizations is more humane and satisfying than under bureaucratic arrangements. Workers in the post-bureaucratic organization are more trusted, and, since they enjoy greater scope to become involved and participate in decision-making, are increasingly 'empowered'.

In contrast to bureaucratic organizations, where managers seek to secure the compliance of their subordinates by enforcing obedience to formal rules, under post-bureaucracy this is supplanted by a concern with articulating a shared culture. What do we mean by '**organizational culture**'? It comprises the unwritten, tacit and informal norms, values and beliefs that influence behaviour in organizations. When we join an organization, whether it is a finance company, a sports club or a university, we pick up these unwritten rules from our workmates or colleagues and by observing how people behave, 'how things are done around here'. Organizational culture, then, is intangible; it is influenced by the symbols and stories that mark everyday life in organizations. Since the 1980s, management and business writers have emphasized the benefits of explicitly managing culture as a tool for securing competitive advantage (Peters and Waterman 1982), by winning the 'hearts and minds' of their workers (Kunda 1992; Willmott 1993), and thus gaining their commitment to organizational objectives.

Yet we need to be careful not to assume that the experience of work in the post-bureaucratic organization is better for workers than it is under bureaucratic arrangements. The absence of formal rules and procedures, for example, may increase the propensity for managers to make unfair and arbitrary decisions. A more important criticism, however, concerns the limited evidence for any shift towards a substantially more empowered workforce, suggesting that on this measure at least claims about the advance of post-bureaucracy need to be treated with caution.

Proponents of the post-bureaucracy thesis emphasize its liberating consequences for workers. Bureaucratic organizations are marked by an emphasis on internal career ladders, hierarchical management and narrow, specialized job roles. Under post-bureaucracy, however, it is suggested that workers enjoy more opportunities to shape their own careers and, in the absence of the rigid constraints imposed by bureaucratic structures, hierarchies and rules, have more scope to participate in decision-making. Work in post-bureaucratic organizations also takes place in more diverse locations (see box 6.4).

Box 6.4 The spatial elements of post-bureaucratic organization

A further aspect of post-bureaucracy concerns changes in the spatial organization of work activities. Office workers are commonly based in open-plan, collective offices. Many organizations have instituted 'hot-desking' arrangements whereby individual workers do not have their own dedicated work station; rather they are allocated one when they arrive at their firm's premises. For Felstead and Jewson (2005), collective offices symbolize the post-bureaucratic organization, as the changes in the spatial organization of work reflect and encourage greater cross-functional working, interchangeable job roles, team working and attenuated job hierarchies. Also, developments in information technology permit increasing numbers of people to work from home, or on the move. The ubiquity of mobile phones, the growth of fast, broad-band internet connections and the extensive use of electronic mail arrangements enable many work activities that were previously tied to particular office locations to be undertaken anywhere.

It is claimed that such changes render traditional bureaucratic forms of managerial control redundant. Greater trust between managers and workers leads to greater freedom for employees to work outside the office, free from the direct control of supervisors. Organizations that are marked by the extensive use of opportunities to work from home or on the move rely instead on post-bureaucratic forms of maintaining control, based on the establishment of strong cultures (Felstead et al. 2005). Yet we need to be cautious when interpreting such developments. Although the restructuring of office space, to facilitate collective offices and hot-desking arrangements, is an important, and by no means new, trend, the extent to which people are able to work from home is a rather more limited affair. Although some employers encourage people to work from home, in many workplaces no one does so. Opportunities to work from home are increasing slowly, but White et al. (2004) found that they tended to be limited to certain groups of staff, for example managers and professionals.

The supposed decline of bureaucratic organization also means that the importance of internal career ladders has diminished. Workers, particularly those who are involved in the expanding knowledge-based economy, can liberate themselves from the constraints of working for organizations as employees. Instead they are encouraged to offer their expertise to firms on a contract basis, thus giving them more choice and flexibility in their working lives. Post-bureaucracy, then, involves the development of 'boundaryless' or 'portfolio' careers as described by Arthur and Rousseau (1996) and Handy (1994). Post-bureaucratic employment is not only beneficial for firms, since it enables them to engage labour when they need it, without the requirement to commit themselves to the potential rigidities of hiring staff under an employment relationship, but also held to be advantageous for workers. People increasingly choose to work as 'free agents', as self-employed, temporary contractors who sell their services to a range of firms, thus liberating them from the restrictive 'iron cage' of working in bureaucracies.

There is some support for the 'free agent' thesis. People often do make a deliberate choice to undertake freelance working arrangements because of the freedom and flexibility it gives them, for example to turn down offers of work at times when it is inconvenient. In her study of the UK media industry, Platman (2004) pointed to the important degree of freedom enjoyed by many freelance workers. Yet there are some doubts about the extent to which people undertake self-employed free-lance and other temporary work arrangements as a matter of personal choice. Many workers would prefer permanent positions with employ-ers. Grimshaw et al. (2003) and Kirkpatrick and Hoque (2006) note that freelance workers, and temporary agency staff, often receive worse terms and conditions than those enjoyed by directly employed staff, such as the absence of paid holidays and other benefits. The downside of being a free agent is increased financial insecurity. Although some freelancers can earn large sums, this type of employment contract can add to the climate of employment insecurity which characterizes con-temporary labour markets, as we saw in chapter 4.

Perhaps the most pertinent criticism of this aspect of the post-bureaucracy thesis (that conventional bureaucratic employment relationships are dissolving and being superseded by the inevitable growth of 'boundaryless careers' and 'portfolio' jobs) is that it bears limited relation to reality. While the number of self-employed grew rapidly in the UK during the 1980s, largely because of the absence of employment opportunities during that decade, since the early 1990s it has been relatively stable. In the 2000s, the temporary workforce, already not large, did not grow markedly and is anyway composed largely of vulnerable workers, such as migrant workers for example. **Portfolio** and freelance workers can be found but tend to be confined to some rather specialized areas (computing, media, creative arts) where such work has always been common. Therefore there is no evidence for a major shift to post-bureaucratic employment arrange-ments. Overall, then, there is little evidence for the existence of a post-bureaucratic model of work and employment in contemporary societies.

The changing forms of bureaucratic organization

In this section we expose the post-bureaucracy thesis to rather more explicit critical scrutiny, largely by demonstrating the continuing rel-evance of bureaucratic principles to the design of contemporary organizations. Notwithstanding the rhetoric, evidence for the presence of post-bureaucracy is thin on the ground. Rather than a trend towards the development of post-bureaucratic organizations in contemporary societies, the evidence points to the durability of the bureaucratic model. Aspects of bureaucratic control, for example, not only continue to dominate the way in which organizations are managed, but also are manifest in new ways, like the proliferation of systems for managing employee performance (appraisal, staff review and capability proce-dures). Here, we are concerned with understanding variations within the bureaucratic model, and with how bureaucratic organization has adapted to reflect changing circumstances. We consider how bureau-cratic control is being reconstituted in contemporary organizations and account for the resilience of bureaucracy as the dominant princi-ple of organizational design.

Reconstituting bureaucratic control

Far from disappearing, bureaucratic principles seem to be central to the design of contemporary organizations, particularly when it comes to effecting control over labour. While fashionable change-manage-ment programmes, such as Business Process Re-engineering (BPR), are often advanced as initiatives designed to abate bureaucracy, in practice they do not represent a departure from bureaucratic organi-zational principles. Korczynski (2004) looked at operations in the back offices of two financial services firms and an insurance company which had introduced organizational change initiatives. Bureaucratic principles dominated the way in which work was managed. Much of the labour remained highly routinized and monotonous. Thus change management initiatives like BPR do not imply a departure from bureau-cratic principles in organization; indeed they embody a trend towards the 're-bureaucratization' rather than the 'de-bureaucratization' of organizational life (Korczynski 2004: 111).

The reconstitution of bureaucratic control in organizations is most evident when we turn to the nature of organizational rules. The post-bureaucracy thesis holds that formal rules have become less important, given the greater emphasis on informal, tacit arrangements for co-ordinating activities, such as building trust and shared cultures. As we stated earlier, though, rules are as important as ever in organizations, if not more so. In fact, they increasingly apply to aspects of working life that have hitherto escaped the process of rationalization, particularly in the service sector. The concept of 'emotional labour' (Hochschild 1983) introduced in chapter 4 is relevant here. It refers to efforts by managers in service sector organizations, where the work involves a high degree of interaction with customers, to control workers' feelings and emotions as a source of competitive advantage; making sure that airline cabin crew engage with customers in an appropriate manner, for example by establishing rules to mandate smiling at customers.

The management of emotional labour, then, involves an 'extension of work rules into previously "private" domains' (Alvesson and Thompson 2005: 493). While rules governing how tasks are undertaken may have declined in importance, Thompson (1993) notes how 'feeling rules', developed in an effort to govern the emotional behaviour of workers, have become more prevalent. Rather than being abandoned, bureau-cratic control has been reconstituted in new forms. Weber's 'iron cage'

Organizational control and rules are still of great importance, even in seemingly relaxed situations such as the interaction between waiting staff and diners. The waiting staff are often smiling only because it is a requirement of the job.

of bureaucracy 'is clearly still very much in existence'; only it has now 'unlocked its doors and invited emotion in' (Bolton 2005: 42).

We can also see the reinforcement and reconstitution of bureaucratic control in other aspects of organizational life, for example the concern with managing employee performance more assiduously. Performance management systems, and their array of targets, criteria for determining targets and arrangements for measuring the progress of staff against those targets, through review meetings known as appraisals, are highly bureaucratic in nature. Performance management systems have a significant place in contemporary organizations, through the role they play in establishing work standards, determining ways of measuring them, and then evaluating individual staff against those standards.

The emphasis on rules, order and control, and the use of performance management systems to enforce compliance with organizational standards in the interests of efficiency, are all consistent with the rationalizing imperative of Weber's 'ideal-type' bureaucracy. In some cases large corporations are responding to the emergence of irrationality by attempting to rationalize it (see box 6.5). One of the key weaknesses of the post-bureaucracy thesis, then, is the weight of evidence for the durability of the main principles of bureaucratic organization. Indeed, the development of new 'feeling' rules, and the elaboration of more intensive systems of performance management, point to the reconstitution of bureaucratic organization, rather than its decline.

Box 6.5 Spirituality at work: rationalizing the irrational

Given the supposedly rational character of business organizations, since they are concerned with realizing their goals in the most effective ways possible, it is perhaps surprising that some large corporations are increasingly catering for the spiritual, and thus seemingly highly irrational, needs of their employees. Based on research among managers and professionals in large corporations, Casey (2004) identified a growing level of interest among employees in new age and spiritual ideas. Reports of the use of personal growth programmes, meditation, yoga, feng shui and other spiritual practices, even including fortune-telling and 'shamanic healing', were widespread among the highly skilled and senior staff in the organizations she visited. Why was this happening? It seems that the growth of interest in spirituality was occurring as a response to the overly rationalized and alienating environment in which these people worked. For these disenchanted employees, such 'activities are responses to experienced lackings in overly rationalized, instrumentalized and dispirited bureaucratic organizations and industrially disciplined workplaces'. As a reaction against greater rationalization, they are 'generating a growing oppositional voice and alternative practices' (Casey 2004: 73).

Rather than resisting or ignoring these developments, some large corporations appear to be embracing the increasing interest in spirituality among their staff. Firms, including IBM, Xerox and Apple, support their employees' participation in retreats 'which include yoga, meditation, mind–body work and the like' (Casey 2004: 72). Numerous books have been published that offer advice to managers about how they can take advantage of this 'spiritual turn', including such titles as *Bringing Your Soul to Work* and *Liberating the Corporate Soul*. Consultancy firms offer programmes on spirituality and business. What explains the increasing interest of decidedly rational corporations in the seemingly irrational world of the spiritual? Companies are accommodating and appropriating the interest in spirituality demonstrated by some of their senior staff, part of what Casey (2004) calls a 'strategic, neo-rationalist managerial response'. Whereas in the past bureaucratic organizations would have had little time for such evident irrationality, many large companies are now looking to use spirituality as an additional means of securing greater competitive advantage by enhancing employee commitment. Spirituality programmes give staff a sense of belonging and security, overcoming the alienating effects of working and managing in large bureaucracies. Nevertheless, companies may find it difficult to profit from the rationalization of the irrational in this way. The growing interest in spirituality has come about precisely because of a widespread disenchantment with the highly rationalized nature of organizational life, suggesting that it also generates resistance to corporate practices.

Varieties of bureaucracy

While bureaucratic forms of control continue to be an important feature of contemporary organizations, we should not overlook the extent to which bureaucracy has adapted and evolved. Important changes to the structure of organizations have occurred, particularly as a result of the influence of sophisticated ICT, but they have taken place within a paradigm which is essentially bureaucratic, as Hales (2002) argues. The result is the emergence of new, hybrid types of organization which, while different in many respects from older, more conventional organizational forms, are still bureaucracies nonetheless. Three models of '**neo-bureaucracy**' (Reed 2005) are considered here: the 'bureaucracy-lite' concept; the notion of 'soft bureaucracy'; and the 'customer-oriented bureaucracy' approach.

Colin Hales, the advocate of the first of these models, 'bureaucracy-lite', acknowledges that organizations have undergone important changes, notably reduced levels of hierarchy, but that this does not mean there is a trend towards post-bureaucracy. The main characteristics of bureaucratic organization, principally the importance of formal rules and hierarchical management structures, remain important. What has happened is that hierarchies have been made leaner and therefore rendered more efficient as arrangements for co-ordinating organizational activities. The result is 'all the strength of bureaucratic control with only half the hierarchical calories' (Hales 2002: 64). The development of ICT has played a key part in producing the 'bureaucracy-lite' organization. This is because it enables organizational activities to be co-ordinated efficiently without the need for extensive layers of management. The result is not post-bureaucracy, however. The effect of ICT as a co-ordinating mechanism is to augment the authority and control of senior managers, not devolve them to the workforce (Hales 2002).

The concept of 'soft bureaucracy' (Courpasson 2000) bears some similarities with the 'bureaucracy-lite' model. In particular, it recognizes that organizations have been experiencing significant changes which give the appearance of a trend towards post-bureaucracy, but that these represent the evolution, rather than the repudiation, of the bureaucratic form. The 'soft bureaucracy' concept acknowledges the significant degree to which organizational activities have been decentralized, and the development of greater flexibility. But Courpasson rejects the notion that power and authority have been devolved to the workforce. Instead they remain highly centralized. Responsibility for decision-making is concentrated among top managers who attempt to exercise control in conventional bureaucratic ways. Thus a 'soft bureaucracy' is 'an organization where processes of flexibility and decentralization co-exist with more rigid constraints and structures of domination' (Courpasson 2000: 157).

The third type of neo-bureaucratic approach we should discuss is the idea of 'customer-oriented bureaucracy' developed by Korczynski (2002). This is not so much a distinct organizational form, more a way of conceptualizing the management of work in contemporary organizations that are concerned primarily with delivering services to customers, such as retail, hospitality and call centre operations. The customer-oriented bureaucracy 'points to an essential tension at the heart of contemporary service work' (Korczynski 2002: 66). On the one hand, competitive pressures, and the need to remain efficient, as well as customer expectations for standardized, predictable service, mean that companies have to be formally rational, and manage staff in a way that is consistent with conventional bureaucratic principles. On the other hand, companies are also concerned to make sure that customers secure gratification from their experience of the service encounter, that their relationship with the worker who delivers the service is a pleasurable one, something that, being personal, is unpredictable and not susceptible to rationalization. The customer-oriented bureaucracy concept acknowledges that there are important limits to formal rationalization in the service sector. Managers in customer service organizations must acknowledge, and cope with, the emotional and irrational elements in personal relationships between customers and workers. Indeed, in as much as it generates pleasurable experiences for customers (involving, for example, joking, gossip or mild flirting), these elements are to be welcomed. But all this exists alongside a concern with rationalizing the service encounter, standardizing it (for example through scripts that employees are meant to learn and use), and rendering it more predictable, given the efficiency rationale that underpins managerial interventions. If you think of some of the experiences you have had while dealing with customer service departments through semi-automated telephone systems, you are likely to uncover such tensions.

The resilience of bureaucracy

There is little evidence of a paradigm shift from bureaucracy to post-bureaucracy in contemporary societies. While elements of the post-bureaucratic model are clearly present in many organizations, the decentralization of some activities for example, they exist within organizational design frameworks that are still broadly bureaucratic in nature. In some places we can identify a process of greater bureaucratization, such as in the case of an expanding scientific consultancy where a 'soft' form of bureaucracy had developed (Robertson and Swan 2004). Elsewhere, Hodgson (2004) observed a process of 're-bureaucratization' occurring in a telephone bank, as managers reacted to the potential risks that went with giving workers too much discretion. As a result, the project management approach was configured in a way that enabled greater predictability of, and control over, work tasks.

Thus we should reject over-simplistic, linear approaches to organizational change that posit a straightforward trend from bureaucracy to post-bureaucracy. Elements of the post-bureaucratic model exist to varying degrees in many organizations, but they do so within an overall design framework which is largely bureaucratic. Added to this, the bureaucratic form is a more sophisticated, complex and adaptable phenomenon than is generally portrayed by proponents of the post-bureaucracy thesis. As we have already observed, bureaucratic organization is not monolithic. Its variability, and its capacity to evolve and adapt to changing circumstances, mean that bureaucracy continues to be a major influence on organizational design in contemporary societies.

Bureaucracy has endured for sound managerial reasons. Hierarchical structures and formal procedures continue to be important means of securing organizational objectives. They remain essential methods for co-ordinating activities, maintaining control and effecting compliance. But du Gay (2005) points out that bureaucratic organization also embodies certain positive values, notably consistency, equity and fairness. Management decisions are more likely to be perceived as legitimate, and thus secure the consent of the workforce, where they are based on formal procedures. However, a values-based defence of bureaucracy, one that stresses how it enables organizations to function efficiently, by promoting consistency, equity and fairness, may be misplaced. Managers have a tendency to circumvent the rules where they appear to pose a constraint upon their prerogative. We have already used the growth of equal opportunities policies to illustrate the relevance of formal procedures in contemporary organizations. Whether or not managers pay heed to them in practice, however, is quite another matter.

Conclusion

In this chapter we considered the nature of bureaucratic organization, discussed the main features of the post-bureaucratic paradigm, examined the reasons why it is claimed to be superseding the bureaucratic form and emphasized the durability of bureaucracy, highlighting its variability and adaptability as a means of structuring organizations.

While there is evidence that important changes are occurring in organizations – the decentralization of activities for example – they do not imply that bureaucracy has been usurped. The main principles of the bureaucratic paradigm – the existence of formal rules and procedures, hierarchies of authority, management control over subordinates and efforts to secure greater efficiency through rationalization – remain key characteristics of contemporary organizations. Unsophisticated monolithic approaches to organizational change which hold that a straightforward trend from bureaucracy to post-bureaucracy has occurred over-simplify developments.

While the bureaucratic form is clearly advantageous for organizations, its implications for the people who work in them are much more ambiguous. On the one hand, formal rules and procedures help to promote fairness, consistency and transparency in decision-making. The aim of equal opportunities policies, for example, would seem to involve reducing the scope for managers to make arbitrary or irrational decisions that might result in people suffering discrimination on the grounds of, among other things, their gender, ethnicity or age. On the other hand, we have seen that formal procedures, by giving their actions a veneer of acceptability, help to legitimize managerial control. Moreover, they are often not a very good guide to what actually happens in organizations. Equal opportunity policies, for example, are often an 'empty shell' (Hoque and Noon 2004), helping to conceal the existence of discriminatory practices. Workplace cultures and informal, tacit rules are an important influence on behaviour in organizations. In order to understand organizations properly, then, we need to consider not just the formal manifestations of their structures, in the shape of rules, procedures, hierarchies and systems of authority, but also the broader range of influences on behaviour within them, something that is the main focus of chapter 7.

Discussion questions

1. What are the principal characteristics of the bureaucratic form of organization? What are its main advantages and disadvantages?
2. What are the main implications of post-bureaucracy for the ways in which people manage and work in organizations? Can you think of examples of post-bureaucratic organizations?
3. What is meant by the concept of the 'virtual organization'? How is it manifest in practice? How likely is it that, in future, organizations will operate in a more virtual fashion? Are there any obstacles to the further development of virtuality in organizations?
4. Think of an organization with which you are familiar (e.g. a school, college, sports club, employer, voluntary body). What bureaucratic features can you identify? Why do you think they exist, and what effect do they have on how the organization operates?

Further reading

For a brief and highly readable introduction to some of the debates presented in this chapter, we recommend:

Grey, C., *A Very Short, Fairly Interesting and Reasonably Cheap Book about Studying Organizations.* London: Sage, 2005.

For perspectives on management, work and organization, Colin Hales, *Managing Through Organization* (2nd edition; London: Thomson Learning, 2001), and Stephen Ackroyd's *The Organization of Business: Applying Organizational Theory to Contemporary Change* (Oxford: Oxford University Press, 2002) are recommended. *Rethinking the Future of Work: Directions and Vision,* by Colin Williams (Basingstoke: Palgrave Macmillan, 2007), also contains lots of useful material. The standard text on the 'McDonaldization' phenomenon is Ritzer's *The McDonaldization of Society* (Thousand Oaks, Calif.: Pine Forge Press, 2004). For a good critical overview of post-bureaucracy, refer to the book chapter by Alvesson and Thompson in Ackroyd et al.'s *The Oxford Handbook of Work Organization* (2005). Finally, Korczynski's *Human Resource Management in Service Work* (Basingstoke: Palgrave, 2002) offers some good insights into the ways in which the bureaucratic form of organization has been adapted.

7 Managers, workers and behaviour in organizations

The main objectives of this chapter are:

- to examine the main influences on how people behave in organizations
- to assess the influence of human relations thinking on the management of people in organizations, particularly with regard to contemporary human resource management (HRM) techniques
- to consider the significance of behaviour in organizations that does not conform with managerial expectations and standards: organizational misbehaviour as it is often called
- to explore the role played by trade unions both in organizations, and in society at large.

Introduction

While the focus of our attention in chapter 6 was on the structure and design of organizations, notably the characteristics of the bureaucratic organizational form and whether or not it has been superseded by post-bureaucratic arrangements, in this chapter we are concerned with the behaviour of people – managers and workers – in organizations. Managers aim to ensure that their staff comply with organizational standards and work effectively to realize organizational goals. The human relations approach, which is concerned with recognizing the social needs of workers, and with encouraging them to feel that they are involved in decisions that affect them at work, is seen to generate greater loyalty, co-operation and commitment to the organization. The interest in HRM techniques in many contemporary organizations is evidence of its enduring appeal.

But how effectively in reality can managers influence and control the behaviour of their staff, so that it supports organizational goals? Misbehaviour, in the sense of actions that people in organizations undertake which do not correspond with managerial standards and expectations, appears to be widespread. We consider the range of misbehaviour in organizations and its implications for understanding organizational life. Trade union activity can be an additional obstacle impeding managerial efforts to shape and influence the behaviour of employees. Thus a further purpose of this chapter is to analyse the role of trade unions in organizations, and also in wider society, by drawing upon a number of key sociological approaches taken from the work of Marx, Weber and Durkheim. How can the role of unions be interpreted? And is their role in organizations becoming redundant now that people seem to derive their identities from sources other than their work or occupation?

Human relations and human resource management

In contrast to the Weberian perspective (discussed in chapter 6) which emphasizes the importance of written rules, management hierarchies and other structural features that characterize modern organizations, the '**human relations**' approach is informed by a concern with recognizing and satisfying workers' social needs. Human relations principles state that in attempting to realize their objectives, business organizations should secure the co-operation of their staff, for example by trying to improve their job satisfaction or by ensuring that they have opportunities to participate in decisions that affect them at work. In contrast to Taylor (see chapter 4), who emphasized their monetary concerns, the human relations approach recognizes that workers have social needs, as well as economic ones, and that these have to be met if the organization is to function effectively. We examine the main characteristics and the influence of the human relations paradigm and assess the extent to which it informs contemporary approaches to managing people in organizations, principally in the form of HRM techniques.

Understanding human relations at work: Hawthorne and beyond

The human relations approach has its basis in Durkheimian sociology. As we saw in chapter 1, Émile Durkheim was a French sociologist writing in the early part of the twentieth century whose principal concern was with understanding the nature of solidarity in society. You will recall that one of the main features of Durkheimian sociology is the emphasis placed on promoting order and stability in complex industrial societies with their highly differentiated division of labour. The key concern of writers working within a human relations perspective is to devise measures to help integrate workers into the enterprise, by securing their motivation, satisfaction and co-operation with organizational goals. Reports of the experiments undertaken during the 1920s and 1930s at the Western Electric Company's Hawthorne plant near Chicago in the United States were crucial in stimulating interest in the human relations approach.

The Hawthorne studies resulted in two main findings that constitute the basis of the human relations approach. First, the early experiments, particularly those in the Relay Test Assembly Room, suggested that workers perform better when their role is given some acknowledgement. Famously, one group of workers was subjected to various changes in

The Hawthorne effect implies that managers should demonstrate their appreciation for what workers do.

aspects of their working conditions, including the number and duration of rest breaks, the temperature and the lighting in their department. No matter what the change made, the output of the study group rose. Among a control group, whose conditions went unchanged, output also increased. How could such a finding be interpreted? The researchers concluded that, as the objects of study, the workers were encouraged to think of themselves as special. These experiments seemed to demonstrate the presence of a '**Hawthorne effect**'; when workers' efforts are observed, they feel their role is acknowledged, and their performance improves accordingly. A further lesson taken from such experiments was the importance of participation; where workers feel they are involved in, or have some influence over, decisions that affect them at work, they perform more effectively.

The second key finding of the Hawthorne experiments concerns the outcome of later studies undertaken during the 1930s in the Bank Wiring Room. Investigation revealed that workers restricted their output in a way that, from a purely economic perspective, appeared to be irrational, since the greater an individual's output the more they stood to earn. Here, though, the researchers identified the existence of strong informal group norms that governed output. Workers developed informal, collective assumptions about the appropriate levels of effort in order to ensure that the earnings of the group as a whole were maximized, not just those of a few highly productive individuals. The lesson for managers was that workers are not solely motivated by economic concerns; the effective management of staff needs to recognize, and try to influence as necessary, the social factors, such as feelings of solidarity or group identities, that inform people's behaviour at work.

While there is no doubting the significance of the Hawthorne experiments, the research process was marked by a number of major flaws. Supposedly 'uncooperative' workers were sometimes removed from experiments and replaced. The Hawthorne investigators also neglected the economic rationality that informed the behaviour of groups of workers, placing too much of an emphasis on the importance of ill-defined social factors, like 'group sentiment' for example. Also, despite efforts to acknowledge the importance of social factors in understanding organizations, the approach taken by the Hawthorne investigators was surprisingly unsociological. As Rose (1975) points out, little attention was paid to the broader social context within which the company and its workers operated, particularly the growing impact of militant trade union activity.

These criticisms notwithstanding, reports of the Hawthorne experiments had a huge influence on the management of organizations. Although he himself had a relatively minor role in the Hawthorne experiments, Elton Mayo played a key role in popularizing them, not least in his book *The Human Problems of Industrial Civilisation* (Mayo 1933), the success of which 'turned him into a kind of human relations superstar' (Rose 1975: 114). Mayo contended that managerial effectiveness could be enhanced if the social needs of the workforce were respected, since this would encourage more co-operative relations at work. Securing employee co-operation was more productive for organizations than relying upon narrow, instrumentally motivated compliance.

This insight has had an enduring influence on organizational behaviour as a field of study, particularly in the area of motivation at work. See, for example, the appeal of Maslow's 'hierarchy of needs' as the basis for employee motivation. Maslow (1943) argued that once people had satisfied their basic needs, such as food and shelter, they then became concerned with satisfying needs of an ever higher order, with the highest being their need for 'self-actualization', that is the desire to exercise self-control and autonomy over their lives. The implication for organizations is that the effective motivation of workers depends upon recognizing their higher-order needs. Other popular offerings in the extensive 'neo-human relations' genre included McGregor's *The Human Side of Enterprise* (McGregor 1960). He distinguished between an approach to organizing and managing work based on Tayloristic assumptions about workers' needs (Theory X) and an approach that recognized and respected the social needs of workers as human agents (Theory Y).

Human relations thinking has had an enormous influence on the practice of management and on organizational behaviour as a field of study. Yet it was designed primarily to serve managerial ends. Managers were encouraged to use, and take advantage of, the existence of group identities at work and other social dimensions of workplace behaviour, manipulating them to serve organizational goals (Rose 1975).

Human resource management

During the 1960s and 1970s, human relations fell into disrepute. As an ideology of management, it was regarded with suspicion by many workers and trade unionists. In addition, the substantial amount of workplace conflict that marked this period seemed to demonstrate the limited effectiveness of human relations as a managerial tool. Since the 1980s, however, the rise of HRM, which incorporates key aspects of human relations thinking, is evident in the practice of many organizations. However, there is a notable difference between HRM and human relations. As Thompson and McHugh (2002) point out HRM is much less concerned with employee welfare, and places a much greater emphasis on the integration of 'people management' issues with the overall business objectives of the organization.

What are the main features of the HRM approach? Some caution is needed here. Often 'HRM' is used as an umbrella label for managing people in organizations in a way that makes it interchangeable with the term 'personnel management'. A second way of interpreting HRM, and the one we use here, is to view it as a particular approach to managing the workforce, based on five key principles:

- an emphasis on aligning people management practices with the overall business strategy of the organization
- concern with managing people in a way that helps to enhance business performance
- a recognition that improvements in business performance can be secured by interventions designed to involve and increase the organizational commitment of the workforce
- stress on managing organizational culture
- a preference for non-union employment relations arrangements.

Before we consider these features of HRM in more detail, we need to examine the main factors contributing to its rise since the 1980s. First, the development of HRM occurred in a context of changing markets and growing competitive pressures that affected business organizations. Increasing competition encouraged firms to look for new sources of competitive advantage. This led them to emphasize the knowledge, skills and expertise of the people they employ. In as much as they help to ensure these attributes are used effectively, the use of sophisticated people management practices is seen as an essential component of organizational growth. To a large extent, then, the rise of HRM was stimulated by a desire to ensure that the way in which people were managed at work was more supportive of business goals and competitive advantage.

The rise of HRM since the 1980s can also be linked to important political and economic changes that have given organizations greater latitude when it comes to managing their staff. In the UK, for example, Conservative governments of the 1980s and 1990s tried to develop a business climate within which employers could re-assert their 'right to manage', principally by weakening the power of the trade unions. While Labour has made some changes to the legislative framework that would appear to have partially reversed such a trend, its over-all approach remains supportive of the need for businesses to have flexibility over how they manage their staff and for unions to remain weak.

As we have already indicated, HRM is marked by five key princi-ples. First, it is characterized by the alignment of people management practices with the overall business objectives of the organization. The management of staff is not undertaken for its own sake, but is carried out in a way that enables it to contribute to overall business goals. Some companies, like the *Guardian* newspaper, for example, have developed sophisticated diversity management programmes, not nec-essarily because they are socially or morally worthwhile, but because it is thought that they will help to grow the business by making their products and services more appealing to members of black and ethnic minority communities.

Linked to the concern with supporting the overall business strategy of the organization, the second key principle of HRM is the emphasis placed on managing people in a way that enhances business per-formance. How can workers be 'engaged' so they contribute more effectively to their organizations? Studies undertaken in the United States, for example by White et al. (2004), highlight the importance of certain so-called 'high commitment' or 'high performance' prac-tices and business performance. These include: formal team-working arrangements where members of the team are responsible for allocat-ing work between them; functional flexibility, such that workers have the requisite skills to be able to undertake a variety of jobs; mecha-nisms that enable employees to be involved in, and thus influence, decisions that affect them at work; and sophisticated reward arrange-ments, like performance-related pay for example. The use of high commitment practices helps to enhance business performance in two ways: by producing higher-quality staff, who are capable of perform-ing their jobs more effectively; and by increasing workers' sense of engagement with their organization, so they are willing to contribute a greater amount.

Following on from this, the third key principle underlying HRM is the emphasis given to capturing organizational commitment. Securing the co-operation and commitment of staff to organizational goals is viewed as a key means of realizing performance improve-ments. The assumption is that a better-informed, and more involved, workforce will be more committed. There are a number of forms of employee involvement. Direct forms of communication between managers and staff are arrangements whereby information is dissemi-nated by means of notice boards, newsletters, face-to-face meetings and company intranet facilities. Organizations may also operate direct communication arrangements enabling staff to convey information to managers, through the use of attitude surveys and suggestion schemes for example. Many companies, including the Prudential, B&Q and

Pizza Express among others, operate schemes that enable them to communicate with staff indirectly, by informing and consulting with employee representatives. The B&Q scheme, called 'Grassroots', allows elected employee representatives to ask questions about company policy, make suggestions for improvement and raise staff concerns (Hall 2005).

The fourth key principle is the importance accorded to managing organizational culture, through an attempt to manipulate symbols, values and beliefs in the workplace. As we saw in chapter 6, this is consistent with a supposedly 'post-bureaucratic' trend in the management of organizations. One of the main reasons why many organizations are so concerned with managing culture in this way is that it can provide a challenge to trade unions with the aim of reducing their influence (the fifth key principle). Organizations emphasize the co-operative and harmonious nature of relations between managers and workers, and the shared values – based on the desirability of realizing organizational goals – that inform their behaviour. Any conflict is presented as either frictional, down to short-term, easily resolved problems, such as personality differences for example, or the product of external agitators, such as trade union activists. An example is the management style of the multinational courier company studied by Dundon and Rollinson (2004). Characterized by an emphasis on developing a strong organizational culture, it was supported by the use of a range of sophisticated HRM interventions, including an extensive system of direct communication methods. By following such an approach the company attempted to make the role of a trade union unnecessary.

Interpreting human resource management

How far has this HRM approach, in which people are treated as resources to be developed, rather than as commodities to be exploited, become established among organizations though? There are several problems with assuming that HRM, based on the five key principles elaborated above, has transformed the way in which organizations are managed.

First, the prevalence of sophisticated HRM as an approach to managing people at work is rather limited in practice. There are relatively few workplaces in which a 'high commitment' approach to managing staff is evident, and their number does not seem to be growing (Kersley et al. 2006). Many firms find it profitable to employ staff in narrow, specialized job roles, where there are few opportunities to be involved in workplace decisions. See the sandwich factory studied by Holgate (2005), for example. There is also little evidence that the HRM agenda has made much headway in producing healthier working environments (see box 7.1).

Second, we should be sceptical about claims that HRM has been of

Box 7.1 HRM and stress

Short-term financial considerations often encourage managers to concentrate on productivity improvements, at the expense of employee well-being. Yet it is argued that effective HRM can help to reconcile performance pressures with the maintenance of a healthy and safe working environment. The Chartered Institute of Personnel and Development (CIPD) claims that businesses investing in the health and well-being of their staff benefit from greater productivity and profitability.

Yet there are doubts about the extent to which this business case for advancing health and safety at work has permeated the thinking of senior managers. Many people are expected to work in environments that potentially damage their well-being. For example, stress-related illnesses are very common in organizations. Stress can be defined as the adverse reaction people experience when they come under too much pressure, or where the demands placed upon them are excessive. Stress is a major cause of physical and psychological ill-health – a source of heart disease, anxiety and depression, among other things (Boyd 2003). Each year, some half a million people in the UK report that they have experienced ill-health as a result of work-related stress. Research carried out by the Department of Trade and Industry (DTI) found 16 per cent of the workers surveyed – one in every six workers – were working over sixty hours a week. Stress has a detrimental impact on business organizations; it results in increased levels of sickness absence and also has an adverse impact on staff morale. The DTI survey also found one in five men (19 per cent) had visited the doctor because of stress, rising to almost a quarter (23 per cent) of over-40s.

Yet the way many jobs are organized contributes to the ill-health of the workers that undertake them. For one thing, limited discretion at work has been identified as a source of stress-related illness. In addition, increasing work pressures, linked to organizational demands for greater productivity in a more competitive business environment, also contribute to people's ill-health at work. While the aspiration of HRM to manage people in a way that helps to reconcile performance pressures with the well-being of employees is praiseworthy, in practice it is not that easy to achieve.

benefit to employees, by involving, nurturing and engaging them so that they are more committed to organizational goals. There is evidence that HRM practices sit easily alongside more traditional coercive management approaches. The high commitment approach, moreover, is often difficult to maintain in the context of economic pressures. A study by Gratton et al. (1999) of a number of companies who claimed to be at the 'leading edge' of contemporary HRM practice found that financial considerations generally took precedence over good people management.

Third, the significance of employee involvement initiatives should not be exaggerated. Involvement is often limited to the one-way flow of information, from managers to staff, with few opportunities available for the workforce to influence organizational decisions. The study of 'leading edge' companies mentioned earlier found that managers adopted a rather restricted view of employee involvement, limiting themselves to giving information to staff rather than being concerned with responding to their views and suggestions (Gratton et al. 1999). Employees in such circumstances can become cynical and see consultation as a 'sham'.

Finally, Legge (2005) argues that there are problems with the proposition that HRM, through the use of high commitment management practices, has a positive influence on business performance. The relationship between HRM and performance is rather more complicated in practice; firms that are performing well may be in a better position to afford to implement expensive HRM interventions, suggesting that it may be difficult to disentangle cause and effect when it comes to measuring the impact of HRM. In the case of the aircraft manufacturer studied by Danford et al. (2004), performance improvements were the product of greater work pressures, not a more committed workforce.

The enduring influence of human relations thinking is evident in many of the assumptions that characterize best-practice contemporary HRM, particularly the assumption that interventions designed to nurture the co-operation of employees generate greater commitment and better performance, helping to realize organizational goals. However, the extent to which HRM, based on the five key principles described earlier, has taken root is questionable. Besides, even in situations where managers have been able to develop and sustain a strong HRM approach, this does not necessarily mean that they are going to be effective in influencing and shaping employees' attitudes and behaviour, as in the case of the multinational courier company mentioned earlier. Despite the presence of a sophisticated HRM approach, many staff remained unhappy about the lack of influence they had over decisions that affected them at work (Dundon and Rollinson 2004).

Organizational misbehaviour

In 2006 the reported antics of some staff working for the British government's Rural Payments Agency in Newcastle-upon-Tyne provoked a furore. They were alleged to have had sex in the office toilets, participated in fights and break-dancing competitions during working hours and romped around the offices and jumped from filing cabinets while naked. Following a managerial investigation into the allegations, the agency, which is responsible for administering agricultural payments to farmers, acknowledged that some 'inappropriate behaviour' had taken place; it announced that four members of staff had been dismissed, and five others disciplined, as a result. This example helps to focus our attention on behaviour at work that does not correspond with the standards and expectations laid down by managers, or '**organizational**

misbehaviour', things people do at work that they are not supposed to do (Ackroyd and Thompson 1999: 2). The main purpose of this section is to examine this important, but often neglected, dimension of organizational life, drawing on relevant sociological perspectives where appropriate.

Organizational misbehaviour: a framework

Ackroyd and Thompson (1999) provide a useful framework for understanding the range of misbehaviour that occurs in organizations: how workers seek to appropriate, or secure control over, their work, the products of their work, the time they are supposed to be engaged in work, and also their work identities.

One broad area of misbehaviour in organizations concerns efforts by workers to gain control over their work: its pace, its content and its intensity. 'Soldiering' and 'making out' are manifestations of this type of misbehaviour; these terms are used to describe work limitation practices. During the 1940s, 1950s and 1960s, American and British researchers, such as Donald Roy, Tom Lupton and Sheila Cunnison among others, submitted the practice of 'making out' to an extensive degree of sociological scrutiny. They found that workers develop collective assumptions about appropriate levels of effort and output, in order to regulate their earnings, or control the pace of work, in a way that benefits the work group as a whole. The norms spread through the group and the workers limit their pace of work accordingly; one of the authors of this book was told off by the work-team in her first job for working too hard.

This can be described as a form of **'effort bargaining'**. The term captures how workers attempt to regulate, through informal, sometimes tacitly accepted group norms, the amount of work undertaken, or its pace, in exchange for an acceptable level of earnings. It is a type of misbehaviour that is particularly common where pay rates are determined by output levels (piece-rate systems).

The significance of effort bargaining extends rather wider. This is particularly evident from investigations of work and employment relations in small and medium-sized enterprises (SMEs). A particularly interesting study is Monder Ram's (1994) *Managing to Survive*, an analysis of work and employment relations in small Asian-owned clothing firms in the West Midlands region of the UK. Managerial authority was limited by the need to reach accommodations with workers over the pace of work tasks and the earnings they attracted. Supervisors and line managers often turn a blind eye to 'soldiering' in order to keep good relations with their workers and stop them leaving the firm.

A further way in which workers seek to appropriate greater control over aspects of their work is by engaging in acts of sabotage. What do we mean by 'sabotage'? The picture that comes to mind is one of workers deliberately damaging work equipment in order to gain a break from their toil. The narrow approach to sabotage in organizations views it as a purely destructive act. However, there is also a broader, and perhaps more appropriate, way of conceptualizing sabotage that sees it as a form of effort bargaining (Dubois 1979). It exists not simply for destructive reasons, but also because of a constructive urge by workers to alter their working conditions for the better.

For a particularly insightful analysis of sabotage in the contemporary service sector, see Harris and Ogbonna's (2002) study of four firms in the hospitality industry. They found acts of sabotage to be commonplace in the establishments they studied, 'ranging from spitting in consumables, to adding dirt to food, to spoiling guest rooms in a discreet fashion (an unpleasant example including the wiping of a used tissue around the rim of a drinking glass)' (2002: 171). The important thing about these instances of sabotage is that they were not destructive acts undertaken by individual workers just for their own sake, or to gain revenge on rude customers. Rather, they embodied a collective ethos, being underpinned by tacitly accepted group norms about what constituted acceptable behaviour.

A second broad area of organizational misbehaviour concerns the efforts by workers to appropriate the products of their work, through such illicit activities as workplace fiddles, theft and pilferage. Many of the insights about these activities come from sociologists who are interested in the phenomenon of deviance, such as the classic 1970s investigations of bakery workers, among others, undertaken by Jason Ditton (1979).

The sociology of deviance approach has been important in helping us to understand fiddling behaviour in organizations. It holds that particular forms of behaviour that might appear to outsiders as undesirable or abnormal have to be understood from the perspective of those who engage in them. Whether or not a specific type of behaviour is normal is not a matter for determination from those on the outside, but is socially constructed by the actors concerned. This helps to account for the scale of fiddling behaviour in organizations.

The most extensive and well-known study of workplace fiddles is Gerald Mars' *Cheats at Work* (1982). Mars looked at how the characteristics of particular jobs and occupations encouraged certain types of fiddling behaviour. He identified four main categories. Where workers are employed in 'donkey' jobs, being closely supervised by managers, they can only pilfer goods when a particular opportunity arises. The fiddling behaviour of supermarket workers, for example, tends to be reactive and opportunistic, restricted to pilfering isolated items of merchandise. A second category of fiddling behaviour is undertaken by 'hawks'. While this type of activity also has an individualistic orientation, unlike the 'donkeys' those who participate in it enjoy a much greater degree of freedom. In organizations, hawk-type behaviour is generally undertaken by professional and managerial staff who can use their greater autonomy to engage in fiddles, such as over-inflating

Smoking breaks can be used by smokers and non-smokers, junior and senior members of staff alike to gain additional time away from their work. Such levels of 'misbehaviour' are openly accepted.

expenses claims for example. Like the donkey type, people in 'vulture' jobs respond to fiddling opportunities as and when they arise, but they lack the creativity and innovation that marks out the activities of hawks. Where the vulture job differs from the donkey job, however, is that fiddling behaviour, while undertaken on an individualistic basis, takes place within a tacitly agreed framework and may be tolerated, and even encouraged, by managers on the basis that it helps to maintain motivation and job satisfaction. Finally, where fiddling has an unambiguously collective dimension, with the workers involved explicitly co-operating with one another to operate fiddles, it can be likened to the actions of a wolfpack. He cites airport baggage handlers as an example of an occupation in which strong group norms govern fiddling behaviour.

A third broad type of misbehaviour concerns how people try to secure control over the time they are supposed to spend working. The most obvious manifestation of this form of misbehaviour is absence from work. Absence is often a response to difficult working conditions and close management supervision. In the call centre studied by Mulholland (2004), for example, workers sought some respite from excessive work pressures by going absent, either through unauthorized breaks during work time, making use of smoking breaks as an opportunity to leave their work stations regardless of whether or not they smoked, or by reporting sick.

Mulholland's (2004) study also discovered that workers sought some respite from the intensity of their work by pretending to be engaged in telephone sales encounters. This directs our attention to the phenomenon of people going 'absent at work' in Ditton's (1972) pithy phrase. It is important, then, not to equate absence, as a form of misbehaviour, just with non-attendance at work. Workers can be absent from work without leaving the workplace. For an instructive example, see the reported behaviour of some staff within the UK government's Child Support Agency. Pressures of work, the product of constant restructuring initiatives, resulted in excessive stress levels and very low morale. As well as generating a high level of sickness absence, there were claims that staff responded to work pressures by not picking up ringing telephones or by immediately hanging up without responding (Atkinson and McKay 2005).

The fourth type of organizational misbehaviour concerns efforts by workers to exercise control over their identity. We have already seen that organizations are increasingly looking to effect employee compliance with managerial norms through attempts to manage their emotions and culture. The aim is to secure more effective control over the behaviour of workers in organizations by attempting to manipulate their beliefs, values and, ultimately, their identities. Unsurprisingly, then, struggles over identity at work constitute an increasingly important dimension of organizational misbehaviour, as Ackroyd and Thompson (1999) report. See, for example, the case of workplace gossip in box 7.2.

Box 7.2 Gossip in organizations

Gossip is widespread in organizations. It is part of the informal, social fabric of organizations and constitutes an important source of group solidarity. Gossip encompasses all sorts of things that are of interest to the individuals concerned, ranging from discussions about the previous night's television, to conversations about which of their colleagues are engaged in romantic liaisons, and to speculation about future management plans for the organization.

Gossip can be viewed as a form of organizational misbehaviour in two respects. For one thing, it is a way that workers can, collectively, appropriate working time. If they have the time to engage in gossip, they cannot be working effectively. More importantly, the practice of gossip in organizations can be seen as a key way in which people attempt to seek control over aspects of the identity at work, separate from management. Gossip helps to generate and maintain collective social relationships between workers, contributing to the development of organizational sub-cultures and counter-cultures that operate outside managerial control, and are often used to challenge it.

The potentially subversive character of gossip has been identified by some writers, particularly in the United States. One writer, for example, contends that gossip 'poisons' business, and can 'wreak havoc' in organizations (Greengard 2001: 26). The use of gossip can enable workers to mock and undermine the authority of messages disseminated through official, formal communications channels, helping to challenge managerial control. Yet gossip may also operate in ways that are advantageous for managers in organizations. This was evident in a further education college which was going through a major restructuring process. Gossiping activity increasingly focused on the perceived adverse effects of the change initiative, promoting and reinforcing perceptions of insecurity and anxiety, and contributing to the erosion of social solidarity among the workforce. This rendered them more vulnerable and less able to challenge the authority of managers (Tebbutt and Marchington 1997).

So we see that the function of gossip can vary depending upon the context in which it operates. In some circumstances it can help to forge group identity and solidarity in opposition to managerial demands; in others, gossip can undermine it.

There is plenty of evidence that workers seek to develop and maintain their own individual and group identities in a way that is separate from, and sometimes comes into conflict with, the identity fostered by the organization for which they work. Perhaps the most notable way in which workers seek to maintain an identity distinct from that fostered by their organization is through the use of humour, jokes and fun. Humour enables workers to retain a distinctive sense of identity, in opposition to the official corporate culture. Satirical jokes, for example, are often marked by a subversive character, as a means of mocking managerial actions; by helping to subvert the given order of an organization, workplace humour undermines management efforts to control behaviour.

The use of workplace humour to express dissent is a good example of the limits of managerial efforts to enforce particular identities on people in organizations, or to manage culture effectively. Smircich (1983) suggests it is better to view culture as something which an organization *is*, comprising multiple cultures, as well as various sub- and counter-cultures based on occupation, gender, ethnicity, occupation and so on, rather than something an organization *has* that can be easily manipulated by managers. For example, hospital doctors are quite famous for their 'gallows humour', earthy jokes about operations and patients, which runs quite counter to the official caring ethos of the NHS; while nurses like to make satirical jokes about doctors they regard as pompous and arrogant. 'Taking the mickey' is a longstanding British way of ridiculing those in positions of power and authority.

Interpreting organizational misbehaviour

In order to understand and interpret the significance of organizational misbehaviour properly, some key questions need to be answered: why does it happen? To what extent does it demonstrate the resistance of workers to managerial control regimes? Why do managers frequently appear to tolerate it? And has a more assertive managerial approach, associated with the rise of HRM, reduced its prevalence in contemporary organizations?

To begin with, then, how can we account for organizational misbehaviour? Why does it occur? One response to these questions, particularly from a human relations perspective, would be to see misbehaviour as an expression of workers' irrationality. As illegitimate forms of behaviour with the potential to disrupt the organization, the activities we have discussed are seen as counter-productive, and must be eradicated by robust managerial intervention. For example, managers might hope that improved communication channels would help to re-educate workers and instil more appropriate and acceptable standards of conduct. However, the sheer volume of the activities that we can call 'misbehaviour' suggests that simply ascribing them to the irrationality of workers is inadequate. In fact activities such as 'soldiering' and other forms of effort bargaining are evidently rational behaviour for the workers involved, given that they help to regulate work and pay levels.

A better way of accounting for misbehaviour in organizations, one that explains why particular forms of misbehaviour occur under particular circumstances, is to consider specific features of different jobs and how they are managed. Characteristic types of misbehaviour reflect the nature and balance of worker–management relations in organizations, and also the basis of managerial control in the workplace. Different jobs, then, will tend to be marked by different types or patterns of misbehaviour. See, for example, the variations in fiddling behaviour identified by Mars (1982). Absence is a more commonplace manifestation of misbehaviour in some workplaces than in others. In the call centre studied by Mulholland (2004), for example, absence was used by workers as a means of gaining some respite from their onerous and monotonous jobs. As in the case of women clothing factory workers studied by Edwards and Scullion (1982), absence acted as an 'escape valve', as a way of helping to relieve the tedium and the pressures that marked their everyday working life. Where people are already able to exercise a substantial amount of control over their jobs, through collective effort bargains for example, there is less of a need to appropriate working time in this way.

Another way of explaining organizational misbehaviour would be to draw upon a tradition of Marxist sociology. From a Marxist perspective, misbehaviour expresses the conflict between workers and their employers that marks production relations under capitalism, as discussed in earlier chapters. For Marxists, misbehaviour is an inevitable feature of organizational life; it symbolizes the workplace conflict that springs from resistance by workers to managerial control. From this perspective, what we have been exploring in this section is not really 'misbehaviour', but a manifestation of class conflict. Yet not all types of misbehaviour can be equated with conflict and resistance. In many cases, instances of misbehaviour are expressions of frustration, or ways of trying to secure some respite from onerous jobs, not attempts to challenge the prevailing order. Ackroyd and Thompson argue that we need to understand organizational misbehaviour in its own right, and on its own terms, and not just in terms of the contribution it makes to resisting managerial control (Ackroyd and Thompson 1999). This is particularly important when we consider the extent to which managers in organizations often seem to tolerate, or even encourage, misbehaviour.

Box 7.3 Managerial misbehaviour in organizations

One of the reasons why managers may tolerate misbehaviour in their organizations is because they are engaged in it themselves. In 2007, for example, the utility firm Southern Water was fined £20 million by regulators after it was discovered that a previous managerial regime had knowingly and systematically overcharged its customers. In his 1996 book *Dirty Business: Exploring Corporate Misconduct*, the author Maurice Punch is concerned with the phenomenon of managerial misbehaviour. He focuses on ten key cases of corporate misconduct to illustrate the 'dirty side of business', including the 1979 nuclear incident at the Three Mile Island plant in the United States, the 1980s share-dealing scandal involving the Guinness company and the Paris 1974 crash of the McDonnell Douglas DC10 aircraft which cost hundreds of lives. Investigations reveal that in various ways managerial misbehaviour was complicit in all these events. Punch (1996) contends that corporate misconduct is widespread among the senior echelons of organizations. By bringing it to wider attention we are able to develop a different, and more realistic, picture of organizational life than that which is presented in the sanitized, carefully constructed accounts presented for public relations purposes by businesses.

How can managerial misbehaviour be explained? Why does it happen? In order to understand corporate misconduct, we need to enter the 'social world of the manager'. Misbehaviour is essentially a deviant activity, but it may be treated as if it is normal by social actors in specific contexts, in this case managers. Managers operate in complex, uncertain and ambiguous environments and often face conflicting pressures. Paying a migrant worker less than the minimum wage is against the law; but the costs of a pay increase might eradicate the company's profit margin. Tipping untreated toxic waste into a nearby river damages the environment, as well as being against the law. But the costs involved in treating the waste and ensuring that it is disposed of appropriately might be high enough to encourage managers to avoid their environmental obligations. Importantly, such misconduct happens because it does not occur to the managers involved that their activities are illegal, unethical or immoral; they have become part of the everyday routines and practices that are perceived by managers as normal. From the outside, managerial misbehaviour, whether it involves exploiting workers or damaging the environment, strikes us as undesirable. But for the managers involved, such deviant practices, which develop out of the social norms and collectively held assumptions about how business gets done, are viewed as normal.

Why are managers so indulgent towards misbehaviour? For one thing, they may be implicated themselves (see box 7.3). Moreover, managers might tolerate, or indulge, a certain level of misbehaviour because it helps to make their jobs easier. One interpretation of soldiering and other 'games' that characterize organizational life suggests that, rather than being forms of conflict, they should be viewed as activities that help managers in the smooth running of business. The efficient production of goods or delivery of services depends on managers securing the co-operation and consent of their workforce; tolerating a degree of misbehaviour may be a relatively small price to pay if it makes workers co-operate in other respects and helps to ensure that broader organizational objectives are realized.

Finally, how significant is misbehaviour to life in contemporary organizations? There is some evidence that the development of more robust and aggressive approaches to the management of people, linked to the HRM agenda, have eroded the capacity of workers to misbehave. Tighter managerial performance standards and expectations, aided by developments in technology, may have reduced the scope for misbehaviour. The greater emphasis accorded to cultural techniques as a means of managing behaviour implies that workers are less able to hold beliefs and values separate from organizational norms. Nevertheless, dissent and subversion are common in many organizations, to such an extent that it renders the concept of 'organizational culture' effectively meaningless.

Misbehaviour exists even in the most unpropitious circumstances. Workers at Disneyland laboured under a regime marked by tight managerial control over standards of conduct, performance and demeanour; they found opportunities to misbehave nonetheless, including manhandling discourteous customers (Van Maanen 1991). Even in call centres, where managers supposedly exercise rigorous control over workers through the use of sophisticated monitoring devices, workers seem to find opportunities to avoid work, by pretending to be involved in sales encounters for example (Mulholland 2004). Organizational misbehaviour will persist for very good reasons. As long as some jobs are boring, mundane, onerous or simply unengaging, there will always be some motivation for misbehaviour. It is unrealistic to expect management to eradicate organizational misbehaviour completely. Edwards (1979) refers to workplaces as being 'contested terrains' where opposing values and interests clash; therefore control in organizations can never be absolute. Workers always enjoy some space, however limited, to engage in activities that do not accord with managerial expectations. Moreover, they may enjoy some protection in this from their trade unions.

Trade unions and organizations

Trade unions are membership bodies comprised of workers, whose activities include protecting their members' interests, both at work

A strike: the classic way for workers to mobilize resistance against employers.

and in society at large, by winning improvements in pay and conditions from employers for example, or by influencing government policy. Unions not only play a key part in fomenting conflict at work, by mobilizing resistance to management initiatives for example, but also, through reaching agreements with managers over pay and conditions, contribute to promoting order in organizations. Based on Hyman's (2001) framework of analysis, we examine the contribution of four key sociological approaches: Marxism, which emphasizes the class-based nature of unions; a Weberian perspective, in which the focus is on how union activity enhances the market power of particular groups of workers; Durkheimian sociology, which is marked by concern with how union activity can help to promote order both in organizations and in society in general; and postmodernism, which views unions as largely irrelevant in contemporary organizations and societies.

Marxism: unions as class actors

How can Marxism help us to understand the role of trade unions in organizations? It offers some important insights, notably by emphasizing the centrality of class. Critical to Marxism is the role of class struggle under capitalism. Workers, by virtue of being exploited by their capitalist employers, develop a collective awareness of their exploitation and of the desirability of acting together to challenge the terms under which they labour. From a Marxist perspective, unions can be viewed as class actors, agents of the working class, whose activities are directed towards overturning the exploitative capitalist system that privileges employers. Unions can help towards establishing a socialist society.

This class-based analysis of unions has much to commend it. Historically, we can identify plentiful examples of the importance of an anti-capitalist, pro-socialist tradition within union movements. Between the 1880s and 1920s in particular, Marxist ideas exercised a strong influence over union goals, encouraging the development of a radical tendency within many national labour movements. The activities of unions in Italy and France in particular came to be dominated by a Marxist ideology, which still lingers today. Moreover, the perception of the unions as the representatives of a working class seems to accord with the historical experience. In many countries during the first half of the twentieth century, union movements were marked by a proletarian character; the centrality of the miners within national union movements exemplified the working-class basis of the trade unions in practice. Indeed, the long struggle of miners against pit closures in the Miners' Strike of 1984 is sometimes see as the last great manifestation of traditional class conflict, as the miners ranged themselves against their managers and the Conservative government of Margaret Thatcher.

The decline of such evidently proletarian jobs as mining, and other shifts in the occupational make-up of societies, suggest that the importance of class in general, and the existence of a homogeneous working class in particular, may have diminished. Regardless of one's perspective on the significance of class in contemporary societies, though, it is important not to write off the relevance of Marxism as a means of understanding the role of unions in contemporary organizations. One of its key benefits is the emphasis on broader social and political forces and their impact on organizational behaviour. A Marxist approach also helps us to understand how union activists in workplaces can identify particular grievances and use them as a lever to build collective organization and challenge managerial control. It is a valuable tool for explaining the presence of conflict between managers and workers in organizations, and for accounting for the presence of militant union behaviour, as in the case of the Royal Mail for example, where there are a high number of strikes as a result (Gall 2003).

Weber: unions as labour market actors

The second perspective we can draw on to understand the role of unions in organizations comes from the work of Max Weber. A Weberian approach views unions primarily as market actors, bodies that use their collective power, and are prepared to engage in conflict with employers, to defend or improve the labour market rewards of their members. Whereas Marxism sees unions as collective organizations of workers mobilized for primarily political purposes, as part of a broader class struggle leading to socialism, from a Weberian perspective unions use their collective power to achieve narrower, more instrumental goals. Their economic power is derived from the scarcity of their members' skills, so it can be used to enhance the narrow or 'sectional' goals of the workers they represent, for example by getting pay increases for skilled workers. The implication is that union organization benefits workers who are already in relatively privileged labour market positions, the 'labour aristocracy' of skilled workers in particular. Writing at the end of the nineteenth century, Beatrice and Sidney Webb, the first major students of trade unions, highlighted their role as collective bargaining agents. By forming unions, and bargaining over pay with employers collectively, workers could enhance their market power and secure better outcomes than would be possible as individuals.

There is no doubting the significance of a Weberian approach in explaining union activity. A famous series of studies in the 1960s, for example, demonstrated that manual workers joined unions primarily for instrumental purposes, not out of working-class solidarity but because they saw effective union action as an important means of improving their own material well-being (Goldthorpe et al. 1969). More recently, both the British Medical Association and the British Dental Association have used their market power very effectively to conclude agreements securing major improvements in pay and conditions for general practitioners and dentists, arguably to the detriment of the health service in the UK as a whole. The deals were controversial for directing scarce health service resources away from where they were most needed to already well-off professionals.

But what about workers who lack the market power of their skilled or otherwise relatively privileged counterparts? One of the main problems with a market-based emphasis is that vulnerable workers, who lack marketable skills, often find that their interests go unrecognized by unions. Ironically, the very people who most need union protection often find themselves excluded, or their concerns neglected, by trade unions. This is particularly evident when we consider the extent to which, historically, the policies and practices of male-dominated unions contributed to gender disadvantage at work. Bradley (1989) demonstrated that union bargaining priorities often supported and reinforced a gendered division of labour in which jobs performed largely by men were given a higher value than those undertaken by women.

Box 7.4 Trade unions and vulnerable workers

The Trades Union Congress (TUC) is the umbrella organization representing the UK's trade unions. In addition to acting as the voice of the unions in the UK, the TUC has increasingly sought to act on behalf of workers and advance their interests more generally, regardless of whether or not they are organized in a trade union. Among other things, this has encompassed campaigns against excessive working hours, to improve the rights of workers with child-care responsibilities and to publicize poor working conditions in telephone call centres. This shift in the TUC's priorities is illustrative of its attempt to develop a more inclusive, less sectional trade union movement, one that is better able to respond to the concerns of groups of workers who have traditionally not been well catered for by the unions. This includes so-called 'vulnerable' workers, people whose labour market experience is marked by insecurity and other difficulties, such as homeworkers, migrant workers and low-paid workers, people who often hail from black and ethnic minority communities, but whom in the past unions have failed to organize.

In a 2006 report, *The Hidden 1 in 5*, the TUC claimed that vulnerable workers comprised some 20 per cent of the workforce (TUC 2006). The following year, the TUC established a Commission on Vulnerable Employment, consisting of academics and representatives of unions, employers and non-governmental organizations (NGOs). The Commission was instructed to gather evidence to determine the extent of vulnerable employment, to explore its pay and conditions, and to identify measures that could be taken to reduce it and remedy its adverse consequences. This initiative is a good example of how Britain's unions, under the influence of the TUC, may be becoming more inclusive, better able to accommodate the needs and concerns of a more diverse range of workers, not just those who have traditionally been the focus of union action.

However, unions are making greater efforts to develop a more inclusive approach that focuses on protecting and advancing the interests of *all* workers, not just the already relatively privileged sections of the workforce (see box 7.4). They are now concerned with representing the interests of women workers more effectively, for example, often spurred into action by pressure from female union activists themselves. This has meant a concern with developing bargaining priorities relevant to women workers, such as equal pay or flexible working hours. Unions have also introduced policies designed to encourage female participation in union affairs, for example women's committees or special reserved seats for women members on union decision-making bodies. While the Weberian approach offers us important insights into union behaviour, demonstrating the way in which unions use their collective power to advance the material interests of their members, unions inevitably have broader social and political concerns, such as alleviating gender disadvantage at work, and, as Hyman (2001) argues, cannot be viewed just as market actors.

Durkheim: unions and organizational and societal integration

The third sociological perspective we can use to understand the role of unions comes from the work of Émile Durkheim. The influence of

Durkheim's ideas on the human relations tradition of management thinking was discussed at the start of this chapter. Whereas Marxist and Weberian approaches to understanding trade unions are both marked by an emphasis on conflict, a Durkheimian perspective focuses on the role of unions as sources of order. Their activities are seen as contributing to greater social integration and helping to sustain the organic solidarity that characterizes contemporary societies (Durkheim [1893] 1964).

The relevance of Durkheimian sociology in this area became evident during the 1960s in Britain. Growing union militancy was perceived to be having adverse effects on the British economy. Frequent local and short-lived disputes between workers and their managers, mainly about pay, seemingly undermined productivity. Moreover, the understandable desire of managers to prevent disputes from happening, by agreeing to workers' demands for higher pay, resulted in undesirable inflationary pressures in the economy. Policy-makers recommended that organizations needed to recognize the legitimacy of a union presence, rather than try to resist it. Workers were entitled to join trade unions to pursue their interests; but at the same time managers needed to exercise greater control over relations with unions in their organizations, trying, for example, to persuade unions of a common interest in exercising wage restraint. The development of formal procedures for engaging in collective bargaining with unions would help to keep conflict from spreading, preventing disputes that could damage business from spiralling out of control. By reaching agreements with employers over pay and working conditions, within mutually agreed procedures, trade union activity helps to institutionalize conflict, contributing to order and facilitating social integration. Marxists are often critical of the way union leaders operate for this reason.

Does such an approach have any relevance today? The answer to this question would appear to be 'yes'. The importance of developing formal procedures for reaching agreements between organizations and unions as a source of industrial order can be seen in the contemporary emphasis on partnership at work. Many large business organizations, including Tesco, Barclays, and Legal and General, have instituted partnership agreements with trade unions. The aim is to encourage the development of a moderate, constructive form of trade unionism, one that benefits the workforce by ensuring that people have protection and representation at work, but is also advantageous for the business, because it helps to stimulate performance improvements. An example of partnership in action was the construction of London Heathrow Airport's Terminal Five which opened on time in 2008, albeit with some short-lived operational difficulties. The co-operative relationship that existed between the contractor firms and the recognized unions helped prevent disruption. Partnership arrangements, though, are perhaps less advantageous for unions than they might appear. Studies of how partnership operates show that it generally benefits managers rather than workers, suggesting that its capacity to promote integration and order should not be exaggerated. Unions may find partnership attractive, without it leading to increased trust in management. The employees themselves are often sceptical about partnerships, describing them as 'sellouts' by the unions and as 'collusion' with the management. Thus we should be cautious about the capacity of partnership agreements to solve industrial conflicts and promote order and genuine collaboration.

Trade unions: postmodern perspectives

All three of the sociological approaches we have considered so far in this section offer important insights that enable us to understand the role played by trade unions in organizations. The extent to which union activity is marked by an emphasis on class, the market or with promoting societal integration varies over time, from country to country and also between different unions within the same country. Hyman's framework (2001) emphasizes that, in varying degrees, all unions are pressurized to operate as protagonists of the class struggle, as market actors and as forces of social integration. Moreover, an assumption shared by all three perspectives is that the unions have an important role, albeit in different ways. A fourth approach, that of postmodern sociology, sees the unions as increasingly lacking relevance in contemporary organizations.

You will recall from earlier chapters that postmodernists believe that sources of social identity that characterized modern societies – work, occupation, class – have experienced a dramatic decline. Whereas, in the past, people's identities were largely informed by their role in the sphere of production as workers, and thus as members of a specific occupation – coal miner, factory worker, schoolteacher and so on – postmodernists argue that people increasingly derive their identity from their activities as consumers, from the characteristics of their social background – their gender, ethnicity and sexuality – and from their identification with, and participation in, political struggles such as those concerned with environmental protection.

What are the implications for trade unions? As bodies whose activities are rooted in the sphere of production, they would appear to be increasingly redundant in postmodern societies. This is evident in declining support for, and membership of, trade unions. In the UK, for example, union membership fell from 50 per cent of the workforce in 1980 to barely a quarter in 2005. Union decline is particularly evident in the United States. In that country scarcely more than one in ten workers now belongs to a trade union. The diminution of union membership means that many business organizations find that they can avoid having to deal with unions relatively easily. In the UK, for example, in 1980 unions were recognized for collective bargaining in two-thirds of workplaces. By 2004 unions were recognized in under

The increase in numbers of people from minority backgrounds in organizations – and the inequality they can face – offers an important new role for trade unionism.

a third of workplaces, and in just 16 per cent of private sector ones (Kersley et al. 2006). Postmodern sociology holds that trade unionism, as the institutional embodiment of workers' interests in modern societies, is experiencing irreversible decline.

Yet such an approach can be questioned. For one thing, to what extent is union decline really linked to changes in identity formation of the kind proposed by postmodernists? Economic, political and organizational factors appear to have been a more notable cause of the dire state of trade unionism and collective bargaining. Across the advanced industrialized societies, employment growth has increasingly been concentrated in sectors of the economy where unions are weak, such as private services, and declined in areas where they have traditionally been strong, such as manufacturing industry. In many countries, including the UK, Australia, New Zealand and the United States, trade unionism has come under attack from governments keen to pursue policies that support employers and their right to manage employment relationships without interference. Emboldened by such support, many major companies, for example Wal-Mart in the United States and BSkyB in the UK, have devoted considerable amounts of managerial time to resisting the establishment of a union presence in their operations. Union decline, then, is less the product of changes in identity formation and more the result of economic and political change.

A further problem with the postmodern account of union decline is that it fails to recognize how trade unions can strengthen themselves by acknowledging and engaging with different aspects of social identity. With the help of campaign groups and community bodies, they are thus better placed to organize workers in parts of the economy from which they have largely been absent in the past. Efforts to expand union membership often focus on categories of workers with particular social characteristics, minority ethnic groups for example, because these are people who are most likely to suffer from labour market disadvantage. The development of networks of black and minority ethnic members not only helps to enhance union capabilities, by encouraging greater participation, but also means that unions pay greater attention to race equality issues. Healy et al. (2004) show how diversity can help to foster solidarity. Not only is there often a marked relationship between material disadvantage and social identity, but also unions may even benefit from the existence of more diverse patterns of social identity formation.

Conclusion

This chapter has reviewed some major aspects of people's behaviour in organizations. Managerial efforts to promote co-operation and commitment from employees, encapsulated by the human relations approach, constitute one of the most profound influences on the behaviour of workers. The aim is to secure the motivation and loyalty of staff by recognizing their social needs and encouraging their involvement in decisions that affect them at work. The enduring influence of human relations thinking is evident in many of the assumptions that underpin contemporary human resource management techniques. Yet the impact of sophisticated HRM seems to be of rather limited significance. Much contemporary people management practice is marked by rather unsophisticated efforts to maintain managerial control, and to ensure employee compliance, instead of an emphasis on increasing participation and commitment.

Many books dealing with behaviour in organizations focus solely on managerial efforts to shape and influence it. In this chapter we have also been concerned with the activities of workers and managers that do not conform with organizational goals, or employee misbehaviour. We demonstrated the range of misbehaviour that exists in organizations, explained why it occurs and set out the reasons why managers frequently tolerate it. No analysis of behaviour in organizations would be complete without considering the influence of trade unions, bodies that represent the interests of workers. This provided a good example of the way different sociological perspectives can be used to analyse workplace relations. We drew upon a number of perspectives – Marxism, the work of Weber and the tradition of Durkheimian sociology – to elucidate the varied role unions play both in organizations and in the wider economy and society. Unions can be interpreted as class, market and societal actors (Hyman 2001). Where they exist, trade unions play an important part in challenging managerial control in work organizations, enhancing the pay and conditions of their members and enabling managers to secure the co-operation of their staff. It would be a mistake to assume, as postmodern sociologists often do, that profound social changes have made the role of unions redundant. Union decline is more a function of economic, political and organizational trends rather than changes in the way in which people's identities are formed. This implies that unions have an opportunity to renew themselves, by concentrating on organizing workers who suffer from labour market disadvantage for example. Clearly they will continue to exercise an important influence on organizational life for many years yet.

Discussion questions

1. What are the main implications of the development of human resource management (HRM) for the way in which people are managed in organizations? To what extent has the rise of HRM changed people's working lives for the better?
2. What is 'organizational misbehaviour'? What forms does it take? Discuss in your group any examples of organizational misbehaviour you have encountered in jobs you have done. Why does it occur? Can managers in organizations ever eradicate misbehaviour? If not, why not?
3. Compare and contrast the Marxist, Weberian and Durkheimian approaches to understanding the role of trade unions. Which of them is the most useful, and why?
4. How far do you agree with the proposition that changes in business organizations, and in society at large, have rendered trade unions irrelevant?

Further reading

For further details of the human relations approach, and how it developed, see Rose's *Industrial Behaviour* (London: Allen Lane, 1975). The best critical overview of the human resource management phenomenon is Legge's *Human Resource Management: Rhetoric and Realities* (2nd edition; Basingstoke: Palgrave, Macmillan, 2005). For more information about organizational misbehaviour, in all its manifestations, you should refer to Ackroyd and Thompson's 1999 book *Organizational Misbehaviour* (London: Sage). An earlier study of misbehaviour, Mars' *Cheats at Work* (London: Allen and Unwin, 1982) is always well worth a read. Richard Hyman's *Understanding European Trade Unionism: Between Market, Class and Society* (London: Sage, 2001) examines the purpose of unions set against a comparative historical overview of three countries – the UK, Germany and Italy. For more information on trade unions in the UK, go to the website of the TUC (www.tuc.org. uk), which also has lots of information about workplace issues such as stress or employment law.

8 Social divisions and inequalities

This chapter will:

- introduce the concept of social divisions and how they lead to inequality, particularly in workplaces
- discuss how social class as a fundamental division has connections to other social divisions
- show how social divisions are replicated in workplaces
- introduce and discuss the differences between discrimination, prejudice and unfair discrimination
- describe and discuss the legislative framework for addressing unfair discrimination that is in place in the UK
- examine the key social divisions of gender, 'race' and ethnicity, and disability, from a sociological perspective.

Introduction

The issue of social equality is hotly contended and is the centre of debate in pub discussions, over family meals, in conferences and in university seminars. These debates are often dogged by half-truths and myths:

'People are fully protected by legislation';
'Britain is a meritocracy, and those with sufficient ability and endeavour can and will succeed';
'Absolute equality is unrealistic and undesirable, people are not "all the same"!'
'Equality measures stifle the talented and erode competition! They are a brake on progress!'

This chapter uses a sociological approach in order to explore critically the most frequently expressed views on social equality. This approach is critical, political and historically informed, relying on carefully researched evidence. We argue that while it would be inaccurate to claim that no progress had been made towards overcoming social inequality in the past sixty years, such progress has been insufficient and faltering. Moreover, in some instances the gap between the advantaged and disadvantaged is in fact now widening, while in other instances previously privileged groups are beginning to experience the negative impact of social change.

Our society, like most other industrial societies, is deeply divided. Social divisions are rife and pattern UK society in quite specific ways. And, of course, this is what we would expect of any industrial society – people are different from each other, have different skills and abilities, different psychological make-ups, live in different places and have different life experiences. Social divisions are, in part, a reflection of the diversity of our society. All of us participate in reinforcing divisions based on these forms of characteristics: we discriminate between people on the basis of our needs and personal choices. Just think about how you have ended up with your particular friendship group; it is likely that you picked these people as friends because you liked them, had things in common with them, felt comfortable with them and preferred them to other people. In doing this you discriminated against other people. This form of discrimination is not necessarily 'unfair'.

However, some social divisions are generated and reinforced by prejudices and power, and are not a result of the diversity of society. These social divisions, which divide our society on structural and prejudicial lines, are the concern of this chapter. Social divisions based on characteristics that are not alterable by individuals – such as gender, ethnicity, age, disability – have significant consequences for how our society sees itself; for individuals in marginalized, stigmatized or patronized groups; and for business organizations that ignore the power of external social divisions in stratifying and limiting the operation of an organization. Discrimination that is based on such characteristics is unfair discrimination – the people being discriminated against cannot do anything to change these characteristics, and these characteristics have no bearing on what a person is actually like and the contributions they can make to the workplace.

A distinction must be made between discrimination and unfair discrimination. All those who manage or organize workplaces must discriminate. To discriminate is to make a decision. Managers must make decisions which will leave some workers 'winners' while others lose out: who will win promotion or receive specialist training, who will get the job? That kind of decision-making is part and parcel of the work of management; there are decisions which must be made and there is nothing wrong with discrimination as long as it is fair. However, decisions may be made because of prejudice. This term, prejudice, encompasses the notion of pre-judgement: making a decision about an individual, group or community without prior knowledge or experience of them. Negative prejudices can be closely linked to unfair and inaccurate **stereotypes** which categorize the behaviour of entire social groups in one sweeping condemnation: 'women are too emotional . . .'. When prejudices are acted upon, unfair discrimination takes place.

Most people in our society recognize that unfair discrimination is a bad thing, and try to avoid it in their own actions. But despite this general societal attitude of opposing unfair discrimination and supporting equity and equality, we still have persistent patterns of discrimination and inequality. One reason for this is the difficulty in changing organizational behaviour and attitudes. Business organizations, embedded as they are in society, reproduce patterns of discrimination in their actions and policies, and this in turn serves to reinforce unfair discrimination in society. In this chapter we will examine the major forms of unfair discrimination, the social divisions that this discrimination engenders and, using case studies, the impact this has on workplaces.

Social divisions and barriers to equality

Many business studies books, particularly those that focus on employment law, look at three main areas of unfair discrimination that are addressed by legislation and other forms of state action: gender, 'race'/ ethnicity and disability. We concur that these are significant areas that need to be addressed (amongst others), and think that much more must be done to combat unfair discrimination on the grounds of gender, 'race' or ability. Much of the rest of this chapter focuses on these three areas. However, some sociologists argue that underlying and underpinning these three forms of discrimination lies a more fundamental inequality and social division, that based on social class, whereby working-class people are discriminated against. This is apparent just from a cursory glance at employment statistics: working-class women, working-class people from ethnic minorities and working-class people with a disability are all less likely to do well in the labour market than women, people from ethnic minorities and people with disabilities from middle-class backgrounds. Unfair discrimination in each case is being compounded by class, making the discrimination more entrenched and more difficult to overcome.

A fundamental social division: social class

Indeed, many sociologists go further and use class as a fundamental division that explains why forms of unfair discrimination emerge. In feminist theory, particularly the dual-systems theory (for example see Walby 1986), gender relations and class relations are parallel systems that combine in patriarchy to produce the ideas and effects of unfair discrimination. A number of sociologists examining racism consider that this is a product of capitalism: racism is an ideological construct that emerges from the class struggle in capitalist society (for example Miles and Brown 2003). The discrimination against disabled people is, perhaps, most acutely observed in the labour market, and disability rights activists and academics have linked the disabling society we live in with the operation of capitalism (Oliver 1990).

Class has long been a favoured topic among sociologists: whole books have been written about it and there are many disagreements about how it should be defined, classified and measured. We don't have space to give a full account of these complex debates here, but what we

These pictures show homes in London, not that far apart. You probably will have some ideas of the kind of people who might live in each area – where they work, what music they listen to, how they talk, etc. The fact that you have these interpretations helps to prove the continuing significance of class in the UK.

do want is to emphasize the crucial importance of class divisions in our lives. The class position into which we are born has a powerful effect on our 'life chances': where we live, where we go to school, the food we eat, the clothes we wear, our health, the university we attend, our leisure activities, our occupations and career opportunities – all these and more are influenced by our class background.

Indeed, UK society is riven with class divisions. Class is everywhere, and we are socialized into a very sophisticated understanding of class. We 'know' from common sense a lot about class – who falls into which class, how to identify different classes, what material goods are associated with which class, what cultural choices are appropriate for each class, and so on. And our social structures reflect this too – schools, hospitals, churches and other religious institutions, housing, culture and business organization. Class is a result – albeit a complex one – of differences in income and wealth. Differences in income and wealth spring from the way people are differently located in the labour market and from the different roles they fill in the system of production. Those who are excluded from participation in production fare worst in this system and are most vulnerable to poverty.

When social scientists or the government measure social class they use occupational designations to construct a classificatory scheme. These schemes produce an objective measure of social class, and currently the government classificatory scheme describes the UK class structure using the scheme known as the National Statistics Socioeconomic Classification (NS-SeC). This has been used since 2001 for all official statistics and surveys. It replaces Social Class based on Occupation (SC) and Socio-economic Groups (SEG).

> The NS-SeC is an occupationally-based classification designed to provide coverage of the whole adult population. The version of the

classification which will be used for most analyses has eight classes, the first of which can be subdivided. These are:

1. Higher managerial and professional occupations
    1.1. Large employers and higher managerial occupations
    1.2. Higher professional occupations
2. Lower managerial and professional occupations
3. Intermediate occupations
4. Small employers and own account workers
5. Lower supervisory and technical occupations
6. Semi-routine occupations
7. Routine occupations
8. Never worked and long-term unemployed

For complete coverage, the three categories Students, Occupations not stated or inadequately described, and Not classifiable for other reasons, are added as 'Not classified'. (*Social Trends*, 34, 2004, Appendix 1: 227)

You might want to think about where you, your friends and family fit into this scheme.

Class is not just about objective measures – in fact, those objective measures are often counter-productive for analysis, hiding from us the real issues of class. The following two quotations give some sense of the complexities of understanding class:

Class . . . is conceptualized as a dynamic process which is the site of political struggle, rather than as a set of static and empty positions waiting to be filled by indicators such as employment and housing. It is the result of a historical process in which the bourgeoisie became a 'class for itself' through distinguishing itself from its twin others – the aristocracy and the poor (later to be designated 'the working class/es') (Finch, 1993)

Although there have clearly been important social, economic and political changes in both working-class and middle-class life in all classed societies over the last one hundred or so years, my argument here focuses on the relational, rather than the substantive, manifestations of classed existence. (Lawler 2005: 430)

If we start to look at culture as a dynamic relationship and a site of political struggle, we see things in a new light. Recent sociological research on class has shifted from a consideration of structural features and conditions of social stratification and moved to a consideration of cultural constructions of class. One reason for this is the decline in the importance of some structural determinants – economically there are fewer differences between middle-class occupations and working-class occupations; in the middle of society disparities between salaries have decreased. However, at the edges of society the gap between richest and poorest has increased dramatically. A recent study by the Joseph Rowntree Foundation found that the number of 'core poor' households rose from 17 per cent in 1980 to 27 per cent in 2000. In the same period the number of 'asset wealthy' households rose from 17 per cent to 27 per cent (Dorling et al. 2007).

Clearly we can't say that money is no longer significant – it is. However, it is what one does with it that is most significant, and here we can see a significant shift in: (a) sociological theories of class, and (b) societal attitudes. Sociological analysis of class formerly focused on collective aspects – what large groups of people did and thought in terms of group interests. Think about how we used to explain voting patterns – class and tradition dictated, largely, who you would vote for. Now it is much more about interests in terms of the self: who offers the best deal for you and your family? We have seen a shift in society towards more individual modes of explanation and behaviour – particularly in terms of the self. The control and discipline of the self, and the construction of self-identity as a responsible consuming subject now dominate our society, and sociology has started to understand class in this way. This is an aspect of the 'liquid modernity' we discussed in chapter 3.

When we start looking at class in terms of cultural representations of class subjects, we see some disconcerting things. We need to recognize that control and dissemination of culture lies in the hands of the majority – the middle and privileged classes. Representations reflect the concerns of the dominant group in society. What we think of as being objective class divisions are produced in the everyday practices and judgements of the middle class. Central to this, according to sociologist Stephanie Lawler (2005), is a sense of disgust, particularly disgust with the working class, reflected in the contemptuous terms often used about them: plebs, proles, chavs, oiks and so forth. Increasingly, middle-class parents seek private schooling for their children to protect them from contamination by contact with 'rough' working-class pupils. Middle-class identity is based upon the construction of an Other that middle-class selves are not, and that Other is despised and disliked. The middle class forms itself in opposition to a construction of working class-ness: working class-ness forms the constitutive outside to middle-class existence.

> The issue here is not simply about middle-class people 'looking down on' working-class people. Such understandings work to produce working-class people as abhorrent and as foundationally 'other' to a middle-class existence that is silently marked as normal and desirable. But . . . they also produce middle-classed identities that rely on not being the repellent and disgusting 'other'. (Lawler 2005: 431)

If you look at public representations and the media in British society, a common expression you will observe concerning the working class is dislike and disgust (think of the TV comedy programme *Little Britain*'s characters Vicky Pollard or Andy the wheelchair user). And – importantly – this is hardly ever remarked upon. The consequences are immense: class divisions are constructed and perpetuated by structures of power and become fundamental to all social relationships and social representations. As Beverley Skeggs says:

> We require an understanding that goes beyond the 'economic' and exchange to understand the consequences of cultural struggle and how this is part of new marketization, new attributions of value, new forms of appropriation, exploitation and governance, and new selves.
> (Skeggs 2004: 186)

In her own research Skeggs has also explored the way that some members of the working class react to this 'Othering' by seeking to 'disidentify' themselves from being a member of the despised class. She studied young women in Lancashire who were training to be care workers and found that above all they sought ' respectability' to distinguish themselves from 'poor people' (Skeggs 1997). Not all people take such a position, however. Many people who have been interviewed by the authors of this book have, on the contrary, stated how proud they are to be part of the class 'that does the real work in Britain' (Bradley 1999). Among women and men who work in factories, construction companies, shops and hospitals to provide our society with essential goods and services there is a demand for recognition, both economic and cultural, for the valuable work they do. As we saw in the previous chapter, the trade union movement, formed out of the needs of working people for representation, has fought consistently over the centuries for 'a fair wage for a fair day's work'. Many unions now have a particular concern for opening up career paths for their working-class members and preventing discrimination on class grounds as well as those of gender, ethnicity and disability.

The business case against unfair discrimination

It has long been recognized that unfair discrimination is not good for business. Gary Becker's groundbreaking study on the economics of discrimination (1971) starts from the premise that all unfair discrimination is not rational and is therefore a cost to businesses. Given this, employers who do not discriminate will have a competitive advantage over those who discriminate unfairly. Although Becker's work has a high degree of internal validity, his argument fails to recognize the deeply ingrained structural patterns of discrimination, and the way that expectations are socially constructed and reflect gendered social relations. There is a general expectation that women will be less productive than men as they more frequently have caring responsibilities. These expectations become self-fulfilling in the world of gendered work.

However, Becker's arguments have resurfaced in the context of Britain's increasingly diverse and multi-ethnic society and labour force. Recent research by the Equal Opportunities Commission (EOC) revealed that the majority of employers and managers, especially in large organizations, do support the 'business case' for equality and diversity and believe it will help to increase their profits (Bradley et al. 2007). This rests on a number of premises:

1. customers and clients are themselves diverse, so prefer to deal with companies and organizations with a mixed workforce;
2. ignoring the potential of women and BME (black and minority ethnic) workers means that firms will lose out in the 'search for talent', increasingly important in the competitive global marketplace;
3. failure to treat people equally may lead to legal prosecution and expensive tribunal cases;
4. it is good for an organization's image to be seen as a fair employer, and a good record on equality and diversity is good promotional and public relations (PR) material.

However, the EOC research also found that employers, although recognizing the validity of the business case, were not really sure how to implement it, with many saying they found it hard to recruit BME women staff. Moreover, while top managers and HRM staff were greatly in favour of diversity policies, some line managers still held stereotypical and prejudiced views about women and BME citizens, and in their appointment and promotion decisions were often acting to undermine the organization's equality and diversity policies.

Law, work and equality

British law distinguishes between what it calls 'direct' and 'indirect' discrimination and these are important features of much equality legislation. Direct discrimination is said to have occurred when a person treats another person less favourably on the grounds of their 'race' or ethnic origin, age, disability, gender, sexual orientation, religion or belief. Indirect discrimination is said to have occurred when a provision, criterion or practice is applied which disadvantages people due to 'race' or ethnic origin, age, disability, gender, sexual orientation, religion or belief. That provision, practice or criterion may be applied to all workers (and does not directly focus upon a member of a disadvantaged group) but if it does have negative ramifications for a disadvantaged group or individual and there is no legitimate business requirement, then indirect discrimination has occurred. An example of indirect discrimination is when a business requires all its employees to work late on a Friday evening, despite the fact that the religious beliefs of some members of the workforce require that they join others in worship at that time. If there is no legitimate business rationale for the work-late requirement, then indirect discrimination, contravening the Employment Equality (Religion or Belief) Regulations (2003), has occurred.

British law outlaws harassment in the workplace. Sometimes workers might refer to their experience of harassment as 'workplace bullying'. Although most claims of workplace harassment are brought under the specific equality legislation relating to the protection of disadvantaged groups, the Protection from Harassment Act 1997 and the Criminal

Justice and Public Order Act 1994 have also been used successfully. While equality legislation seeking to protect a range of vulnerable social groups makes specific reference to harassment, those who fall outside those groups can make a claim if they can make a case that they are being treated unreasonably and that an abuse of power has taken place.

Although harassment may, in some instances, be difficult to recognize, crucial to the definition is the concept of 'unwanted' behaviour. This can include ridicule and unwanted teasing, for example, and the use of intimidating and insulting language, verbal and physical intimidation, public humiliation, threats or the imposition of unreasonable workloads and deadlines. It can refer to unwanted conduct affecting the dignity of men and women in the workplace. It may be persistent or an isolated incident. Individuals may not always be aware that their behaviour constitutes harassment, because what may be considered to be acceptable behaviour or conduct by one individual/group may not be acceptable and cause distress to another. For example, what some people perceive as joking or banter may be hurtful to individuals if it contains elements disrespectful to women or members of minority groups. Consequently, the important issue is the perception and feelings of the injured individual. However, this is not the sole test. A further test, for example, would be that any reasonable person would find the alleged behaviour wholly unreasonable and unacceptable in the circumstances and context in which it occurred.

It can take a good deal of courage for an unhappy employee to make a claim against their employer, manager or colleagues. They may fear reprisals for their actions. However, it is import to note that, under anti-discrimination legislation, workers are protected from **victimization**. Victimization can be said to have occurred when a person receives unfair treatment and:

(a) they have previously made a complaint about being discriminated against or harassed; or
(b) they intend to make a complaint about discrimination or harassment; or
(c) they have acted or intend to act as a witness or to give evidence in support of another person(s) relating to a complaint about discrimination or harassment.

Victimization can take a variety of forms. It may be that individuals are refused requests for time off, denied promotion or training, ignored by their manager or colleagues, criticized continually for their work or find that their work schedules have been rearranged at short notice and for no reason. If this happens and an organization does not take reasonable steps to prevent it, the organization may be found liable to pay compensation. Individuals who victimize may also be ordered to pay compensation.

Harassment and victimization may be carried out by a manager or employer or by a person's colleagues. In these circumstances, even when the employer is not directly responsible for the act of harassment or victimization, they can be held liable for it. Employers have a responsibility to prevent such acts and, if they do not act accordingly and with sufficient conviction, they may be found to have what is legally called 'vicarious liability'.

In light of the findings of the Macpherson Inquiry into the role of the police, following the murder of black teenager Stephen Lawrence, and the recognition of the reproduction of inequalities within and by institutions, the Equality Act 2006 was introduced, which required that statutory organizations (Local Authorities, the police service, Health Authorities, for example) had a 'duty' to eliminate unlawful discrimination and harassment and to actively promote equality. This meant that public-sector organizations were required not simply to have an equalities policy and respond to any complaints, but also to show they were taking positive steps to promote equality. Duties refer not only to access to employment but also to the provision of social goods and services. Thus far these statutory bodies have a general duty of responsibility to eliminate inequalities associated with 'race', gender, age and disability, but it is likely that inequalities associated with sexual orientation and religion and belief will be added to that responsibility. Public authorities will be subject to detailed requirements, which are known as specific duties. This will require that they publish an equality scheme stating their equality goals with regard to gender, 'race' and disability, how they plan to achieve these and how they monitor and review their equality progress. Universities are also bound to such 'duties'.

We noted in the above discussion that this legislation relates to a number of different forms of discrimination. In the next section of this chapter, we shall go on to discuss three of these in more detail: ethnicity, gender and disability. Although there are common elements between these three, there are also issues specific to each one. Formerly they were looked after by three separate bodies, the Commission for Racial Equality (CRE), the Equal Opportunities Commission (EOC) and the Disabilities Commission. These were replaced in 2007 by a single body which covers all types of discrimination and inequality, the Equality and Human Rights Commission (EHRC). There is much disagreement as to whether this is a positive development. On the one hand, the enlarged commission may have more power and clout, and will be able to investigate how two or more types of disadvantage may operate together (what is now called 'intersectionality' and which will be illustrated in the following sections). On the other hand, there are fears that the strength of advocacy for each separate form of disadvantage may be lost or that one particular form may dominate at the expense of the others. The EHRC is very new and its effectiveness will be judged in coming years. One point that needs to be made, though, is that each type of discrimination has different parameters, as explored here, and may need different policies to address it.

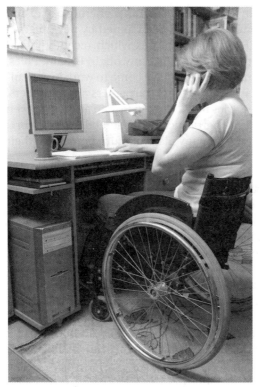

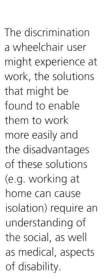

The discrimination a wheelchair user might experience at work, the solutions that might be found to enable them to work more easily and the disadvantages of these solutions (e.g. working at home can cause isolation) require an understanding of the social, as well as medical, aspects of disability.

'Race' and ethnicity

Parameters

As discussed in chapter 3, we live in an increasingly multi-ethnic world, as globalization encourages the movement of firms and workers between countries. Like many countries, however, the UK has a long history of migration, inwards and outwards, as a consequence of our colonial history. Thus some of the largest ethnic minority groups in Britain are migrants from former colonies: the Indian subcontinent and the Caribbean islands. Though migration of these groups goes back to the eighteenth and nineteenth centuries, the major period of immigration was during the post-war reconstruction period, when citizens from these colonies were actively recruited to fill shortage areas in the economy: nursing, transport and factory work.

Subsequently many other groups have added to the multi-ethnic variety of Britain's major cities, some coming in as economic migrants to fill continuing labour shortages (such as Filipina nurses and domestic servants, Indian and Pakistani doctors), others as refugees and asylum seekers from the world's wars and trouble spots. Despite strict control over immigration imposed since the 1970s, many of these economic and political migrants have been welcomed for the skills and resources they possess. Chinese, Turks, Kurds and Bangladeshis have enriched the culture of our society by providing restaurants offering cheap and novel 'ethnic' foods. Recently they have been joined by new migrant groups from the Eastern European countries which recently joined the European Union and thus gained rights to work in Britain. Poles, Hungarians, Romanians and Bulgarians have come to work in agriculture or to offer their craft skills as builders, carpenters and plumbers. Low wages in their own countries make work in Britain attractive, even in low-paid work such as strawberry-picking or hotel domestic work. However, as we saw in chapter 3, many plan to return home with their savings, particularly as their own economies develop.

The presence of both new and old ethnic minority communities in the UK has unfortunately been attended by conflict and controversy. Racist and xenophobic attitudes among some members of the white indigenous population led to calls for curbs on immigration and resulted in the positing of minority populations as 'second-class citizens'. They have suffered widespread disadvantage in the labour market. BME Britons are much more likely to be unemployed; they are clustered into low-paid dead-end jobs, often those rejected by the majority population; they are under-represented in managerial and professional roles; the work of Anthony Heath has shown that many groups suffer an 'ethnic penalty' in that they do not gain the same rewards from their educational achievements and qualifications (Heath and Cheung 2006).

However, it is important to note that there are major differences between the BME communities. The Indian and Chinese communities have employment profiles much closer to those of whites and are slightly more likely than whites to be in managerial jobs, although this is often in the ethnic business sector of small firms serving their own communities. Increasingly, however, young Britons of Indian and Chinese origin are succeeding in professional areas, such as the finance sector, medicine or engineering. By contrast, Bangladeshis are among the most disadvantaged groups. The unemployment rate among Bangladeshi men of working age in 2002 was 20 per cent, compared to the national male average of 5 per cent. Even more shockingly, the rate for the 18–24 age group was 41 per cent, compared to 12 per cent. Bangladeshi men are highly concentrated into two occupations: transport (as taxi drivers) and restaurant work (as owners or waiters). While 27 per cent of white men work in two sectors (hotels, transport and distribution), 81 per cent of Bangladeshi men work within them. Bangladeshi women have the lowest economic activity rate, at 27 per cent in 2001, compared to a national average for women of 70 per cent.

Explanation

As the above examples suggest, it is difficult to make generalizations about ethnic discrimination, as different BME communities are differently positioned in the labour market, partly in relation to the circumstances of their migration: when they came, what jobs they entered into upon arrival, what their occupational and class position was in their country of origin. However, we can draw out a few general points.

When these patterns of disadvantage were first discerned in national surveys carried out by PEP (Political and Economic Planning) (Smith 1977; Brown 1984), it was suggested that these might be partly related to language difficulties or lack of skills among the migrant groups. However, when it subsequently became apparent that the same patterns were appearing among the 'second-generation' of BME citizens (those born and educated in Britain), this explanation no longer held water. Research into matched pairs of applicants with similar qualifications revealed that jobs were offered to the white people, not to African-Caribbeans or Asians, though the Caribbeans might get as far as interview if they had English-sounding names. These and other studies suggested that racial prejudice and stereotyping were common. More recent research continues to show the effects of such prejudices. For example, research in the NHS by John Carter (1999) showed that black staff had to apply for promotion many more times than whites before they succeeded and that they were more likely to undergo disciplinary procedures. Bradley et al. (2007) found that black Caribbean women were perceived as too aggressive and 'mouthy' to be suitable management material, even though many of them reported how they had trained young white men in their jobs who were then promoted over them. Meanwhile Muslim women who chose to wear Islamic dress found it more difficult to find employment than those who chose western clothing, and found that if they started to wear the hijab (headscarf) after not doing so at first they were then treated with suspicion by their workmates, clients and customers.

Indeed Tariq Modood (2005) has mounted a vigorous argument that religion is now a greater source of discrimination than skin colour, a position that gains some affirmation from the rise of Islamophobia, following the terrorist attacks on the World Trade Center and the London Underground. He points out that, while in the past it was black Caribbean youth who were stopped and searched on the streets, young Asian men are now viewed as the dangerous troublemakers. However, we would suggest that racism and xenophobia can take many different forms. While Muslim groups are certainly targets of racism, so too are members of other visible minorities; a black skin still triggers off stereotypes which sociologists such as Miles and Brown (2003) demonstrate are rooted in past colonial attitudes which viewed non-white peoples as inferior, childlike and lacking in intelligence.

Particularly vulnerable to the impact of racism and xenophobia are recently arrived migrants, such as refugees from Somalia, sub-Saharan African countries or the Middle East. These refugees and asylum seekers lack legal rights to protect them and live in fear of exportation, which makes them prey to exploiters such as gang-masters or pimps who take advantage of them. As they lack the right to employment they may be lured into illegal work or the sex industry. Even legal entrants such as the East Europeans may be vulnerable because of their unfamiliarity with the culture and its rules. The terrible story of the twenty-one Chinese cockle-pickers who were drowned in Morecambe Bay in February 2004 illustrates the dangers that confront illegal and temporary economic migrants.

At the other end of the scale we can see how class can offset some of the disadvantages of ethnic origin (just as it can also compound them). For example, the Indians who were expelled in the 1970s from Kenya and Uganda came from privileged class backgrounds, owning their own businesses or working as professionals in education, banking or medicine. Although many of the original migrants experienced an initial occupational downgrading, forced to work as taxi drivers or hosiery workers, they were able to pass on some of their **cultural capital** to their children, who achieved well in education. Thus many British Indians have regained their original class position, accounting for their relative labour market success. Even so, evidence suggests that Asian graduates have to undergo many more interviews than whites before finding a job (Modood et al. 1997).

Legislation

Legislation relating to racial discrimination dates back to 1976, when the Race Relations Act made it illegal to cause or allow racial harassment. The Race Relations Act makes discrimination on grounds of 'race' unlawful in education, training and employment; provision of goods, facilities and services; disposal and management of property. 'Race' in this Act is defined as 'race', colour, nationality, ethnic or national origin. The Race Relations Act was amended in 2000 to prohibit racial discrimination in many public functions including policing, and to place a new duty on public authorities to promote racial equality.

In July 2003 the government implemented the European Union (EU) Directive on Race which introduces a minimum standard of protection from race discrimination and harassment across Europe. This will benefit UK citizens who wish to travel, live or work in the EU. The Directive has led to more changes to the Race Relations Act. Outlined below is the legal framework from 19 July 2003.

There is legal protection from direct discrimination, i.e. treating a person less favourably than another on grounds of 'race', colour, nationality, ethnic or national origin, and from indirect discrimination. Indirect discrimination is defined in two ways: either in the applying of a condition or requirement which adversely affects people on grounds of their colour or nationality, causes a detriment and cannot be justified, or in the application of a provision, criterion or practice that puts or would put people, on grounds of their 'race' or ethnic or national origin, at a particular disadvantage and which is not a proportionate means of achieving a legitimate aim. The legislation also prohibits victimization (unfair treatment because a person has made a complaint of racial discrimination) and harassment (i.e. unwanted conduct that has the purpose or effect of violating another person's dignity or creating an intimidating, hostile, degrading, humiliating or offensive environment).

With this new legislation, the burden of proof has also changed. Formerly the person alleging discrimination was obliged to provide proof, which was, for example, difficult in cases where decisions about appointment or promotion were made and the complainant was not present at the discussion. However, now courts and tribunals deciding on complaints of discrimination on grounds of 'race' or ethnic or national origin must, once the facts of the complaint have been established, uphold the complaint unless it can be proven by the employer that the discrimination did not occur. As well as the protection afforded to individuals, the Race Relations Amendment Act (RRAA) 2000 requires public authorities to have due regard when performing their functions to eliminate unlawful racial discrimination.

In December 2003, regulations came into force in order to end discrimination on the basis of religion or belief. The regulations cover discrimination, harassment and victimization in work and vocational training. They make it unlawful to behave in a way that violates someone's dignity, such as calling someone names because they are of a particular religion. They also outlaw harassment that is not personal but makes the atmosphere difficult for someone because of their religion.

Case study 8.1 A double discrimination: ethnic and gender hierarchies at work

As we stated earlier in the chapter, forms of discrimination may come together to compound disadvantage. Following research by the EOC (Botcherby and Hurrell 2004; Bhavnani 2006) which found that young BME women were faring less well in the labour market despite being better qualified, more aspirational and harder-working than their white counterparts, Bradley et al. (2007) studied the impact of workplace cultures on Black Caribbean, Pakistani and Bangladeshi women. Although the case-study organizations in their research all had strong equalities policies on paper, these did not always translate into fair practice. Despite senior management and HR staff showing real commitment to equality, women reported that they had experienced sexist and racist discrimination and prejudice from line managers who often favoured white candidates for promotion. Women had been denied access to training which would help them to develop their careers, had been turned down repeatedly in promotion applications on grounds that continually shifted, had seen less-qualified staff promoted over them, and had not been given adequate guidance or mentoring to equip them to progress. Skills which they had, such as speaking several languages, or experience of managing in a family business, were often ignored.

Some had been denied jobs on the basis of their dress (a woman was told that she could not have a job in a lingerie department because she wore a headscarf). Though it is good EO practice to have a gender and ethnic mix on interview panels, many reported only being interviewed by white males. Provision of mentoring and role models is an important issue which could easily be adopted by managers to make their organizations more diversity friendly:

> Girls around my age we're actually struggling to find our feet in the professional environment and we don't really have anybody to look up to. There's lot of men, but the women have suffered because they had this stigma attached to them.

> When I went for the job I looked at my two interviewers and they were Black and I thought, I must have this job. So it was motivating and inspiring and warming to see two Black women in that position. Seeing them in that position and thinking, yes, okay, we can do it.
> (Bradley et al. 2007: 5, 14)

Bradley et al. also found that in many cases women felt excluded and marginalized by the informal relationships within the workplace culture. Much workplace interaction centred on after-hours visits to pubs, which Caribbean and Muslim women felt uncomfortable taking part in. Official workplace events also often involved alcohol or gambling which are forbidden in the Muslim religion. Pakistani and Bangladeshi women often had no place to say their prayers and were persistently questioned about their cultural practices, such as fasting for Ramadan, in ways which made them appear strange and different.

Why should these things matter? The women were very well aware that a lot of networking went on in pubs and at social events from which they were excluded. Networking is generally acknowledged as crucial in making your way in organizations: making contacts, picking up vital information or knowledge about opportunities, making an impression on your peers and your seniors. This was one reason why the women failed to progress up the hierarchy. Some progressive organizations are helping with this by providing mentors or setting up black networks which offer support to BME women; however, even then they may still feel like outsiders in their work-groups. A common theme among the women in the study was a desire to work in an organization that was friendly and welcoming, where they could feel comfortable.

Many of the organizations were making genuine attempts to change their cultures and open up career paths for BME women. Nonetheless the compound effects of ethnicity with gender (which will be explored in the next section) meant that in most of the organizations there were very few women in senior posts and hardly any black women.

Case study 8.2 'Young, gifted and black' – that's not where it's at . . .

> Teachers have the power to throw young people out of school without giving them substitute education. The statistics show that a disproportionate number of young people that are excluded are black males. Education empowers people and gives you the skills to become successful. Young people who are thrown out of school and denied their education are not empowered for the business world.
>
> (Richardson 2007: 155)

While research shows that racism and discrimination within organizations have negative effects on minority citizens, workplaces alone are not responsible for patterns of racial disadvantage. Factors outside the workplace have an important role, which reminds us of the need to view business organizations in their social context. One of the major issues in the UK today is widespread unemployment among young minority men, and, as the quotation above suggests, the problems start in the school system and surrounding neighbourhoods.

Tell It Like It Is (Richardson 2007) is a collection of essays exploring the educational underachievement of young black boys and, as the book argues, how schools fail black children. This arises from a classic study by Bernard Coard (1971) which showed how many Caribbean children were wrongly categorized as educationally subnormal (ESN). Despite various attempts to remedy this, such as the government's Aim Higher Scheme, these problems persist many decades later:

> When African and Afro-Caribbean children enter the school system at five they do as well as white and Asian children in tests. By eleven their achievement levels begin to drop off. By sixteen there has been a collapse. 48 per cent of all 16-year-old boys gain five GCSEs, grades A to E. Only 13 per cent of black boys in London achieve this standard.
>
> (Abbott 2007: 105)

This failure at school leads to low self-esteem among many of the boys, who then turn to other areas of their lives to find success and fulfilment and the key cultural value of 'respect'. As many live in deprived areas, there is a danger that they will get dragged into gang culture, and thence into fighting and violence, criminal activity, drug-taking and drug-dealing. Many come from single-parent families and lack positive male role models, or guidance from what Elijah Anderson (1997), in a study of young African-Americans, calls 'old heads', that is experienced community leaders who can help youngsters through the troubles of adolescence. Instead they may aspire to emulate rich young drug-dealers who display the status symbols (cars, clothes, girlfriends) they covet.

A young black man, Craig Cameron, reflecting on his own experiences, analyses the processes that lead towards these depressing outcomes:

> I was always a very bright student, but I felt that I was treated differently because I was a black male while the culture and atmosphere and the majority of the teachers were middle class and white. Although my overall experience of school was positive, whenever I was in trouble or the school was trying to sanction me I found I was being treated more harshly than others. I feel this was a reflection of how society generally stereotypes black men. Afro-Caribbean boys are seen as aggressive and confrontational.

These stereotypes often arise from misperceptions of a different cultural style:

> Within my culture people can express themselves in a loud and enthusiastic, passionate way. That is how my parents are, and that's how I know how to be . . . The way we behaved was misunderstood at school and regarded as rudeness, aggression and bad attitude.
>
> (Richardson 2007: 157)

Craig himself did not drop out of school, partly, he explained, because of his respect for his mother and her example. But he also spoke of the void left by the lack of a positive male role model such as a father or older brother and suggested that many of his friends filled that void by joining a gang:

> For them it was almost like having the family that they never had at home, and it is a reaction to how they were treated at school and how society generally sees them.
>
> (Richardson 2007: 158)

Contributors to the book stress the importance of getting more BME teachers into schools where black children are in a majority; altering the curriculum to make it more inclusive, useful and relevant to children from a different culture; identifying the strengths of BME children and helping them to acquire the skills that they may lack. It is also important to fight against racial stereotyping and misunderstandings, put more resources into schools in deprived areas and ensure that minority parents have access to the information they need to steer their children successfully through the education system.

As the contributors to *Tell It Like It Is* point out, these school dropouts are then trapped into a way of life which may lead to long-term or permanent labour market exclusion. It is not easy to find even low-skilled work with limited qualifications, a messy CV and possibly a criminal record, especially if you are black or Asian. It is important that ways are opened up through lifelong learning and late-entrant schemes to reintegrate people back into work, and that organizations respond sympathetically to such schemes. If solutions are not found, the whole of society will continue to suffer the negative results of such patterns of unemployment and exclusion, such as the prevalence of drug-fuelled crime (muggings and robberies) and street violence such as the series of killings of young teenagers in London and the North-West which occurred in 2008 while we were writing this book.

Gender

Parameters

> An equal society protects and promotes equal, real freedom and substantive opportunity to live in the ways people value and would choose, so that everyone can flourish. An equal society recognizes people's different needs, situations and goals and removes the barriers that limit what people can do and can be.
>
> (The Equalities Review 2007: 6)

Gender discrimination, the vast majority of which is against women, is a persistent phenomenon in the world of business in the UK and elsewhere, despite decades of legislation and action. It takes a range of forms, from blatant prejudice such as refusing to promote or appoint women, to subtle undermining of women in workplaces by marginalizing them or assigning them to lesser or demeaning roles. Frequently this form of discrimination is attached to women's reproductive role (see case study 8.3).

Case study 8.3 '£60k payout for "useless" pregnant sales executive'

A sales director has won nearly £60,000 compensation after her boss told her she would be 'useless' because she was pregnant. When Louise Manning, 39, of Chelmsford, Essex, announced her pregnancy she was told she would 'never be the same again'. Earlier in the year an employment tribunal in Ashford, Kent, ruled managing director Nicholas Medlam and Safetell, based in Dartford, had sexually discriminated against her 24 times. Yesterday it ordered Medlam and Safetell to pay £20,509 in loss of earnings and £37,100 in compensation but rejected a claim of constructive dismissal.

(*Guardian* Friday 2 May 2008)

What the Americans call 'maternal profiling' of this kind – that is, refusing to employ or promote a woman because she is pregnant or might become so – is illegal, but is apparently widespread in the UK. Sir Alan Sugar exemplified this when he questioned Katie Hopkins, a single mother and leading candidate to become his apprentice, about her childcare arrangements and whether they would be compatible with working for him. Employers should not ask interviewees about their domestic arrangements, but subsequent to Sir Alan's statement of his views about working mothers, many employers admitted that they avoid appointing young women who were married and likely to give birth. This is one example of a very marked 'maternal penalty' that operates against working mothers, who often see their careers lose momentum while their children are young.

At the heart of gender discrimination lies the gendered division of labour. Men and women perform different tasks in the labour market (see chapter 4) such that we can identify men's work, women's work and work that is gender-neutral using Hakim's terminology (Hakim 2000). Work is thus segregated between the sexes, and this **segregation** is not only horizontal – between occupations – but also vertical – within occupations. The result is a gender pay gap (currently around 20 per cent in the UK), and a structural situation where men are much more likely than women to be in positions of power in organizations.

It is frequently argued, even by university undergraduates, that gender inequality has been overcome. In reality, despite thirty years of legislation specifically designed to eradicate it, gender inequality persists. Although the gap may have narrowed, it still exists between the experiences and treatment of men and women, particularly in relation to work, paid and unpaid. Women are clustered in low-paid low-status jobs, excluded from powerful posts and bear responsibility for the bulk of housework. Surveys continue to show that women carry out about 70 per cent of domestic labour with men cherry-picking the tasks that they like to 'help' with.

The 'second wave' of feminism produced increased pressure for social change and for legal protection for women in the 1960s and 1970s. A substantial body of legislation relates to sex inequality and this covers the rights of both men and women. In addition to the duties now incumbent on statutory authorities enshrined in the 2006 Equality Act (see below), legislation going back thirty years has sought to ensure sex equality, particularly with regard to employment.

While the Sex Discrimination Act (1975) and the Equal Pay Act (1970) were designed to protect both men and women from discrimination, it is women who have historically faced most disadvantages in the workplace and women who have most frequently had cause to call upon the Acts for protection (though men also use them). The gender pay gap, though reduced, continues to exist. Government statistics suggest that, if we use internationally comparable measures based on mean earnings, women's average hourly pay (excluding overtime) was 17.2 per cent less than men's pay in 2007. This represents a reduction of 12.2 per cent in the pay gap between men and women since the Equal Pay Act came into force in 1975; not insignificant, but not enough (ONS). According to the EOC in 2007 the average full-time, hourly wage for a man was £14.08, while for a woman it was £11.67. Women who work part-time are in a worse situation, earning only £8.68 per hour, or 61.6 per cent of the rate for men working full-time.

The reduction of the pay gap is not the only measure of progress. The roles and responsibility women take up in the workplace are also of significance. In 1975 women made up only 2 per cent of workplace managers; by 2007 that figure increased to 30 per cent (The Equalities

Review 2007). In addition women are accessing forms of work, particularly in the professions, which were exclusively male preserves. These include medicine, dentistry and the legal profession (Bradley et al. 2000). Despite such positive trends, progress has been slow to the extent that, unless decisive new action is taken, it is estimated that the gender pay gap will continue for at least another generation (The Equalities Review 2007).

Explanation

In spite of attempts to legislate for gender equality, the stereotype as to what is appropriate 'feminine' and 'masculine' behaviour continues to have a major impact on popular culture. Sexist ideologies, which promote the apparent 'naturalness' of male and female social roles, result in the gender 'pigeon-holing' of both men and women. This ideology of gender is deeply entrenched in British culture and has been internalized by those affected by it; men and women believe in gender stereotypes, even when they are disadvantaged by them. The relationship between the ideology of a 'natural' gender order and the workplace is mutually reinforcing; men and women make choices and are persuaded to make choices about their paid and unpaid work on the basis of such ideologies, while at the same time the world of work mirrors and reproduces gender stereotypes.

Once again we see continuity and change: stereotypes about what constitutes 'women's' and 'men's' work have been challenged, but nevertheless persist. Gender pay gaps can be explained, in part, by the ghettoization of women into low-paid, temporary and part-time work which mirrors their 'natural' domestic ability, while they continue to carry the majority of responsibility for domestic, unpaid work in the home. Women are still perceived as 'natural carers', both in the home and in the workplace, and are over-represented in poorly paid cleaning, catering, caring, cashiering and clerical work (all the Cs!).

While legislation can be used to increase the wages of such workers and in doing so change the perception of the value of that work, gender equality, particularly in terms of pay, is unlikely to be brought about unless women are willing and able to force their way into male employment, climb career ladders and take senior positions of responsibility. A significant barrier to this is that gender stereotyping has an impact on the ambitions and expectations of both men and women and affects the types of jobs they choose. The EOC claims that only 2 per cent of childcare workers are men and less than 1 per cent of plumbers are women. By contrast, despite the trend towards women entering the professions which were once male strongholds, they have tended not to reach senior positions. In high-profile decision-making jobs women are poorly represented: in 2007 only 9 per cent of senior judges and 10 per cent of senior police officers were women (The Equalities Review 2007).

Pregnancy, or the possibility of it, continues to be treated as a threat to business interests. As a consequence, more than 200,000 women a year in Britain experience illegal dismissal or disadvantageous treatment at work because of their pregnancy (see case study 8.3). As with most equality legislation, the emphasis to prove injustice lies with the 'victim' (The Equalities Review 2007). Inadequate or insufficient social care (compared to the kind of state nursery provision which is available in Scandinavia and France) has had a major impact on women's ability to access employment. Almost four out of ten mothers have left a job or been unable to take a job because of their parenting responsibilities. The same is the case for over one in ten fathers, and two in ten carers experience similar difficulties.

There are long-term consequences for those who opt out of employment. Five out of six recently retired women are not entitled to the full basic state pension based on their own contributions. The value of time spent caring for children or other family members is not recognized by the state and can contribute to women's poverty in retirement, as many women do not pay full national insurance contributions and consequently reach retirement age with an inadequate pension: older women are much more likely to live in poverty than older men (The Equalities Review 2007).

A further significant cultural barrier to female equality is the continued cultural sexualization of women. In the workplace this can result in the sexual harassment of women in employment which continues to be a major problem. Again it is for the women involved

The sexualization and trivialization of women's roles in the workplace can be found in popular culture, such as the stereotypical fancy-dress 'doctors and nurses'.

to understand their experience and to seek recompense from employment tribunals. In doing so, these women face a number of potential dangers. They face ridicule, of being portrayed as kill-joys or 'frigid' if they reject unwanted sexual attention. Stop for a moment and consider the popular humorous portrayal of nurses, for example. The vast majority of nurses in Britain are women and they are relentlessly portrayed in popular culture as sexually available, their uniforms seen less as a badge of professionalism and more an expression of sexual desirability.

Legislation

The Equal Pay Act (1970) stipulated that people should be paid the same regardless of their sex. Women and men have a right not to be paid less than someone of the opposite sex doing the same work in the same organization. They also have the right to equal pay for work which can be considered to be of equal value to that done by a colleague of the opposite sex in the same employment. The Sex Discrimination Act (1975) protects workers from all forms of discrimination on the grounds of sex and from sexual harassment. As we saw earlier, sexual harassment is where there is unwanted conduct on the ground of a person's sex or unwanted conduct of a sexual nature and that conduct has the purpose or effect of violating a person's dignity, or of creating an intimidating, hostile, degrading, humiliating or offensive environment for them.

The Employment Rights Act (1996) (amended by the Employment Act 2002) and the Sex Discrimination Act (1975) provide women with rights and protection during pregnancy. Women cannot be legally dismissed because of pregnancy, and have the right to paid leave for antenatal classes and to work in an environment which is safe for their unborn baby and themselves. They have the right to return to the job they left prior to pregnancy, unless this is genuinely impossible (for example, the job no longer exists).

In 2006 the British New Labour government launched a drive to increase flexible working practices in employment. As we saw in earlier chapters, this can mean anything from part-time and **flexi-working** to homeworking. The advantages of flexible working can be significant for employers and employees alike, as it can reduce absenteeism, increase productivity and reduce stress among staff, particularly where people are attempting to manage home and work arrangements. Many women workers interviewed by the authors of this book have stated that they would not be able to hold their jobs if it was not for their rights to flexibility. Although flexi-working has allowed many women to have children and continue with their employment, spells working part-time still put them at a disadvantage in the promotions race.

Case study 8.4 A gender-neutral recruitment process?

As we have seen, there is a problem with women receiving equal treatment in the recruitment process; women face prejudice in terms of their skills, commitment to work and the possibility of their (perceived) caring responsibilities conflicting with their work. Is there a solution to this? A gender-neutral recruitment process, where women's and men's abilities to carry out the job tasks are the sole focus, could be a solution.

Anette Fasang's 2006 study of women musicians working for a symphony orchestra examined just such a recruitment process (Fasang 2006). Auditions for German orchestras are gender-neutral in that candidates perform from behind a screen. Selections for orchestra positions are made from these auditions. Yet despite women applicants making up 50 per cent of applications, the national average of female musicians employed in German symphony orchestras was only 28.5 per cent. This has nothing to do with the quality of female performers! On closer inspection this gender-neutral recruitment process was flawed in a significant way: not all applicants were invited for interview and audition, and the selection for these stages was distorted by discriminatory practices.

Fasang's analysis of questionnaires administered to female orchestra musicians reveals that factors other than their musical ability are significant in explaining their selection for interview: women are discriminated against in selection based on their written applications. Once women get past this first stage, there is no statistical difference between men and women in gaining a post. Fasang also found that if a woman applicant had a father who was also a musician they were more likely to be invited for interview; having a musician mother made no difference.

Why is this happening? Male musicians are the majority of an orchestra (over 70 per cent) and they may perceive women co-workers as 'a threat to their own status in a traditionally male occupation, and therefore react in a hostile way to female applicants' (Fasang 2006: 807). The obvious conclusion is that a gender-neutral recruitment process has to be neutral at every stage for it to be fair and effective.

Case study 8.5 Why consent to discriminatory practices?

It is sometimes stated that women 'are their own worst enemies', in that they appear to stick to 'typical' female job choices. For example, attracting and retaining women to work as police officers is difficult, and there is a widely held perception that this is due to the nature of the work, the shift system and other working practices. Front-line policing is represented as 'demanding, unpredictable, potentially dangerous and often conflictual' (Dick and Cassell 2004: 52). But we can question these representations – they stress the masculine side of policing and may not be an accurate reflection of the realities of police work. Indeed, researchers have found that front-line police work is mundane and boring, though the portrayal that comes across is of relentless 'fire-fighting' that requires 'every officer to work a harsh, rotating five-week shift system and the preparedness to stay behind at work or return to work at short notice' (2004: 54). Many women police officers agree with this portrayal and offer accounts of their work that are similar to male police officers. We could describe these women police officers as being complicit in forms of discrimination that work against them; they are unlikely to resist the working practices that marginalize them and consent to a version of the world that compromises their interests.

Dick and Cassell investigated this situation using the work of French **post-structuralist** Michel Foucault (see chapter 1) and carrying out a **discourse analysis**. This sociological perspective looks at the social world as a series of constructions; in this case it is policing that is being socially constructed by those who carry out this work. Specifically, Dick and Cassell looked at the construction of policewomen's identities, and found that these identities are developed against a background of the widely held social knowledge that police forces are sexist institutions. To represent themselves as 'modern women' who are not 'lackeys' to male power, these women constructed their police role in the same way as men. Such a strategy both defends against charges of being subordinate, and probably confers on women acceptance by their colleagues. But the result is the persistence of working practices that operate against women's interests and prevent many women officers who return from maternity leave from taking up front-line duties. Dick and Cassell conclude that '[a]t present, working practices that produce excessive demands on police officers' time are the key reproducers of the dominant discourses that operate to disadvantage working mothers in particular' (2004: 69).

Case study 8.6 Glass ceilings: pay, promotion and gender

As we have seen, the gender pay gap is still significant. The difference between male and female pay can be explained in a number of ways, but a persistent and convincing explanation is that many women have shorter working careers, due to taking breaks for child and other care responsibilities, and, by and large, access only to lower-paid, low-progression jobs. A remedy for this state of affairs would be for more women to have professional careers (Witz 1992). Solicitors are highly paid professionals, but women solicitors receive on average 58 per cent the pay of men solicitors. This is far below what we would expect, even if we take into account the gender pay gap. Not only are women solicitors not receiving the same pay as men, they are not even getting close. Why?

A recent sociological study of solicitors by Victoria Wass and Robert McNabb investigated this, using statistical data provided by the Law Society Annual Pay Survey (Wass and McNabb 2006). They followed it up using qualitative interviews. Their research found that the main determinant in a solicitor's pay rate was their level in a company, and that promotion to higher levels was determined by experience in a range of settings, particularly office management, recruitment of clients and supervision of junior staff. The research revealed that there was a significant difference in the hours worked by women and men depending on their child-care responsibilities: men and women without children were working the equivalent of an extra day each week. Significantly, this extra work was not chargeable, i.e. case-based work; it was non-chargeable work such as attending meetings, managing the office, meeting prospective clients and supervising junior colleagues. This experience provides solicitors with important aspects of their reputation. All the women solicitors interviewed in the research 'considered that women, and most especially mothers, were at a disadvantage in establishing themselves on this reputation track' (2006: 303). In a profession where the average working week for a partner is fifty-two hours, women have to prove their commitment by working even longer hours. Solicitors who want to spend time with their children are at a significant disadvantage, although their pay will be high.

This research shows that the 'long hours' culture of solicitors creates a glass ceiling for women (and also, to a lesser extent, for men who want to spend time with their children). But it also reveals that the social closure facing women in the law has shifted from entry to progression.

Disability

Parameters

Defining disability is not straightforward, and much of the subsequent sections will show that debates about the meaning of disability are at the heart of our understanding and response to it. Legally, disability is defined as a person's physical or mental impairment that might have a long-term effect on their ability to carry out day-to-day activities (paraphrased from the Disability Discrimination Act (DDA) 1995 Section 1(1)). From this perspective, disability can be open or hidden, chronic or acute, a result of genetics, accident, disease or ageing. Disability can range from the experience of being a paraplegic confined to a wheelchair to dyslexia, from chronic rheumatism or back pain to depression or anorexia, from deafness to epilepsy.

Disabled people are marginalized in society and the labour market, and are routinely ignored by politicians, academics, trade unions and employers' organizations. Having a disability is seen as something that stigmatizes individuals, and many disabled people reject identifying themselves as disabled, preferring to describe themselves as 'ill'. Yet disability is very prevalent in our society: there are 8.5 million disabled people in the UK, of whom 6.8 million are of working age. And disability is something that is likely to affect all of us personally at some point in our life, either through the ageing process or through acquiring or having a physical impairment from accident, injury or disease. Given this widespread occurrence, the avoidance and marginalization of disability needs to be explained.

Explanation

> It is society that disables us and disabled people are an oppressed social group.
>
> (Vic Finkelstein)

Disability has not been a major concern for social scientists, legislators or employers. This is finally changing with recent legislation and a growing body of academic work which explores how attitudes towards disabled people create a social division. The main reason that disability has become more noticed is because disabled people themselves have organized and agitated for equal rights, fairness and justice. The formation of the British Council of Organizations of Disabled People in 1981 was a 'key milestone' that led to national campaigns for anti-discrimination legislation (Shakespeare et al. 1996: 1). Disabled people have used direct action such as blockades and occupations, as well as more traditional campaign methods such as political lobbying, to assert their presence and promote their struggle for equality. But central to much campaigning has been a focus on exposing prejudicial attitudes towards disability and discussing the bases and meaning of disability.

Disability, for many years, was studied by the medical profession and was defined and conceptualized by doctors and scientists. The 'medical model' sees disability as a consequence of impairment, and as an objective thing that can be measured. For example, individuals may have an impairment such as poor eyesight that leads to a disability of blindness, and a handicap of being unable to negotiate and orient themselves in much of the social environment (Martin et al. 1988: 7). Disability rights activists strongly challenged the medical model, arguing in favour of a social model. The social model sees disability as disadvantage that results from a disabling society. Impairments are not what disable people: society is the cause by failing to provide access to buildings for people with mobility problems or Braille textbooks for blind people. The social model emphasizes the material and social factors that create barriers in the lives of disabled people, and the ideology of **disablism** that promotes prejudice against people with impairments.

> The social model suggests that people with impairment are disabled by society, not by our bodies. The main 'problem' of spinal injury is not a failure to walk normally, but a failure to gain access to buildings if one uses a wheelchair. The difficulty of deafness is not inability to hear, but the failure of society to provide Sign Language interpretation and to recognize deaf people as a cultural minority. (Shakespeare et al. 1996: 2)

From this perspective what becomes defined as a disability is shaped by social meanings which become attached to particular impairments, both physical and mental. An impairment is 'a physical fact, but a disability is a social construction' (Braddock and Parrish 2001: 12). So understanding disability requires a sociological, or at least a social, perspective to show how it is socially constructed and defined rather than biologically determined.

However, in more recent years the social model has faced challenges from some disability studies academics. Tom Shakespeare was a staunch defender of the social model for many years, but has recently moved away from this position, describing the social model as 'an outdated ideology' (Shakespeare and Watson 2002). In his recent book *Disability Rights and Wrongs* (2006), a radical review of disability studies and politics, Shakespeare explains his position: the social model 'relies on an overly narrow and flawed conception of disability' (2006: 9). Without a consideration of how impairment can have significant effects on the lives of individuals, the social model becomes dogmatic and inflexible. Instead, Shakespeare proposes understanding disability as a result of an interplay of relational and contextual factors. Rather than creating a dichotomy of impairment and disability, whereby impairment is related to bodies and disability is about society, a relational approach would see the connections between these two things. Disability is about experience and social relations: some factors are intrinsic to the person, such as the form of impairment, but other external factors interact with these – social attitudes, disabling or enabling environments, the social class of the individual, and so on. For Shakespeare, this perspective can lead to a progressive politics and an inclusive approach to disability, rather than what he sees as fragmented and hierarchical disability rights organizations which provide narrow political agendas. The need for an inclusive and progressive political movement is important:

Minority ethnic communities have sometimes felt ignored by disability groups dominated by the majority population. Lesbian and gay disabled people have experienced homophobia, or have felt unwelcome in disability organizations. (Shakespeare 2006: 75)

Legislation

The Disability Discrimination Act (DDA) makes it unlawful for people defined as having a disability to be discriminated against in employment; access to goods, facilities and services; the management, buying or renting of land or property; and in education. The DDA was passed in 1995 to introduce new measures aimed at ending the discrimination which many disabled people face in their everyday lives. Under the DDA, discrimination occurs where: a disabled person is treated less favourably than someone else; the treatment is for a reason relating to the person's disability; and there is a failure to make a reasonable adjustment for a disabled person.

There are also measures in the DDA covering harassment and victimization. The Disability Equality Duty is a new way of helping the public sector make a real, positive change to the lives of disabled users and employees, ensuring that they are treated fairly and equally. The most recent legislation relating to harassment on the grounds of disability is the Disability Discrimination Act of 1995, which has introduced the concepts of less favourable treatment and failure to make reasonable adjustments. It is unlawful for employers to discriminate against current or prospective workers who have a disability or who have had a disability in the past. Harassment is not referred to as a separate issue under disability legislation. However, harassing a disabled person on account of disability will almost always amount to a detriment under the DDA.

This legislation was extended in 2001 by the Special Education Needs and Disability Act (SENDA), which has now been incorporated into the DDA. This important amendment was designed to ensure that people with a disability had equal access to all levels of education. This is obviously important as education is so crucial for labour market success. The provisions of SENDA were:

- an education institution should not treat a disabled person 'less favourably' for a reason relating to their disability
- an institution is required to make 'reasonable adjustments' if a disabled person would otherwise be placed at a 'substantial disadvantage'
- adjustments should be 'anticipatory'
- the legislation applies to all admissions, enrolments and other 'student services', which includes assessment and teaching materials.

Across Great Britain, 45,000 public bodies are covered by the Disability Equality Duty (DED). These bodies under the specific duties were required to produce and publish a Disability Equality Scheme by December 2006. The DED is meant to ensure that all public bodies – such as central or local government, schools, health trusts or emergency services – pay 'due regard' to the promotion of equality for disabled people in every area of their work. Like the gender and race duties, however, the disability duty does not apply to the private sector, a major limitation of the current legislation. Government has preferred to take a voluntarist approach to private firms, persuading them to follow good practice from the public-sector organizations. The argument is that the provisions might be too costly and impair profitability of private businesses. But is it fair that public organizations should have to shoulder extra costs from equality provision, while the private sector gets away free, especially when the government requires public-sector organizations to pay their way?

Case studies

The sociology of work and employment has a patchy record when it comes to disability research. There are few systematic and sustained case studies, and disabled workers are still not a mainstream topic for sociological analysis. However, there is a long tradition of disability researchers and disabled rights activists providing critical perspectives on the world of work as experienced by disabled workers.

Given that a large amount of disability research in the social sciences is informed by the social model, which to some extent derives from a Marxist perspective, it is not surprising that capitalism is placed centre stage in many studies. For example, Alan Roulstone surveys recent research into disability and work and concludes that globalized capitalism with 'its emphasis on compressing time and space ... unpredictable and fast moving capital flows, the central role of information, the complex global–local interaction, represents major challenges for disabled workers and jobseekers' (Roulstone 2002: 636). This becomes visible in the employment policies and effects that impact on disabled workers, notably the insistence on early return to work or the necessity of disabled people to find work despite the UK having the highest rates of occupationally related illness in the EU and the longest hours of work (2002: 629). Overall, Roulstone concludes that, where new patterns of employment may be detrimental to all workers, they are increasingly harsh for disabled workers and jobseekers.

This is despite the introduction of legislation designed to give rights and protection to disabled workers. Deborah Foster's recent research examined the experiences of disabled employees in public-sector workplaces as they negotiated workplace adjustments that the DDA required. This legislation places a duty on employers to make 'reasonable adjustments' to the physical environment and/or to employment arrangements (hours of work, allocation of duties) to ensure that a disabled person is not put at a 'substantial disadvantage' (Foster 2007: 69). Foster notes that for the first time disabled employees had the chance to challenge discriminatory practices. She interviewed a group of twenty disabled employees, using a qualitative approach to give a 'voice' to participants – an important consideration seeing that disabled people have been consistently ignored and marginalized by academics (Barnes and Mercer 1997). Focusing on the way that employees tried to get new arrangements put in place through negotiation, she found that negotiation processes were ad hoc and difficult, often because of managers lacking any training in disability awareness. Over half of Foster's interviewees reported bullying leading to stress and ill health as a result of trying to change their working conditions:

> The teacher was initially absent from work because of a physical impairment, although the actions of her headmaster, who continually pressurized her to return to work and blamed her for the financial and organizational problems faced by the school, led to depression. The teacher also experienced a number of crises in her personal life while on sick leave which, instead of eliciting support from her headmaster, led to calls for her to resign. One incident involved the headmaster calling a special meeting of school governors and parents to gather signatures for a letter of no confidence in the teacher, which he then sent to the Local Education Authority (LEA). The teacher commented:
>
> 'It's interesting who signed . . . There was a mother whose child was in my class, who happened to be a parent-governor at the time, her name is on the letter . . . even the caretaker signed . . . I was allowed to hold a copy of this letter in my hand for about five minutes . . . I requested a copy . . . but haven't been furnished with one'.

When in a position to return to work the teacher requested she return on a half-time job-share basis as an adjustment. However, despite advice from the LEA that this was possible, the school:

> 'really wanted to make it difficult. They said I could start work immediately because I was fit to return to work. But they couldn't effect the job share until half term so I'd have to go back to work on a full-time basis for at least a month, and boy, did they try to break me in that month. It was a concerted effort by everyone.'

The job share was eventually granted, although she found that other teachers had been instructed not to co-operate with her and she was allocated work that a junior staff member would normally do. In this case the headmaster later admitted he knew nothing about the DDA; the bullying she experienced only stopped when amendments to the legislation in 2004 introduced the concept of disability harassment. Indeed, a survey by the teachers' union NASUWT in 2000 suggests that misunderstanding of the DDA is widespread in the school sector (Foster 2007: 73–4).

Foster's research reveals a depressing catalogue of employer intran-
sigence, prejudice, stereotyping and plain ignorance: even routine
facilities like car parking were denied:

> 'I went to the chappy in charge of the car park and asked if I could have
> a saved parking space in the office car park. Most of the spaces there
> were for top management but there were three disabled spaces. . . . I
> was told, while sitting in a wheelchair, that disabled spaces were only
> for disabled people. I asked him how much more disabled he would
> like me to be? I was quite shocked by his response, I had a blue badge
> [nationally recognized disabled parking permit] at the time.' (2007:
> 76–7)

Although some employees did get what they had requested, in *all* cases
respondents noted that this was only after delays in implementation.

Foster's research shows where organizations are going wrong, and
presents some simple and straightforward solutions. The core problem
is that disability is seen as an individual problem, and the legislative
framework reinforces this by making change contingent upon an
individual making a complaint and requesting changes. Instead,
'[o]rganizations collectively need to "own" and positively promote
policies aimed at eliminating discrimination against disabled employees' (2007: 79). This needs to be coupled with education and training,
particularly among line managers, to challenge myths and stereotypes
attached to disability.

Conclusions

In this chapter we have considered the evidence for the continuation
of patterns of disadvantage and discrimination, which we argue are
deeply embedded in our society's structures and cultures, despite
popular misconceptions that 'we are all equal now'. We reviewed the
range of legislation and policies designed to deal with discrimination
in the workplace, focusing particularly on the recent equalities duties
which have been introduced in the public sector and are obligatory.
Government prefers to take a voluntarist stance and work by persua-
sion with the private sector.

We suggested that social class, which arises from the way work is
organized in capitalist economies, underpins many of these forms of
disadvantage. Britain is a society deeply divided by class; however, class
is too controversial, sensitive and complex an issue to be resolved by
legislation. Other forms of disadvantage may be helped by legislation,
however, and we have considered three types of unlawful discrimination, those based on gender, race/ethnicity and disability. We should,
however, be mindful of other less remarked-on forms of discrimination: those of age, sexual orientation, and religion and belief. These also
appear in organizations and workplaces and they too are unlawful. As
suggested, legislation can make an impact in addressing unfairness at

work, but, as the case of young Caribbean men shows us, we have to place work relations within their broader social context.

Coping with discrimination and seeking fairness in all the processes associated with labour market opportunity – recruitment and selection, performance and appraisal, promotion and rewards – is a major challenge for contemporary managers. As this chapter has revealed, many forms of discriminatory practices are deeply rooted in informal workplace cultures; it may take time to bring about the changes needed to ensure that all sorts of people are treated with respect and dignity at work and allowed equal chances to develop their capabilities.

Discussion questions

1. What is the business case for opposing unfair discrimination?
2. Are discriminatory practices in organizations the result of institutional structures, personal prejudices or societal influences?
3. Does employment legislation provide adequate protection against unfair discrimination for employees?
4. What are the causes of prejudice and discrimination in society?

Further reading

There is an enormous amount of literature on social inequality. Finding one's way around this is an art in its own right. In order to make the task easier we suggest some key textbooks and then focus on 'race', disability and social class.

There are a number of useful books which deal generally with social divisions. Geoff Payne (ed.), *Social Divisions* (London: Palgrave, 2000) and Shaun Best, *Understanding Social Divisions* (London: Sage, 2005) both provide general overviews. Harriet Bradley's *Fractured Identities* (2nd edition; Cambridge: Polity, 2009) provides a comprehensive analysis of the relationship between social inequalities, social stratification and identity.

A. Ansell and J. Solomos, *Race and Ethnicity* (London: Routledge, 2008), provides an insight into definitions, forms of discrimination and harassment and the impact of racial inequality for individuals and communities. Toby Shelley, *Exploited* (New York: Zed Books, 2007), examines how economic liberalization has accelerated economic migration resulting in the exploitation and enslavement of some of the world's most vulnerable men, women and children.

New theories of racism are evolving: the notion of environmental racism suggests that black and vulnerable ethnic groups face greater peril from their 'natural' environment as a direct result of social and political policy. The aptly named *There Is No Such Thing as a Natural Disaster: Race, Class, and Hurricane Katrina*, edited by Chester Hartman and Gregory Squires (Abingdon: Taylor and Francis, 2006), provides an insight into these ideas.

Dave Byrne's book *Social Exclusion* (Maidenhead: Open University Press, 2005) provides an insight into the notion that many are excluded from full participation in society as a result of poverty and powerlessness. The work focuses particularly on issues of class and 'race' and age inequalities, and argues that neoliberal economic policy has both increased the number of those excluded and widened the gap between rich and poor. He uses health inequalities to demonstrate how social inequality limits the life chances and life length of those who face poverty and powerlessness.

Tom Shakespeare's *Disability Rights and Wrongs* (London: Routledge, 2006) provides a useful insight into key theories of disability such as the social and medical models. In addition it looks at the role of the state and charities in supporting those with special needs. The author critically explores the role of scientific research and practice which looks to eliminate disability and argues that an improvement in the political and economic power of the disabled is preferable. The experience of disability and the perceptions of disabled people are often hidden in our society: Shakespeare looks at a range of issues which have too long been neglected by academics, for example intimacy, sexuality and reproduction.

Reports, statistics and a lot of other interesting material can be found on the EHRC website at www.equalityhumanrights.com.

9 Work, community and action

This chapter will

- explore the many meanings and definitions of the term 'community'
- present some examples of different forms of community and highlight their relevance to the world of work
- consider how to carry out research on communities and give examples of actions based within different types of community
- look at the involvement of trade unions in the community unionism movement
- introduce the notion of 'corporate social responsibility' and explore its potentials and limitations.

Introduction – defining community

> Community can be the warmly persuasive word to describe an existing set of relationships, or the warmly persuasive word to describe an alternative set of relationships. What is most important, perhaps, is that unlike all other terms of social organization (state, nation, society, etc.) it seems never to be used unfavourably.
>
> (Williams 1983: 76)

Raymond Williams is right: 'community' is a word that has no negative connotations. Almost anything and everything which is associated with the concept of community is improved by that association. In popular usage community signifies a physical place, such as a village or neighbourhood, including a more abstract sense of 'belonging' embedded in close and stable relationships. In idealized versions, which often play to nostalgic longings, locality and 'belonging' overlap to denote a bounded and harmonious community of interests. We talk about academic communities (although we know academics are often arguing with each other) and we talk about the business community (although most businesses are in fierce competition with one another). We also talk of community leaders, community associations, 'care in the community', ethnic minority communities, community arts, the 'decline of community' and so forth. Thus, community is an important organizing and motivating factor. Yet despite the apparent universal approval of the term, and its application to many parts of social life, community is a complex and slippery concept. Do we mean a physical grouping of people when we talk of community? Or are we gesturing towards some imagined entity that we think we are a part of – a community of academics or a political community? And sometimes we use community as a description of how we do things – we can act as a community in a community fashion. There are complexities and difficulties associated with the concept of community – problems of definition are at the centre of debates and we will explore this in the body of the chapter. Whilst it may be the case that community is an unstable concept to use within sociological theory and analysis, it is, nevertheless, a concept which has been and is continuously being used in social life.

Sociologists have always had an interest in community, and examining community and communities is still an important part of sociological research. The meaning of 'community' is notoriously slippery and open to interpretation. In their classic text, *Community Studies*, Bell and Newby (1971) explore different definitions of the concept of community. They note that one commentator, G. A. Hillery Jr (1955), identified no fewer than ninety-four definitions of community. Hillery was ultimately able to reduce those ninety-four definitions to just sixteen, but on further reflection argued that the only common denominator was that 'all of the definitions deal with people. Beyond this common basis, there is no agreement' (quoted in Bell and Newby 1971: 27).

The most widely used common sense definitions of community refer to locality and to common interest and these two factors have been of value in academic research. The idea of belonging is integral to other uses of the term, such as in the ideas of occupational and organizational communities or ethnic minority communities. In each case it suggests membership of a group which is distinguished by shared characteristics, values, interests and goals. Belonging to a community carries with it the sense of closeness, warmth, protection and engagement. In a way, community carries the values associated with family life into a larger unit.

Bauman (2001) suggests that, whilst community always seems to be 'a good thing', its inclusive qualities are only meaningful with reference to what it excludes. What is a place of security for those who 'belong' can be an alien and unfriendly environment for those who do not conform or identify with the majority or the mainstream within it. Also, it may be closed to outside influence and possibilities for change. Even for those who 'belong' to any named community, the realities of social change, inequality and power relations within social groups mean that the warmth of community, its promise as a 'feel good' condition, is elusive in practice and uneven in distribution. Moreover, a community can be split, as happened to close-knit occupation communities during the Miners' Strike of 1984, when the miners who went back to work were ostracized by the strikers and their families. There were other subtleties of inclusion and exclusion during this long-lasting dispute, as shown in the case of the women who worked together against pit closures (see box 9.1).

Box 9.1 Women and their support of the Miners' Strike: 'One of us and not one of us'

Women played a central part in the battle to save mining communities during the 1984–5 British Miners' Strike. The strike lasted for a full year and during that time groups of women worked to sustain mining families who were living without an income. According to research carried out by Spence and Stephenson (2007; 2009), while women worked co-operatively during the strike, there was disagreement about who could legitimately join their community of resistance. While women activists were often dubbed 'Miners' Wives' by the British press, many had little or no connection with mining while others were indeed the close relatives of striking miners. This was a source of conflict within the support groups. While some mining women were happy to see 'outsiders' join their ranks, welcoming women activists from environmental groups and socialist groups, others had a policy of allowing only those whom they saw as 'legitimate' mining women to participate. This question of who was 'one of us' and who was not was a major cause of conflict between support groups. When re-interviewing women twenty years after the conflict, Spence and Stephenson found that this issue of the legitimacy of community membership continued to rankle with some former activists.

Community studies

Community studies rely heavily on an ethnographic approach and emerged in the USA in the years between the First and Second World Wars. This was no coincidence. The disruption of those wars and the emergence of fascism and communism had led social scientists to attempt to disentangle the complexity of social relationships, allegiances, identities and geographies of people in specific set localities.

The genre of community studies carried on into and after the Second World War as sociologists became more aware of the complexity of social divisions and less complacent about the inevitability of a liberal path towards 'progress' – a position which was hard to sustain in the face of nuclear bombs and the Holocaust. Researchers were motivated by the desire to build a new post-war world which would not repeat the mistakes of the past. If it was not going to happen as a result of some inevitable path of human history, then human agency would be necessary to construct it. It is in this mould that the Institute of Community Studies and Social Policy was developed in Bethnal Green in London, with the intention of studying an urban locality in order to provide information to government directly for the purposes of informing social policy.

Methodologically the community studies approach focused on a particular small town, village or city in an attempt to understand how different types of localities 'worked', what problems were experienced and how were these overcome. They relied on observation and the collection and classification of data. Community studies researchers have usually lived, or spent a great deal of time, in the town or village under study. Many have been emotionally as well as physically close to what they are studying. This means that they tend to be sympathetic to the people they are studying. A variety of methods can be used to gather data, such as documentary sources and surveys, but there is a special emphasis on participant observation and upon conversation with key informants. The books and articles which result tend to be highly readable, lively and full of graphic description, and sometimes short on theory.

Two classic community studies projects were carried out by the Lynds in the USA and they provide an insight into how such work was done. The Lynds were originally interested in surveying religious provision and practices in 'Middletown', a small American town, but realized that to do so in any meaningful sense, they would need to understand the social context and the relationship between religious and other social practices. They therefore adopted a social classification system derived from anthropology to organize their data as follows: getting a living; making a home; training the young; using leisure; engaging in religious practices; engaging in community activities. This system provided a cultural framework within which the features of the life of one geographical community could be mapped (Lynd and Lynd 1929; 1937).

Family and Kinship in East London (Young and Willmott 1957) is probably the most famous British community study. It had a strong social policy remit – to explore the impact on traditional family and kinship relations of moving inner-city working-class families into new housing estates. Following the Second World War, social policy had been designed around the notion that people should be moved out of older housing in the cities and into these estates. The book explores family and kinship patterns of those living in Bethnal Green, a working-class area populated almost entirely by manual workers. The second part of the book focused on social relations in 'Greenleigh', in Essex, a new London County Council housing estate, typical of the type of estate to which Bethnal Greeners were relocated.

In studying Bethnal Green, Young and Willmott 'discovered a village in the middle of London'. Bethnal Greeners claimed to 'know everyone': most people in the area were connected by kinship ties to a network of other families, and through them to a host of friends and acquaintances. The picture of life depicted by Young and Willmott was different from the prevailing view of what a modern city was like, though it would now be familiar to us through television 'soaps' such as BBC1's *Eastenders*. Residents of Bethnal Green were not a group of alienated individuals but rather an ordered community held together by kinship and family ties and neighbourhood groupings. By contrast, working-class families that had been moved to new council estates in an attempt to improve their social conditions found themselves lonely and the object of suspicion. They missed the warmth, communal solidarity, familiarity and friendship which was apparent in the old working-class, inner-city communities.

Family and Kinship in East London provides a very rich insight into family life. So too do a range of other community studies such as Rees' (1950) work on Welsh country life, Norman Dennis et al.'s 1956 classic study of the coal community 'Ashton', *Coal is our Life*, and Stacey's (1960) study of Banbury. These works have in common a tendency to focus on the loss of a way of life precipitated by technological progress and urbanism.

The legacy of community studies has been a rich one in terms of the now historical information which we have inherited from the studies, about particular places and times. However, it has its limitations. One weakness, possibly resulting from the researchers' sympathy for their respondents and the attempt to capture a waning social world, is the danger of over-romanticizing community life. Cornwell (1984), when studying the East End of London, sought to dig beneath the outward appearances and descriptions of community life and found that there was a distinct difference between 'public' and 'private' accounts of community life. Private accounts were more likely to tell of conflict and difficulties in family, kinship and neighbourhood relations. Think of *Eastenders*! Cornwell concludes that Young and Willmott's work relied too heavily on a public account and therefore gives an overly rosy account of community life.

Young notes that women provided a less positive picture of community life than did men. This raises the important point that community, even the same community, is not experienced in the same way by all people – community is a highly gendered concept (see box 9.5). Similarly class and race are significant social divisions which impact upon how community is experienced. Members of ethnic minorities often find the doors of the majority community closed to them.

A characteristic of the community studies tradition is that each study focuses on one geographic area, and as a consequence its findings and conclusions are not easily translated into broader policy or theory: they tend to be specific to that community, set within time and space. Linked to this, another key problem is that the studies tended to focus on geographic communities as if they exist in isolation, while ignoring the wider economic and political forces which shape their existence and the community relations within them.

Although the community studies approach had its heyday between the mid 1920s and the mid 1960s, it is a tradition which continues today, and to good effect. For example, Dennis et al.'s (1956) approach to a mining community can be found in the work of David Waddington who considers the impact of the Miners' Strike and pit closures on what are now ex-mining communities.

Occupational communities

Notions of community are also invoked in the work and practices of social institutions, where people must communicate and co-operate in order to pursue institutional goals. This is the sense of community most relevant to this book. Professional workers in particular are said to develop their own 'occupational communities' with their representative bodies, such as the BMA for doctors or CIPFA for accountants. Alongside this, organizations try to establish their own types of communities and cultures, embodying their corporate values and goals. In this way, organizational life develops its own type of community life and this is sustained through shared organizational values.

We can distinguish two different, but linked, types of occupational communities. There are communities of employees inside an organization; sometimes these extend to cover the entire organization, more frequently they are discrete groups of employees who share some characteristics such as gender, class, skill, age or a combination of these. External occupational communities emerge in the physical locality surrounding a single employer (as in a coal mining community which exists around a single mine) or a group of employers (such as a shipyard community, where a number of shipyards will exist in one locale). Of this second type there are two forms: traditional (such as coalfield communities) and emerging (new occupational communities), for example creative industries which have been located in distinctive areas of cities.

Communities emerge in the work and practices of business organizations, where people must communicate and co-operate in order to pursue institutional goals. This is sustained through shared organizational values. As we saw in earlier chapters, the development of organizational culture has been promoted within management as an instrumental means of achieving organizational cohesion. In the context of the operation of power in organizations and the structural inequalities which have traditionally been based upon essential differences between individuals and groups, it is perhaps not surprising that the notion of organizational communities has not been universally accepted.

This is contested terrain which has implications for institutional life. Japanese multinational companies, for example, have attempted to enforce a set organizational culture in an attempt to develop a community of compliance. At Nissan UK, the car manufacturer has attempted to inculcate workers into a company culture known as the 'Nissan Way'. Critics argue that the imposed rules of this 'community' serve the interests of the employer exclusively as they are geared towards absolute loyalty to the company, the encouragement of competition between workers, unquestioning hard work and ambition, and suspicion of trade unionism and worker collectivism (Garrahan and Stewart 1992). Research suggests that these attempts to enforce a particular set

Communities within organizations can be formed of those who share certain characteristics, e.g. gender, class, skill, age, ethnicity or a combination of these.

of community relations and attitudes have not been entirely successful: while some employees have adopted the 'Nissan Way', others have critically rejected this, viewing it as manipulation, and have sought to encourage the development of a critical and worker collectivist community culture in its place.

Traditional occupational communities have been dependent for their existence on a (usually single) source of employment, and when that employment ends the community is threatened. The pattern of deindustrialization across the UK from the later 1970s onwards shows how such traditional communities have declined and changed. Many social theorists have linked this decline in community to a decreasing relevance of social class in people's lives, social atomization, increased individualism and a big challenge to masculinity, as most traditional occupational communities were structured around a gendered division of labour where male household members would be the main earners.

Is community in decline?

The decline or perceived decline of community is seen by politicians and policy-makers as being highly significant for the breakdown of social cohesion, for welfare dependency and for increased criminality. Academics who have predicted or described the breakdown of community cohesion have attracted attention from politicians and policy-makers.

Robert Putnam's book *Bowling Alone* (2000) attracted a great deal of media and political attention, not just in America but in many Western nations, when he claimed that civic disengagement was characteristic of the modern age and that this would have a profound impact on social cohesion. He claimed that people were disengaged from what he called civic life and demonstrated that through reference to a range of indicators including voting, political activity, newspaper readership, and participation in local associations such as sports clubs (hence the title of the book) and Parent Teacher Associations (PTAs). This disinclination to engage with civic society was an indicator of a decline in Americans' **social capital** and similarly a decline in community relations and social cohesion. Americans were more and more isolated, experiencing less and less social connectedness, even choosing to spend leisure time alone.

Box 9.2 Social capital

The central premise of Putnam's theory of social capital is that networks have value. Social capital refers to the collective value of all social networks (who you know) and the inclinations that arise from these networks to do things for each other (norms of reciprocity). Social capital helps you to get by, but for some people it also helps them to get on. Right now at university you are developing your social capital – making friends, forming networks and making contacts. Your friends will help you to get by, but some of the social capital you acquire, for example meeting a prospective employer, will help you to get on, by providing you with contacts for future employment.

The term 'social capital' emphasizes not just warm and cuddly feelings, but a wide variety of quite specific benefits that flow from the trust, reciprocity, information and co-operation associated with social networks. Social capital creates value for the people who are connected and – at least sometimes – for bystanders as well.

Social capital works through multiple channels and mechanisms:

- information flows (e.g. learning about jobs, learning about candidates running for office, exchanging ideas at college, etc.) depend on social capital
- norms of reciprocity (mutual aid) are dependent on social networks
- bonding networks connect folks who are similar and sustain particularized (in-group) reciprocity
- bridging networks connect individuals who are diverse and sustain generalized reciprocity
- collective action depends upon social networks (e.g., the role that the black church played in the civil rights movement) although collective action can also foster new networks
- broader identities and solidarity are encouraged by social networks that help translate an 'I' mentality into a 'we' mentality.

Putnam provides a number of examples of social capital: looking after a neighbour's house; e-mail exchanges amongst a cancer support group; 'The motto in TV soap *Cheers* "where everybody knows your name" captures one important aspect of social capital' (Robert Putnam's website, www.bowlingalone.com).

For Putnam, participation in civic and community life is the bedrock of American democracy and democratization: civic disengagement led to political apathy, a decline in the institutions of community and local democracy, increased intolerance of others and decreased trust. Putnam represents an ongoing tradition in sociological theory – less popular in the UK than in the USA – that of functionalism (see chapter 1). This theory suggests that societies and the institutions inside them represent an expression of collectively held norms and values; when collective action and participation decline, these norms and values, the 'social glue' of society, weaken and a number of negative consequences emerge.

A range of factors have been blamed, such as changes in family structure, with more people living alone and suburban sprawl, which has fractured the spatial integrity of people's life, meaning that they travel further to work. This increases time pressures in working people's lives and also means that people do not necessarily shop or enjoy leisure within their geographic community. Electronic entertainment, especially television, has privatized leisure time and separated us from one another. One of the most significant changes identified by Putnam was that, while older Americans had the habit of civic engagement, the current generation did not. Young people lived increasingly privatized, isolated and, according to some, self-preoccupied lives. Technology, such as social networking sites and mobile phone texting, offers new ways of connecting people, but does so without promoting the physical closeness which is so central to community.

Putnam's work has been significant for politicians and policy-makers not least because it suggests that supporting community life and civic engagement might be more productive in the long run than the targeting of 'problem individuals'. The UK government even collects

Local shops forced to close: a more common sight as people begin to shop outside of their geographic community.

statistics on social capital, and connects a lack of social capital to poverty and social exclusion. Thinking about social capital provides informal educators, community workers and other service providers with a rationale for their activities. It also provides a powerful argument for spreading resources across communities in order to build social and community cohesion rather than concentrating the bulk of resources on groups and individuals who present the strongest social problems (currently the received thinking among many policy-makers). It is not just those who are disadvantaged or who are seen as problems who must be engaged in community life, but also the majority, who are unlikely to be experiencing multiple disadvantage, will not be engaged in criminal activity, and will be (or have been) engaged with education systems and the world of work.

Putnam's work is not without its critics. For French sociologist Pierre Bourdieu the concept of social capital simply cannot be understood in isolation, or without analysis of a wider context. For him, talking about social capital without thinking about issues such as access to resources, power and social position simply makes no sense – in fact, it's worse, as it serves to hide the fact that disadvantage in society is generated by structures of power, not by how many people you talk to in a day or have in your address book.

Bourdieu does use the concept of social capital, but only in combination with analysis of other forms of capital, and only in the context of capitalism. It is a capitalist society that makes capital significant – a point that Putnam seems to miss! Bourdieu's account is critical, not normative; he offers a critique of society, not just a validation of it. He identifies four categories of capital – each person in society will possess differing amounts of these:

social capital – valued social relations between people (who you know)

economic capital – money and property (what you have)

cultural capital – kinds of legitimate knowledge (what you know); we all know things, but some forms of knowledge are much more valued than others socially, and knowledge is valued differently in different places

symbolic capital – honour and prestige (your status in the eyes of others).

We can understand social divisions and discrimination much better by using this fourfold typology: to really understand it you have to look at all forms of capital. Think about how it applies to yourself. Think about what coming to university is about. Are you here to gain knowledge, or are you here to improve your social capital, symbolic capital and cultural capital such that you'll end up improving your economic capital and utilizing these resources in your career? Or both?

Revitalizing communities

The definition of community which relies upon place and interest has been challenged by a new set of interpretations: in this perspective, community is something which is done, which is consciously or unconsciously made or unmade. This definition of community as something that 'is done' was first articulated by Raymond Plant (1974). Plant's ideas take the understanding of community beyond geography and common interest. Community from this standpoint is a process, it is activism and it is self-conscious; it is a set of ongoing constructed social relationships. From this standpoint, community is perceived not so much as a material common interest people share, but rather as relating to the ongoing process of human interaction and the meanings and values people associate with their actions. You only have to consider the vitality and dynamism of the social networks and relationships that people enter into all the time to see the relevance of this approach to thinking about community. In London, for example, increasing numbers of foreign migrant workers mean that organizations within the ethnic and nationality-based communities to which they belong have taken on a new importance as sources of welfare advice and support (Datta et al. 2007). See box 9.3 for insights into how new technology affects human interaction, with the implications for community it entails.

Box 9.3 New technology and 'virtual' communities

We have already referred to Putnam's argument concerning the decline of civic engagement, with the adverse consequences for community life it implies. However, it is important not to think about the concept of community in too narrow a way, but rather as an ongoing process of human interaction. This is evident when we think about the implications of new technology, particularly the internet, for our understanding of what community means. Social networking sites, such as Facebook, Bebo and MySpace allow people with shared interests, in music for example, to initiate and maintain contact with each other, without them necessarily having to meet physically. The internet offers enthusiasts of all kinds, be they science-fiction fans, film enthusiasts or aficionados of particular types of music, the opportunity to form and maintain communities of interest unimpeded by the constraints of geography. Through these shared interests people can construct quite strong personal and intimate linkages with people they have never come face to face with. People's engagements with these sites can become very passionate, for example in disagreements over different types of music and their values. Many people post blog entries in the middle of the night! By this reckoning, it would be mistaken to say community is in decline; rather, under the influence of new technology, our understandings of what community means, and how communities operate, are having to change.

The notion of community as something which we 'do' has had a major impact on the study of the subject. For example Waddington's work on the community of Worksop Vale utilizes definitions of community as both a thing and a process (see box 9.4). Waddington sees Worksop Vale as a material, established geographic community in which people shared common work, family and class ties. At the same time, in his examination of the regeneration of Worksop Vale, community is something which is being 'done'.

Box 9.4   Worksop Vale: deindustrialization, community decline and regeneration – the community studies approach

Dave Waddington and his colleagues have carried out a series of studies into post-industrial mining communities. Waddington et al. look in detail at the political and economic factors which brought about pit closure, while utilizing a community studies approach to exemplify the impact of closure on social relations within Worksop Vale, a small colliery village.

The defeat of the National Union of Mineworkers in the 1984–5 strike resulted in an acceleration of the process of mine closures across the national coalfield. Post-industrial mining communities, such as Worksop Vale, have been devastated by high levels of long-term unemployment, poverty, social exclusion and a decline in community resources. Both voluntary and government agencies have long recognized a significant increase in both youth crime and the abuse of drugs and alcohol, generally (Coalfields Task Force 1999; Critcher et al. 1991; Waddington et al. 2001; Waddington 2004).

Of prime concern for Waddington and his colleagues are the high levels of unemployment symptomatic of the post-industrial experience, and the consequential effects of depopulation, alongside a decline in the services and material conditions within the community. The researchers draw attention to the dramatic and negative impact on community and individual morale (Waddington et al. 2001; Waddington 2004). This stems from the dismantling of established relationships that coincide within redundant occupational communities and is, they argue, the primary problem facing such communities (Waddington et al. 2001). This process is accelerated by the loss of what they call 'focal points of social contact', such as pubs, Working Men's Clubs and the local shops, all of which are sites of social interaction. Additionally, the people suffer the loss of community rituals that allow collective community engagement, and the celebration of industrial identity. As a consequence, people report a disconnection with the very community that once defined all aspects of their lives. At the heart of this disconnection is the loss of important sources of social support, opportunities for communal interaction, and the pride associated with an industrial identity based on the demanding work of mining (Waddington et al. 2001).

In a later study, Waddington (2004; 2005) explores how people in Worksop were attempting to regenerate community alliances through the identification of common needs and goals. The population of those active in developing and making community had changed. While some were mining people, others were outsiders who had come to Worksop Vale in an attempt to find or make community. The co-operation and common endeavour displayed by these groups, in identifying common needs, fighting absentee landlords and seeking funding to re-establish focal points of social interaction, had established a new set of community relationships. To that end, community was being regenerated both materially and socially.

Community is being self-consciously constructed by those who have chosen to remain in the area, alongside those who have chosen to move to the area, attracted by the notion that they might enjoy positive supportive social relations in a former mining community. Spence and Stephenson's (2009) account of women's engagement in supporting the Miners' Strike shares Waddington's view of community as a self-conscious active process. Waddington's group of regeneration activists were actively recreating community relations in order to develop a more cohesive and supportive social environment. Similarly the women in Spence and Stephenson's study were 'living community' (see box 9.5).

Box 9.5 Women activists in the Miners' Strike, 'doing and living community'

The notion of 'mining community' has a powerful resonance in the British popular culture. Writers such as Dylan Thomas and D. H. Lawrence have written about mining communities, while seminal research works, such as Dennis et al.'s (1956), have similarly informed policy-makers and academics. These communities have been depicted as geographically isolated, with a heavy if not exclusive dependence on mining as the major industry. They are characterized by a sharply defined gendered division of labour, since women had been barred from pit work, while being a miner's wife involved heavy burdens of domestic work. These are self-contained and self-sufficient communities. Key institutions of home, union and industry support and maintain what are highly disciplined self-contained and self-sufficient communities. Beynon and Austrin (1994) claim that historically harsh working conditions led to the development of a deep commitment to trade unionism and that mining unions developed an early form of welfare state within mining communities, offering social, educational and leisure care.

British mining had been in decline for some time when in 1984 the Thatcher government announced an accelerated closure programme. The miners' union, the National Union of Mineworkers, led a year-long strike in defence of mining. Union, miners and activists argued that 'defence of community' was at the heart of the dispute; however, research reveals the complexity of definitions and understandings of the notion of community.

By the time of the dispute, the overlapping of geographical and common interest forms of community (e.g. common employment) was relatively rare. Pit closures meant that many miners lived in isolation from one another; many had become 'industrial gypsies', travelling to find work. 'Mining communities' in the traditional vision were more history than fact. Women had experienced many changes also; many women from the pit villages had found employment and the gendered division of labour was not as marked as it had been, though women still found themselves disadvantaged in terms of access to political power. Few women had climbed the ladder in the Labour Party and the union was still men-only. This illustrates how community is a gendered experience. Men and women were living in the same geographic community with shared common interests but their experience of that community life was profoundly different, profoundly unequal.

Despite these changes, mining women activists were quick to refer to community when defending the industry. Reference to community gave women's involvement a legitimacy which might have been lacking had this been merely an 'industrial dispute'. Women were inspired and educated by an understanding of what mining communities had been. This imaginary version of community life drew in mining and non-mining women. In some instances mining women were informed by older female relatives about past disputes and the collectivism characteristic of mining communities historically.

Women's activism during the dispute 'created community; they lived community, through the sharing of common problems' (Shaw and Mundy 2005), through the development of food kitchens and through collective endeavour in working to meet the varied needs of the community. In doing so they created a community of activism, of process, community which can best be understood as a verb rather than a noun (Spence and Stephenson 2009).

Community unionism

In contrast to the Nissan example discussed above, some workers' groups have also utilized the concept of community in order to win political advantage. In recent years trade unions in a number of countries, including the UK, United States and Australia, have sought to move 'beyond the workplace' and to work more closely with communities in order to represent the interests of disadvantaged groups.

During the nineteenth and twentieth centuries, unions sought to improve the lot of their members as workers, through the development of class-based political parties and through campaigns for legal and social change. The primary core business of the trade union has been to represent the interests of their employed membership, not those of the broader communities, or people outside of paid employment. Similarly the political strength of unions has rested with the union members and employees and the threat of industrial action, such as strikes and working to rule, was very much a work-based phenomenon, the business of the worker, the union and the employer only. In periods of high levels of employment, unions have been able to rely on white, male, full-time and skilled workers for their core membership. As a consequence the interests of female, BME and unskilled workers were neglected, and they tended not to share the benefits won by 'core' workers. As Holgate (2005) points out, the primary aim of unions in the twentieth century was to ensure improved material rewards in the workplace for already relatively privileged groups of workers.

A decline in trade union influence and membership was brought about by the neoliberal policies adopted by the advanced capitalist nations in the 1980s (see chapter 3) and brought the unions to a point of crisis. Membership fell dramatically and trade unions became politically impotent. They were forced to re-think their agenda in an attempt to bring about renewal, and part of that process was to recognize that unionism should reach 'beyond the workplace', that is, work for social justice in a more general sense to support and empower vulnerable people, which might then influence the political agenda and bring about change. In return the unions sought support for workplace political campaigns and attempted to increase union membership and the vitality of the union movement as a whole. What emerged was a new direction in union strategy which has come to be known as community unionism.

Community unionism seeks to represent the interests of previously neglected workers while simultaneously giving trade unions the power to raise the question of economic and social justice. Three main types can be identified. The first type of community unionism involves efforts by unions themselves to develop a more community-based orientation. In the UK two trade unions, representing iron and steel workers and garment workers respectively, merged to form a new union which they actually called 'Community'. Both predecessor unions had deep roots in specific industrial communities but, because of economic change, membership levels were dwindling. As Wills (2001) shows, the focus on community was designed to stem decline by helping to sustain workplace organization. Perhaps the best-known example of how a trade union has sought to become more community oriented concerns the efforts of the Service Employees International Union (SEIU) in the United States with its Justice for Janitors campaign (see box 9.6).

Box 9.6 Community unionism in action: Justice for Janitors

Since 1985 the American SEIU Justice for Janitors movement has helped low-wage workers achieve social and economic justice. Formed in Denver, USA, the goal of the campaign has been to support low-paid (often migrant) service workers to achieve a living wage, job security and improved working conditions. In cities across the USA, 225,000 janitors are part of the campaign.

Justice for Janitors' action exists 'beyond the workplace' as the campaign has sought and secured support from a broad base of public bodies such as political and community and religious groups. The campaign has taken on an international dimension, supporting workers in similar situations abroad and being joined by those workers in days of industrial action.

In the United States a second type of community unionism has emerged in the form of bodies that operate in areas marked by pronounced labour market disadvantage. Since they are based outside the workplace, these 'community labour organizations' differ from traditional trade unions, but nonetheless operate in ways that support working people and help to revitalize the labour movement, as Black (2005) describes. Perhaps the best-known examples of this type of community unionism are the growing numbers of immigrant worker centres, organizations that work to improve the prospects of poorly paid, vulnerable and disadvantaged people, often along ethnic lines.

The third type of community unionism involves joint initiatives between traditional labour unions and like-minded community organizations. Such coalitions work to raise awareness of labour market disadvantage, and campaign for effective ways of reducing it. The London Citizens group and its London Living Wage campaign has been one of the most effective of its type in the UK (see box 9.7).

Box 9.7 The London Citizens and the London Living Wage campaign

The London Living Wage (LLW) campaign is supported by trade unions and by community, political and religious groups. London is an extremely expensive city to live in, with higher-than-average transport, housing and food costs. Campaigners argue that there is a need for a living wage to be paid to all London workers and that there is a gap between the National Minimum Wage (NMW) and the wage level required to live within London. As a consequence many London workers live in poverty. The Greater London Authority argues that around one in five workers fall into this category. In 2007 the NMW stood at £5.52 while the London Living Wage (as calculated by the Low Pay Commission) stood at £7.20 per hour, a gap of £1.68 for each hour worked. (For more information, see www.london. gov.uk/mayor/economic_unit/workstreams/living-wage.jsp.)

The LLW campaign began in 2001 and is led by London Citizens. London Citizens is the capital's largest and most diverse alliance of active citizens and community leaders. London Citizens has over eighty-three member organizations, including faith congregations, schools, student organizations, community associations, trade union branches and resident groups. Members share a commitment to taking action for the common good, and helping people of all backgrounds and ages to become active leaders who can then shape the public life of the city.

London Citizens is a broad-based coalition of citizens and organizations which share common goals and is supported by trade unions, local and national, and provides a prime example of community unionism in action in the UK. By joining together through London Citizens, local organizations across the city have created an influential people's organization with the power to create positive change in their communities. (For more information, see www.londoncitizens.org.uk/.)

Although there are different types of community unionism, and the definition of community unionism continues to be debated, broadly it can be taken as relating to the efforts of trade unions to engage with communities, in terms both of localities and of interest groups, and to encourage community through social action ('doing community'). Any attempt to provide a definition is complicated by the slippery nature of the concept of community. To restate what was said at the outset, community is used to describe a common interest or a geographic locality but it can also be understood in an active sense, that is community as something that is 'done', a way of organizing and acting. We can see each of these three definitions at play in community unionism, and it can be seen that they are complementary, not mutually exclusive of each other. For example, the Justice for Janitors campaign focused on the needs of a vulnerable group of workers (common interests) but widened the campaign to other service workers with similar problems. At the same time it sought to build support at a broader level from other groups with an interest in social justice, locally, nationally and internationally; community was taken beyond the workplace and beyond locality.

In other instances trade unions have sought to target particular geographic areas in an attempt to reach marginalized and vulnerable workers. For example, unions in Sunderland set up a stall in the shopping centre to recruit new types of members. Buses have also been used to spread the union message. This is in direct contrast to previous union strategies, as the focus is locality as opposed to industry. This strategy seeks to empower and engage local groups and support local leaders in their attempt to improve social and economic conditions.

Although much of this is hailed as new, Fine (2006) points out how poor communities in the USA in the 1960s were organized by the United Auto Workers Union and civil rights movement activists, most notably the Black Panthers, and the term 'community unionism' was actually used at that time.

While it is potentially a radical step for unions, there are some limits to the development of community unionism in the UK. For one thing, in contrast to the United States, community unionism has been slow to take off. Also there has been insufficient focus on retired workers, on the skills and political commitment of former trade unionists and on the needs of post-industrial communities which once relied so heavily on a trade union presence. There is a tendency for the debate to be limited to a narrow focus on how community unionism can help to revitalize unions rather than support the communities in which they operate. As a consequence older communities and workers with little prospect of employment have not been the object of attention for either trade unions or academic researchers. For community unionism to be effective, it has to be reciprocal, 'sustaining relationships with community groups to help local life *as well as* fostering trade union growth' (Wills and Simms 2004: 66). Yet the unemployed, especially the redundant and retired, even those who have enjoyed a long association with trade unionism and trade union practice, are largely neglected both by the trade unions and by the debate. This neglect means that a valuable community and union resource is neglected, as the case of the New Herrington Banner Partnership reveals (see box 9.8).

Box 9.8 The New Herrington Banner Partnership: the importance of trade union heritage and culture within communities

The Durham Miners' Gala has been an annual event in the North East of England since 1871 and while it has altered in form and place over the years, the core elements remain unchanged. Mining communities parade their lodge banner through the streets of Durham in what can best be described as part picnic, part political rally, part community get-together.

Hudson (1995) records how it was predicted that the Durham Miners' Gala would die with the communities which celebrated it, once pit closures occurred, as there would be little interest in either unions or mining identity in the future. Despite these dismal predictions, resurgence in the Gala began to take place in the early 2000s. Research suggests that, despite the end of mining, unionism continues to have a role within mining communities of the region. The role is both practical (among other things, in terms of the organization of the Gala itself) and symbolic, in the cultural, social and political importance it has to those activists in mining communities who work collectively to engage with mining and union heritage and culture.

A significant indication of the resurgence of mining communities and their commitment to the union and industry has been the commissioning of new lodge banners. The New Herrington Banner Partnership (NHBP) was formed in 1999, with the specific purpose of raising the funds to commission a replica banner to replace the one damaged in 1986. For many in New Herrington, the Gala was the last remaining link to the complex matrix of influences that had defined their lives: occupation, class, community and trade union. In 1986, with the disintegration of the old banner due to high winds, that link was broken (Stephenson and Wray 2005).

The Partnership is made up of a small group of people, former miners and the wives of miners, community workers, trade unionists and local people who wished to regenerate their community but who had little or no direct connection with mining. It is important to note that the two people at the centre of the NHBP were the former Lodge Secretary, and his wife who had been very active during the dispute and was a trade unionist in the garment industry. The Lodge Secretary continues to be seen in his trade union role by local people, who come to him for help and hold him in high regard. Despite the fact that the local mine closed twenty years ago and there is no employer or viable employment nexus, the echo of a trade union structure remains here: the depth of respect for and reliance on unionism continues to leave its mark on the community which sustained the union and which was sustained by the union for generations.

While the NHBP has made little material difference to the lives of those living in New Herrington, it has been instrumental in uniting local people in a common purpose and in remembering heritage with pride. To that extent it has been highly valuable in rebuilding social cohesion in an economically depressed environment.

The Partnership points to the importance of non-crisis based community union activity and the ongoing role of older and retired workers in an environment experiencing economic hardship. The New Herrington Banner Partnership provides some important new directions in the community unionism debate. Unionism is more than simply a contractual relationship between workers and union. In this instance the union historically provided political and practical education to an industrial community, and with it the principles and practices of collectivism and union politics, principles which came to provide a blueprint for action. This level of influence and mutual support (union for community and community for union) has not died with the employment relationship. Communities which have relied on unions for long periods do not end their commitment to the union or their need for guidance and protection. Both community and activists offer the trade union movement pockets of energy and opportunity and challenges for the future.

This last example points to the wider meaning of community in social and political activism. Visions of 'alternative communities' have

Community activism is often inspired by issues such as damage to the local environment, and campaigns commonly confront powerful organizations, such as a large supermarket.

often been pursued as ways of living whose values differ from the mainstream. Such communities not only have been imagined, but also have been the subject of social experiments in co-operative living. Frequently, activists in social and community contexts, including welfare, educational and employing organizations, adopt a position which runs counter to the mainstream or the norm being promoted by powerful voices.

For example community activists may oppose the building of a supermarket which threatens the livelihoods of small local shops, may resist the development of green spaces or, as happened recently in the Bristol area, demonstrate against a plan to turn a popular and well-used cycle path into a new bus route. In such situations we have a plurality of representatives of different communities jockeying for power in an effort to assert the primacy of their own systems and values.

Business in the community: the rise of corporate social responsibility

One such representative group is the 'business community'. How far can the activities of business help to support, sustain and revitalize communities? Within the business world there has been a pronounced growth of interest in the concept of corporate social responsibility (CSR). Underpinning CSR is the idea that business organizations have duties and responsibilities not just to their shareholder owners, but also to the communities in which they operate. Businesses are thus answerable to a broad range of stakeholders, including their staff, customers, suppliers and members of communities affected by their activities. There is nothing new about businesses acting to support their local communities. In the nineteenth and twentieth centuries, paternalist employers, Quaker firms such as Cadburys for example, were noted for investing in housing and recreational facilities for their staff. Corporate philanthropy, in the form of charitable donations, also has a long history. Since the early 1990s, however, the resurgence of CSR has been a particularly noteworthy development (Crane et al. 2008; Vogel 2005). This is evident in a number of respects: the development of the 'fair trade' movement; the increasing interest in 'socially responsible investment'; and the keenness of business organizations to demonstrate their environmental credentials by becoming 'carbon-neutral', which we spoke of in chapter 3. So what is CSR, why has it risen to prominence and how significant is it?

The World Bank offers a useful definition of CSR. It 'is a term describing a company's obligations to be accountable to all of its stakeholders in all its operations and activities. Socially responsible companies consider the full scope of their impact on communities and the environment when making decisions, balancing the needs of stakeholders with their need to make a profit' (quoted in Doane 2005: 217). A number of important issues arise from this definition. There is the belief that firms have to demonstrate accountability, not just to their shareholders, but also to a broader range of stakeholders. CSR also embodies a concern with considering the impact of business activities on communities and the environment. Finally, there is an assumption that firms can effectively balance the twin objectives of profitability and social responsibility when undertaking their activities.

CSR activities tend to be concerned with certain issues, notably those relating to human rights, labour standards and environmental protection. There are indications that human rights considerations play a part in influencing corporate behaviour. The US multinational PepsiCo, for example, withdrew its investment from Myanmar (Burma) in response to concerns about human rights violations under the military dictatorship there (Vogel 2005). Companies have also made efforts to improve labour standards in the developing countries from which they source their products. Established in 1998, the UK's Ethical Trading Initiative (ETI) is a body largely consisting of companies such as Tesco and Marks & Spencer. It publishes a 'Base Code' which, among other things, requires its members to use suppliers that respect the right of workers to join trade unions and that pay workers a 'living wage', defined as 'enough to meet basic needs and to provide discretionary income'. Many major multinational companies, such as Nike, which source products from countries where the cost of labour is relatively cheap, have developed their own corporate codes of conduct which their suppliers are expected to respect. With regard to the environment, the implications of climate change have encouraged major companies, for example satellite broadcaster BSkyB, to commit themselves to becoming 'carbon-neutral', thus reducing the amount of carbon dioxide released into the atmosphere. The operator of the rail link under the English Channel, Eurostar, emphasizes the environmental benefits of travelling by rail, and using its services, as opposed to going by air.

Major firms often publish CSR policies. The insurance company Aviva's policy, for example, covers how it aspires to conduct its business; its relationships with its customers, suppliers and staff; human rights issues; health and safety matters; relations with the community; and the impact of its activities on the environment (Whitehouse 2006: 285). The influence of CSR is evident elsewhere: in the rise of the 'fair trade' movement for example. Fair trade products, such as coffee and bananas, have become staple features of UK supermarkets. Underlying the fair trade concept is the belief that the people directly responsible for growing or making products, small Caribbean banana producers for example, should receive a price for their produce that provides them a decent standard of living. A growing number of businesses specialize in fair trade produce, such as the organic chocolate firm Green & Blacks. The fair trade movement is a prime example of how CSR has grown in importance since the early 1990s.

Having discussed what CSR means, how are we to account for its increasing prominence? We might expect that external factors have played a part in encouraging businesses to act in more socially responsible ways, such as pressure for change from consumers, campaign groups, governments and international bodies. It is widely believed that consumer pressure has impelled companies to become more socially responsible; that firms have promoted CSR more vigorously because their customers expect it. However, the proposition that people's consumption decisions are increasingly being influenced by whether or not a business is socially responsible is not borne out in practice (Doane 2005). Look at the popularity of the cheap flights offered by airlines like Ryanair and EasyJet, for example, something that supposedly greater environmental awareness doesn't seem to have eroded.

The activities of NGOs have generally had more of an effect on company behaviour. In the United States, for example, campaigns run by NGOs such as Global Exchange, and the public awareness they generate, have forced multinational companies to deal more effectively with the issue of labour standards in their supply chains. In box 9.9 we consider how new communities of interest have developed to contest some of the adverse consequences of globalization.

Box 9.9 Globalization, mobilization and 'transnational advocacy networks'

When considering the role of business in the community, it is important not to overlook the extent to which firms have been pressed to operate in more socially responsible ways by communities of activists, who have mobilized to challenge what they see as the adverse consequences of globalization, such as the power of multinational companies, the erosion of labour standards, environmental degradation and human rights abuses. The book *One No, Many Yeses*, by Paul Kingsnorth is a very readable study of the rise of the anti-globalization struggles around the world, which really came to worldwide prominence as a result of the protests at the 1999 meeting of the World Trade Organization in Seattle (Kingsnorth 2003). The global anti-sweatshop movement, encompassing bodies such as Global Exchange in the United States and Labour Behind the Label in the UK, and represented by international bodies like the Clean Clothes Campaign, is a particularly prominent example of what Keck and Sikkink (1998) call a 'transnational advocacy network'. These networks comprise loosely affiliated groups of campaigners, activists and advocacy bodies, operating across national borders, who share a common goal. The many and diverse groups making up the global anti-sweatshop movement, including human rights organizations, consumer groups, churches, student bodies, trade unions and policy institutes, share the aim of improving labour standards in garment factories around the world (Micheletti and Stolle 2007). Internet technology facilitates these activities, for example by publicizing demonstrations or mounting electronic petitions. The development of the global anti-sweatshop movement, as a prominent transnational advocacy network, demonstrates how communities of interest emerge, evolve and develop in response to prevailing circumstances. Far from declining, communities, as sites of human interaction, are changing, not least because of the social, political and economic transformations forged by globalization.

Initiatives by governments and international bodies have also encouraged firms to change their behaviour in more socially responsible ways. In the UK, for example, the Department for International Development (DfID) supported the establishment of the ETI. The UK government has also reformed company law to strengthen the reporting obligations on companies with regard to issues such as the impact of their activities on the environment. International bodies have also attempted to encourage greater CSR. The 2000 'Global Compact' published by the United Nations, for example, is a 'framework for businesses that are committed to aligning their operations and strategies with ten universally accepted principles in the areas of human rights, labour, the environment and anti-corruption'. A voluntary initiative – firms are under no obligation to comply with the Compact – the principles include a commitment on the part of business to supporting and protecting internationally proclaimed human rights, ensuring that child labour is abolished, and taking greater responsibility for protecting the environment.

While external factors, particularly pressure from NGOs and initiatives undertaken by governments and international bodies, have had some effect in encouraging businesses to adopt CSR, there is also a well-attested business rationale for promoting CSR. The business case is founded on the belief that firms can secure greater competitive advantage, through increased sales and better relations with customers for example, by engaging in CSR. There is, in Vogel's phrase (2005), a 'market for virtue'. We should expect firms to act in a virtuous, socially responsible and ethical manner because it is in their interest to do so.

There is a growing consensus among major firms that CSR is good for business, and not just an act of selfless generosity. In theory, CSR activities can enhance a firm's reputation, helping it to attract customers and retain key staff, and, by demonstrating the effectiveness of voluntary action, enable it to avoid potentially burdensome government regulation. Reputational issues seem to be a particularly important driver of CSR initiatives. According to a manager from the engineering firm Rolls-Royce: 'everyone is in a competitive market and if companies' reputations start to suffer because they are not doing what they should be doing then investors and customers will go elsewhere' (Whitehouse 2006: 287). CSR offers firms an opportunity to highlight the distinctiveness and attractiveness of their brand as a means of securing competitive advantage. A manager from a leading retailer explained the rationale behind its CSR policy: 'at a time when companies find it increasingly difficult to differentiate themselves, we are all buying in the same markets, we are all buying at the same cost price, the ability to differentiate oneself through conducting one's business in a socially responsible way is another way you can actually work it through' (Whitehouse 2006: 289). CSR programmes have become increasingly commonplace because business organizations see them as advantageous, as a source of competitive advantage.

Finally in this section, how should we interpret CSR? What has been its impact, and how effectively has the business case encouraged firms to behave in more socially responsible ways? One critical interpretation of CSR comes from the free market right, and is strongly associated with the famous US economist Milton Friedman who died in 2006 (see box 9.10).

Box 9.10 Milton Friedman and corporate social responsibility

Friedman believed that, unless there were direct and tangible benefits, businesses shouldn't be concerned with improving the communities in which they operate. Getting involved in CSR activities adds to business costs, reduces the return to shareholders, diminishes economic prosperity and thus ultimately impoverishes society. Friedman maintained that 'the only one responsibility of business towards society is the maximization of profits to the shareholders within the legal framework and the ethical custom of the country' (Garriga and Melé 2004: 53). Whatever you think of his views, at least Friedman was consistent in his disdain for social responsibility of any kind. As Naomi Klein recounts in her book *The Shock Doctrine*, he gave economic advice to the leaders of countries with distinctly unsavoury human rights records. In 1975, for example, he was happy to travel to Chile and advise General Pinochet's military dictatorship, which had tortured and murdered tens of thousands of political opponents after toppling the previous democratically elected government in a *coup d'état* two years before (Klein 2008: 81).

The bulk of the criticism of CSR is that it is of marginal significance when set against the overall activities of business and that, where it does exist, it has little practical effect, suggesting that the business case for acting in a socially responsible manner is overstated. Companies either tend to invest heavily in CSR activities only where they do not damage profitability, or use them as a means of improving their business. Much activity is simply marketing dressed up as CSR; initiatives by supermarkets in the UK which reward schools with equipment when customers spend so much money in their stores should really be seen for what they are: attempts to increase sales. Socially responsible activities that are perceived to be too costly, or too damaging to the business, however desirable, tend to be neglected. The giant retailer Tesco promotes itself as a highly socially responsible company. Yet it has been subject to substantial ongoing criticism that its expansion programme actually damages communities, by forcing the closure of local shops in areas where it opens new stores. In 2008, Tesco also faced newspaper allegations that it uses complex avoidance schemes to reduce its tax liability in the UK, claims that it vigorously denies. While undeniably lawful, is it 'socially responsible' for a company to employ sophisticated tax avoidance arrangements which reduce the amount of revenue that a government has to fund schools and hospitals? A company may claim to be socially responsible, by announcing that it is moving towards becoming carbon-neutral for example, or by stating its commitment to fair trade, but as a business it is primarily concerned with making a profit. After all, managers of public companies have a legal duty to conduct their affairs in the interests of shareholders.

A related criticism of CSR is that it has little practical effect. CSR initiatives are, by their nature, voluntary arrangements; firms are under no obligation to abide by their own policies. Investigations into labour practices in Bangladeshi factories, where workers make garments for UK retailers including Primark, have revealed violations of the ETI's Base Code. The oil company BP promotes itself as a highly socially responsible company, yet it has been alleged that its operations have been detrimental to, and have even displaced, local communities in some of the countries where it operates, for example Turkey and Azerbaijan (Doane 2005). These criticisms highlight the weakness of the business case for CSR; businesses exist primarily to make a profit for their shareholders, and their interests and those of the communities in which the business operates may come into conflict. Is it too much to expect a company like Primark, whose business model is based on retailing cheap clothing, to be a model of social responsibility, given that its success depends to a large degree on sourcing goods at a low cost, with all that implies for labour standards? On the other hand, perhaps we should recognize that businesses are at least trying to do something, however limited the effects, and encourage them to continue such efforts.

Conclusion

While a number of definitions and approaches have been identified here, it is important to recognize that research which explores the concept of community may draw on and utilize a range of definitions of 'community'. Many of these meanings may be useful in exploring relations within organizations. So we may ask, is there a sense of belonging, a community in a workplace? Is the workplace embedded in a local geographic community? If so, does that sense of belonging and common interest transfer into the workplace and influence workplace relations? Are senior managers and HRM staff actively trying to 'do community', to manufacture a sense of belonging? Do occupational loyalties and identifications help or hinder the development of an organizational community? Who is included and who is excluded from workplace communities? How is the trade union involved?

We have argued in this chapter that the notion of community may make a useful contribution to the study of relations within and surrounding workplaces. Arguably the recreation of a sense of belonging is increasingly important in an ever-changing and fragmenting global economy.

Discussion questions

1. Reflecting on your own lifestyle, what communities do you think that you belong to? What are the characteristics of these communities? Are they based on geography, social identity, a shared interest or something else? How do the people making up these communities interact with each other?
2. To what extent do you agree with the proposition advanced by Putnam that civic engagement has declined?
3. How likely is it that greater community engagement will help to revive the fortunes of the trade unions?
4. Why has corporate social responsibility become such an important feature of business life? What are the main advantages and disadvantages to becoming more socially responsible for businesses?

Further reading

Most research and writing on community falls into three basic categories: theoretical work on what constitutes a community, how they work or fail and what they can achieve; an exploration of the experience of community life and the problems communities face; and finally, strategies for supporting, developing and regenerating community. Graham Day's *Community and Everyday Life* (London: Routledge, 2006) is highly recommended as it manages to bridge the gap between the three categories. It examines theories of community, explores the experience of the decline of working-class community life and the reasons for this, and provides a critical insight into strategies for conflict resolution and community regeneration.

A concise but comprehensive insight into the theory of community is provided by Gerard Delanty, *Community* (London: Routledge, 2006), part of the Routledge Key Ideas series. Delanty provides an insight into the meaning of community and the likely positive and negative impacts of what have come to be called 'virtual communities', to which people 'belong' through their use of communication technologies such as the internet. For an American perspective on the decline of traditional communities, see Robert Putnam's book *Bowling Alone* (New York: Simon and Schuster, 2000). A good article on community unionism is the one written by J. Wills and M. Simms (2004), 'Building reciprocal community unionism in the UK', published in the journal *Capital and Class* (82, 59–84). See D. Vogel's *The Market for Virtue* (Washington, D.C.: Brookings Institution Press, 2005) for insights into the corporate social responsibility phenomenon.

John Flint and David Robinson (eds.), *Community Cohesion in Crisis? New Dimensions of Diversity and Difference* (Bristol: Policy, 2008), examine the impact of social change, such as immigration, worklessness and poverty, on community cohesion. Their work critically examines the role of the state in supporting and maintaining community life.

The work of community development, its problems and dilemmas are explored in a range of texts. A good introduction to the strengths and weaknesses of this approach is provided by Margaret Ledwith and Jo Campling in *Community Development: A Critical Approach* (Bristol: Policy, 2005). Keith Popple, *Analysing Community Work* (Buckingham: Open University Press, 1995) and Marjorie Mayo and Jo Campling, *Cultures, Communities, Identities: Cultural Strategies for Participation and Empowerment* (Basingstoke: Palgrave, 2000), investigate how ordinary people can be empowered as a result of engagement with their community.

10 Conclusion – looking to the future

In this final chapter we will

- offer some reflections on the importance of sociological analysis for making sense of work, employment and business
- situate these reflections within the wider context of neoliberalism and capitalism and, from a sociological perspective, examine the challenges, problems and limitations associated with these
- argue that society should be the starting point for our analyses, not the individual or the market
- consider the trends and challenges that face business, organizations and society.

At the start of this book we argued that to understand business you need to understand society. Everything we see around us is profoundly social, and understanding the connections between individual things – business organizations, people, ideas – and wider society reveals underlying structures and causes that explain why things are the way they are. The world of work and business is structured by social forces external to it, and is in turn responsible for structuring much of the society that surrounds it. This is visible in many ways, not least of which is the operation of the division of labour in society and the labour market.

We then went on to look at how we can use this framework to explain work, organizations and the actions of people and communities. A sociological approach makes us challenge our assumptions, particularly those that claim things are natural, obvious or 'common sense'. It can help us to identify how power operates, and to examine the interplay between individual and society and the ways that this is mediated. Structure and agency are interrelated and mutually interdependent: agency works through structure and structure works through agency. Our actions are affected by social structure and social structure is affected by our actions (Giddens 1984).

We saw that societies have changed over time, and that different types of society have different forms of economic and social organization. Society affects the types of business organization that exist at a given stage of time and development; currently the supposed drive towards a knowledge-based economy and the impetus of economic globalization are contributory factors to changes in the labour market and labour process. The dominant neoliberal climate evident in many parts of the world engenders particular forms of work and types of worker, and organizations reflect this in their structure, function and culture, although we noted that some changes have been overstated. Communities, too, are affected by economic contexts and the types of work organizations that are located within them and, in turn, communities contribute to the kinds of work culture inside organizations. And as society changes, particularly as some traditions are set aside or challenged, people's aspirations change and we see more demands for fairness and equality: this is reflected in ongoing equal opportunities campaigns and new legislation (see chapter 8). Our sociological perspective reveals a complex interplay between individuals, organizations, social structures, economic forces and society as a whole, with lines of effect operating in many directions.

Using a sociological approach to understand work, organizations and business means applying social theory to the world; this provides a framework where concepts can be used to describe a range of phenomena, and then connected using models or ideal types. It also means carrying out and appraising research that uses appropriate methods: the systematic analysis by sociologists of work has revealed the tenacious grip that work has on us, and the way that work has become a major organizing principle in social life. Sociological analysis allows us to break down the complexity of work into its main components, and to consider the relationship between effort, skill and identity. We need to be flexible and see theory in a dynamic relationship with research into the 'real' world, and flexible in applying a range of methods to look at things from a number of different angles; this allows us to get beneath the surface of things to analyse potential causes and contexts of social phenomena.

One of the strengths of sociological analysis is that it allows us to identify problems through research and theory, but also suggests ways that we can start to address, perhaps even solve, social problems. The argument we have presented throughout this book is that a critical sociological approach, and a critical engagement with the social world, is appropriate, indeed vital, to understand fully work, organizations and business. This argument is supported by a study of papers published in business and management journals (Dunne et al. 2008). The authors found that most of the articles fail to deal with the broader social issues, such as distribution of wealth, the environment and equality, or to consider the ethical and political aspects of business. One of the authors, Stefano Harney, has argued that the failure of business schools to teach their students about these issues has directly contributed to the economic crises of 2008, by failing to challenge the culture of greed and selfishness that developed in the business and financial world, such as the huge bonuses paid to city traders (*Times Higher Education*, 26 September 2008). Traders and hedge fund dealers made billions of dollars selling risky loans and then offsetting risks to banks and investors, using their billions to buy yachts, jets, luxury fashion goods and tropical holidays in exclusive spas. Dunne et al. call for business schools to adopt a more responsible and critical stance in educating their students.

Our theoretical perspective, therefore, is a 'critical theory' (see also Bradley et al. 2000: 197): critical in the sense that it offers a critique of existing approaches and understandings of workplaces, proposes alternatives to the existing structures of power and domination, and challenges orthodoxies and myths surrounding work and business. As a result, we are better able to understand the often complex range of factors that influence business activities. The critical approach encourages us to be wary of over-simplistic accounts of life in business organizations, and also helps us to think about business in a more reflective, questioning manner. It ensures that, rather than remaining as bystanders, we are better placed to act as agents who can effect change and improvement.

If anything, the need for a critical sociological approach is even more pressing now, as Harney is arguing. The challenges that we face, both in society as a whole and in the world of business and enterprise, are more significant, more immediate and more global than at any other time. The rapid decay of the environment suggests we have less time than we thought available to work together to build a better world and a sustainable global economy. We will summarize a number of these challenges, those we feel are most pressing and relevant, but we need to place these in a wider context to understand their importance, their antecedents and their possible outcomes. Given the business focus of this book, it is not surprising that we identify capitalism, and the dominant neoliberal phase of capitalist development, as being the most significant context for our analysis.

Capitalism and neoliberalism

Neoliberalism has become the dominant mode of economic thought and life in UK society, so much so that some commentators have described it as being now 'common-sense' (Harvey 2005; Thompson 2008). In UK society we can see its influences reaching out into many, perhaps most, aspects of social and individual life: marketization of public services; the selling of state assets to 'free' them from the restricting hand of government; privatization in the education, health and defence sectors of government – areas formerly seen as being sacrosanct from this; and an increasing emphasis on personal choice, personal possessions and personal gains. As one commentator puts it, 'A society of "individualized" human beings has taken shape, driven by commodification and the spread of markets' (Rutherford 2006: 26). Neoliberalism has been very successful from an economic point of view: GDP has doubled in the past thirty years, personal incomes have tripled in the past fifty years. The majority of the UK population have been provided with affluence and individual choice in a wide range of areas. However, we should note that the economic crises of 2008, with the collapse of major financial institutions in the USA and UK, have suggested that neoliberalism has its limits. In fact we shall argue that we have perhaps become rather too complacent about the possibility of unchecked prosperity and economic growth.

With this economic transformation has come a social transformation. Sociologist Anthony Giddens argues that we have become a 'post-traditional' society where traditional structures, notably of deference and social class, have been broken away from (Giddens 1991). Our new selves are constantly encouraged to be self-reflexive and to continually work on ourselves, fashioning new identities through consumption. But this sense of freedom is, in part, illusory: we have no freedom but to consume, and the social structures and identities that formerly nurtured the self and communities are dwindling, leaving individuals atomized in an increasingly risky and competitive environment. As the boundaries of older social categories have been challenged and breached – particularly those of state, class, the family and community – sociology has had to find new theories and conceptual apparatus to make sense of our changing society. A report by the thinktank Compass went so far as to argue that neoliberalism fosters systemic loneliness, growing numbers of psychologically damaged children, eating disorders, alcoholism, drug addiction and widespread mental health problems (Rutherford and Shah 2006: 15). The report went on to describe a 'social recession' with symptoms of shameful and personal failings that we experience in the privacy of our homes. This may be overstating the situation, but it does remind us that capitalism has social as well as economic consequences.

Sociology tells us that people are social beings and that the things we see in the world are embedded in society; social structure and social action are in interplay with each other, and social groups and group formation are major components of social life and society. Our needs are formed socially, we achieve value and construct our identities socially, and we achieve freedom by being part of social groups and networks. Our social interdependence is the defining feature of human beings. Neoliberalism, however, looks in the opposite direction. It makes the individual and their personal needs and goals the main unit for analysis and action. The contradictions between the imperatives of neoliberalism and the way that society works are already visible in a number of areas.

Although we may think that neoliberalism is just 'common sense' or natural, it isn't and this means that we can investigate it to take a critical look at its central ideas, its course and consequences. Neoliberalism has been criticized by many on the left since its inception in the early 1980s, but it is still with us and belief in it appears to be stronger than ever, particularly if we examine the rhetoric of politicians and business leaders. As Thompson notes 'it hovers [in the body politic] almost unnoticed in its productive inventiveness' (Thompson 2008: 68). Neoliberalism has pervasive effects on us and the way we think. We are told that we have become neoliberal subjects with neoliberal subjectivities living in a culture where consumption has become increasingly significant: the pressure to consume and to define self and others by consumption is unavoidable. We think in neoliberal ways and we reach for neoliberal explanations and solutions to social problems. The market is the answer – now what is the question?

At the heart of neoliberalism is a belief in the logic of the market and the need for free, unrestrained and unregulated markets. Where markets don't exist they need to be created, for that is the best way for individuals to interact with each other to meet their needs. The state needs to take a back seat and merely maintain the institutional framework, notably the money system; anything further is unnecessary and inappropriate meddling in the market which, according to this theory, is perfectly capable of looking after itself. Writing this conclusion in the summer of 2008 with the credit crunch biting, major financial institutions failing and a recession looming, this rhetoric of 'the logic of the market' rings hollow.

Given the stress in neoliberal thinking on consumerist selves, it is also significant that major high street retail areas across Britain have reported falling sales over the summer, as people have responded to the threat of recession by 'tightening their belts' and being more careful how they spend. Hotels and restaurants have suffered in particular, as people economize by staying at home. This shows both how social actors can consciously change their behaviour in response to altered social circumstances, and how social selves can be reconstructed.

The critique of neoliberalism

Proponents of neoliberalism argue that the system will generate a better future for all participants through promoting freedom in a free market. A critical sociological approach starts to question whether this really could be possible and argues that it cannot achieve its promise for social, political and, perhaps surprisingly, technical reasons.

Socially, we can see an exacerbation of social inequalities and social divisions. British society is becoming divided on material lines more rapidly and more significantly than at any other point in modernity. The gap between rich and poor is wider than ever before: in 1997 the top 10% of earners held 47% of the UK's personal wealth; in 2008 this had grown to 54%. In the late 1980s the average CEO of a FTSE 100 company in the UK earned 17 times their average employee's salary; in 2008 that same CEO now earns 75 times his average employee's pay. Some CEO salaries dwarf this: Sir Terry Leahy, CEO of Tesco, earns £6,267,360, which is 526 times the average Tesco salary of £11,918 (*Guardian*, 12 September 2008). The pay of chief executives of the thirty biggest UK companies rose by 33% in 2007–8 alone (Toynbee in *Guardian*, 5 August 2008). And, perhaps predictably, the tax burden in UK society has increasingly fallen on the lowest paid: the bottom 10% of earners pay 38% of their earnings in direct and indirect taxation, the top 10% just 34%. Research carried out by UK accountancy firm Grant Thornton in 2006 found that Britain's fifty-four billionaires paid a total of £14.7 million in income tax on their combined wealth of £126 billion. They estimate that 60% of UK billionaires paid no income tax at all (Maidment 2006). On the basis of these figures the Inland Revenue is losing at least £1 billion a year in 'avoided' income tax from UK billionaires, a sum equivalent to the annual UK government budget for student grants!

Socially it seems unlikely that a system that generates such injustice and such disregard for so many can maintain its legitimacy. In UK society, divided though it is, there is a generally held value of fairness and a concern for social justice: unfairness, injustice and massive inequality are not desired outcomes for most people. The growing gap between rich and poor, and the increasing emphasis on consumption as a marker of social worth places an increasing strain on societal integration. For example, it is argued that some young unemployed men from disadvantaged backgrounds respond to being excluded from the wealth they see around them by turning to crime such as burglary and mugging. This in turn makes the lives of the rest of society less secure: you or your friends may well have experienced the theft of mobile phones or MP3 players. In addition, the tensions between the desire of many people for strong and well-funded publicly controlled institutions, such as the NHS and schools, and a system that promotes deregulation and marketization may well come into conflict soon. Since the neoliberal turn began, we have seen consistent opposition and resistance to the neoliberal agenda, not just from trade unionists and public sector workers but from concerned communities across the board.

Politically, too, a neoliberal agenda presents problems. Sociologists have examined the way that governments achieve legitimation, and broadly agree that it can only be achieved by general consent: we need to allow governments to govern us, but expect in return protection, security and a broad respect for social values and the rights of citizens. When governments fail to protect or provide for citizens, or ignore their core values and rights, when a state fails to achieve its purpose, a legitimation crisis will arise. Such a crisis would impact on markets just as much as on the state: the state, after all, is still the source of the central financial system. A neoliberal agenda requires states to withdraw from many areas, but to maintain order so that production and consumption continue to increase. Where a neoliberal agenda is not popular or uppermost in people's minds, then this will need some degree of force, overt or covert, to achieve that goal. In a state which curtails freedom and represses its population, individuals are unlikely to be willing and productive employees, or even consumers, and the concept of a 'free' market is lost.

However, the technical reason, namely that the 'logic' of the market that is at the centre of neoliberal thinking and neoliberal practice is actually a mirage, is perhaps the most pressing problem for neoliberalism. The idea that market forces, and the logic of the market, will self-regulate and tend towards equilibrium is certainly overstated and may even be simply wrong. Economic theory conceptualizes markets as being (mostly) in equilibrium that reflects an overall balance of economic forces. So when market forces change, markets change. For example, bad news about a company will make its share price fall because demand for its stock will fall, good news will make it rise; an increase in demand for a commodity will make its price rise and a decrease will make it fall. Neoliberalism assumes that markets – commodities, stock or labour – are regulated by the combined activities of individual actors, all of whom have access to the same information and who collectively will come up with the best possible response to certain conditions. This idea – that markets are made up of masses of individuals who can process information in the most rational way – is at the heart of neoliberalism and also at the heart of neoliberal opposition to state intervention in markets. Put simply, a state is simply not smart or flexible enough to process that amount of information in the best possible way; only a mass market can do that.

Markets should not, under neoliberal economic theory, crash (or boom) in the unpredictable and erratic way that they do. However, in fact, markets are sometimes driven by public emotions (such as fear or panic), not rational evaluation of information about risks and benefits. They also respond to social pressures that are reflections of concerns unrelated to the actual value of products or availability of goods. Contrary to neoliberal predictions, markets are inherently unstable. That few people ever mention this is testament to the power of those who benefit from such market fluctuations and the operation of the free market in general.

As to how long this can continue, it appears that some nations like China, where neoliberalism as an economic strategy has been embraced (albeit in a form 'with Chinese characteristics' (Harvey 2005)), are considering bringing in restrictions on unfettered markets as an attempt to restrain the juggernaut. The boom in China's economy has largely bypassed small business owners and has not advantaged workers: unemployment has skyrocketed in recent years. Those who have profited from the boom 'have been transnational profit seekers and those domestic power holders who abuse public positions for private gains. These two groups are connected to one another' (Chun 2008: 10). China has seen a rise of commodity fetishism 'accompanied by a deep and pervasive sense of alienation in a society trapped in naked greed, harsh competition, hysterical consumerism and a broad commodification of human values' (2008: 11). The failure of the marketization of China's health care system led to millions of people being unable to afford care, and the Chinese government are currently bringing in new policies to rebuild social security and provide at least some protection for labour – in the face of strong opposition from transnational corporations.

In China there are increasing numbers of protests and demonstrations as workers challenge the development of neoliberal market capitalism. During the 2000s, the number of labour disputes in China rose dramatically, as people mobilized to oppose job losses, fight against non-payment of wages and struggle for better working conditions. As a result, the government and the state-controlled Chinese trade union confederation have come under increasing pressure from the growth of new independent workers' organizations and other groups. A sociological perspective, one that recognizes the important ways in which markets are rooted in a dynamic social environment, is therefore vital to understanding the development of capitalist market relations in China. The Chinese economy is changing rapidly, but so are its social relationships, and both affect each other.

China's adoption of neoliberalism has produced dramatic social and economic change, a situation mirrored by many former communist Eastern European countries. The Baltic states in particular have embraced deregulation, marketization and free markets with great fervour. In contrast, many Western European countries, the UK being the exception, have not followed a strong neoliberal path: efforts to deregulate labour markets in France and Italy have been relatively muted and the Greek government's attempt to privatize state assets has been met with extremely vocal opposition.

Even in the UK, despite decades of neoliberal rhetoric, there has been a remarkable reluctance to embrace all aspects of neoliberalism. Marketization of public services has taken place, to some extent, but public support for public institutions such as the NHS remains high. The limits of a market-based approach, and the importance of developing a sociological understanding, are evident when we consider what's been happening to employment, work and organizations. Following the neoliberal, free market perspective, with its emphasis on choices made by individual actors in a deregulated economic environment, we would expect employment arrangements in the UK to have become increasingly marketized. In other words, rather than taking conventional jobs within an organization, with the prospect of long-term employment in return for a regular weekly or monthly salary, we would expect people to operate more as self-employed contractors, hiring themselves out on a temporary basis to companies that want to make use of their expertise in exchange for a one-off fee. For organizations, there are obvious benefits in reducing the numbers of workers they directly employ; hiring people on a temporary basis, from the external labour market, should offer them more flexibility, and also help to reduce costs, by ensuring that people are engaged only when their input is absolutely necessary.

Yet, contrary to popular belief, there has been no trend towards the marketization of employment in this way in the UK (McGovern et al. 2007). Organizations exhibit a marked preference for employing people directly; and do not rely on the external labour market for staff as much as might be expected. While there are economic benefits in keeping employment arrangements internalized, the reduced 'transaction' costs associated with administering a potentially vast range of different contracts in particular, there are important sociological reasons why the market has not transformed employment in the way that many people anticipated. For organizations, internal systems of incentives and control, like arrangements that link pay to performance for example, seem to be particularly valued methods of maintaining organizational effectiveness. This is further evidence attesting to the durability of bureaucratic methods of managing organizations, as outlined in chapter 6.

For workers there are also benefits to being directly employed by an organization; work is an important source of social cohesion. In chapter 7, for example, we saw that workplace gossip can help to generate and maintain collective social relationships between people at work. The atomized individual so beloved of the free market is, in fact, a social animal. McGovern et al. (2007) also demonstrate the ongoing influence on business organizations of that staple of sociological analysis: social class. Class, it seems, continues to exercise an important effect over many aspects of employment, including pay and other benefits. In order to understand work, organizations and businesses properly, then, we need to look beyond the market, and recognize the value of sociological enquiry.

During the 1990s, fuelled by the advance of neoliberal capitalism, the balance between many people's jobs and their lives outside paid employment became more uneven. People in full-time employment saw their working hours rise, and work in general became more intensive. Since the early 2000s, however, the average number of hours people work has slightly decreased; and it also seems that the general trend of work intensification has come to a halt. While the reasons for this are complex, it does seem that societal factors have had an important part to play in ameliorating work pressures. Demands from workers for better work–life balance have influenced government policy in the UK, through legislation making it easier to work more flexibly for example, and have also inspired businesses to improve their own flexible working provision. An example of this is the recent improvement to the arrangements for paid maternity leave, with diminished requirements for eligibility and an increased leave period (now thirty-nine weeks). Yet there is an asymmetric aspect to this, where those employed in lower-paid jobs experience poorer work–life balance. For example, working-class women are less likely to have been in jobs which provide occupational maternity benefits more generous than those provided by the state, or to have been in continuous employment for twenty-six weeks (the requirement for statutory maternity pay). Employees in prestige organizations (for example lawyers and financiers) are even entitled to have their gym fees paid during their statutory leave. Here it is social class and gender relations that are being reproduced in poor employment practices, so that those least able to resist the pressure to provide more work, mainly due to economic insecurity, are those who experience the worst work–life balance. This is a further example of how the operation of business organizations is influenced by aspects of the dynamic social context which they inhabit.

Challenges

Neoliberalism creates a number of challenges for us as a society, for organizations and for individuals. We have already discussed the challenge of societal integration when the gap between rich and poor is rapidly widening and when many of the wealthiest people are withdrawing from civil society by buying themselves out of health, education and social services. Reversing this trend is not impossible, but in a climate of marketization and privatization it will be difficult. But this may be a minor problem compared to that of global warming and the social, political and economic consequences it will bring about.

Tackling climate change is a pressing problem, and one that needs immediate and concerted action. Social awareness is on the rise, as is evident from the growth of 'transnational advocacy networks' (see chapter 9), and societal values are shifting towards a concern for sustainability and 'green' options. From a sociological perspective, climate change will bring about social change: global migration is almost certain to increase, insecurity of energy resources will lead to shortages and privation for many, and maintaining standards of living may become difficult. To achieve concerted global action on climate change there needs to be co-ordination and co-operation at an international level. However, the decline of the nation-state and the rise of global capital has altered the balance of power: can capitalism really provide a sustainable future given its inexorable drive for expansion and profit? And can the market, operating at the global level, really provide a mechanism that can tackle climate change, particularly given its instability and irrationality? As Naomi Klein points out (Klein 2008) the US government response to the devastating hurricane Katrina in 2005 may be the model for future disaster relief – only the wealthy received appropriate aid and the poor were left to fend for themselves:

> Unless a radical change of course is demanded, New Orleans will prove to be a glimpse of a dystopian future, a future of disaster apartheid in which the wealthy are saved and everyone else is left behind (Klein 2006)

Organizations face significant challenges that arise directly from the context of unstable global capitalism. Markets shift and change and as new global players emerge these markets become increasingly competitive and saturated. The rise and growth of economies like Russia, India and, most significantly, China place our own economy under pressure, and also make us more vulnerable to external economic fluctuations and fortunes. A new global order is coming into being and with it a new balance of power which does not necessarily benefit the UK economy.

The 2008 Olympic Games provided an opportunity for China to show the world how great its recent economic and technological progress has been. The Bird's Nest Stadium and the Water Cube required investment which the UK in 2012 will be unable to afford when it hosts the games. The extraordinary displays at the opening and closing ceremonies demonstrated that China can also excel in creative and cultural production, utilizing cutting-edge computer technologies and a hyperdisciplined workforce. The fact that China gained more medals than the USA and Russia was also a symbol of its desire to become dominant as a world power and indicated the level of resources it is prepared to devote to gaining this objective. However, China's rapid development places great strains on its natural resources and environment. To feed the power needs of one city alone, Shanghai with its glittering light displays and new skyscrapers, the output of seventeen power stations is needed.

The emerging world players, China and India, along with other developing nations, put great emphasis on ICT and technological innovations as a strategy for growth, training graduates for these areas and building new 'cybercities' such as the suburbs that lie outside Delhi and Beijing. The faith in the 'technological fix' is replicated around the globe. Indeed, organizations need new forms of work to generate more profit. New technologies can be an aid in driving down costs, and can make production more efficient. However, new technologies bring with them new challenges. The replacement of humans with machines creates a problem for a labour market and there are social consequences to automation. In addition, the deployment of new technology, particularly ICTs, creates a need for new types of workers, and creates new workplace cultures and new challenges for management. Indeed, the increasing use of ICTs in workplaces generates new social formations and types of workers. As we saw in earlier chapters, this brings advantages for some highly skilled knowledge workers with computer expertise who can command high salaries in the market. But it also requires the growth of a 'cybertariat' of low-paid call centre and data-processing workers to carry out monotonous and repetitive jobs, which also generate health problems, such as damage to sight or repetitive strain injuries. Many young people, even those with good qualifications, find themselves trapped in these unrewarding jobs.

Education and training are seen as vital for a new knowledge-based economy, and we can see a number of government interventions aimed at trying to increase the skill level of the UK workforce; most recently the UK government announced it was raising the school leaving age to eighteen. Yet we can see the education system being placed under increasing strain from privatization and marketization forces: city academies sponsored by businesses, top-up fees for university students and more skills focus in university degrees are all aspects of this.

Despite this, every year sees more undergraduates entering universities as a university degree becomes an entry-level qualification for more and more careers.

This may be of direct relevance to you: perhaps you are a reader whose decision to come to university and study was inspired, in part, by a desire to provide a more secure future for yourself through education. We are often told that education is the best way for people to improve their life chances, their earning potential and their career prospects (this is an arguable point: most social mobility comes from marriage between social classes). However, education in itself cannot protect against the insecurity and risk that the future holds. As capitalism expands and becomes more unstable through global competition for shrinking resources, particularly energy resources, global warming and other environmental problems put government, corporations and international organizations under greater strain, and international economic policies impose a neoliberal agenda on governments, forcing them to withdraw from labour market control, employment and welfare provision and subsidizing education and training. Our levels of protection are dropping: getting a degree is one way of trying to improve one's security through gaining a better position in the labour market, but this needs to be placed in the context of a more competitive and global labour market with more participants, where employers can ask for much more while offering less.

One of the many things that sociology shows is the almost infinite capacity of humans to adapt and change in different environments and circumstances, as we illustrated with the example of the response of British people to the credit crunch that began in 2007. Challenging situations throw up innovative individuals and communities; problems are addressed and coped with, although rarely solved once and for all. It helps if solutions are visible in other places, or alternative ways of doing things can be examined and compared. The expansion of capitalism around the globe has diminished possibilities for comparisons: it looks as if there is only one way to organize work and enterprise. But, as we said at the outset of this book, the idea that what we see in front of us is somehow 'natural' or inevitable is a product of how we learn, and are encouraged, to see the world. It need not be this way, and increasing global competition, impending global catastrophe from climate change and the rise in global population may be catalysts for dramatic social and economic change. The direction of change remains uncertain, but it is not necessarily utopian to hope that it will be away from the endless cycle of exploitation and appropriation that we have seen over the last two centuries.

Glossary and abbreviations

Ageism: unfair discrimination against older people.

Alienation: in Marxist theory a condition that arises from working in capitalism. Humans should perform creative, transformative work that fulfils their potential, but instead perform work that serves only to satisfy subsistence needs. People are therefore alienated from their work, each other and from their true being.

Anomie: sense of normlessness where individuals are unsure of their role and place within society.

ASHE: Annual Survey of Hours and Earnings.

BMA: British Medical Association.

BME: black and minority ethnic.

Bourgeoisie: in Marxist theory the social class that owns the means of production. Other sociologists use this term interchangeably with 'middle class'.

BPR: Business Process Re-engineering is an approach to managing organizations in which organizational goals are best achieved by re-designing organizations so that the focus is on operating processes that add value to the firm, by meeting the needs of customers, eschewing hierarchical and unwieldy decision-making structures.

Bureaucracy: a form of administration where decisions and processes follow fixed and rational rules.

Bureaucratization: the process whereby fixed rules become increasingly significant in more and more aspects of everyday life.

Call centre: a workplace where telephone and electronic communications such as emails are handled by workers. Call centres can be run to sell products or services (telemarketing), or to process and handle customer requests, often for product support.

Capitalism: an economic system where goods are produced and sold for a profit in a free market, the profits being retained by the owner of the productive process. In the contemporary world capitalism has come to dominate most societies and the global economy.

CBI: Confederation of British Industry.

CIPFA: Chartered Institute of Public Finance and Accountancy.

Class: social class is the principal form of stratification in our society. Class is, ostensibly, a result of ownership of material goods and money. However, sociologists identify class as a set of characteristics that include culture, status, occupation and lifestyle.

Community: a catch-all term for collective groupings. Formerly 'community' referred to groups with shared characteristics in a specific location. More recently society has begun to recognize quite disparate and loose communities that are based on shared consumption or lifestyle choices, or shared religious and cultural characteristics. Occupational communities are geographical communities that are based on a shared form of employment.

Concepts: abstract ideas that describe objects in the social world.

Conscience collective: that part of our consciousness that we have in common with the rest of society.

Consumer society: a society where emphasis and focus is placed on consumption rather than production.

Consumption: the use of goods and services.

Corporate social responsibility (CSR): the idea, and subsequent actions, according to which organizations consider the impact of their business on the environment, communities, employees and other stakeholders. CSR initiatives may include carbon balancing initiatives, providing free or subsidized community facilities or being involved in charity or development work.

Corporatism: a term that refers to the incorporation of employers' and trade union representative bodies into state policy-making processes; often used as a means of moderating the wage demands of the latter.

CRE: Commission for Racial Equality.

CRS: contract research staff.

Cultural capital: the term used by French sociologist Pierre Bourdieu to describe the various kinds of knowledge that an individual may possess. Cultural capital is a key indicator of social class position.

DDA: Disability Discrimination Act.

DED: Disability Equality Duty.

Degradation of work: see deskilling.

Deregulation: an ideological position and process whereby legislation that restricts the free operation of capital is removed.

Deskilling: the process by which knowledge of work practices and work autonomy are removed from the worker and passed to management or machines.

Disability: the condition that results from an individual being excluded or disadvantaged in society as a result of having a physical or mental impairment.

Disablism: prejudice against people with impairments.

Discourse: specifically, discourse is any complex linguistic construction. However, sociologists often use the word 'discourse' to refer to the framework of ideas and concepts that underpins a form of thought. For example, 'management discourse' refers to the dominant mode of thought by which people conceptualize and understand management.

Discourse analysis: the analysis of speech and texts to identify underlying patterns and structures of thought, i.e. discourses.

Discrimination / unfair discrimination: discrimination is unfair when the people being discriminated against cannot do anything to change the relevant characteristics, and these characteristics have no bearing on what a person is actually like and the contributions they can make to the workplace.

Disenchantment: in modernity, the process through which things become more explicable by rational means; the replacement of magical and mystical explanations with scientific ones.

Displacement: a feature of the degradation of work (see labour process theory), where less skilled, cheaper labour displaces more skilled, expensive labour.

Division of labour: the way that society assigns and distributes tasks to its members, the allocation of jobs and roles. In a globalized world, a new international division of labour becomes visible.

Dot com: a company whose business is internet-based.

Dramaturgical: the work of Canadian sociologist Erving Goffman revealed the dramaturgical aspect to social life; we are constantly acting out our social roles as if we were actors on a stage performing a drama.

DTI: Department of Trade and Industry.

Economy: the system of production and exchange in any society. Western industrial societies are capitalist economies, and the economic institutions of such societies are powerful, influential and highly specialized.

Effort bargaining: attempts to control amount, pace and intensity of work.

EHRC: Equality and Human Rights Commission.

Emotion work/labour: work that requires individuals to present specific emotions, such as happiness or empathy. The term comes from the work of Arlie Russell Hochschild whose work investigates how emotions have become commodified in contemporary society.

Employment: doing things and getting paid.

Environment: the physical world that we are located within. Sociological studies of the environment often focus on the interaction between the human and the natural, particularly how environmental issues, such as global warming, pollution and ozone depletion, are constructed and dealt with by experts.

EOC: Equal Opportunities Commission.

EPA: Equal Pay Act.

Equal opportunities (EO): the state of affairs where no individual is disadvantaged due to personal, fixed characteristics such as gender, age, sexuality, impairment, religion. Equal opportunities policies are an attempt by organizations to ensure fairness in employment processes and recruitment.

Ethnicity: cultural norms and values which are shared by a group, thus making a distinct and identifiable ethnic group.

ETI: Ethical Trading Initiative.

EU: European Union.

Family-friendly: organizational policies that are designed to help employees with caring responsibilities are sometimes described as being family-friendly. The UK government has made a number of attempts to promote such policies as an adjunct to formal social policy.

Feminism: a political movement that seeks to end male dominance in society. In sociology, a perspective that places gender at the heart of social and cultural analysis.

Feminization: an increase of women in the labour market, a decrease of traditional 'male' jobs in manufacturing and an increase in forms of employment that are traditionally seen as women's jobs, such as service sector work.

Feudalism: an economic system that preceded capitalism. Peasants work the land, and landowners collect rent and produce, and expect military service from their tenants. Feudal society is characterized by a network of ties of dependence throughout the social hierarchy.

Flexibility: a concept that is applied to a range of different phenomena but is primarily concerned with labour market and organizational flexibility. Labour market flexibility is the ability of a labour market to respond to the demands of business and employers in providing appropriate workers at the right price. Organizational flexibility refers to the ability of an organization to adapt to changing circumstances.

Flexible firm (core/periphery): firms that divide workforces into a 'core' and 'periphery' group, where the core experience standard employment conditions and the periphery are employed on short-term or temporary contracts. This arrangement is an aspect of organizational flexibility.

Flexible specialization: multi-tasking in team work situations.

Flexi-working: working patterns that are adjusted to suit the needs of individuals. Examples include flexitime, part time, job sharing, home-working and staggered hours.

Forces of production: in Marxist theory, history is driven forwards by the contradictions and resolution of contradictions between the forces of production – those things that make production work such as means of production and labour power – and the relations of production: how production is socially organized.

Fordism: the production system introduced by Henry Ford and characterized by mass production, moving assembly lines and repetitive working practices. Fordist mass production is related to the construction and exploitation of mass markets.

FTC: fixed-term contract.

G8: the group of eight leading industrialized nations (USA, UK, France, Japan, Italy, Germany, Canada, Russia).

GDP: gross domestic product, a measure of national income and output.

Gender: a social construction that creates and defines sex roles, attitudes and behaviours for males and females.

Globalization: processes operating on an emergent global level which over time are compressing the distances between people and places within different societies and which increase the sense that we live in a single world. There can be economic, social, political and cultural accounts of globalization, depending on which particular aspects of the relations between 'people and places' we focus on.

Habitus: the way individuals calculate and determine future actions based on existing norms, rules and values representing actual conditions.

Hawthorne effect: people changing their behaviour simply as a result of being observed. The term comes from a 1930s study of factory workers whose output went up when working conditions were altered in both positive and negative ways.

Homeshoring: moving customer service jobs out of high-overhead call centres, often located in a country different from where the customers are, and into workers' homes.

Homeworking: work that is mainly carried out in the home or with the home as a main base.

HRM: human resource management is an assertive approach to managing workforces in which people-management issues are integrated with the overall needs of the business. HRM theory sees staff as resources to be developed and enthused so that employees will have a greater commitment to, and thus be more productive in, a business.

Human agency / agency: the degree of free will that individuals are able to exercise in social action.

Human relations: an approach to workforce management in which the social needs of the workers are respected in order to promote efficiency and managerial effectiveness.

ICT: information and communication technology.

Ideal type: a concept that is constructed to reflect the main traits and parameters of any social phenomenon; it is subsequently used to analyse concrete cases. Ideal types are 'ideal' because they are constructed from ideas, not real, existing cases. However, real, existing cases can conform quite closely to ideal types.

Identity: the sense of self and distinctive characteristics that a person has. Identity has many sources: occupation, gender, class, ethnicity and so on. Many sociologists now see identity as a process, something that is always being worked on, rather than as something that is fixed and given.

Ideology: collectively held ideas or beliefs that are widespread in a social group. For Marxists, ideologies are reflections of ruling-class interests and are used to legitimize existing hierarchies and forms of domination.

ILO: International Labour Organization.

IMF: International Monetary Fund.

Individualization: a process by which people come to feel and be seen as more separated from one another. Individualization is associated with the modernization of societies.

Industrialism: expresses the main ideas of industrial societies – an advanced division of labour, a tendency towards democratic government and a rational approach to forming social institutions.

Information society / knowledge society: a society where the production of knowledge has become more significant than the production of goods. Central to this process is information and communication technology.

IT: information technology.

JIT: just in time. A production regime where raw materials, workers and parts are delivered to the point of production at the time when they are needed.

JIWIS: Job Insecurity and Work Intensification Survey.

Job polarization: visible when new jobs being created are increasingly divided between good, stable and rewarding, and poor-quality, low-paid and insecure.

Knowledge-based economy: an economy based on a highly educated, highly skilled workforce who can act as 'knowledge workers' in specific sectors of the economy such as ICT and finance.

Knowledge work: work that draws on a body of theoretical (specialized and abstract) knowledge, which is used under conditions of relative autonomy.

Labour market: a place where employers and employees interact to make arrangements with each other. These arrangements are usually governed by some form of contractual obligation.

Labour process: a term used to describe the bringing together of labour power (work), raw materials and tools or equipment that facilitate work.

LEA: Local Education Authority.

Leisure society: a society where leisure activities become increasingly important to both individuals and social institutions.

LFS: Labour Force Survey.

McDonaldization: the process whereby more and more aspects of society come to be dominated by the ethos and methods of the fast-food industry. The five basic dimensions of this process are efficiency, calculability, control, predictability and the irrationality of rationality.

Means of production: a Marxist term that refers to the actual physical equipment and premises that make production possible (factories, raw materials, machines, etc.).

Meritocracy: the idea that people get assigned to occupations within the social hierarchy on the basis not of their birth, but of their merits (talents, capabilities, skills, hard work).

Migration: globalization has brought about increased levels of migration, the movement of people around the globe. Whilst migration has always been a feature of human societies, the economic migration engendered by globalization is a recent phenomenon.

MNC: multi-national corporation.

Mode of production: the way that a society organizes its division of labour, technical and human resources at any given time. Marxist theory identifies successive modes of production: primitive, ancient, Asiatic, feudal, capitalist, to be followed by socialist and communist.

Modernity: the epoch that western industrial societies entered at the time of the industrial revolution. Modernity is characterized by rationalization, disenchantment and more ordered social organization.

Multi-skilling: the ability to carry out a range of tasks on a specific project.

Neo-bureaucracy: organizations that have attempted to free themselves from the constraints of traditional bureaucratic forms have embraced the idea of neo-bureaucracy. There are three principal modes: bureaucracy-lite, in which organizations attempt to flatten hierarchies; soft bureaucracy, where organizations combine flexibility with centralized control; customer-oriented bureaucracy, where the needs of customers are highlighted in customer–employee interactions.

Neoliberalism: a political perspective which holds that the deregulation of markets (including labour markets), reductions in taxation, and the privatization of state assets are essential sources of economic competitiveness.

NES: New Earnings Survey.

NGO: non-governmental organization.

NMW: National Minimum Wage. At 1 October 2008 the UK NMW was £5.73 per hour for workers aged 22 and over, £4.60 per hour for workers aged 18–21 and £3.40 per hour for workers aged 16 to 17.

Norms: rules and regularities that we expect to see in the behaviour of others; embodiments of social values and the moral order of society.

Occupational community: an internal occupational community is the group of workers inside an organization who share a sense of identity or allegiance. An external occupational community is located in a geographic region where employment is dominated by a single industry or employer (e.g. shipyard or coalfield communities).

ONS: Office for National Statistics.

Organizational culture: comprises the unwritten, tacit and informal norms, values and beliefs that influence behaviour in organizations.

Organizational misbehaviour: deliberate breaking of workplace rules, restriction of work effort, theft from or sabotage in an organization. Organizational misbehaviour is commonplace, often minor and often tolerated or ignored by managers and colleagues.

Patriarchy: power of the father, and the social system that emerges from this.

Pluralism: a perspective on employment relations that recognizes that employers and employees may have conflicting interests, but that these can be resolved to the mutual benefit of both by means of formal procedures, bargaining relationships with trade unions in particular.

Portfolio (career): a work trajectory where an individual will have a number of different career paths; these can be concurrent or successive.

Post-bureaucratic: a challenge to classical or traditional forms of bureaucratic organization. There are three main forms of post-bureaucratic organization: inter-organizational networks, network enterprises and virtual organizations.

Post-Fordism/post-Fordist: features of a post-Fordist society – societies that have departed from the Fordist mode of organizing production – include the rise of MNCs, individuation of culture and media, and emphasis on consumption not production. In organizations and businesses, features include an increase of women in the workforce, decline of trade unions, increase in service sector work, production organized around team work, focus on quality, JIT, multi-skilling, job insecurity.

Post-industrial: where an industrial society is one that is oriented towards production, a post-industrial society is one that is oriented towards the consumption of goods and services. A transition has occurred, from a manufacturing- to a service-sector-based economy. This brings about significant changes in society, particularly in terms of social class and gender relations.

Postmodernity: a period, following modernity (and connected to post-Fordism), characterized by social fragmentation, lack of faith in progress and rationality, and relativism.

Post-structuralist: ideas that are based on structuralism (the idea that there are underlying and/or hidden structures that govern thought, social action and social structure) but step towards a relativist position.

Privatization: the process by which state-owned or state-managed enterprises and institutions are transferred to the private sector.

Proletariat: originally the class of labourers in capitalist society who own no property and subsist through selling their labour power.

Protestant ethic: sociologist Max Weber described the attitude of early capitalist entrepreneurs (whom he identified as being part of the Protestant community) as being a focus on the importance of hard work, reinvestment of profits and an ascetic lifestyle. This forms the basis for the work ethic of western industrial societies.

R&D: research and development.

Race: the narrow definition of this term is the now discredited idea that the human population can be divided into distinct biological groups with fixed characteristics. More frequently it is used in very loose ways to describe different ethnic or national groups.

Rationality: the application of reason and logic to a specific issue. Rationality does not indicate truth, but does indicate a consistent and reasoned approach. Formal rationality, where rules and regulations are consistently applied, is the cornerstone of bureaucracy and bureaucratization.

Rationalization: this process brings rationality into more and more aspects of the social and personal world. It is coupled to disenchantment and associated with modernization.

Reflexive modernity: a theory describing the situation in late modernity in which individuals have increased ability to reflect on their own conditions of existence. This makes us more aware of the risks that surround us, hence the connection to the risk society thesis.

Relations of production: see forces of production.

Resistance: informal and formal opposition to management control by workers.

Risk / risk society: contemporary society can be seen as a risk society, as we become increasingly aware of risks that face us and increasingly uncertain as to how to deal with these risks.

SCELI: The Social Change and Economic Life Initiative.

Scientific management: see Taylorism.

Segregation, vertical and horizontal: referring to the gendered division of labour, horizontal segregation is the clustering of women and men into different occupations, and vertical segregation is the concentration of women in lower tiers in each occupational hierarchy.

SENDA: Special Education Needs and Disability Act.

Social capital: the collection of networks, resources and connections that an individual has amassed in their social interactions.

Social division: any significant fault line that divides society. Most notable are social class, disability, gender, sexuality and ethnicity.

Social exclusion: the condition of being excluded from society normally as a result of poverty.

Social structure: constraints on individuals that arise from social forces and institutions external to the individual. Persistent social patterns such as norms, values and rules, social institutions such as the economy, education system and judicial system, and constructed ideologies are all examples of social structures. Many theorists see structure as inextricably linked to agency.

Solidarity: French sociologist Émile Durkheim described two forms of social solidarity – the 'glue' that binds society together – pertaining to two types of society. More basic societies exhibit mechanical solidarity, where people cohere because they resemble one another. Advanced industrial societies cohere through organic solidarity, where people recognize their dependence on others because of difference.

Stereotypes: an exaggerated description of a specific social group. Stereotypes are often prejudiced and their deployment is at the heart of much unfair discrimination in organizations.

Strikes: the temporary withdrawal of labour by a group of workers, undertaken in order to express a grievance or to enforce a demand.

Taylorism: F. W. Taylor designed a scientific management strategy in which the mental and manual aspects of labour were wholly separated, allowing much greater management control over the labour process. The 'scientific' aspect of this comes from the focus on precise measurement of effort and tasks.

Team work: a central component of JIT working, team work refers both to the organization of workers into distinct teams which carry out a range of roles in production processes and the ethos of 'our team first, my interests second' that management want employees to adopt.

Telesales: a form of work where sales representatives use telephones to sell goods and services to customers. Usually based in call centres.

Telework: a form of homework where workers use ICT to carry out their core tasks.

Trade union: an organization set up and run by workers to protect their interests, carry out pay negotiations with employers and defend individual workers.

Tripartism: a term used to refer to arrangements that facilitate the involvement of three parties – the government, unions, employers – in economic and social policy-making.

TUC: Trades Union Congress.

Unemployment: the condition where individuals want paid employment but cannot find it. Unemployment is inevitable in a capitalist economy: as businesses start up or go bust, there is movement of workers into and out of employment. However, involuntary unemployment occurs when there are no jobs available for a large number: most industrial societies have a significant number of involuntary unemployed citizens.

Union derecognition: the act of an employer who decides not to maintain union recognition.

Union recognition: the act of an employer who agrees to enter into a formal relationship, usually involving collective bargaining, with a trade union.

Upskilling: the idea that, through team working and multi-skilling, workers will increase their skills level.

Verstehen: a sociological method that involves the reconstruction of the meanings and motivations of an actor – an empathetic understanding.

Victimization: deliberate negative actions taken against an individual who has made a formal or informal complaint in the workplace.

Virtual organization: organizations and businesses that have no physical presence and operate solely using ICT.

Vocation: more than a career, a vocation is something that an individual is 'called' to and is a career path they feel compelled to follow.

Voluntarism: a term that is used to describe the absence of state intervention in relations between employers and their employees, and between employers and trade unions.

Welfare capitalism: in contrast to neoliberal capitalism, this mode of governance attempts to balance the needs of capital with a strong welfare state and centralized social institutions. Often associated with Scandinavian countries.

Working class: a social class broadly composed of people involved in manual occupations.

Work intensification: increasing the amount of work and range of tasks that a job comprises.

Work–life balance: specifically the balance between an individual's work and their personal life. More generally, work–life balance refers to a range of 'family-friendly' social and organizational policies designed to increase social cohesion and family life whilst not inconveniencing business.

References

Abbott, D. 2007: 'Teachers are failing Black boys', in B. Richardson (ed.), *Tell It Like It Is: How our Schools Fail Black Children*. Stoke on Trent: Trentham Books, 108–11.

Abercrombie, N., Warde, A., Deem, R. and Penna, S. 2000: *Contemporary British Society*. Cambridge: Polity.

Abrams, F. 2002: *Below the Breadline: Living on the Minimum Wage*. London: Profile Books.

Ackroyd, S. 2002: *The Organization of Business: Applying Organizational Theory to Contemporary Change*. Oxford: Oxford University Press.

Ackroyd, S. and Thompson, P. 1999: *Organizational Misbehaviour*. London: Sage.

Adkins, L. 1995: *Gendered Work: Sexuality, Family and the Labour Market*. Milton Keynes: Open University Press.

Adler, P. S. 1999: 'Building better bureaucracies'. *Academy of Management Executive*, 12, 4, 36.

Alvesson, M. and Thompson, P. 2005: 'Post-bureaucracy?', in S. Ackroyd, R. Batt, P. Thompson and P. Tolbert (eds.), *The Oxford Handbook of Work Organization*. Oxford: Oxford University Press, 485–507.

Anderson, E. 1997: *The Code of the Streets*. New York: W. W. Norton.

Ansell, A. and Solomos, J. 2008: *Race and Ethnicity: The Key Concepts*. London: Routledge.

Arendt, H. 1959: *The Human Condition*. New York: Doubleday.

Aron, R. 1991: *Main Currents in Sociological Thought 2*. London: Penguin.

Aronowitz, S. and DiFazio, W. 1994: *The Jobless Future. Sci-Tech and the Dogma of Work*. Minnesota: Minnesota University Press.

Arthur, M. and Rousseau, D. 1996: *The Boundaryless Career*. Oxford: Oxford University Press.

Ashkenas, R., Ulrich, D., Jick, T. and Kerr, S. 1995: *The Boundaryless Organization*. San Francisco: Jossey-Bass.

Atkinson, A. and McKay, S. 2005: *Child Support Reform: The Views and Experiences of CSA Staff and New Clients*. Department of Work and Pensions Research Report No. 232. London: HMSO.

Atkinson, J. 1984: 'Manpower strategies for flexible organisations'. *Personnel Management*, August, 28–31.

Baldamus, W. 1961: *Efficiency and Effort. An Analysis of Industrial Administration*. London: Tavistock Publications.

Barnes, C. and Mercer, G. 2005: 'Disability, work and welfare: challenging the social exclusion of disabled people'. *Work, Employment and Society*, 19, 3, 527–45.

    (eds.) 1997: *Doing Disability Research*. Leeds: The Disability Press.

Bauman, Z. 1989: *Modernity and the Holocaust*. Cambridge: Polity.

    1998: *Work, Consumerism and the New Poor*. Milton Keynes: Open University Press.

    2000: *Liquid Modernity*. Cambridge: Polity.

    2001: *Community: Seeking Safety in an Insecure World*. Cambridge: Polity.

    2004: *Wasted Lives: Modernity and its Outcasts*. Cambridge: Polity.

2006: *Liquid Times: Living in an Age of Uncertainty.* Cambridge: Polity.

2007: *Consuming Life.* Cambridge: Polity.

Beck, U. 1992: *Risk Society.* London: Sage.

1999: *What Is Globalization?* Cambridge: Polity.

2000: *The Brave New World of Work.* Cambridge: Polity.

Beck, U., Giddens, A. and Lash, S. 1994: *Reflexive Modernization. Politics, Tradition and Aesthetics in the Modern Social Order.* Cambridge: Polity.

Becker, G. S. 1971: *The Economics of Discrimination.* Chicago and London: University of Chicago Press.

Bell, C. and Newby, H. 1971: *Community Studies: An Introduction to the Sociology of the Local Community.* London: Allen and Unwin.

Bell, D. 1973: *The Coming of Post-industrial Society.* New York: Basic Books.

Berg, I., Freedman, M. and Freeman, M. 1978: *Managers and Work Reform.* New York: Free Press.

Best, S. 2005: *Understanding Social Divisions.* London: Sage.

Beynon, H. 1973: *Working for Ford.* Harmondsworth: Penguin.

Beynon, H. and Austrin, T. 1994: *Masters and Servants: Class and Patronage in the Making of a Labour Organisation. The Durham Miners and the English Political Tradition.* London: Rivers Oram Press.

Bhavnani, R. 2006: *Ahead of the Game: The Changing Aspirations of Young Ethnic Minority Women.* Manchester: Equal Opportunities Commission.

Biswas, N. 2008: 'Streetwise, techno-savvy and hungry for it: my cousin embodies the spirit of modern India'. *Guardian,* 9 April.

Black, S. 2005: 'Community unionism: a strategy for organising in the new economy'. *New Labour Forum,* 14, 3, 24–32.

Blastland, M. and Dilnot, A. 2007: *The Tiger That Isn't: Seeing Through a World of Numbers.* London: Profile.

Blauner, R. 1964: *Alienation and Freedom. The Factory Worker and His Industry.* Chicago: University of Chicago Press.

Bolton, S. C. 2005: *Emotion Management in the Workplace.* Basingstoke: Palgrave Macmillan.

Botcherby, S. and Hurrell, K. 2004: *Women and Men in Britain: Ethnic Minority Women and Men.* Manchester: Equal Opportunities Commission.

Bourdieu, P. 1998: 'The essence of neoliberalism'. *Le Monde Diplomatique,* December (available at http://mondediplo.com/1998/12/08bourdieu, accessed 31 July 2008).

Boyd, C. 2003: *Human Resource Management and Occupational Health and Safety.* London: Routledge.

Braddock, D. L. and Parrish, S. L. 2001: 'An institutional history of disability', in G. L. Albrecht, K. D. Seelman and M. Bury (eds.), *Handbook of Disability Studies.* Thousand Oaks, Calif., and London: Sage, 11–68.

Bradley, H. 1989: *Men's Work, Women's Work.* Cambridge: Polity.

1996: *Fractured Identities. Changing Patterns of Inequality.* Cambridge: Polity.

1999: *Gender and Power in the Workplace. Analysing the Impact of Economic Change.* Houndmills: Macmillan.

2007: *Gender.* Cambridge: Polity.

2009: *Fractured Identities 2nd Edition.* Cambridge: Polity.

Bradley, H., Erickson, M., Stephenson, C. and Williams, S. 2000: *Myths At Work.* Cambridge: Polity.

Bradley, H. and Healy, G. 2008: *Ethnicity and Gender at Work.* Basingstoke: Palgrave.

Bradley, H., Healy, G., Forson, C. and Kaul, P. 2007: *Ethnic Minority Women and Workplace Cultures: What Does and Does Not Work.* Manchester: Equal Opportunities Commission.

Braverman, H. 1974: *Labour and Monopoly Capital. The Degradation of Work in the Twentieth Century*. New York: Monthly Review Press.

Brook, K., 2004: 'Labour market data for local areas by ethnicity. Technical report'. *Labour Market Trends*, October, 405–16.

Brown, C. 1984: *Black and White Britain*. London: Heinemann.

Brown, R. 1997: *The Changing Shape of Work*. London: Macmillan.

Brown, R. K. 1992: *Understanding Industrial Organisations. Theoretical Perspectives in Industrial Sociology*. London: Routledge.

Bryson, C. 2004: 'The consequences for women in the academic profession of the widespread use of fixed term contracts'. *Gender Work and Organization*, 11, 2, 187–206.

Buckingham, S. and Turner, M. 2008: *Understanding Environmental Issues*. London: Sage.

Burchell, B., Ladipo, D. and Wilkinson, F. (eds.) 2002: *Job Insecurity and Work Intensification*. London: Routledge.

Burns, T. and Stalker, G. 1961: *The Management of Innovation*. London: Tavistock Publications.

Byrne, D. 2005: *Social Exclusion*. Maidenhead: Open University Press.

Carter, J. 1999: 'Ethnicity, gender and equality in the NHS', in R. Barot, H. Bradley and S. Fenton (eds.), *Ethnicity, Gender and Social Change*. London: Macmillan, 45–59.

Casey, C. 1995: *Work, Self and Society. After Industrialism*. London: Routledge.
        2004: 'Bureaucracy re-enchanted? Spirit, experts and authority in organizations', *Organization*, 11, 1, 59–79.

Casey, C. and Alach, P. 2004: '"Just a temp?" Women, temporary employment and lifestyle'. *Work, Employment and Society*, 18, 3, 459–80.

Castells, M. 2000: *The Rise of the Network Society*. Oxford: Blackwell (2nd edition).

Castles, S. and Miller, M. 1998: *The Age of Migration*. London: Macmillan.

Cavendish, R. 1982: *Women on the Line*. London: Routledge.

Chandler, A. 1962: *Strategy and Structure: Chapters in the History of the Industrial Enterprise*. London and Cambridge, Mass.: MIT Press.

Child, J. and McGrath, R. 2001: 'Organizations unfettered: organizational form in an information-intensive economy'. *Academy of Management Journal*, 44, 6, 1135–48.

Chun, L. 2008: 'China: changing the rules of the game'. *Soundings*, 39, 7–19.

Clegg, S. 1990: *Modern Organizations: Organization Studies in the Postmodern World*. London: Sage.

Coalfields Task Force 1999: *The Coalfields Task Force Report: A Progress by the Government*. London: Department of Environment, Transport and the Regions.

Coard, B. 1971: *How the West Indian Child is Made Educationally Subnormal*. London: Beacon Books.

Cockburn, C. 1985: *Machinery of Dominance. Women, Men and Technical Know-how*. London: Pluto Press.

Cornwell, J. 1984: *Hard-Earned Lives: Accounts of Health and Illness from East London*. London: Tavistock.

Courpasson, D. 2000: 'Managerial strategies of domination. Power in soft bureaucracies'. *Organization Studies*, 21, 1, 141–61.

Crane, A., McWilliams, A., Matten, D., Moon, J. and Siegel, D. (eds.) 2008: *The Oxford Handbook of Corporate Social Responsibility*. Oxford: Oxford University Press.

Critcher, C., Waddington, D. and Wykes, M. 1991: *Split at the Seams? Community, Continuity and Change after the 1984–85 Coal Dispute*. Milton Keynes: Open University Press.

Cunnison, S. and Stageman, J. 1993: *Feminizing the Unions*. Aldershot: Avebury.

Danford, A., Richardson, M., Stewart, P., Tailby, S. and Upchurch, M. 2004: 'Partnership, mutuality and the high-performance workplace: a case study of union strategy and worker experience in the aircraft industry', in G. Healy, E. Heery, P. Taylor and W. Brown (eds.), *The Future of Worker Representation*. Basingstoke: Palgrave Macmillan, 167–86.

Datta, K., McIlwaine, C., Evans, Y., Herbert, J., May, J. and Wills, J. 2007: 'From coping strategies to tactics: London's low-pay economy and migrant labour'. *British Journal of Industrial Relations*, 45, 2, 404–32.

Davies, P. L. and Freedland, M. R. 1993: *Labour Legislation and Public Policy: A Contemporary History*. Oxford: Clarendon Press.

    2007: *Towards a Flexible Labour Market: Labour Legislation and Regulation since the 1990s*. Oxford: Oxford University Press.

Day, G. 2006: *Community and Everyday Life*. London: Routledge.

Delanty, G. 2006: *Community*. Key Ideas. London: Routledge.

Dennis, N., Henriques, F. and Slaughter, C. 1956: *Coal is our Life: An Analysis of a Yorkshire Mining Community*. London: Tavistock.

Department of Employment 1985: *Employment. The Challenge for the Nation*. Cmnd 9474, London: HMSO.

Department of Trade and Industry 2003: *Guidance on Teleworking – As Agreed by TUC, CBI and CEEP*. www.dti.gov.uk.

Dick, P. and Cassell, C. 2004: 'The position of policewomen: a discourse analytic study'. *Work, Employment and Society*, 18, 1, 51–72.

Dickens, L. 2000: 'Still wasting resources? Equality in employment', in S. Bach and K. Sisson (eds.), *Personnel Management*. Oxford: Blackwell (3rd edition), 137–69.

Dickens, R., Gregg, P. and Wadsworth, J. (eds.) 2003: *The Labour Market under New Labour: The State of Working Britain 2003*. Basingstoke: Palgrave Macmillan.

Dickens, R. and Manning, A. 2003: 'Minimum wage, minimum impact', in R. Dickens, P. Gregg and J. Wadsworth (eds.), *The Labour Market under New Labour: The State of Working Britain 2003*. Basingstoke: Palgrave Macmillan, 201–13.

Ditton, J. 1972: 'Absent at work: how to manage monotony'. *New Society*, 21 December, 679–81.

    1979: 'Baking time'. *Sociological Review*, 27, 1, 157–67.

Doane, D. 2005: 'Beyond corporate social responsibility: minnows, mammoths and markets'. *Futures*, 37, 215–29.

Dorling, D., Rigby, J., Wheeler, B., et al. 2007: *Poverty, Wealth and Place in Britain, 1968 to 2005*. Bristol: Policy Press.

du Gay, P. 1996: *Consumption and Identity at Work*. London: Sage.

    (ed.) 2005: *The Values of Bureaucracy*. Oxford: Oxford University Press.

Dubois, P. 1979: *Sabotage in Industry*. Harmondsworth: Penguin.

Dundon, T. and Rollinson, D. 2004: *Employment Relations in Non-Union Firms*. London: Routledge.

Dunne, S., Harney, S. and Parker, M. 2008: 'Speaking out: the responsibility of management intellectuals'. *Organization*, 15, 271–82.

Durkheim, E. [1893] 1964: *The Division of Labour in Society*. New York: Free Press.

Edgell, S. 2006: *The Sociology of Work: Continuity and Change in Paid and Unpaid Work*. Thousand Oaks, Calif.: Sage.

Edwards, P. and Scullion, H. 1982: *The Social Organisation of Industrial Conflict*. Oxford: Basil Blackwell.

Edwards, R. 1979: *Contested Terrain: The Transformation of the Workplace in the Twentieth Century*. London: Heinemann.

Ehrenreich, B. 2002: *Nickel and Dimed: Undercover in Low-Wage USA*. London: Granta.

2006: *Bait and Switch: The Futile Pursuit of the Corporate Dream.* London: Granta.

The Equalities Review 2007: *Fairness and Freedom: The Final Report of the Equalities Review.* London: HMSO.

Erickson, M. 2002: 'Science as a vocation in the 21st century: an empirical study of science researchers'. *Max Weber Studies*, 3, 1, 29–52.

Esping-Andersen, G. and Regini, M. (eds.) 2000: *Why Deregulate Labour Markets?* Oxford: Oxford University Press.

Fasang, A. 2006: 'Recruitment in symphony orchestras: testing a gender neutral recruitment process'. *Work, Employment Society*, 20, 4, 801–9.

Fayol, H. 1949: *General and Industrial Management.* London: Pitman.

Felstead, A. and Jewson, N. 2000: *In Work, At Home: Towards an Understanding of Homeworking.* London: Routledge.

Felstead, A., Jewson, N. and Walters, S. 2005: *Changing Spaces of Work.* Basingstoke: Palgrave Macmillan.

Fincham, B., 2007: '"Generally speaking people are in it for the cycling and the beer": bicycle couriers, subculture and enjoyment'. *Sociological Review*, 55, 2, 189–202.

Fine, J. 2006: *Worker Centres: Organising Communities at the Edge of the Dream.* Ithaca, NY: ILR Press.

Flint, J. and Robinson, D. 2008: *Community Cohesion in Crisis? New Dimensions of Diversity and Difference.* Bristol: Policy.

Foster, D. 2007: 'Legal obligation or personal lottery?: employee experiences of disability and the negotiation of adjustments in the public sector workplace'. *Work, Employment and Society*, 21, 1, 67–84.

Frenkel, S., Korczynski, M., Shire, K. and Tam, M. 1999: *On the Front Line: Organization of Work in the Information Society.* Ithaca, NY: Cornell University Press.

Galbraith, J. K. 1992: *The Culture of Contentment.* London: Sinclair-Stevenson.

Gall, G. 2003: *The Meaning of Militancy: Postal Workers and Industrial Relations.* Aldershot: Ashgate.

Gallie, D., Marsh, C. and Vogler, C. (eds.) 1994: *Social Change and the Experience of Unemployment.* Oxford: Oxford University Press.

Garrahan, P. and Stewart, P. 1992: *The Nissan Enigma: Flexibility at Work in a Local Economy.* London: Cassell.

Garriga, E. and Melé, D. 2004: 'Corporate social responsibility theories: mapping the territory'. *Journal of Business Ethics*, 53, 51–71.

Gavron, H. 1966: *The Captive Wife. Conflicts of Housebound Mothers.* London: Penguin.

George, S. 1999: 'A short history of neo-liberalism: twenty years of elite economics and emerging opportunities for structural change'. Conference on Economic Sovereignty in a Globalising World, Bangkok, 24–26 March 1999 (available at www.globalexchange.org/campaigns/econ101/neoliberalism.html, accessed 31 July 2008).

Ghose, A. K. and International Labour Office. 2003: *Jobs and Incomes in a Globalizing World.* Geneva: International Labour Office.

Giddens, A. 1984: *The Constitution of Society.* Cambridge: Polity.

1990: *The Consequences of Modernity.* Cambridge: Polity.

1991: *Modernity and Self Identity.* Cambridge: Polity.

Goffman, E. 1959: *The Presentation of Self in Everyday Life.* Harmondsworth: Penguin.

Goldthorpe, J., Lockwood, D., Bechhofer, F. and Platt, J. 1969: *The Affluent Worker in the Class Structure.* Cambridge: Cambridge University Press.

Goos, M. and Manning, A. 2003: 'McJobs and MacJobs: the growing polarization of jobs in the UK', in R. Dickens, P. Gregg and J. Wadsworth (eds.), *The Labour Market*

Under New Labour: The State of Working Britain 2003. Basingstoke: Palgrave Macmillan, 70–85.

Gorz, A. 1999: *Reclaiming Work. Beyond the Wage-Based Society.* Cambridge: Polity.

Gouldner, A. W. 1954a: *Patterns of Industrial Bureaucracy.* New York: Free Press.

1954b: *Wildcat Strike. A Study in Worker–Management Relations.* New York: Harper Torchbooks.

Gratton, L., Hope-Hailey, V., Stiles, P. and Truss, C. 1999: *Strategic Human Resource Management: Corporate Rhetoric and Employee Reality.* Oxford: Oxford University Press.

Greengard, S. 2001: 'Gossip poisons business'. *Workforce,* July, 24–8.

Grey, C. 2005: *A Very Short, Fairly Interesting and Reasonably Cheap Book About Studying Organizations.* London: Sage.

Grey, C. and Garsten, C. 2001: 'Trust, control and post-bureaucracy'. *Organization Studies,* 22, 2, 229–50.

Grimshaw, D., Earnshaw, J. and Hebson, G. 2003: 'Private sector provision of supply teachers: a case of legal swings and professional roundabouts'. *Journal of Education Policy,* 18, 3, 267–88.

Guardian newspaper 2007: 'Special report: bananas to UK via the Channel islands. It pays for tax reasons', 6 November.

Hakim, C. 1996: *Key Issues in Women's Work: Female Heterogeneity and the Polarisation of Women's Employment.* London: Athlone.

1998: *Social Change and Innovation in the Labour Market: Evidence from the Census SARs on Occupational Segregation and Labour Mobility, Part-Time Work and Student Jobs, Homework and Self-Employment.* Oxford and New York: Oxford University Press.

2000: *Work–Lifestyle Choices in the 21st Century: Preference Theory.* Oxford: Oxford University Press.

Hales, C. 2001: *Managing Through Organization.* London: Thomson Learning (2nd edition).

2002: '"Bureaucracy-lite" and continuities in managerial work'. *British Journal of Management,* 13, 1, 51–66.

Hall, M. 2005: 'Using a multi-level consultation framework: the case of B&Q', in J. Storey (ed.), *Adding Value through Information and Consultation.* Basingstoke: Palgrave Macmillan, 240–53.

Hammer, M. and Champy, J. 1993: *Reengineering the Corporation.* London: Brealey Publishing.

Handy, C. 1994: *The Empty Raincoat.* London: Hutchinson.

Harris, L. and Ogbonna, E. 2002: 'Exploring service sabotage: the antecedents, types and consequences of frontline, deviant, antiservice behaviors'. *Journal of Service Research,* 4, 3, 163–83.

Hartman, C. and Squires, G. 2006: *There Is No Such Thing as a Natural Disaster: Race, Class, and Hurricane Katrina.* Abingdon: Taylor and Francis.

Harvey, D. 2005: *A Brief History of Neoliberalism.* Oxford: Oxford University Press.

Hausbeck, K. and Brents, B. 2006: 'McDonaldization of the sex industries? The business of sex', in G. Ritzer (ed.), *McDonaldization: The Reader.* Thousand Oaks, Calif.: Pine Forge Press (2nd edition), 103–17.

Healy, G., Bradley, H. and Mukherjee, N. 2004: 'Individualism and collectivism revisited: a study of black and minority ethnic women'. *Industrial Relations Journal,* 35, 5, 451–66.

Heath, A. and Cheung, S. 2006: *Ethnic Penalties in the Labour Market: Employers and Discrimination.* DWP Research Project 341. Leeds: HMSO.

Heckscher, C. 1994: 'Defining the post-bureaucratic type', in C. Heckscher and A. Donnellon (eds.), *The Post-Bureaucratic Organization – New Perspectives on*

Organizational Change. London: Sage, 14–62.

Hillery, G. A. 1955: 'Definitions of community: areas of agreement'. *Rural Sociology*, 20, 1, 111–23.

Hirst, P. and Thompson, G. 2001: *Globalisation in Question: The International Economy and the Possibilities of Governance*. Cambridge: Polity.

Hochschild, A. R. 1983: *The Managed Heart: Commercialization of Human Feeling*. Berkeley: University of California Press.

Hodgson, D. 2004: 'Project work: the legacy of bureaucratic control in the post-bureaucratic organization'. *Organization*, 11, 1, 81–100.

Holgate, J. 2005: 'Organizing migrant workers: a case study of working conditions and unionization in a London sandwich factory'. *Work, Employment and Society*, 19, 3, 463–80.

Hoque, K. and Noon, M. 2004: 'Equal opportunities policy and practice in Britain: evaluating the "empty shell" hypothesis'. *Work, Employment and Society*, 18, 3, 481–506.

Hudson, M. 1995: *Coming Back Brockens*. London: Vintage.

Huff, D. 1973: *How to Lie with Statistics*. Harmondsworth: Pelican.

Hughes, J. A., Sharrock, W. W. and Martin, P. J. 2003: *Understanding Classical Sociology: Marx, Weber, Durkheim*. London: Sage.

Huws, U. 2003: *The Making of a Cybertariat: Virtual Work in a Real World*. London: Merlin.

Hyman, J., Scholarios, D. and Baldry, C. 2005: 'Getting on or getting by? Employee flexibility and coping strategies for home and work'. *Work, Employment and Society*, 19, 4, 705–25.

Hyman, R. 2001: *Understanding European Trade Unionism: Between Market, Class and Society*. London: Sage.

International Labour Organization 1990: *Telework. Conditions of Work Digest.* 9, 1.

Irwin, A. 2001: *Sociology and the Environment*. Cambridge: Polity.

Jones, P. 2003: *Introducing Social Theory*. Cambridge: Polity.

Kanter, R. 1977: *Men and Women of the Corporation*. New York: Basic Books.

Keck, M. and Sikkink, K. 1998: *Activists Beyond Borders: Advocacy Networks in International Politics*. Ithaca, NY: Cornell University Press.

Kelly, J. 1998: *Rethinking Industrial Relations*. London: Routledge.

Kerr, C., Dunlop, J., Harbison, F. and Myers, C. 1962: *Industrialism and Industrial Man*. London: Heinemann.

Kersley, B., Alpin, C., Forth, J., et al. 2006: *Inside the Workplace: Findings from the 2004 Workplace Employment Relations Survey*. London: Routledge.

Keynes, J. M. and Royal Economic Society (Great Britain) [1936] 1974: *The Collected Writings of John Maynard Keynes, Vol. VII: The General Theory of Employment, Interest and Money*. London: Macmillan for the Royal Economic Society.

Kingsnorth, P. 2003: *One No, Many Yeses: A Journey to the Heart of the Global Resistance Movement*. London: Free Press.

Kirkpatrick, I. and Hoque, K. 2006: 'A retreat from permanent employment? Accounting for the rise of professional agency work in UK public services'. *Work, Employment and Society*, 20, 4, 649–66.

Klein, N. 2006: 'Disaster capitalism'. *Guardian*, 30 August.

——— 2008: *The Shock Doctrine. The Rise of Disaster Capitalism*. London: Penguin.

Korczynski, M. 2002: *Human Resource Management in Service Work*. Basingstoke: Palgrave.

——— 2004: 'Back-office service work: bureaucracy challenged?', *Work, Employment and Society*, 18, 1, 97–114.

Koser, K. 2007: *International Migration: A Very Short Introduction*. Oxford: Oxford University Press.

Kumar, K. 1978: *Prophecy and Progress.* Harmondsworth: Penguin.

Kunda, G. 1992: *Engineering Culture: Control and Commitment in a High-tech Corporation.* Philadelphia: Temple University Press.

Lawler, S., 2005: 'Disgusted subjects: the making of middle-class identities'. *Sociological Review,* 53, 3, 429–46.

Ledwith, M. Campling, J. and British Association of Social Workers 2005: *Community Development: A Critical Approach.* Bristol: Policy.

Legge, K. 2005: *Human Resource Management: Rhetoric and Realities.* Basingstoke: Palgrave Macmillan (2nd edition).

Levitas, R. 2005: *The Inclusive Society?* London: Palgrave.

Lienhard, J. 1998: *The Engines of our Ingenuity: No. 1366. Rain, Steam and Speed.* www.uh.edu/engines/epi1366.htm (accessed November 2008).

Lindsay, C. and McQuaid, R. W. 2004: 'Avoiding the "McJobs": unemployed job seekers and attitudes to service work'. *Work, Employment and Society,* 18, 2, 297–319.

Lynd, R. S. and Lynd, H. M. 1929: *Middletown: A Study in Contemporary American Culture.* New York: Harcourt Brace.

    1937: *Middletown in Transition.* New York: Harcourt.

Lyon, D. 2000: *Postmodernity.* Milton Keynes: Open University Press.

Maidment, P. 2006: 'The U.K.'s billionaires'. *Forbes Magazine,* 12 July.

Mars, G. 1982: *Cheats at Work.* London: Allen and Unwin.

Martin, H., Meltzer, H. and Elliot, D. 1988: *The Prevalence of Disability Among Adults.* London: HMSO.

Martinez, E. and García, A. 2000: *What is 'neo-liberalism'? A brief definition.* www.globalexchange.org/campaigns/econ101/neoliberalDefined.html (accessed November 2008).

Marx, K. 1973: *Surveys from Exile.* Harmondsworth: Penguin.

    1975: *Early Writings.* Harmondsworth: Penguin.

Marx, K. and Engels, F. [1848] 1967: *The Communist Manifesto.* Harmondsworth: Penguin.

Maslow, A. H. 1943: 'A theory of human motivation'. *Psychological Review,* 50, 370–96.

Mayo, E. 1933: *The Human Problems of an Industrial Civilisation.* New York: Macmillan.

Mayo, M. and Campling, J. 2000: *Cultures, Communities, Identities: Cultural Strategies for Participation and Empowerment.* Basingstoke: Palgrave.

McGovern, P., Hill, S., Mills, C. and White, M. 2007: *Market, Class and Employment.* Oxford: Oxford University Press.

McGregor, D. 1960: *The Human Side of Enterprise.* New York: McGraw-Hill.

McIntosh, S. 2003: 'Skills in the UK', in R. Dickens, P. Gregg and J. Wadsworth (eds.), *The Labour Market under New Labour: The State of Working Britain 2003.* Basingstoke: Palgrave Macmillan, 248–61.

Micheletti, M. and Stolle, D. 2007: 'Mobilizing consumers to take responsibility for global social justice'. *Annals of the American Academy of Political and Social Science,* 611, May, 157–75.

Miles, R. and Brown, M. 2003: *Racism: Second Edition.* London: Routledge.

Modood, T. 2005: *Multicultural Politics: Racism, Ethnicity and Muslims in Britain.* University of Minnesota Press & Edinburgh University Press.

Modood, T., Berthoud, R., Lakey, J., et al. (eds.) 1997: *Ethnic Minorities in Britain: Diversity and Disadvantage.* London: Policy Studies Institute.

Morris, S. and Lawrence, F. 2007: 'A foreign worker's lot: a squalid caravan to sleep in, scraps to eat and £102 a month. Bulgarians reduced to scavenging for food. Employer ordered to stop trading by watchdog'. *Guardian,* 15 August.

Moynagh, M. and Worsley, R. 2005: *Working in the Twenty-First Century*. Leeds: Leeds University / ESRC.

Mulholland, K. 2004: 'Workplace resistance in an Irish call centre: slammin', scammin', smokin' an' leavin''. *Work, Employment and Society*, 18, 4, 709–24.

Murray, J. 2007: 'College voices'. *Guardian*, 8 April.

Nohria, N. and Berkley, J. 1994: 'The virtual organization: bureaucracy, technology and the implosion of control', in C. Heckscher and A. Donnellon (eds.), *The Post-bureaucratic Organization – New Perspectives on Organizational Change*. London: Sage, 108–28.

Oakley, A. 1974: *The sociology of Housework*. London: Robertson.

Office for National Statistics 2006: *Focus on Gender*. London: Office for National Statistics. www.statistics.gov.uk/focuson.

Oliver, M. 1990: *Politics of Disablement*. London: Macmillan.

Parsons, T. 1951: *The Social System*. London: Routledge & Kegan Paul.

Payne, G. (ed.) 2000: *Social Divisions*. London: Palgrave.

Peters, T. and Waterman, R. 1982: *In Search of Excellence*. New York: Harper and Row.

Philpott, J. (ed.) 1997: *Working for Full Employment*. London: Routledge.

    2006: 'Teleworking, trends and prospects'. *Impact*, 16, August, 24–7.

Piore, M. and Sabel, C. 1984: *The Second Industrial Divide*. New York: Basic Books.

Plant, R. 1974: *Community and Ideology: An Essay in Applied Philosophy*. London: Routledge & Kegan Paul.

Platman, K. 2004: '"Portfolio careers" and the search for flexibility in later life'. *Work, Employment and Society*, 18, 3, 573–99.

Pollert, A. 1981: *Girls, Wives, Factory Lives*. London: Macmillan.

    1988: 'The flexible firm: fixation or fact?' *Work, Employment and Society*, 2, 3, 281–316.

Popple, K. 1995: *Analysing Community Work*. Buckingham: Open University Press.

Pringle, R. 1989: *Secretaries Talk*. London: Verso.

Pugh, D. and Hickson, D. 1976: *Organization Structure in its Context: The Aston Programme 1*. London: Saxon House.

Punch, M. 1996: *Dirty Business*. London: Sage.

Putnam, R. D. 2000: *Bowling Alone. The Collapse and Revival of American Community*. New York: Simon and Schuster.

Quah, D. 2003: *Digital Goods and the New Economy*. London School of Economics, Economics Department website, http://econ.lse.ac.uk/staff/dquah/index_own.html (accessed September 2008).

Ram, M. 1994: *Managing to Survive*. Oxford: Blackwell.

Ramesh, R. 2007: 'India outsources outsourcing'. *Guardian*, 13 October.

Ramus, C. and Montiel, I. 2005: 'When are corporate environmental policies a form of greenwashing?' *Business and Society*, 44, 377–414.

Reed, M. 1992: *The Sociology of Organizations*. Hemel Hempstead: Harvester-Wheatsheaf.

    2005: 'Beyond the iron cage? Bureaucracy and democracy in the knowledge economy and society', in P. du Gay (ed.), *The Values of Bureaucracy*. Oxford: Oxford University Press, 114–40.

Rees, A. D. 1950: *Life in a Welsh Countryside. A Social Study of Llanfihangel yng Ngwynfa*. Cardiff: University of Wales Press.

Richardson, B. 2007: *Tell It Like It Is: How Our Schools Fail Black Children*. Stoke on Trent: Trentham Books.

Ritzer, G. 2004: *The McDonaldization of Society*. Thousand Oaks, Calif.: Pine Forge Press.

    2007: *Contemporary Sociological Theory and its Classical Roots: The Basics*. New York: McGraw-Hill (2nd edition).

Rius 2003: *Marx for Beginners*. London: Pantheon Books.

Robertson, M. and Swan, J. 2004: 'Going public: the emergence and effects of soft bureaucracy within a knowledge-intensive firm'. *Organization*, 11, 1, 123–48.

Rose, M. 1975: *Industrial Behaviour*. London: Allen Lane.

—— 1994: 'Skill and Samuel Smiles', in R. Penn, M. Rose and J. Rubery (eds.), *Skill and Occupational Change*. Oxford: Oxford University Press, 281–335.

Ross, A. 2003: *No-Collar: The Humane Workplace and its Hidden Costs*. New York: Basic Books.

Roulstone, A. 2002: 'Disabling pasts, enabling futures? How does the changing nature of capitalism impact on the disabled worker and jobseeker?' *Disability and Society*, 17, 6, 627–42.

Roy, D. 1960: '"Banana time". Job satisfaction and informal interaction'. *Human Organization*, 18, 4, 158–68.

Rubery, J., Cooke, F.-L., Earnshaw, J. and Marchington, M. 2003: 'Inter-organizational relations and employment in a multi-employer environment'. *British Journal of Industrial Relations*, 41, 2, 265–89.

Rutherford, J. 2006: 'In search of the good life'. *Red Pepper*, 147, November, 26–7.

Rutherford, J. and Shah, H. (eds.) 2006: *The Good Society: Compass Programme for Renewal*. London: Compass / Lawrence and Wishart.

Sachs, W. (ed.) 1993: *Global Ecology: A New Arena of Political Conflict*. Halifax: Fernwood Publications.

Saunders, P. 1990: *Social Class and Stratification*. London: Routledge.

Sennett, R. 1998: *The Corrosion of Character: The Personal Consequences of Work in the New Capitalism*. New York: W. W. Norton & Co.

—— 2003: *Respect: The Formation of Character in an Age of Inequality*. London: Allen Lane.

Shakespeare, T. 2006: *Disability Rights and Wrongs*. London: Routledge.

Shakespeare, T., Gillespie-Sills, K. and Davies, D. 1996: *The Sexual Politics of Disability. Untold Desires*. London: Cassels.

Shakespeare, T. and Watson, N. 2002: 'The social model of disability: an outdated ideology?' *Research in Social Science and Disability*, 2, 9–28.

Shaw, M. and Mundy, M. 2005: 'Complexities of class and gender relations: recollections of the women active in the 1984–5 Miners' Strike'. *Capital and Class Special Edition*, 87, Autumn, 151–75.

Shelley, T. 2007: *Exploited: Migrant Labor in the New World Economy*. New York: Zed Books.

Shiva, V. 1995: 'Biotechnological development and the conservation of biodiversity', in V. Shiva and I. Moser (eds.) *Biopolitics*. London: Zed Books.

Skeggs, B. 1997: *Formations of Class and Gender: Becoming Respectable*. London: Sage.

—— 2004: *Class, Self, Culture*. London: Routledge.

Smircich, L. 1983: 'Concepts of culture and organisational analysis'. *Administrative Science Quarterly*, 23, 2, 339–58.

Smith, D. 1977: *Racial Disadvantage in Britain*. Harmondsworth: Penguin.

Smith, P. and Morton, G. 2006: 'Nine years of New Labour: neo-liberalism and workers' rights'. *British Journal of Industrial Relations*, 44, 3, 401–20.

Social Trends, 34, 2004.

Spence, J. and Stephenson, C. 2007: 'Female involvement in the Miners' Strike 1984–1985: Trajectories of Activism'. *Sociological Research Online*, 12, 1.

—— 2009: 'Side by side with our men? Women, community and the British Miners' Strike'. *International Labour and Working Class History*, 75, Spring.

Stacey, M. 1960: *Tradition and Change: A Study of Banbury*. Oxford: Oxford University Press.

Steger, M. B. 2003: *Globalization: A Very Short Introduction*. Oxford: Oxford University Press.

Stephenson, C. and Wray, D. 2005: 'Emotional regeneration through political action in a post industrial mining community'. *Capital and Class Special Edition*, 87, Autumn, 175–201.

Taylor, P. 1999: *Hackers*. London: Routledge.

Taylor, P. and Bain, P. 1999: 'An assembly line in the head: work and employee relations in the call centre'. *Industrial Relations Journal*, 30, 2, 101–17.

Taylor, P., Baldry, C., Bain, P. and Ellis, V. 2003: '"A unique working environment": health, sickness and absence management in UK call centres'. *Work, Employment and Society*, 17, 3 435–58.

Tebbutt, M. and Marchington, M. 1997: '"Look before you speak": gossip and the insecure workplace'. *Work, Employment and Society*, 11, 4, 713–35.

Thompson, G. 2005: 'Interfirm relations as networks', in S. Ackroyd, R. Batt, P. Thompson and P. Tolbert (eds.), *The Oxford Handbook of Work Organization*. Oxford: Oxford University Press, 508–29.

    2008: 'Are we all neoliberals now? "Responsibility" and corporations'. *Soundings*, 39, 67–74.

Thompson, P. 1983: *The Nature of Work. An Introduction to Debates on the Labour Process*. London: Macmillan.

    1993: 'Postmodernism: fatal distraction', in J. Hassard and M. Parker (eds.) *Postmodernism and Organizations*. London: Sage, 183–203.

Thompson, P. and McHugh, D. 2002: *Work Organisations: A Critical Introduction*. Basingstoke: Palgrave (3rd edition).

Touraine, A. 1971: *The Post-industrial Society*. New York: Random House.

Toynbee, P. 2003: *Hard Work: Life in Low-Pay Britain*. London: Bloomsbury.

Trades Union Congress (TUC) 2006: *The Hidden 1 in 5 – Winning a Fairer Deal for Britain's Vulnerable Workers*. London: TUC.

Travis, A. 2007: 'From foreign fields to UK streets – the anatomy of an £8 billion industry'. *Guardian*, 21 November.

Van Maanen, J. 1991: 'The smile factory: work at Disneyland', in P. Frost, L. Moore, M. Louis, C. Lundberg and J. Martin (eds.), *Reframing Organizational Culture*. London: Sage, 58–76.

Vogel, D. 2005: *The Market for Virtue: The Potential and Limits of Corporate Social Responsibility*. Washington, D.C.: Brookings Institution Press.

Waddington, D. 2004: *Developing Coalfield Communities: Breathing New Life into Worksop Vale*. Bristol: Policy.

    2005: 'With a little help from our friends'. *Capital and Class Special Edition*. 87, Autumn, 201–27.

Waddington, D., Critcher C., Dicks, B. and Parry, D. 2001: *Out of the Ashes? The Social Impact of Industrial Contraction and Regeneration on Britain's Mining Communities*. Norwich: HMSO.

Walby, S. 1986: *Patriarchy at Work*. Cambridge: Polity.

    2007: 'Introduction: theorising the gendering of the knowledge economy: comparative approaches', in S. Walby, H. Gottfried, K. Gottschall and M. Osawa (eds.) 2007: *Gendering the Knowledge Economy*. Basingstoke: Palgrave, 3–21.

Warhurst, C. and Thompson, P. 2006: 'Mapping knowledge in work: proxies or practices?' *Work, Employment and Society*, 20, 4, 787–800.

Warner, M. and Witzel, M. 2004: *Managing in Virtual Organizations*. London: Thomson Learning.

Wass, V. and McNabb, R. 2006: 'Pay, promotion and parenthood amongst women solicitors'. *Work, Employment and Society*, 20, 2, 289–308.

Waters, M. 2000: *Globalization*. London: Routledge (2nd edition).

Webb, J. 2006: *Organisations, Identities and the Self.* Basingstoke: Palgrave Macmillan.

Weber, M. 1947: *The Theory of Social and Economic Organization,* (trans. A. Henderson and T. Parsons, ed. by T. Parsons). New York: Free Press.

  [1905] 1958: *The Protestant Ethic and the Spirit of Capitalism.* New York: Charles Scribner's Sons.

  [1921] 1978: *Economy and Society I.* Berkeley: University of California Press.

White, M., Hill, S., Mills, C. and Smeaton, D. 2004: *Managing to Change?* Basingstoke: Palgrave Macmillan.

Whitehouse, L. 2006: 'Corporate social responsibility: views from the frontline'. *Journal of Business Ethics,* 63, 279–96.

Wickham, J. 2007: 'Irish mobilities', in S. O'Sullivan (ed.), *Contemporary Ireland: A Sociological Map.* Dublin: University College Dublin Press.

Williams, C. 2007: *Rethinking the Future of Work: Directions and Visions.* Basingstoke: Palgrave Macmillan.

Williams, R. 1983: *Keywords.* London: Flamingo.

Williams, W. M. 1963: *A West Country Village: Ashworthy.* London: Routledge & Kegan Paul.

Willis, P. 1981: *Learning To Labour. How Working Class Kids Get Working Class Jobs.* New York: Columbia University Press.

Willmott, H. 1993: 'Strength is ignorance; slavery is freedom: managing culture in modern organizations'. *Journal of Management Studies,* 30, 4, 515–52.

Wills, J. 2001: 'Community unionism and trade union renewal in the UK: moving beyond the fragments at last?' *Transactions of the Institute of British Geographers,* new series, 26, 4, 465–83.

Wills, J. and Simms, M. 2004: 'Building reciprocal community unionism in the UK'. *Capital and Class,* 82, 59–84.

Wilson, F. 2004: *Organizational Behaviour and Work.* Oxford: Oxford University Press (2nd edition).

Witz, A. 1992: *Professions and Patriarchy.* London: Routledge.

Woodward, J. 1965: *Industrial Organization: Theory and Practice.* London: Oxford University Press.

Wright Mills, C. 1959: *The Sociological Imagination.* Oxford: Oxford University Press.

Young, M. and Willmott, P. 1957: *Family and Kinship in East London.* Harmondsworth: Penguin.

Index

Note: Abbreviations used in the index: BME workers = black and minority ethnic workers; CSR = corporate social responsibility; HRM = human resource management

Abbott, D. 215
Abrams, F. 134
absence at work 184–5
absence from work 151, 184, 187
academic workers 125–7, 130
accidents, workplace 136
Ackroyd, S. 182, 187–8
action, Weber's ideal types of 13–15, 34
Adams, D. 36
administrative theory of management
    147
affective action 13
age discrimination 200
    cult of modernity and 39–40
    equality legislation and 94, 208
    labour markets and 88–9, 94
ageing, disability through 225
ageism *see* age discrimination
agrarian societies 8, 31, 32–3, 79
    see also preindustrial economy
agriculture sector
    average weekly earnings 84
    employment patterns 42
    environmental dilemmas 70
    relative size in 2006 83
air stewardesses 67, 132
air travel 69–70, 254
Alach, P. 129
alienation 6, 33, 34, 35, 136–7
Anderson, E. 215
anomie 10–11, 37
anti-discrimination legislation *see*
    equality legislation
anti-globalization movement 255
anti-social behaviour 24
    see also crime; organizational
      misbehaviour
anti-sweatshop movement 255
Anuta 40–1

The Archers (radio soap) 70
Arendt, H. 113, 116, 137
Aronowitz, S. 140
aropa (compassion/love/affection) 41
asylum seekers 211–12
Atkinson, J. 156–7
authority
    bureaucratic organizations and 145
    organizational misbehaviour and 186
    see also control
authority rewards, work 122
axial principle 43

Baldamus, W. 117, 133
banana trade 55–6
Barnes, C. 87
BASE (Business and a Sustainable
    Environment) 71–2
Bauman, Z. 46, 152, 234
Beck, U. 40, 114–15, 140
Becker, G. 205
behaviour in organizations 173–98
beliefs, employment equality legislation
    94, 206, 208, 213
    see also religion
Bell, C. 234
Bell, D. 42, 43
Berkley, J. 160
Beynon, H. 153
bicycle couriers 127–8
Biswas, N. 65–6
black and minority ethnic (BME)
    workers
    trade unions and 193, 196
    unfair discrimination 200, 209–16
      business case against 205–6
      equality legislation 206, 208,
        212–13
      gender hierarchies 211, 213–14

labour markets 86–7, 210–12, 213–14, 216
see also migrant workers
Blauner, R. 137
Bolton, S. C. 132
boundaryless careers 163–4
Bourdieu, P. 5, 58, 242
typology of capital 242
bourgeoisie 5, 6, 32, 33
Bradley, H. 118
Braverman, H. 33, 100, 101, 102, 103, 147
Brents, B. 149–50
Brown, G. 89, 90
Brown, R. 79–80
Bryson, C. 130
bullying *see* harassment
Burberry 53–4
Burchell, B. 135
bureaucracy-lite 168
bureaucratic organization 144, 145–53, 154, 170–1
changing forms 164–70
labour markets and 98–9
Weber's analysis of 14, 34, 35–6, 145–8, 150–1
Burns, T. 154
business
in the community 252–8
the environment and 68–70, 71–2, 253–4, 255
globalization and 50–8
modernity and 39–40
performance–CSR relation and 256–8
performance–discrimination relation and 205–6
performance–HRM relation and 178–80, 181
reason for studying 1–2, 260–2
reputation 256
social typologies and 31
strategy–HRM relation and 178
see also organizations; work
Business Process Re-engineering (BPR) 155–6, 165
business schools 261–2

call centres 53, 57
homeshoring 106
misbehaviour in 184, 187
work in 103, 107–10, 130
calling, work as 125–7
Cameron, C. 215–16

capitalism 31
consumer society 47
the environment and 60, 68, 269, 271
feminism and 19
future challenges for 271
labour market regulation and 92–3
Marxist theory of 4–7, 19, 30, 32–4, 103
alienation 6, 33, 34, 136–7
disabled workers and 228
unions as class actors 190–1
neoliberal 58–60, 93, 262–9
scientific management and 100–1, 102
social capital and 242
social divisions and inequalities under 201
unemployment and 91
Weber's account of 33–6, 41, 138
work ethic in 138, 139–40
careers 163–4
carers
gender (in)equality 219, 220, 224
meaning of work and 116
Casey, C. 122–4, 125, 129, 167
Cassell, C. 222, 223
Castells, M. 61, 159
Castles, S. 63
Champy, J. 155–6
Chandler, A. 147
childcare 219, 220, 224
Chinese economy 57, 58, 266–7, 269
choice, work and 128–30, 267–8
civic society 239–42, 243
class *see* social class
coalmining communities 234, 235, 237, 244–6, 250–1
Coard, B. 215
cocaine trade 56–7
collective bargaining 191–3, 194–6
collective laissez-faire doctrine 92
collective offices 163
communications
globalization of 52, 53
human resource management and 178–9, 180–1
organizational misbehaviour and 187
see also information and communication technology
communism 5, 6, 30, 33, 41
community
business in 71–2, 252–8
decline of 239–42, 244, 250–1, 263

community (*cont.*)
  defining 233–4, 243–6, 249
  Marx's ideals 33
  occupational 136, 234, 235, 238–9
  organizational 238
  as something that is done 243–6, 249,
    251–2
  studies 235–7
  trade unions 245–52
community activism 243, 246, 251–2,
    254–5
community unionism 246–52
competition, global 53–4, 75, 98
computers 72–5
  see also information and
      communication technology
concepts, sociological 2, 3
conflict
  functionalism and 10–11
  Marxist theory of 6–7, 32–3, 187,
    190–1
  organizational misbehaviour and
    187
  post-industrial society and 43, 44, 45
  unions as class actors and 190–1
  unions as source of order and 194
  see also industrial relations
conscience collectives 8, 9
consumer culture 124
consumer pressure, CSR 254
consumer society 31, 47, 48, 78
  neoliberalism and 263, 264, 265, 266
  self-identity and 118
contentment 133
contract research staff (CRS) 125–7
contracts of employment 92, 94, 125,
    130, 164
contradictions, Marxist theory 32–3
control
  alienation and 137
  bureaucratic organizations and 145–8,
    149–50, 151–2, 164–7, 170, 171
  call centre workers and 109
  neo-bureaucratic organizations and
    168, 169
  organizational misbehaviour and
    185, 187
  post-bureaucratic organizations and
    161–2, 163
  scientific management and 101, 147
co-operation
  human resource management and
    179, 181

organizational misbehaviour and 189
  post-bureaucratic organizations and
    161
core employees 156, 157
core unemployment 91–2
Cornwell, J. 237
corporate cultures 122–5
  see also organizational culture
corporate misconduct 188
corporate social responsibility (CSR)
    71–2, 252–8
corporatism 273
Courpasson, D. 168–9
craft-based production 102, 103, 137
critical theory 262
cultural capital 212, 242
cultural construct, class as 203, 204–5
cultural homogenization 52
cultural relativism 21
cultural style, racial discrimination and
    216
culture
  corporate 122–5
    see also organizational culture
  within communities 250–1
  workplace 214
customer-oriented bureaucracy 168,
    169

dangerous work 136
data 3
  collection methods 23–6, 228, 236
  UK government statistics 82–3
decision-making
  employee involvement in 178–9,
    180–1
  unfair discrimination and 200
de-differentiation, consumer culture
    124
degradation of work (deskilling) 44, 73,
    94–6, 102–3, 148
de-humanization
  of bureaucracy 152–3
  Weber's analysis of 14
deindustrialization 244
  see also post-industrialism
demand-deficient unemployment 91
deprivations of work 133
deregulation 58, 59
  labour markets and 89, 90, 92–5, 98–9,
    267
deskilling (degradation of work) 44, 73,
    94–6, 102–3, 148

deviance
  fiddling behaviour 183–4
  managerial 188
diasporas 62–3
Dick, P. 222, 223
DiFazio, W. 140
disability 200, 224–31
  defining 224–5
  direct discrimination 206
  equality legislation and 208, 209, 225,
    227–9, 230
  labour market participation and
    87–8, 228–30
  social class and 201
Disability Discrimination Act (1995)
  (DDA) 227, 228–9
Disability Equality Duty 227–8
disablism 226
disaster relief 269
discourse 21–3, 223
discrimination 200
  business case against 205–6
  direct 206, 212
  disability 87–8, 200, 201, 206, 208,
    209, 224–31
  ethnic 86–7, 200, 205–6, 208, 209–16
  gender *see* gender (in)equality
  indirect 206, 212
  labour markets and 82, 86–9, 94–5
  legislation against 82, 94–5, 206–8,
    212–13, 218, 221, 227–9, 230
  unfair 200–1, 205–6
disenchantment 14, 34–5
disgust 204
displacement of labour 102
diversity, business case for 205–6
division of labour 7–9, 36, 78–9
  degradation of work 102
  gendered 19–20, 218, 219, 245, 246,
    277
  international 42, 52
  organizing mechanism *see* labour
    markets
  post-Fordist 103
  preindustrial 40
dogma of work 140
domestic labour *see* housework
dot com collapse 135
dramaturgical perspective 15, 16
drug crime 215, 216
drug trade 56–7
du Gay, P. 40, 124–5
dual-systems theory 201

Dunne, S. 261–2
Durham Miners' Gala 250–1
Durkheim, Émile 7–10, 30–1
  human relations and 174, 194
  social typologies 30–1, 36–7, 47–8
duty, work as 125–7

Eastern European countries 64, 210, 267
economic migration 63–6, 75, 209–10,
  269
economic motivation for work 119, 120,
  126–7
economic power, unions 192
economy, the
  2008 crisis 261–2, 263, 264
  functionalist analysis of 11
  globalization and 51–8
  knowledge-based 50–1, 60–2, 75, 270
  Marxist analysis of 4–6, 32–4
  Neoliberalism and 58–60, 93, 262–9
  preindustrial 40–1
  social typologies and 31, 32–6
  in a tribal society 40–1
EDF, sustainability 69
education
  knowledge-based economy and 62,
    96, 97, 98, 270–1
  labour markets and 95, 97, 98, 271
  people with disability and 227
  post-industrial society and 43, 44, 45,
    48
  racial discrimination in schools 215–16
  sociological 261–2
education workers
  disabled teacher case study 229
  work-to-rule 151
  working time 131
Edwards, R. 147–8
effort, defining work 117
effort bargaining 182–3, 187, 189
email 73–4
emotional action 13
emotional labour 67, 131–2, 165–6
empathetic understanding (*verstehen*)
  15
employee–employer relations
  corporate cultures and 123–5
  emotional labour and 132
  flexibility and 130
  harassment and 207–8, 213, 229
  labour markets and 80, 82, 92, 93
  low-wage jobs and 134–5
  telework and 105

employee involvement 178–9, 180–1
employee–manager relations
    behaviour in organizations and
        173–98
    bureaucratic organizations and
        145–8, 151–2, 165–6, 170, 171
    harassment and 207–8, 213
    neo-bureaucratic organizations and
        168, 169
    post-bureaucratic organizations and
        161–2, 163
employment
    marketization of 267–8
    work as 113–14, 115–16, 117, 141
    see also unemployment; work
employment contracts 92, 94
    fixed-term 125, 130
    freelance workers and 164
employment equality legislation 82,
        94–5, 206–8, 212–13, 218, 221,
        227–9, 230
energy resources 68, 69, 72
Engels, F. 5
enterprise culture 124–5
environment, the 60, 68–75, 76, 253–4,
        255, 269, 270, 271
equal opportunities
    bureaucratic organizations and 152,
        153, 171
    double discrimination and 213–14
Equal Opportunities Commission
        (EOC) 205–6
    see also Equality and Human Rights
        Commission (EHRC)
Equal Pay Act (1970) 82, 218, 221
equality, lack of *see* social divisions and
        inequalities
Equality Act (2006) 208, 218
Equality and Human Rights
        Commission (EHRC) 94–5,
        208
equality legislation 82, 94–5, 206–8,
        212–13, 218, 221, 227–9, 230
equalizing processes, enterprise 124
Erickson, M. 126
Esping-Anderson, G. 99
Ethical Trading Initiative (ETI) 253,
        257
ethnicity *see* black and minority ethnic
        (BME) workers
European Union (EU)
    Directive on Race 212
    knowledge economy 60–1, 62

migrants 64
    working time 93, 131
extrinsic rewards, work 119–20

fair trade movement 254
family life
    community and 241
    family-friendly policies 94
    gender (in)equality and 219, 220, 221,
        224
    non-standard work and 130
    social research methods and 24, 25,
        236–7
    socialization and 10
    see also work–life balance
Fasang, A. 222
Fayol, H. 147
Felstead, A. 107
feminism 4, 16–20, 23, 153, 201
feminization 62, 66–7
feudalism 32–3, 36
fiddling behaviour 183–4, 187
Fincham, B. 127–8
Finkelstein, V. 225
First World War 235
fixed-term contracts (FTCs) 125, 130
flexibility
    cult of modernity and 39–40
    labour markets in 92, 93, 94, 98–9,
        103–4
    non-standard work and 128–30, 221
    post-bureaucracy and 155, 156–7
    postmodernity and 46
    team working and 103–4
flexible firms 156–7
flexible specialization 96
flexible working 221, 268
    see also flexibility
Flexible Working Regulations 94
Ford, H. 101
    see also Fordism
Ford workers, de-humanization 153
Fordism 101–2, 103, 156
Foster, D. 228–30
Foucault, M. 22–3, 74, 223
free market ideology 92–3, 256–7
    see also neoliberalism
freelance workers 163–4
    see also self-employment
frictional unemployment 90, 91
Friedman, M. 256–7
fun, work as 127–8
functionalism 4, 7–12, 20, 24, 241

Galbraith, J. K. 131
gangs 215, 216
García, A. 58
gender (in)equality 201, 217–24
  anti-discrimination legislation and
    82, 94–5, 206, 208, 218, 221
  bureaucratic organizations and 153
  business performance and 205–6
  community and 237, 245, 246
  ethnic hierarchies and 211, 213–14
  feminism and 16–20, 201
  feminization of economic activity
    and 66–7
  labour markets and 81–2, 86, 99, 192,
    211, 213–14, 218
  meaning of work and 116
  non-standard work and 125, 128–9,
    130, 219, 221
  pay gap and 86, 218, 219, 224
  trade unions and 192, 193
  work–life balance and 268–9
gendered division of labour 19–20, 218,
    219, 245, 246, 277
gendered knowledge 96
gendered skills 96
George, S. 59–60
Giddens, A. 37, 40, 55, 263
glass ceilings 224
global warming *see* climate change
globalization 50–8, 75–6
  CSR and 254–5
  disabled workers and 228
  environmental catastrophe and
    68–70, 76, 269, 271
  future challenges for 269–70, 271
  migration and 62, 65–6, 75, 209, 269
Glucksmann, M. 33
goal displacement 151
Goffman, E. 15, 16, 25
Goos, M. 97
Gopalakrishnan, K. 57
Gorz, A. 116, 139–40
gossip 185–6
Gouldner, A. W. 151–2
government legitimacy 265
government policy
  community life and 241–2
  CSR and 255
  education and 270–1
  flexible working and 268
  labour markets and 89–90, 91–5, 98–9
  neoliberalism and 59–60, 93, 262–6,
    267–9

government statistics 82–3
Grandad's Back in Business (TV series)
  39–40
green issues *see* environment, the

habitus 5
hackers 74–5
Hakim, C. 81
Hales, C. 168
Hammer, M. 155–6
harassment 206–8, 212, 213, 220–1, 227,
  229
Harney, S. 261
Harris, L. 183
Harvey, D. 58, 59
Hausbeck, K. 149–50
Hawthorne effect 175
Hawthorne experiments 174–6
health problems *see* ill-health
health services 186, 192, 211, 266, 267,
  269
Heckscher, C. 155
heritage, mining 250–1
Hewlett Packard (HP) 105, 106
hierarchies, bureaucracy 145, 147, 155,
  168, 170
hierarchy of needs 176
higher education
  contract research staff in 125–7
  knowledge-based economy and 62,
    270–1
  post-industrial society and 43, 44, 45
  qualifications 96
  sociological 261–2
historical materialism 4
Hochschild, A. R. 67, 131–2
Holocaust 152, 235
homeshoring 106
homeworking 73, 104–7, 163
horizontal segregation 218
hot-desking 163
housework
  gender (in)equality and 218, 219
  meaning of work and 115–16
human relations (HR) 174–7, 181, 187,
  194
human resource management (HRM)
  176–81, 189
human resource services 159
human rights 253, 257
humour 186
Hurricane Katrina 269
Huws, U. 73

Hyman, J. 130
Hyman, R. 190, 195

ideal type(s) 13–15, 34
  bureaucracy 145–6, 148, 150–1, 154, 167
  post-bureaucracy 155, 160
  virtual organizations 160
identity
  neoliberalism and 263
  organizational misbehaviour and 185–6
  police work and 223
  postmodern social constructionism and 20
  social class 204
  trade unions and 195, 196–7
  work and 117, 118–19, 120–1, 122–5, 129–30, 140, 223
ideologies 140
ill-health
  call centre workers and 108–10
  dangerous jobs and 136
  disability and 229
  sickness absence management and 151
  stress-related 180
  work intensification and 135
impairment, disability and 225–6
income (in)equality 84, 85, 95, 99
  challenges of 269
  class and 202, 203
  critique of neoliberalism and 264–5
  gender and 86, 218, 219, 224
  see also wage discrimination
Indian economy 57–8, 270
individualization 58, 263, 282
indulgency 152
industrial bureaucracy 153
industrial relations
  labour markets and 92
  post-industrial   44, 45
  see also conflict
industrial sector
  employment by 83
  wage variation by 84
industrialism 8–9, 31, 36–7
inequality *see* social divisions and inequalities
information and communication technology (ICT) 72–5, 76, 96
  bureaucracy-lite organizations 168
  community and 241, 255

future challenges 270
newly industrializing economies 270
outsourcing of IT jobs 135
post-bureaucratic organizations 157, 159, 160–1, 163
teleworking 73, 76, 104–7
virtual communities 243
virtual organizations 160–1
information society 78
Infosys 57
intensification, work 134, 135, 268–9
international division of labour 42, 52
  see also globalization
internet 72–5
  community activism and 255
  virtual communities and 243
inter-organizational networks 158, 159, 161
interpretive sociology 4, 12–15, 20, 25
  see also Weber, Max
intrinsic rewards, work 120–8
involuntary unemployment 90, 91–2

Jewson, N. 107
job insecurity 135
job polarization 95, 97–8
job seekers 98
Jones, D. 98
Just In Time (JIT) 103–4
Justice for Janitors movement 247, 248, 249

Kerr, C. 36
Keynes, J. M. 90, 91
Kingsnorth, P. 255
kinship 236–7
Klein, N. 257, 269
knowledge
  cultural capital and 242
  degradation of work and 102
  post-industrial society and 43, 44, 45
  as power 74–5
  skills and 95, 96
knowledge relativism 21
knowledge society 277–8
knowledge work 95, 96
knowledge-based economy 50–1, 60–2, 75
  education and 62, 96, 97, 98, 270–1
  labour market and 95–110, 271
Korczynski, M. 165, 169
Kumar, K. 37–8

labour 116
  division of *see* division of labour
  movement of *see* migration
  power of 4–5, 6–7, 33
  see also work
labour markets 78–82
  BME workers and 80, 86–7, 210–12,
    213–14, 216
  definition 79
  deregulation of 89, 90, 92–5, 98–9, 267
  disabled workers and 87–8, 228–30
  gender (in)equality in 81–2, 86, 99,
    192, 211, 213–14, 218
  globalization and 53–4
  in the knowledge-based economy
    95–110, 271
  neoliberalism and 93, 267–8
  non-standard work and 128–9, 267
  regulation of 82, 89, 90, 92–5, 98–9
  social class and 81, 202, 212
  trade unions and 80, 92, 93, 191–3
  UK data 82–9, 90
  UK policy 89–90, 91–5, 98–9
  Unemployment and 80–1, 89, 90–2,
    98, 99
labour process theory 33, 95–6, 137
language 21–3, 223
Lawler, S. 204
Lawrence, S. 208
Lawson, N. 60
legislation
  CSR 255
  equality 82, 94–5, 206–8, 212–13, 218,
    221, 227–9, 230
  flexible working 268
  minimum wage 99
  working time 93
leisure society 43, 44, 78
liberal feminism 18, 20, 153
Lienhard, J. 38
lifestyle
  consumer society and 47
  environmental dilemmas and 68,
    69–70
  low-waged workers and 134–5
  migration and 65–6
  in a tribal society 41
lifetime jobs 114, 140
London Citizens 249
London Living Wage (LLW) campaign
  248–9
low-waged workers 134–5, 248–9
  see also income (in)equality

Lynd, H. M. 236
Lynd, R. S. 236

MacJobs 97
'making out' 182
male role models 215, 216
manager–employee relations *see*
    employee–manager relations
managerial misbehaviour 188–9
Manning, A. 97
manufacturing sector
  average weekly earnings in 84
  global economy and 53–4
  post-Fordism and 46, 156
  post-industrial society and 42, 45
  relative size in 2006 83
market, the
  for labour *see* labour markets
market power, unions 192
Mars, G. 183–4
Martinez, E. 58
Marx, Karl, and Marxism 4–7, 19, 20
  Theory of alienation 6, 33, 34, 35,
    136–7
  On bureaucratic organizations 147–8
  degradation of work 103
  disabled workers and 228
  meaning of work 113
  organizational misbehaviour and 187
  scientific management and 100
  social typologies and 30, 31, 32–4, 35,
    47–8
  unions as class actors and 190–1
Maslow, A. H. 176
mass production 101–2, 153, 156
maternity benefits 94, 268
Mayo, E. 176
McDonaldization 148–50
McDonald's Corporation 48–9, 97
McGregor, D. 176
McJobs 97, 98
McNabb, R. 224
meaning, interpretive sociology 12–15,
  34–5
means of production 4–5
mechanical solidarity 8, 30–1
medical discourse 22
medical model, disability 225–6
medieval times 32
men
  bureaucratic organizations and 153
  feminism and 17, 18–20
  gender stereotyping and 219

men (*cont.*)
  gendered division of labour and
      19–20, 218
  male–female pay gap and 86, 218,
      219, 224
  non-standard work and 130
  trade unions and 192
mentoring 214
Mercer, G. 87
meritocracy 37
middle class-ness 204
migrant workers
  Britain and 63–4, 209–12, 243
  community and 243
  community unionism and 248
  Ireland and 64, 65
  labour markets and 80, 210–12
migration 62–6, 75, 209, 269
  see also migrant workers
Miller, M. 63
Mills, C. W. 2, 30
minimum wage 99, 134–5, 248
mining communities 234, 235, 237,
      244–6, 250–1
minority ethnic workers *see* black and
      minority ethnic (BME) workers;
      migrant workers
misbehaviour, organizational 173,
      181–9
mobile working 73
modernism 37, 46
modernity 14, 20–1, 22–3, 37–40
  organization structures 157
  reflexive 31, 40, 46–7, 48, 114–15
Modood, T. 211
money, as motivation for work 119, 120,
      126–7
moral order, society as shared 8–12, 36
morally contested work 136
motivation
  human relations approach 176
  interpretive sociology 12–15, 34–5
  to work 119–30, 137–42, 268
Moynagh, M. 73
Mullholland, K. 184
multi-ethnic society 209–10
  unfair discrimination 205–6
  see also black and minority ethnic
      (BME) workers
multinational corporations (MNCs) 52,
      238–9, 253, 255, 266
multi-skilling 96, 104
Muslim groups 211

national minimum wage (NMW) 99,
      134–5, 248
National Statistics Socio-economic
      Classification (NS-SeC) 202–3
nation-state, globalization and 54–5,
      269
neo-bureaucracy 168
neoliberalism 50–1, 58–60, 93, 262–9
network enterprises 159
networks
  post-bureaucratic organizations and
      158, 159, 161
  social capital and 240
  social divisions and inequalities and
      214
  transnational advocacy 255
  virtual 243
new age ideas 167
New Herrington Banner Partnership
      (NHBP) 250–1
New Labour
  modernity and 39
  neoliberal economic policy and 59
  workfare and 37
Newby, H. 234
newly industrializing countries 52,
      57–8, 266–7, 269–70
Nissan 246–7
Nohria, N. 160
non-governmental organizations
      (NGOs) 254
norms 10
  effort bargaining and 182
  social cohesion and 241
  work ethic and 138–40

observation, community studies 236
occupational communities 136, 234,
      235, 238–9
occupations, feminization 66–7
office space, organization 162–3
offshore activities
  in a global economy 53, 54
  or homeshoring 106
  IT jobs and 135
  see also outsourcing
Ogbonna, E. 183
Olympic Games 270
online activities 73, 243
  see also internet
orchestral musicians 222
organic solidarity 9, 30–1, 194
organizational communities 238–9

organizational culture 162
    community and 238–9
    double discrimination and 214
    human resource management and
        179
    organizational misbehaviour and
        186, 189
    see also corporate cultures
organizational misbehaviour 173, 181–9
organizations
    behaviour in 173–98
    bureaucratic 14, 34, 35–6, 144,
        145–53, 154, 164–71
    community 238–9
    CSR and 71–2, 252–8
    culture *see* organizational culture
    future challenges for 269–70
    post-bureaucratic 144, 154–64,
        169–71
outsourcing
    inter-organizational networks and
        158, 159
    IT jobs and 135
    see also offshore activities

Parry, B. 40–1
partnerships, union–management
        194–5
part-time work 128–9, 219
patriarchy 18–19
Patrick, N. 74–5
pay *see* wage discrimination; wage
        distribution; wage levels; wage
        variation
PCs (personal computers) see ICT
pensions, gender inequality 220
people management 173–98
    see also employee–manager relations
performance management systems
        166–7
peripheral employees 156–7
Plant, R. 243
pluralism 124
police work 222–3
portfolio careers 163, 164
post-bureaucracy 46, 144, 154–64,
        169–71
post-feminism 46
post-Fordism 31, 46, 103
    identity construction 122–4
    post-bureaucracy and 156
post-industrialism 31, 42–6, 48, 51, 244
post-materialism 46

postmodern feminism 17–18, 23
postmodern social constructionism 4,
        20–3
postmodernism 46–7
    trade unions and 195–7
postmodernity 31, 46–7, 51, 157
post-structuralism 122–4, 223
post-traditional society 263
post-war community studies 235, 236
poverty
    community unionism and 248–9
    future challenges and 269
    gender inequality and 220
    low-waged workers and 134
    social capital and 242
    see also wealth, inequalities
power
    degradation of work 101, 102
    discourse 22–3
    feminist analysis of 19–20, 23
    knowledge and resistance and 74–5
    neo-bureaucratic organizations and
        168, 169
    organizational misbehaviour and
        186
    post-bureaucratic organizations and
        162
    social capital and 242
    social class and 204–5
pregnancy 217–18, 220, 221, 223, 268
preindustrial economy 40–1
prejudice 200
    acting on *see* discrimination, unfair
private property 33
privatization 58, 267
procedures *see* rules and procedures
production systems
    degradation of work and 102–3
    Durkheim's analysis of 8–9
    Fordist 101–2, 103, 156
    Just In Time 103–4
    Marxist theory of 4–7, 32–4, 103
    post-Fordist 103, 156
    Taylorism and 100–1
proletariat 5, 6, 32–3, 190–1
promotion
    BME workers and 211, 213–14
    gender inequality and 219, 221, 224
Protestant work ethic 35, 113, 138–40
public services, marketization 267
Punch, M. 188
punishment-centred rules 152
Putnam, R. 239–42

Quah, D. 61
qualifications 96
qualitative social research 23–6, 229
quantitative social research 23–4, 25,
    26, 236

R&D (research and development) 61, 96
race discrimination 209–16
    equality legislation and 94–5, 206,
        208, 212–13
    social class and 201
    see also black and minority ethnic
        (BME) workers
Race Relations Acts 212–13
radical feminism 18–19, 20, 153
Ram, M. 182
rational action 13, 14, 34
rationality and rationalization 14, 15,
    34–5
    bureaucracy and 145–8, 151, 167–8
    customer-oriented 169
    McDonaldization and 148–50
recruitment
    ethnicity and 214
    gender-neutral 222
reflexive modernity 31, 40, 46–7, 48,
    114–15
refugees 211–12
Regini, M. 99
regulation/deregulation 58, 59
    labour markets and 89, 90, 92–5, 98–9,
        267
relativism 21
religion
    double discrimination and 214
    employment equality legislation
        and 94, 206, 208, 213
    identity construction and 123
    Muslim groups and 211, 214
    Protestant work ethic and 138
reputational issues, CSR 256
research and development (R&D) 61, 96
research methods 23–6, 228, 229, 235–7
resistance
    bureaucratic organizations and 167–8
    corporate cultures and 123–5
    emotional labour and 132
    organizational misbehaviour and 187
    power and 74–5
retail sector, de-differentiation 124
    see also consumer society
retired workers, unionism 250, 251
retirement, gender inequality 220

rewards, work 119–28
rich–poor gap *see* wealth, inequalities
Richardson, B. 215, 216
risk society 114–15
Ritzer, G. 44, 148–9
role models 214, 215, 216
Rolls-Royce 256
Rose, M. 139
Roulstone, A. 228
Roy, D. 25
rules and procedures
    bureaucracy and 146, 148, 151–2, 153,
        165–7, 168, 170, 171
    post-bureaucracy and 155, 157,
        161–2, 165
Rutherford, J. 262, 263

sabotage 182–3
salaries *see* wage discrimination; wage
        distribution; wage levels; wage
        variation
satisfactions of work 133
SCELI survey 24, 119–20, 139
school teachers
    disabled 229
    working time and 131
    work-to-rule 151
schools
    disability discrimination and 229
    labour markets and 95
    post-industrial society and 43
    racial discrimination and 215–16
    socialization in 9, 10
science, post-industrial society 43, 44,
        45
scientific management 100–1, 102, 103,
        147
scientific workers, motivations 125–7
Second World War 235, 236
secularization 34–5
self
    neoliberalism and 264
    social class and 204
    work and 118–19, 120–1, 122–3,
        124–5, 140
self-employment 73
    neoliberalism and 267
    post-bureaucratic organizations and
        163–4
Service Employees International Union
        (SEIU) 247, 248, 249
service sector
    average weekly earnings 84

bureaucratic organizations and 152, 165–6, 169
community unionism and 247, 248, 249
consumer society and 47
customer-oriented bureaucracy and 169
emotional labour and 67, 132, 165–6
feminization of work in 67
Fordism and 103
job insecurity and 135
low-waged workers and 134–5
organizational misbehaviour in 183
post-industrial society and 42, 44, 48
relative size in 2006 83
teleworking and 73
see also knowledge-based economy
Sex Discrimination Act (1996) 82, 218, 221
sex industry, McDonaldization 149–50
sexual equality *see* gender (in)equality
sexual orientation
    direct discrimination and 206
    employment equality legislation about 94, 208
sexualization of women 220–1
Shah, H. 263
Shakespeare, T. 225, 226–7
Shiva, V. 72
shopping 47, 124
    see also consumer society
sickness *see* ill-health
Skeggs, B. 204–5
skills 95–6
    degradation of work (deskilling) and 44, 73, 94–6, 102–3, 148
    future challenges and 270–1
    ICT and 73
    meaning of work and 116, 117
    post-Fordism and 103
    in post-industrial society 43, 44, 48
    work ethic and 139
smoking breaks 184
social action, ideal types 13–15
social capital 240, 242
Social Change and Economic Life Initiative (SCELI) survey 24, 119–20, 139
social class 201–5
    ethnicity and 212
    feminism and 19, 201
    labour markets and 81, 202, 212

Marxist theory of 5, 6–7, 19, 32–3, 190–1
Neoliberalism and 263, 268
organizational misbehaviour and 187
as passive identity 118
post-industrial society and 43
trade unions and 190–1, 205
work–life balance and 268–9
social cohesion 239–42, 250–1, 268
social construct
    disability as 226
    work as 116
social constructionism 4, 20–3
social contact, focal points of 244, 245
social divisions and inequalities 199–200
    disability and 200, 201, 206, 208, 209, 224–31
    equality legislation and 82, 94–5, 206–8, 212–13, 227–9, 230
    labour markets and 81–2, 86–9
    Marxist theory of 32, 33
    Neoliberalism and 264–5
    race and ethnicity and 200, 201, 205–6, 208, 209–16
    social class and 201–5, 212
    unfair discrimination and 200–1, 205–6
social identity 118–19
social inclusion/exclusion 37
    feminism and 19
    labour markets and 86–9
    neoliberalism and 265
    social capital and 242
social inequalities *see* social divisions and inequalities
social justice 265
social model, disability 226, 228
social networking sites 243
social research methods 23–6, 228, 229, 235–7
social responsibility, corporate 71–2, 252–8
social structure, importance of 1, 2
social typologies 30–1
    post-industrialism and 42–6, 48
    postmodernity and 46–7
socialism
    Marxist theory of 6, 33, 35
    Weber on 35–6
society
    reason for studying 1–2, 260–2
    sociological analysis of 3
    sociological theories of 3, 4–23
socio-economic classification 202–3

sociological analysis 2–3, 260–2
sociological imagination 2, 30
sociology
  2008 economic crisis and 261–2
  classical sociology 31, 32–41, 44, 46,
    47–8
  climate change 68, 69, 253–4, 269
  definition of 2
  methods 23–6, 228, 229, 235–7
  theories 3, 4–23, 24, 26
  see also sociological analysis
soft bureaucracy 168–9
'soldiering' 182, 187, 189
solicitors, gender inequality 224
solidarity 8, 9, 10, 30–1, 36, 174, 194
spatial organization, offices 162–3
Special Education Needs and Disability
    Act (2001) 227
specialization 8–9, 36, 79
  degradation of work and 102
  flexible 96
  preindustrial 40
Spence, J. 235, 245
spirituality 167–8
sport, functions 9, 10
staff–employer/manager relations *see*
    employee–employer relations;
    employee–manager relations
Stalker, G. 154
state, the
  Marxist theory of 7
  Neoliberalism and 264, 265, 266
statistics, UK government 82–3
  see also data
Stephenson, C. 235, 245
stereotyping 200
  gender 219
  racial 211
  see also discrimination
stress
  call centre workers and 108–10, 184
  dangerous jobs and 136
  disability and 229
  human resource management and
    180
  job insecurity and 135
  morally contested work and 136
  organizational misbehaviour and
    184, 185
strikes
  Miners' Strike (1984) 234, 235, 244,
    245–6
  post-industrial society and 45

structural unemployment 91
supra-national bodies/institutions 52,
    55
  CSR 255
  see also European Union (EU)
sustainability 69, 71–2
sweatshops 255
symbolic capital 242
symbolic interactionism 25–6

Tata 57
tax burden 264–5
Taylor, F. W. 100
  see also Taylorism
Taylor, P. 74, 75, 108–10
Taylorism 100–1, 102, 147
team work 9, 10, 103–4
  human resource management and
    178
  identity construction and 123
  network enterprises and 159
technology
  alienation and 137
  degradation of work through 102–3
  future challenges for 270
  ICT *see* information and
    communication technology
  post-industrial society and 43, 44, 45,
    48
  for preservation of the environment
    72–5
  virtual communities and 243
telesales 96
teleworking 73, 76, 103, 104–7
temporary work
  gender (in)equality and 219
  neoliberalism and 267
  post-bureaucratic organizations and
    163–4
  reasons for offering 134
  reasons for taking 125, 128, 129
Tesco 55–6, 257, 264
Thatcher government 58, 59, 92, 93,
    245–6
theories, sociological *see* sociology,
    theories
Thompson, G. 263
Thompson, P. 182, 187–8
Touraine, A. 42
Toynbee, P. 107–8, 134–5, 264
trade unions
  class and 190–1, 205
  community unionism and 246–52

degradation of work and 102–3
employee behaviour in organizations
    and 173–4, 177–8, 179, 189–97
Ethical Trading Initiative and 253
global resourcing and 54
labour markets and 80, 92, 93, 191–3
Marxist theory of 33, 190–1
mining communities and 245–6,
    250–1
neoliberalism and 58, 247
post-industrial society and 45, 244
postmodern account 195–7
as source of order 193–5
work-to-rule and 151
Trades Union Congress (TUC) 192–3
traditional actions 13, 14, 34
traditional society 31, 40–1, 263
training 95, 98, 270
    see also education
transnational advocacy networks 255
tribal society, case study 40–1
Tribe (TV series) 40–1
tripartism 282
trust 161–2
Turner, J. M. W. 37–8
typologies *see* social typologies

UK government policy *see* government
    policy
unemployment
    BME workers and 210, 215, 216
    community decline and 244
    community unionism and 250
    consumer society and 47
    definition 90
    globalization and 55
    labour markets and 80–1, 89, 90–2, 98,
        99
    neoliberalism and 265, 266
    work ethic and 138–9
    workfare and 37
unions *see* trade unions
universities *see* higher education
upskilling 95, 96

verstehen 15
vertical segregation 218
victimization 207–8, 213
violence 19
virtual communities 243
virtual organizations 158, 160–1
vocation, work as 125–7
voluntarism 283

voluntary unemployment 90, 91
vulnerable workers 192–3

Waddington, D. 244–5
wage discrimination 82, 86, 99, 218,
    219, 224
    see also income (in)equality
wage distribution 84–5
wage levels
    Ethical Trading Initiative and 253
    job polarization and 97, 98
    London Living Wage campaign and
        248–9
    low-waged workers and 134–5
    national minimum wage and 99,
        134–5, 248
wage variation, by industrial sector 84
Walby, S. 60–1
war, community studies and 235, 236
Wass, V. 224
wealth
    inequalities 59–60, 202, 203, 220,
        264–5, 269
    work ethic and 138
Webb, J. 118
Weber, Max 12–15
    analysis of secularization 34–5
    On bureaucracy 14, 34, 35–6, 145–8,
        150–1
    On labour markets 80, 191–3
    On unions 191–3
    On vocation 125
    social typologies 33–6, 41, 47–8
    Theory of work ethic 35, 113, 138
websites, use of in book 27
welfare capitalism 283
welfare state 58, 59, 60, 265
well-being, threats to 135–6
    see also ill-health
West, the, 'modernity' of 38, 39
western culture, spread of 52
Western Europe, rise of capitalism 138
    see also European Union (EU)
Whitehouse, L. 256
Wickham, J. 64–5
Williams, R. 233
Willis, P. 81
Wilmott, P. 236–7
women 217–24
    bureaucratic organizations and 153
    community and 234, 235, 237, 245,
        246
    emotional labour and 67, 132

women (*cont.*)
  feminism and 16–20
  and feminization of economic
      activity 51, 62, 66–7
  and knowledge 96
  labour markets and 81–2, 86, 99
      ethnicity and 211, 213–14
  male–female pay gap 86, 218, 219, 224
  meaning of work and 116
  non-standard work and 125, 128–9,
      130, 219, 221
  and pregnancy 217–18, 220, 221, 223,
      268
  and sexualization 220–1
  and skills 96
  trade union representation and 192,
      193
Woolworths 256
work
  as calling 125–7
  choice and 128–30, 267–8
  defining 115–17, 141
  degradation of 102–3
  dogma of 140
  Durkheim's sociology and 7–10, 30–1
  as duty 125–7
  as employment 113–14, 115–16, 117,
      141
  feminist sociology and 17, 19–20
  feminization of 67
  as fun 127–8
  ICT and 72–5
  identity and 117, 118–19, 120–1,
      122–5, 129–30, 140, 223
  industrialism and 8–9, 31, 36–7
  intensification 134, 135, 268–9
  in a knowledge-based economy
      99–110
  labour markets *see* labour markets
  Marxist theory and 4–7, 30, 32–4, 113
  Modernity and 14, 20–1, 22–3, 37–40,
      46–7, 48
  motivations to 119–30, 137–42, 268
  nature of 78–110
  negative consequences of 131–7,
      141–2
  non-standard 128–30, 219, 221, 267

  part-time 128–9
  post-industrialism and 42–6, 48
  postmodern social constructionism
      and 23
  postmodernity and 46–7
  preindustrial 40–1
  reason for studying 1–2, 260–2
  in a risk society 114–15
  sociological methods and 23–6
  as vocation 125–7
  Weber's account of 14–15, 33–6, 41,
      113
  see also unemployment
work ethic 35, 113, 138–40
work–life balance 76, 94, 128–30, 268
worker–employer/manager relations
      see employee–employer
      relations; employee–manager
      relations
workfare 37
workforce changes
  feminization 51, 62, 66
  migration 51, 52, 62–6, 75, 209, 269
  see also labour markets
working class
  community studies and 236–7
  cultural representation of 204–5
  labour markets and 81, 191–2
  Marxist theory of 5, 6, 32–3, 190–1
working time 131, 268
  legislation 93
workplace behaviour 173–98
workplace culture 214
workplace harassment 206–8, 213,
      220–1, 227, 229
workplace injuries 136
workplaces, feminist sociology 19–20
Worksop Vale, community 244–5
work-to-rule 151
Worsley, R. 73

xenophobia 210, 211–12

Young, M. 236–7

zweckrational action 13, 14, 34
zweckrational organization 14